Contents

List of tables

List of figures

List of plates

Glossary of Irish terms and proper names

ard-fheis (plural ard-fheiseanna), national conference (of a political party)

Ceann Comhairle, speaker or chairperson (of the Dáil)

Clann na Poblachta, republican party in existence 1946–65

Clann na Talmhan, small farmers' party in existence 1939–65

cumann (plural cumainn), branch (of a political party), term employed in Fianna Fáil particularly

Cumann na nGaedheal, forerunner of Fine Gael

Dáil Éireann, directly-elected lower house of parliament to which Irish government is answerable

Fianna Fáil, largest party in Ireland

Fine Gael, second largest party in Ireland

Oireachtas, parliament (has two houses: Dáil and Seanad)

Seanad Éireann, indirectly-elected upper house of parliament

Sinn Féin, republican party

Tánaiste, deputy prime minister

Taoiseach, prime minister

Teachta Dála, Dáil deputy

Abbreviations

ACA	Army Comrades' Association (the Blueshirts)
AGM	annual general meeting
DUP	Democratic Unionist Party
EPP	European People's Party (pan-European grouping of christian democratic parties)
FF	Fianna Fáil
FG	Fine Gael
GAA	Gaelic Athletic Association
ICA	Irish Countrywomen's Association
ICMSA	Irish Creamery Milk Suppliers Association
IFA	Irish Farmers' Association
IRA	Irish Republican Army
MEP	Member of the European Parliament
NI	Northern Ireland
OMOV	One member one vote
PDs	Progressive Democrats
PR	proportional representation
SDLP	Social Democratic and Labour Party (constitutional nationalist party in Northern Ireland)
SDP	Social Democratic Party (Britain)
SF	Sinn Féin
STV	single transferable vote
TD	Teachta Dála
UUP	Ulster Unionist Party

About the authors

Michael Gallagher is an associate professor in the Department of Political Science, Trinity College, University of Dublin, where he teaches courses on Irish politics and on political parties. He has written on Irish, European and Japanese politics. He is the co-editor of *Politics in the Republic of Ireland* and of two books in the *How Ireland Voted* series on Irish elections, author of *The Irish Labour Party in Transition*, co-author of *Representative Government in Modern Europe* and co-editor of *The Referendum Experience in Europe*.

Michael Marsh is an associate professor and Head of the Department of Political Science, Trinity College, University of Dublin, where he has taught courses on research methods, electoral behaviour and political parties. He has published many articles in professional journals on Irish and European political behaviour, and his co-edited books include *Modern Irish Democracy* and *How Ireland Voted 1997*. He is co-principal investigator for the 2002 Irish Election Study.

Preface

Days of Blue Loyalty is a study of the membership of Fine Gael. No member of that party will need to be told what the title alludes to, but for those for whom the significance of the phrase is opaque, we should explain that since 1933 the colour blue has been associated, initially rather controversially, with Fine Gael. The core of the book consists of analysis of a survey of the party's membership that we conducted in the autumn of 1999, when we posted questionnaires to around 3,600 members of the party. Pessimists told us that we would be lucky to receive 500 replies, but they had under-estimated the helpfulness of Fine Gael members, for we eventually attained a response rate of about 50 per cent.

In writing this book we have incurred many debts. The Fine Gael party responded warmly and positively to our initial proposal for the survey and gave us every assistance in administering it. Both the party's general secretary when we began our planning, Jim Miley, and the then party leader John Bruton supported the venture, even though they were aware that a searching examination of the age profile, activity levels and political views of members had the potential to show aspects of the party in an unflattering light. We appreciate their openness and cooperation and, for what it is worth, we believe that their willingness to facilitate this venture reflects well on the party. Jim Miley's successor as general secretary, Tom Curran, and the party's national director of organisation Terry Murphy have had to bear the brunt of our requests for information, access to meetings and documentation, and time that they could ill afford. They have both been unflaggingly helpful and we thank them very warmly. We would also like to thank Liz Gorman and Eileen Kelly, who from their base in head office have helped us on a number of occasions, and Simon King, who supported the idea of a survey when this was still in an embryonic state. Fine Gael head office was also very helpful in pointing us in the direction of some very evocative photographs, and we would also like to thank Gerry Mulligan and Michael Daly for their assistance in finding photographs from the extensive records of the Irish Independent and Séamus Helferty from UCD's library for processing our late request for pictures so rapidly. We are most appreciative of all those who gave permission for their photographs to be used without charge: G. A. Duncan, Colm Henry, Independent Newspapers Ltd., The Irish Times, Lensman Press Photo Agency, Mrs Brone McGuire, and the family of the late Bill St Leger.

Before the questionnaire was finalised in 1999, earlier versions were piloted at meetings of three branches around the country – one in Munster, one in rural Leinster and one in Dublin. In addition, we were given access to a number of candidate selection conventions in Connacht and Leinster in 2001, which provided an invaluable opportunity to meet some of the members who had completed our surveys and to see intra-party competition at its most fascinating. We thank all those members and public representatives at branch meetings and selection conventions who made us welcome and offered us both their hospitality and their insights.

Surveys cost money, and we could not have carried out this research without a grant awarded, more years ago than we are comfortable to recall, by the Social Science Research Council of the Royal Irish Academy. We gratefully acknowledge this support, and we hope that at some stage it may become possible for us to extend this research to the other political parties in Ireland. We believe that the state of the political parties in any country is an important factor in the quality of democracy there, and at a time when the standing of the Irish political system is increasingly questioned we feel it is all the more vital that we have as much information as we can gather on the health of the parties that are central to that democracy.

Within the academic community our thanks go to the Political Studies Association of Ireland, and especially its president Yvonne Galligan and secretary Gary Murphy, for their support. The PSAI, the professional organisation of Irish political science, has associated itself with this publication and we are pleased that the book bears its imprint. Ronan Murphy and Caroline O'Flanagan played a vital role in administering the survey itself, Miriam Nestor contributed in the collation and sorting of the questionnaires, and Mike Robbins, Caroline O'Flanagan and Aidan Marsh all helped to code the replies. Pat Seyd and Paul Whiteley organised a conference in Sheffield in May 2000 at which we shared some of our findings, to our benefit at least, with researchers conducting similar studies in Britain, Canada, Denmark, the Netherlands and Norway. In the final stages we received valuable comments from John Garry, Gail McElroy and Jane O'Mahony, each of whom read the entire manuscript at very short notice and suggested many areas where improvement could be made. We hope that the final version does justice to their advice. Michael Marsh would also like to thank his wife Kathryn and his family for their endless patience at his frequent physical and mental absences, as well as considerable practical help. James Marsh gave advice at the production stage and designed the cover.

Most of all, we wish to express our gratitude to the 1,722 members of Fine Gael from Malin Head to Carnsore Point, from Belgooly to the Bog of Allen, from Dingle to Daingean, from Clew Bay to Carlingford Lough, from the wind-lashed roads of Durrus to the leafiest suburbs of Dublin, who took the trouble to fill in our 22-page questionnaire. Not all of those who responded felt that we had focused on the really important issues: one member grumbled "22 pages of questions and never touched on cattle prices". However, the care and commitment with which so many members completed what may have seemed an interminable series of queries was very evident, and we are more than happy to express our appreciation for the willingness of so many members to assist in our enquiries. Without this assistance, there would have been no book. Party members – not just those of Fine Gael but of all parties – are in many ways the unsung heroes of democracy, and this book gives them the attention they deserve. Special mention must go to the member who supplied our title in response to the final question in our survey, when we asked members to write in any further comments they had – though we must admit that we have truncated the phrase used. The member wrote: "Days of blue loyalty over". Whether this is an accurate assessment, readers will have to judge for themselves.

Michael Gallagher and Michael Marsh
Dublin, January 2002

1 Introduction

This is a book about the Fine Gael party and its members. We have been working on this project for several years, and when we have talked about it to friends and colleagues, or indeed to complete strangers, the same questions have been thrown at us repeatedly. In essence, we have been asked: why study the members of any political party? Why study Fine Gael? Those who are interested in politics and political parties cross-nationally may ask what they are likely to find interesting about a book on the members of any Irish party; those who are interested in Irish politics generally may ask why Fine Gael is of particular interest. Why study the members of Fine Gael?

One simple answer would be that information on Fine Gael members is interesting for its own sake. Given the almost complete lack of hard facts about members of Irish political parties, this study is a little like a map-making expedition by early explorers who could be certain that whatever they discovered would by definition be new information. The voyage would be worthwhile even if the landscape turned out to be undramatic. Thus, prior to this study, no-one knew how many members of Fine Gael are older than 55 (nearly half of them), whether Fine Gael members favour dropping Irish neutrality (they don't), which former Taoiseach they admire most (Garret FitzGerald) or how exactly they feel their own party differs from Fianna Fáil (in many ways or in none, as we shall see in chapter 8). Fine Gael has been the second largest party in Ireland ever since the early 1930s and it has been in government on six occasions since then, supplying the prime minister and a substantial number of the ministers each time (see Appendix D). Hence Fine Gael is a major player in Irish politics, and any new knowledge about Fine Gael, we might reasonably assume, is important and interesting in itself.

However, information on Fine Gael members should ideally have a value that goes beyond merely satisfying our curiosity about the lie of a hitherto unknown land. Our assumption in appealing to thousands of members of Fine Gael to give an hour or so of their time to this project by completing a questionnaire (as well as devoting many hours of our own time) is that studying Fine Gael should also tell us quite a bit about Irish politics. Indeed, by comparing our findings with the results from similar studies in other countries, we may be able to throw light on some aspects of modern politics generally. Put simply, the argument is this: political parties are very central to politics because of the range of important roles they play, and what goes on within political parties therefore has the potential to shape many aspects of the political process. If something is going wrong within the political parties – and many people in many countries have suggested that this is the case – then the whole democratic process may be in trouble. We will not be so hyperbolic as to suggest that a study of the Fine

Gael party amounts to a "health check on Irish democracy", but we do believe that the quality of democracy depends to a significant degree on the quality and vitality of the political parties in that democracy and that this book will throw considerable light on that.

WHY STUDY POLITICAL PARTIES?

Political parties are essential to contemporary liberal–democratic political systems of the sort that we find across the developed world, but they are not necessarily very popular. The very word "party", indeed, has connotations of "part" and can be traced back to the Latin word *partire*, meaning to divide. Being loyal to a "party" used to be – and perhaps still is by some – contrasted with being loyal to the nation as a whole, until parties became just about respectable a couple of centuries ago and much of the odium of the word was transferred to "faction".[1] Even so, parties know that they are rarely loved, and some deliberately take a name that avoids using the word "party". The two main Irish parties, Fianna Fáil and Fine Gael, have names that connote representing the nation as a whole, with "party" relegated to their subtitles ("The Republican Party" and "United Ireland Party" respectively).[2]

What is it, then, that parties do that makes them indispensable to politics and therefore worth writing a book about? The list of things that parties do is virtually endless, but we can pick out five especially important functions that they perform.[3]

First, parties structure the political world. They dominate governments and parliaments, which would work very differently, or perhaps wouldn't work at all, without them. They also structure the political world for many voters, who see politics in terms of the fortunes of parties as much as the fate of issues; this is especially true at election time. Individual voters don't have the time to work out their view on every political issue, and many simply trust their party's judgement on issues about which they haven't thought deeply.

Second, parties recruit the political elite. Although in some countries ministers may come from outside parliament, that is not the case in Ireland. Anyone who wants to be an Irish government minister must first be a TD (member of the Dáil) belonging to one of the parties in government.[4] And in order to become a party TD, he or she must first be selected as a Dáil candidate by that party. In all the Irish parties, and especially in Fine Gael, ordinary members play a major role in candidate selection. Therefore, if the members have certain expectations – or biases – about what qualities a parliamentary candidate should possess or about what a TD should do (for example, whether the most important role for a TD is legislating in parliament or solving problems on behalf of individual constituents) then these expectations will feed through into the recruitment process. The calibre of TDs and of ministers will be affected by the preferences of the candidate selectors. So will their backgrounds: for example, if the candidate selectors decide to pick more women, then there will be more women in parliament and probably eventually in government, while if the selectors don't want female candidates for one reason or another, then there will be few women at the top in politics. And it might be that the candidate selectors have firm policy views and will favour aspiring candidates who share these views. In Fine Gael, all party members have a direct voice in the selection of candidates, so the preferences of members have the potential to make a major impact. In this book, we will examine those preferences.

Third, parties help to socialise the political elite. They provide the milieu within which the elite – TDs, cabinet ministers – operate. Politicians will often come to look at the political world from the party's perspective. In countries such as Ireland where politicians cannot afford to become detached from the "grass roots", the views of ordinary members will be impressed on members of parliament, including ministers, firmly and regularly. Politicians will not necessarily accept all the advice they get from party members, but they probably won't ignore it all either. In this book we explore the views of Fine Gael members on a number of political issues, enabling us to draw inferences about the kind of messages Fine Gael politicians are likely to hear from the membership. We will also see just how much contact there is between members and politicians.

Fourth, parties put forward manifestos and political programmes that aim to give direction to government. These programmes are not, like the programmes of interest groups, concerned with just a single issue; on the contrary, parties aggregate interests and try to come up with coherent packages of policies that span the whole range of government activity. In this book we will look at the amount of power that Fine Gael members feel they have over party policy, and the amount of power they would like to have. We will talk about the kind of policy areas that are most important to Fine Gael members and the sort of policies that Fine Gael members would like their own party to prioritise.

Fifth, parties perform what has been termed a linkage role between rulers and ruled, between the state and civil society. They have been described as "ambassadors to the community" on behalf of the party.[5] More broadly, they constitute the main mechanism by which voters are linked to the formal political world: to parliament, to the state bureaucracy, to the structures of government. Information flows via parties both upward from citizens to the state and downward in the other direction. However, in virtually every developed country there has been a lot of speculation over the last twenty years to the effect that parties may no longer be performing this linkage role very effectively. Some writers see parties as having become virtually a part of the state, due in particular to the large public funding now received by parties in most countries.[6] Others call attention to what seems to be a decline both in party membership and in the activism levels of those members who remain. Parties are accused of turning inwards and of failing to engage with society. In this book we will discuss membership trends within Fine Gael, examine the level of party activity, find out how many members are becoming less active (or more active) and why this is happening, and look at the range of groups outside Fine Gael that party members belong to.

This list of some of the most important functions that political parties perform nowadays implicitly indicates some of the things that can "go wrong" with parties, preventing them from operating effectively. As we have said, the fear that this is happening has recently become a cause of concern in many countries. Regarding the first role of parties, structuring the political world, their position is still largely unchallenged, in Ireland and elsewhere, notwithstanding the significant number of independents who manage to get elected to the Dáil.

However, when it comes to recruiting and socialising members of the political elite, and also when it comes to producing policy proposals, there is plenty of scope for problems to arise. If ordinary members are frozen out of the process of candidate selection, with the party leadership or the national executive making all the decisions, then there may well be resentment among the rank and file, who may refuse to work for the candidates foisted upon them. In practice, most parties in Europe give members at least some role in candidate selection, and some have gone further by allowing every member a vote in the process – Fine Gael took this step in the mid-1990s. The potential disadvantage of allowing members to have a powerful voice in the selection of a party's election candidates is that members may "distort" the outcomes by picking candidates who are not electorally appealing.

This has been argued for many countries. In Britain in the 1980s, for example, it was suggested that left-wing "extremists" dominated local Labour organisations and were ensuring that only individuals who accepted their worldview, one that had little appeal for most potential Labour voters, were selected as candidates. In the 1990s, the focus of criticism switched to the Conservatives, whose membership was said to be dominated by elderly, out-of-touch Eurosceptics who were determined to select like-minded candidates. Studies of the members of these parties enabled these claims to be systematically investigated.[7] There are many other cases where it has been argued that the views and priorities of members result in less than ideal candidates being selected. For example, in Belgium the leaders of the Liberal party wanted to increase the party's appeal to Catholic voters, but the anti-clerical members of the party, who had great say in candidate selection, were generally unenthusiastic about picking Catholic candidates. In the Dutch parties, members have a preference for candidates with roots in their region, whereas the national leadership of the party is more concerned about national-level ability.[8] Thus if the members of a party have real power in it, they might pick candidates whom either the voters or the leaders (or both) don't want, and they may do their best to get the party committed to the policies they like, which may not necessarily be the policies that would win most votes for the party. Alternatively, the membership may be highly divided over some key issue, preventing the party from presenting a united front and damaging its image in the eyes of the voters. In this book, we shall be exploring the political views of Fine Gael members, seeking their views about why so few women are selected as Dáil candidates, and asking them about what they see as the most important role of a TD. This should enable us to judge whether the members' views are making a difference to the background or calibre of those selected to carry the Fine Gael standard into electoral battle and whether there is a problem here that needs to be rectified.

The linkage role, as we have already said, is widely identified as one that parties are no longer performing effectively. Richard Katz has asked whether this linkage role has now become a "vestigial function", and speculates that increasingly both parties' desire for members, and citizens' desire to be party members, are likely to decline.[9] From the perspective of parties, it has been argued that the "costs" of members – of the sort we outlined in the previous paragraph – may increase, as those members who joined parties for reasons other than the promotion of policy find other and more appealing outlets for their time, leaving the ranks of party membership dominated by those with very definite policy priorities. Members may be a cost in purely financial terms: the negligible membership fees paid barely cover the costs of maintaining records on members and sending regular mailings to them. Moreover, members do not seem to be as necessary as in the past for election campaigning, so it is said, given the wider reliance on the mass media as a means for parties to communicate their message to the public.[10] Hence, it is argued, parties can manage electorally just as well without members, and they may evolve into bodies that continue to dominate formal politics but do not facilitate citizen involvement and do not serve to link the people to the political system. Thus we shall examine the role of ordinary Fine Gael members both within the party and within the wider Irish society, to see why they joined the party in the first place, what they do within the party, and how strongly implanted they are within networks in their community and elsewhere.

Studying political parties, we hope we have established, is something worth doing, but the question might still be asked: of all the parties in all the world, why study Fine Gael? As with many social science projects, the explanation lies in a combination of academic ideals and the art of the possible. We believe that political parties are important, and that the role of members within parties and within society is especially important. A study of Irish parties specifically is, of course, partly a matter of convenience, but in many ways Ireland is any case an ideal context in which to seek the answers to certain questions about political parties. The Irish electoral system, PR-STV, which we explain more fully later in the chapter, allows voters to make a choice among parties and a choice among candidates within each party – or, indeed, to make a choice without regard to parties. The degree of intra-party choice allowed to the voters gives an incentive to candidates to build up a personal organisation that is loyal to them as well as to the party – or even loyal to them *rather than* to the party. In this, there are resemblances to politics in the USA, where candidates need to construct their own personal electoral machinery to have any hope of winning election. In that way Ireland constitutes a valuable case study, as we might find that membership is predominantly party-oriented or predominantly candidate-oriented, or perhaps it manages to be both party- and candidate-oriented at the same time.

Ideally, we would have preferred to conduct a study of all the Irish parties simultaneously, an option followed recently by researchers in other small democracies such as Denmark, the Netherlands and Canada. However, resource constraints confined us to one party, and this led us to Fine Gael. We learned that Fine Gael would be willing to facilitate the kind of study we had in mind, and, moreover, that party's centralised register of members made systematic sampling easier, as we outline in more detail in Appendix A. We launched our survey on the Fine Gael membership in the autumn of 1999.[11]

RESEARCH ON IRISH PARTY MEMBERS

As things stand, ordinary party members don't have a very high profile in Irish society. Occasionally, it is true, they might find themselves in the spotlight. In February 1982, for example, in the middle of one of the many challenges to the leadership of Charles J. Haughey, Fianna Fáil members around the country were contacted by Haughey supporters during the "night of the long phone calls" and urged to put pressure on their local TD before the meeting at which the parliamentary party would decide Haughey's fate. Haughey's popularity among the rank and file members helped him to survive this particular "heave". In Fine Gael, when Michael Noonan and Jim Mitchell launched a challenge to the leadership of John Bruton in January 2001 they said that they had come under pressure from ordinary members to do this. Within Labour, any coalition deal made by the leaders with another party must be ratified by a conference of the membership before the party can go into a coalition government.

With these exceptions, party members are generally out of sight and out of mind as far as the rest of Irish society is concerned. They become a bit more visible to everyone else at election time, perhaps huddled together in the vicinity of polling stations handing out leaflets or escorting candidates on a door-to-door canvass. (We might wonder, though, whether these people are really party members at all or whether they are simply personal supporters of a party candidate – our findings on this point will be discussed in chapter 5.) When the party leader addresses the faithful in his or her televised speech at the party's annual conference, those members in the hall can be relied upon to applaud at the appropriate places and produce a standing ovation at the end. Presumably, though, there is more to being a member than simply cheering on cue and being a foot-soldier at election time. Or is there? As we shall see, members do have other parts to play, yet many of them also feel that some people high up in the party see them as no more than a source of money and free labour.

As we have already pointed out, members can make a big difference – they really are the life and soul of a party. What motivated them to join the party, what kind of people they are, how much time they are willing to devote to party work, how much influence they seek over party policy, what political views and priorities they bring to their role in decision-making within the party – all these things will affect the nature, vitality and direction of the party. As things stand, though, before the present study was undertaken very little was known about party members in Ireland. None of the parties has extensive archives, though in recent years the two major ones have at least made some of their past records available to researchers. The Fine Gael archive at University College Dublin contains minutes of the parliamentary party up to 1949 and the party's standing committee (the inner executive of the party) up to 1945, as well as material relating to general elections up to 1969.[12] Some of this material has been used by Peter Mair,[13] but the archive does not contain recent party records, nor is there any particular focus on members in what is available.

In the 1970s Tom Garvin and Peter Mair studied party organisation in specific Dublin constituencies, while in the 1960s Mart Bax and Paul Sacks, utilising a more anthropological approach, examined the activities of TDs and their political machines in counties Donegal and Cork respectively.[14] Each of these studies has something to say about the backgrounds, views, motivations or activities of members in the area that was studied, and we shall be referring to them in the chapters that follow. However, valuable as they still are in many respects, none of them would claim to be able to offer anything like a portrait of the entire membership of any party. In 1997 Richard Dunphy conducted what was then the only survey of a party's nationwide membership, sending a questionnaire to each branch secretary and elected representative of Democratic Left. His study throws valuable light on the perspectives of activists of this party, but the party was a small one (only 150 questionnaires were sent out) and was to merge with Labour just eighteen months after his survey.[15]

In recent years full-scale studies of party members have been undertaken in a number of countries. In Britain there have been major examinations of the Labour Party and the Conservatives, and somewhat smaller ones of the Liberal Democrats and the Greens.[16] Researchers in Canada, Denmark, the Netherlands and Norway have been able to conduct studies of the members of all the parties in their own country.[17] This is not the place to present a lengthy description of the findings of these projects, but we shall refer to them from time to time in this book as points of comparison with Fine Gael, in order to give us some idea as to whether the backgrounds, views, changing activity levels and so on of Fine Gael members are typical of or are out of line with patterns elsewhere.

These studies of members in other countries all employed the methodology of the large scale sample survey, and we did the same. As we explain in detail in Appendix A, we sent out around 3,600 surveys to members, deliberately over-sampling branch secretaries, and we sent secretaries an additional 1-page questionnaire asking for some information on their branch. This was done partly so that we could get information on branches rather than just on members, and partly because we expected a higher response rate from secretaries. Since secretaries are more active than the average member, this means that the more active members are over-sampled, but by weighting responses appropriately (as described in Appendix A) we take account of this. We received replies from about half of our sample. Most of the questions that we asked were "closed" – that is, respondents were asked a question and invited to tick one of a small number of boxes to indicate which of a fixed set of options they agreed with (see

Appendix B for the detailed questionnaire). A few questions were "open", meaning that respondents were invited to answer a question – such as how they feel Fine Gael differs from its main rival Fianna Fáil – in their own words. The responses to open questions tend to be more difficult to analyse quantitatively but can be seen as "richer" in that respondents are not compelled to accept the framework offered by the researchers but can instead present their own thoughts in their own way. We will quote some of the answers to open questions when we come to discuss such areas as why members say they are becoming less (or more) active, what changes members feel should be made to the Irish political system, what steps Fine Gael should take to attract more members or better candidates, and how Fine Gael could make better use of its existing members. As we explained in the preface, the title of this book came from one such answer, from a member who wrote in response to our invitation to members to make "additional comments" that the "days of blue loyalty are over".[18] Whether this member is right remains to be seen.

THE INSTITUTIONAL CONTEXT

In the next chapter we will present a history of the Irish party system and especially of Fine Gael. Here we give a brief overview of the institutional context of Irish politics by describing the most important political institutions.

The Irish political system is one of parliamentary government. As in most west European countries, the people vote at general elections for members of the lower house of parliament and this house itself then elects the government. Parliament (the Oireachtas) itself has two houses, the Dáil and the Seanad. The Dáil is directly elected by the people; these elections must take place every five years. At the time of our survey, in the autumn of 1999, the most recent election had been in June 1997, so the survey took place at about the mid-term of the government's life. It is the Dáil that elects the government and to which the government is answerable; the upper house, the Seanad, is indirectly elected and has little power.[19] Elections are the key battleground of Irish politics and the next election, however far off it may be, is the main focus for much political discussion and comment. However, election turnout has declined steadily since the 1960s, and, at around 66 per cent, is now lower in Ireland than in most other west European countries.

One particularly distinctive feature of Irish elections, which we have already mentioned, is the electoral system of proportional representation by means of the single transferable vote (PR-STV), a system that is used in only one other country – Malta – to elect the lower house of parliament.[20] The Dáil contains 166 members (known as TDs) who are elected from multi-member constituencies, each of which returns either 3, 4 or 5 TDs. At the 1997 election, for example, the 166 TDs were elected from 41 constituencies; each constituency returned about 4 TDs on average. The average constituency was contested by twelve candidates: 3 from Fianna Fáil, 2 from Fine Gael, 1 from Labour, and 6 from the ranks of smaller parties and independents. Under PR-STV, voters are able to rank all candidates on the ballot paper in the order of their choice, by awarding a first preference to their favourite candidate, a second preference to their second choice, and so on. Voters can vote along party lines if they wish (recording a 1 for their first choice Fianna Fáil candidate, a 2 for their second choice Fianna Fáil candidate, and so on), but they can also vote on the basis of factors that cut across party lines, such as candidates' policy stances on specific issues, candidates' geographical bases, candidates' gender, or indeed any other factor. This engenders competition among candidates: not just among candidates of different parties but also among candidates of the same party. In many constituencies, a Fianna Fáil or a Fine Gael TD might well perceive the main threat to their seat as coming not from a rival party but from a rival candidate from within their own party.[21] Defenders of PR-STV emphasise the power it gives to the voters to determine who their representatives should be; critics argue that it is responsible for a pattern of behaviour among TDs that is detrimental to the quality of governance. We shall return to this debate in chapter 8 when we review Fine Gael members' attitudes to the political system in general and the electoral system in particular.

DAYS OF BLUE LOYALTY: AN OVERVIEW

In the following chapters of this book we shall present and discuss our findings. First, in chapter 2, we give a history of the Fine Gael party, exploring the record, the ethos and the myths of the party since its foundation. The traditions of the party are frequently invoked at party meetings and they also colour the nature of the responses to some of the questions we asked, so it is important to try to understand how members might perceive these. In chapter 3 we will consider the historical role of members within the party. Chapter 4 outlines the demographic profile of party members and compares this with the pattern of Fine Gael support in the wider electorate, examines some trends in membership, and looks at evidence on why people become members. While members don't appear to differ markedly from Fine Gael voters, they do tend to come from families with an established tradition of Fine Gael membership; this rather narrow and exclusive recruitment pool might well be seen as a problem for the party.

In chapter 5 we examine patterns of activity: the sort of activities engaged in by members, and the difference between more active and less active members. Not all activity takes place within formal organisational structures. In general, activism levels are higher than we might have expected, and party activists seem to be performing a valuable linkage role, keeping national politicians in touch with local concerns and ensuring that the party's presence is felt in a variety of arenas. At the same time there are clear signs of decline, which may become more pronounced in the years ahead given that older members are more active than younger ones. Chapter 6 considers the impact of party members: both their internal impact (examining their views about how much influence they have and should have within party structures) and their external impact, the effect their activity has on electoral support for the party. Members, especially active ones, do seem to be an electoral asset for a party. When we asked members whether they are content with their current role in the party, we found a degree of dissatisfaction, although their demands are not revolutionary; members, it appears, would like more involvement but they do not seek complete control.

In chapter 7 we consider the political views of Fine Gael members on a range of questions, including Northern Ireland, the European Union, the role of the Catholic church in Irish politics, and left–right issues. Some issues have the potential to divide the party, while on others there is a high degree of consensus. The views of members do not seem greatly different from those of Fine Gael voters generally. The left–right spectrum has meaning for members, and they are willing to place the main Irish parties somewhere on this spectrum, but we do not find evidence of an ideological underpinning for the political views that members hold. Chapter 8 discusses Fine Gael members' perceptions of the Irish party system. Fine Gael members feel themselves to be closer on the left–right spectrum to Fianna Fáil than to Labour, but they feel markedly warmer towards Labour than towards Fianna Fáil. Members are generally satisfied with the operation of the political system and do not see a need for fundamental change here. In this chapter, too, we probe the relationship between Fine Gael and Fianna Fáil to find out exactly what differences Fine Gael members see between the two parties. For many members, the ethos of the parties is the key difference rather than any policy stance; others do cite a particular policy area, such as Northern Ireland; while for some Fine Gael members there is simply no significant difference between the two parties. In chapter 9, the conclusion, we draw the threads together and consider the implications of our findings.

2   The Fine Gael party 1922–2002

Fine Gael, like the Irish party system generally, has not always proved easy to understand in terms of the categories into which political scientists usually slot west European parties. In particular, its relationship to its traditional adversary Fianna Fáil has been an abiding puzzle. Is the competition between these two parties in some way a conflict between right and left (in which case, which is right and which is left) or does the right–left conflict have nothing to do with their battle? Is there an urban–rural or a religious–secular component to the struggle, or perhaps a nationalist–internationalist or traditional–modern dimension? Or are the two parties really Tweedledum and Tweedledee, two peas born from the same pod and kept separate only by the dictates of history and the personal ambitions of politicians?

This book does not set out to provide definitive answers to these questions – something that would require a different study altogether – but our exploration of the political worldview of Fine Gael members will throw a great deal of light on what differences, if any, they perceive between the two main parties in the Republic of Ireland. In an ideal world, of course, our research would have embraced the members not only of Fine Gael but also of all the other parties in the state. However, for reasons already explained, limitations on resources confined us to a study of the membership of just one party.

In summary, for those who are very pressed for time and require the briefest of thumbnail sketches of Fine Gael, there are three central facts to bear in mind. First, Fine Gael was the second largest party in the state at each of the 22 general elections from 1932 to 1997 inclusive, averaging 30 per cent of the votes at each election (see Figure 2.1). Second, during the 70 years between the general elections of 1932 and 2002, Fine Gael spent only 18 years in government, always as the major component in a coalition that also included Labour (see Appendix D for details). Third, Fine Gael is a member of the pan-European People's Party group that embraces christian democratic parties from around Europe.

We will now proceed to examine Fine Gael's history in more detail. In doing this, we are not aiming to offer an exhaustive history of Fine Gael, let alone of the Irish state.[1] What we will do is outline the most important developments in the party's history, with particular emphasis on the early years when in many ways the mould was set. It was in that period that the party tradition was founded and the party spent ten years in office, yet it was also in that period that it was overtaken by Fianna Fáil and relegated to the second place in the Irish party system that it still occupies. In surveying the party's record, we can usefully bear in mind that all parties have their "myths". By this term, we do not mean beliefs that are untrue. Rather, the term refers to "shared stories about the past – stories which, *regardless of their veracity*, have helped to shape political

Figure 2.1: Support for main parties at Irish elections 1922–97

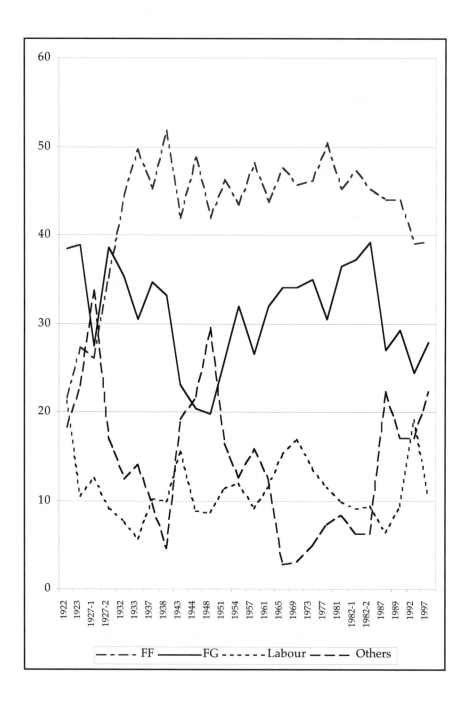

identities" within the party.[2] Such myths, as Lawrence explains, help to give party activists a sense of continuity and "to place themselves within an unfolding, seamless history of political commitment".[3] Some of the central "myths" that Fine Gael members adhere to strongly today were born in the early years of the independent Irish state, as we shall see.

ORIGINS

The origins of Fine Gael go back to the foundation of the state. The party was founded in 1933 by a merger between three existing groups, but its existence can be understood only against the background of the events of 1921–22, when an independent Irish state was formed and immediately plunged into a civil war. Indeed, Tom Garvin argues that Fianna Fáil and Fine Gael represent a tradition that long predates the civil war, and that there is a strong degree of continuity between the two main parties of the twentieth century and the nationalist movement that dominated Irish political life during the nineteenth century. Both Fine Gael and Fianna Fáil, he suggests, can be seen as internal factions of the "pan-nationalist" party that dominated nineteenth-century Irish politics.[4]

First, let us present the straightforward historical background of the early years of the Irish state. Ireland was ruled as a colony of Britain from Tudor times until the start of the nineteenth century, when the Act of Union made it, on paper at least, a fully-participating member of the United Kingdom on the same terms as England, Scotland and Wales. However, even though we don't have the survey evidence to prove this, it is clear that most Irish people felt no particular sense of belonging to or identifying with the United Kingdom, and in practice Ireland was ruled in a quasi-colonial manner by senior British politicians operating from Dublin Castle. These two phenomena, of course, reinforced each other; a feeling of being governed rather than participating fully in self-government led to sporadic attempts, sometimes violent ones, to achieve greater autonomy for Ireland within the United Kingdom or even complete independence, which disinclined the British authorities to relax the top-down nature of rule, and this in turn did nothing to reduce what in later times would come to be called Irish alienation from the state.

Matters began to move rapidly in the early years of the twentieth century. In 1912 the House of Commons passed a Home Rule bill that would give substantial autonomy to an Irish parliament, still operating within the United Kingdom, once it came into existence in 1915. However, events during the first world war changed the picture completely. In 1916 the "easter rising", an attempted insurrection by a small group of nationalists who aspired to an independent Irish republic, was crushed militarily, but the heavy-handed treatment of the surviving rebels, several of whom were executed, led to an upsurge in public support for the small party most closely associated with the rebellion, Sinn Féin (Ourselves). At the next United Kingdom general election, in December 1918, almost all the seats in today's Republic of Ireland were won by Sinn Féin, on a platform that committed its elected members not to take their seats in the British parliament at Westminster but instead to remain in Ireland and create Dáil Éireann, which would be the parliament of an independent Irish republic.

The first Dáil was duly set up in January 1919, but its legitimacy was not recognised by the British and there followed a low-level guerrilla struggle, known as the war of independence, which continued until a truce in July 1921. This was followed by negotiations between the British government and the leading Irish nationalist politicians – all members of Sinn Féin – on a treaty establishing the future relationship between Ireland and Britain; the Irish wanted a completely independent all-Ireland republic, while the British wished neither to concede complete independence to any part of the United Kingdom nor to abandon the million or so unionists, nearly all of them Protestant, who were a majority in the north-east of the island. The unionists were adamantly opposed to the prospect of coming under the rule of an Irish parliament and wanted the whole island to remain within the United Kingdom.

Up to this point the Sinn Féin elite was broadly united, but the treaty negotiations precipitated the split that led to the creation of today's Fianna Fáil and Fine Gael. After a period of intensive negotiation, the Irish envoys, under heavy pressure from the British side, put their names to a treaty (generally known ever since in Ireland as the Anglo–Irish Treaty, or just "the Treaty") that gave Ireland substantial autonomy but not everything that Sinn Féin had wanted. Different reactions to the Treaty brought about the split. Opponents, the anti-Treatyites, the tradition from which Fianna Fáil sprang, believed that the Treaty fell unacceptably short of the national demand because of three aspects in particular. First, its terms required members of the Irish parliament to take an oath to the British monarch; second, Britain would retain control of a number of Irish ports; third, the six counties of north-eastern Ireland would be able to decide their own fate, which as everyone knew meant that they would remain within the United Kingdom and the island would become formally partitioned.

Supporters of the Treaty, the pro-Treatyites, from whom Fine Gael emerged, took a different view of the Treaty. They did not, on the whole, regard it with unqualified enthusiasm, but their rationale for accepting it was that it was the most that could be wrested from the British; that the alternative to accepting it would be a return to military repression by the British; and that even though it did not contain everything the Irish wanted, what it conceded could be used to gain more. The last point was expressed by Michael Collins, one of the two leaders of the pro-Treatyite side, who said that even if it did not itself amount to freedom, it represented freedom to achieve freedom – as indeed, in the long term, it did.

When the Treaty was brought back to Dublin in December 1921, the cabinet, all of whose members belonged to Sinn Féin, voted 4–3 in favour of accepting it. The Dáil debated it the following month, and this time the vote was 64–57, again in favour. The anti-Treaty politicians withdrew from government. An election was set for June 1922, and as it approached the fragile unity that Sinn Féin still just about retained came steadily closer to breaking. The two wings of the party agreed to fight the election on a joint platform, but with attitudes to the Treaty forming the major cleavage within the electorate, it was impossible to prevent voters differentiating firmly between pro- and anti-Treatyite candidates.

The results marked a clear win for the pro-Treatyites and for parties that stood outside the treaty divide, notably Labour and the Farmers' Party. Anti-Treaty candidates fared poorly almost everywhere.[5] Within a month a civil war had broken out, the anti-Treatyites launching a military campaign to try to over-throw the government. The number of people killed was not great by compari-son with some modern conflicts, and it has been suggested that much of the population stood aside from the conflict and regarded it with detachment as if it were a large faction fight between the two wings of Sinn Féin.[6] Nevertheless, some of the actions of both sides caused abiding bitterness. Anti-Treatyites car-ried out a policy of murder and sabotage, not only against combatants but also against civilians whom they accused of collaborating with government forces. On 7 December 1922 they shot two pro-Treaty TDs, one (Seán Hales) fatally, and the following day the government had four anti-Treaty prisoners (one from each province) shot without trial. Altogether 77 anti-Treaty prisoners were executed during the civil war.

The relevance of these events for the subsequent development of the Irish party system is clear. Fine Gael, and indeed Fianna Fáil, did not emerge from a movement organised around a social cleavage such as class or religion. Its roots lie in the broad, cross-class pan-nationalist movement called Sinn Féin that dom-inated Irish politics from 1916 to 1922. That party split, not over a right–left or church–state issue but, at least in the first instance, over a narrow constitutional issue. (Once the disagreement had extended into the violence of the civil war, the pro-Treatyites maintained that the real issue at stake was no longer a narrow one – it was now whether the Irish people had the right to decide matters of pol-icy for themselves or whether opponents of a policy had the right to use violence to prevent the implementation even of policies for which the people had indi-cated their support.)

These circumstances must be understood if we are to understand the nature of early twenty-first century Fine Gael and what distinguishes it from Fianna Fáil. The party was born with a strong commitment to upholding the institu-tions of the state against anti-democratic challenges, in a context where the sur-vival of liberal-democracy seemed under grave threat. It was not committed to any particular position on the left–right spectrum, or indeed to any particular policy stances on the mundane issues of quotidian political life. By the same token, its differences with Fianna Fáil were largely confined to the single issue on which the split had come.[7] In the eyes of the pro-Treatyites, the anti-Treaty camp had been dishonest in claiming that a better deal than the Anglo–Irish Treaty could have been obtained, and cynical and anti-democratic in plunging the country into civil war rather than abide by the verdict of the people that the treaty, whatever its imperfections, should be accepted as the basis from which a fully independent Irish state could be achieved. The perception of the anti-Treatyites was that the treaty represented a betrayal of what those killed in the war of independence had fought for, that the pro-Treatyites' occupancy of office was not legitimate, and that the people had voted for the treaty at the June 1922 election only under duress. The atrocities carried out by both sides during the civil war intensified the mutual antipathy. The scene was set for the scenario of a party system dominated by two parties that often seemed to differ little or not at all on most current political issues, yet identified each other as their main rival and as a party that must always be an opponent, never an ally or a partner.

EARLY YEARS

The pro-Treaty forces, Fine Gael's predecessors, remained in office for the first decade of the new Irish state. When the first two pro-Treaty leaders died in August 1922 – Arthur Griffith through illness, Michael Collins shot in an ambush at Béal na mBláth – leadership fell onto the shoulders of William T. Cosgrave, who was then aged 42. He became President of the Executive Council (prime minister). By nature a modest and practical man not given to theatrics or grandstanding, Cosgrave had been elected to Dublin Corporation as a Sinn Féin candidate as early as 1909 and was Minister for Local Government in the administration set up by the first Dáil in 1919.[8] The pro-Treaty forces now gathered themselves into a party, Cumann na nGaedheal (usually translated as "League of Gaels"), and this party governed until 1932. The party was born in circumstances that augured ill. It was due to be launched at a "preliminary conference" on 7 December 1922, but it was when coming from this meeting that the two pro-Treaty TDs, Hales and Pádraic O'Máille, were shot. When this in turn was followed by the Mountjoy executions, news of the conference was suppressed and the public launch was deferred until April 1923.[9] It was not especially strong electorally – it never won as many as 40 per cent of the votes and once fell below 30 per cent – but its task of forming a government was made much simpler by the abstention from the Dáil of the anti-Treatyites until 1927.

Government in this first decade was anything but easy. The political class was on what would now be termed "a steep learning curve"; it was entirely new to the task of governing, and in the circumstances performed creditably. The absence of the anti-Treaty TDs, even if this gave Cumann na nGaedheal an artificial Dáil majority and thus ensured it of a firm hold on government, was testimony to the sizeable section of the electorate whose attitude to the institutions of the state was one of non-cooperation or grudging obedience. In addition, the reliance on military forces to win first the war of independence and then the civil war brought problems of its own. Government moves to demobilise the large number of soldiers who were no longer needed once the conflict had ended provoked discontent, perhaps even consideration of a coup, among those affected, and led to the so-called "army mutiny" of 1924 in which the subsequent Fine Gael leader Richard Mulcahy was compelled to leave government. This affair definitively affirmed the supremacy of the civil authorities over the military; it also reflected the growing dominance of Kevin O'Higgins, the deputy prime minister and Minister for Home Affairs. O'Higgins not only managed to get Mulcahy, one of his rivals, removed from office; he also asserted himself against the prime minister. Although Cosgrave was supposedly ill throughout the crisis, Regan suggests that "it would seem that Cosgrave was confined to his bed by O'Higgins, not by his doctor; and there he stayed until the danger of compromise passed".[10]

In these difficult circumstances, the Cumann na nGaedheal government that ruled the new state until 1932 generally performed solidly if not always very imaginatively. In many ways the administrative system carried on much as before. The government's economic policy "relied heavily on agriculture as the engine of economic growth",[11] which led logically to a free trade policy, as the main market for Ireland's farm produce remained Britain. This was popular with large farmers but was less so among those who attached priority to the creation of indigenous Irish industry, something that it seemed could be achieved only by the introduction of tariffs and protective quotas to reduce competition from imported goods. The Minister for Finance, Ernest Blythe, was a firm believer in balanced budgets, and in 1924 he reduced expenditure by the simple though astonishing expedient of cutting the old age pension from ten shillings to nine shillings a week.

Cumann na nGaedheal's first four years of rule consolidated Irish independence, no mean achievement, but government policy had managed to alienate one sector of society after another and at the June 1927 election it slumped to 27 per cent of the votes. Despite this, it remained the largest party, but it was only narrowly ahead of the main anti-Treaty party, Fianna Fáil. Fianna Fáil had been formed in July 1926 by the more pragmatic anti-Treatyites. The initial rationale of the policy of abstaining from the Dáil had been that this would bring down the institutions of the state, undermining their legitimacy by withholding support, but the more politically aware anti-Treatyites, notably Seán Lemass and eventually their leader Eamon de Valera, realised that this policy was not going to pay dividends. The formation of Fianna Fáil marked the split among the anti-Treatyites between those who would adhere to this abstentionist policy come what may, and those who preferred to take the fight against Cumann na nGaedheal into parliament.

For the moment, the continued abstention of the Fianna Fáil TDs, together with the fragmentation of the party system, enabled Cumann na nGaedheal to remain in office as a minority government. Everything changed a few weeks later, following the IRA's assassination on 10 July 1927 of Kevin O'Higgins, the second most powerful – some said the most powerful – figure in the cabinet; as well as being deputy prime minister (Vice-President of the Executive Council) he was both Minister for Justice and Minister for External Affairs. In response, the government introduced new legislation that would require candidates at future elections to declare that, if elected to the Dáil, they would take the oath required under the Treaty. On 11 August the deputies of Fianna Fáil took their seats in the Dáil, signing their names as required in the book containing the oath while maintaining that they were not in fact taking any oath. This changed the political picture completely. With only 47 seats out of 153, the Cumann na nGaedheal government was vulnerable to defeat at any time. After it survived a confidence motion on the casting vote of the speaker later in August, it dissolved the Dáil and fresh elections took place in September. Cumann na nGaedheal's vote rose and it formed another government which, with support from Farmers' Party TDs as well as a number of pro-Treaty and ex-Unionist independents, was able to remain in office for a full term.

Election results thus far showed that Cumann na nGaedheal consistently had more support than its main opponent, but things went wrong during the course of this government, which to date remains the last single-party government from the pro-Treaty tradition. During this period the pro-Treatyites allowed themselves to be overtaken by the political grouping that they had decisively beaten in 1922. The behaviour of Cumann na nGaedheal during the 1923–32 period was a classic illustration of the fate that befalls a party that neglects the centre ground. The political scientist Anthony Downs, writing in the 1950s, outlined a model of the way in which the parties in a 2-party system would behave if they were "rational" – in other words, if they wanted to maximise their votes. Assuming that most voters' opinions are somewhere near the centre of the spectrum, with fewer voters holding extreme opinions, it would make sense for the parties to position themselves as close as possible to the centre. To be precise, they would try to place themselves in policy terms at exactly the same place as the "median" voter, the one who is right in the middle.[12] Throughout the first decade of the independent Irish state, the key dimension of political conflict was the one marked by assertive nationalism and economic protectionism at one end and, at the other end, satisfaction with the Treaty as an end in itself and with economic subordination to Britain. In 1922, the pro-Treatyites were clearly closer to the median voter on this the spectrum than the anti-Treatyites were. However, instead of holding fast to this position, and perhaps looking to encroach on anti-Treatyite territory and drive their opponents further to the republican fringes, the pro-Treatyites ceded the centre ground to Fianna Fáil.

The central achievement of the state in this period, and one for which the Cumann na nGaedheal government could take a good deal of the credit, was, as Tom Garvin puts it, "the establishment of a free political order, essentially republican and democratic, in a society with a long tradition of primitive hatred of government". Ironically, as he points out, "Success in this has been so total that Irish people do not realise what an achievement it has been".[13] The Cumann na nGaedheal government was something of a victim of this lack of appreciation. To a population that was impatient to see rapid improvement in the quality of life following the achievement of independence, the government conveyed a sense of complacency and inertia. On two specific issues it handed the initiative to Fianna Fáil: development of the Treaty, and the establishment of industry. In both cases there was a heavy irony, because Fianna Fáil now embraced the position with which one of the original pro-Treaty leaders had been closely associated. In each case Cumann na nGaedheal's approach was to have damaging long-term consequences.

The Treaty, as we have seen, was described by Michael Collins not as a satisfactory end-point but as "freedom to achieve freedom". The clear implication was that the government of an independent Irish state would be able to throw off the remaining shackles, both symbolic and practical, that prevented Ireland being seen as fully sovereign. Yet, during its time in office, Cumann na nGaedheal did not seem interested in pursuing this approach. Fianna Fáil, in opposition, demanded the removal of remaining symbols of a subordinate relationship to Britain, such as the existence of the Governor–General (representing the crown) as head of state and the oath of fidelity to the monarch that all TDs had to take. If Cumann na nGaedheal had moved on these issues it could have cut some important ground from under Fianna Fáil's feet. Instead, it became a more and more dogged defender of the Treaty in all its aspects, arguing that it would be a breach of faith with the British to seek to amend it. Indeed, even after Fianna Fáil won power in 1932 and started dismantling those aspects of the Treaty to which it objected, Cumann na nGaedheal still tried to stop the tide of change by arguing strenuously in the Dáil against these steps.[14] What for Michael Collins had been a means to an end seemed to have become an end in itself for his successors in the pro-Treaty party, leaving Fianna Fáil a clear run to capitalise on the issue. Cumann na nGaedheal's approach consolidated its support among former unionists and the most moderate nationalists, but in reality these people had no-one else to vote for anyway and the centre ground on the nationalist spectrum was ceded to Fianna Fáil.

Along with Michael Collins, the other main pro-Treaty leader in 1921–22 had been Arthur Griffith. One of Griffith's most cherished ideas had been the development of a native Irish industry, and his belief was that while in its fledgling state it would need to be protected against competition from more industrially advanced countries. To this end, he advocated the use of import quotas to limit the amount of specified goods that could come into the country and tariffs to make imports uncompetitively expensive. By the late 1920s this was an issue that divided the two main parties, with Fianna Fáil committed to Griffith's policy and Cumann na nGaedheal as the proponents of free trade, on the ground that if Ireland discriminated against exports from other countries, they in turn would introduce measures against exports of agricultural produce from Ireland with disastrous consequences for the entire economy. Protectionism was introduced on a large scale by Fianna Fáil after it came to power in 1932, and there is still some debate on whether it was a short-term success and a long-run failure and on whether it was abandoned too soon or too late.[15] Either way, it clearly struck a chord in the economically depressed times of 1927–32, and was another issue on which Fianna Fáil appeared to be the party with positive ideas for change and development while Cumann na nGaedheal acquired the image of being the party that could not come up with anything better than the status quo.

Although Downs was not to outline his model until thirty years after these events, its logic is no doubt grasped intuitively by vote-seeking politicians in most countries: it does not make sense to move, in policy terms, towards one end of a spectrum if this simply firms up one's support among the few voters at the extreme while losing the support of a large number of voters in the centre. Exactly why Cumann na nGaedheal behaved in this electorally irrational fashion remains a mystery. Perhaps its leaders simply miscalculated the tenor of public opinion and did not realise that most voters wanted a more assertive nationalism than the party was offering. Perhaps, as the party leaders of the time might have said, Cumann na nGaedheal put the country first and paid little heed to the electoral cost to itself – or, a slightly different explanation, perhaps its leaders concentrated on governing and paid insufficient attention to party politics. Alternatively, it may be that its powerful backers insisted on the continuation of existing policies. Large farmers, a strong element in the party's support base, were aware that adoption of protectionist measures would prompt retaliation from Britain against Irish agricultural exports. Former unionists, though few in number, were wealthy, and Cumann na nGaedheal was in receipt of extensive but secret funding from them throughout the 1920s; whether, as has been alleged, this money impinged on ministerial selection or even policy is not known.[16] The party's approach no doubt served the broader function of helping to integrate the former unionists and supporters of the Irish Parliamentary Party into the political system, but at a significant and perhaps permanent electoral cost to itself.

By 1932 Cumann na nGaedheal had acquired a conservative image. Its reaction to the worldwide economic slump of the late 1920s was to cut spending and raise taxes, and its support base, hitherto perhaps fairly broad, now became more firmly linked to the most prosperous sections of society.[17] As the 1932 election approached, it adumbrated pay cuts for teachers and the gardaí, established a military tribunal that could impose the death penalty and launched a prosecution of the Fianna Fáil newspaper the *Irish Press* before the tribunal, and raised taxes further. It fought the 1932 election on a platform that warned of chaos if Fianna Fáil won, accusing Fianna Fáil of being "un-Catholic", little more than stooges of the gunmen of the IRA, and the dupes of the phantom legions of communists that it convinced itself were striving to take over the country. In the event, the 5-seat lead it had enjoyed over Fianna Fáil at the previous election was transformed into a 15-seat deficit; Fianna Fáil took power; and from then till the present day, the pro-Treaty tradition has consistently trailed behind Fianna Fáil in electoral popularity (see Figure 2.1).

At the start of the twenty-first century, what is the significance of these developments? As we said earlier, some central Fine Gael "myths" date from this period. Needless to say, the dramatic events of the period from 1921 to 1932 can be read in more than one way. Each historian, indeed, will have his or her own interpretation of the period. Supporters of Fianna Fáil would cherish a very different set of myths from those shared by Fine Gael members; they might see the behaviour of the anti-Treatyites as characterised above all by consistency and a refusal to compromise on their fundamental principles regarding national sovereignty. Their reading of the past would be essential to an understanding of the Fianna Fáil membership of today. For many members of Fine Gael, the party with which we are primarily concerned in this book, the lessons to be drawn from the first decade of the state, whose status as "myths" is confirmed by their presence as a leitmotiv in Fine Gael speeches and election rhetoric in subsequent decades, might be:

> Cumann na nGaedheal defended the institutions of the state when these were under threat from those using or condoning violence.
>
> Cumann na nGaedheal was always prepared to take necessary but unpopular decisions in the national interest, even when this was at a cost to itself in electoral terms.
>
> Cumann na nGaedheal espoused a moderate and realistic brand of nationalism rather than an extreme one.
>
> Cumann na nGaedheal was a party of honesty and integrity, always prepared to tell the people the truth about what was achievable rather than make irresponsible promises.

These perceptions, as we shall see in chapter 8, still have resonance today when members of Fine Gael come to think about how their party differs from Fianna Fáil. Perceptions of the past are all the more relevant given the high proportion of current Fine Gael members who come from families whose support for the pro-Treaty side goes back to the civil war, as we shall see in chapter 4.

THE FOUNDATION OF FINE GAEL

Cumann na nGaedheal was relegated to opposition by the 1932 election result, and it remained there for a further 16 years. De Valera called a "snap" election in January 1933, and Cumann na nGaedheal now found itself 29 seats adrift of Fianna Fáil. This election was the most tense ever to take place in the state. After coming to power, the new Fianna Fáil government had released many IRA prisoners jailed under Cumann na nGaedheal, and some of these were now involved in attempts to break up Cumann na nGaedheal meetings, using the slogan "No free speech for traitors". At election meetings around the country there were running battles between members of the IRA and of the Army Comrades' Association, soon to be known as the Blueshirts. Turnout reached a record level, and the polarisation of the electorate into two sharply-divided blocs was clearly evident in the pattern of vote transfers.[18]

By now Cumann na nGaedheal was very much on the defensive. It had proved to be a negative opposition party, and its initial naive hopes that a newly-elected Fianna Fáil government would soon destroy itself through impetuosity and inexperience proved illusory. Consequently, when the idea of a merger with other opposition forces was floated, many in the party found this an attractive prospect. Cumann na nGaedheal merged with two other groups. The first was the National Centre Party, which was led by two nationally-oriented political figures, Frank MacDermot and James Dillon, but was primarily a large farmers' party. In some ways, indeed, it was a revival of the Farmers' Party that had existed throughout the 1920s and had consistently supported Cumann na nGaedheal in government, so a merger between these parties was reasonably logical. The third element in the fusion was a different matter. The Blueshirts (modelled on Mussolini's Blackshirts), known formally as the Army Comrades' Association (ACA) and then as the National Guard, had come to prominence in the summer of 1932, and in July 1933 their new leader General Eoin O'Duffy endorsed a scheme to replace the existing party and parliamentary systems by corporatism along the lines of Italian fascism. Ernest Blythe, who wore the blue shirt with enthusiasm after the merger, saw a possible organisational benefit in joining up with the ACA; since it would never be possible to get responsible businessmen, professional people or farmers to do the arduous and tedious local work for the party, the "young men and boys" of the ACA would be ideal to undertake these chores.[19] The reasons why the colour blue was selected (on Blythe's suggestion) in preference to the original idea, grey, are not entirely clear. Blue was regarded as the national colour during most of the nineteenth century, and moreover the whole design of the shirts was similar to those of the sky blue regulation-issue garda shirts of the time, which may have boosted the appeal of blue since the ACA perceived itself as a kind of auxiliary police force.[20]

Thus, given Cumann na nGaedheal's defence of the institutions of the state while it was in power, it was remarkable that O'Duffy became the leader of the new party. This appears to have come about partly because some of the leading members of Cumann na nGaedheal were pessimistic about the prospects of success under the solid but unspectacular leadership of Cosgrave and hoped that the flamboyant O'Duffy might do better, while, from the National Centre Party perspective, allowing the leadership to go to O'Duffy made the merger look less like a takeover by Cumann na nGaedheal than might have been the case if a Cumann na nGaedheal TD had become leader. Nevertheless, it was a bizarre decision. For one thing, O'Duffy was not even a TD. For another, many of the Cumann na nGaedheal leaders were aware of O'Duffy's record as police commissioner and knew that he was erratic and unreliable at the very least. They may or may not have known that in autumn 1931 O'Duffy and some of his associates, fearful of the consequences for them if Fianna Fáil came to power, had apparently done some serious planning for a military coup against the Cumann na nGaedheal government.[21] William T. Cosgrave, in recommending the merger to Cumann na nGaedheal members, took pains to avoid the faintest hint of recommendation of O'Duffy personally.[22] Meanwhile, the National Centre Party leaders Dillon and MacDermot agreed to an O'Duffy leadership of the party before either of them had even met him, which reflected poorly on their judgement.[23]

The new party was called "Fine Gael – United Ireland Party". The name was something of a compromise, with Cumann na nGaedheal and the Blueshirts in favour of an Irish-language name while the National Centre Party wanted "United Ireland Party".[24] Exactly what the Irish name meant was, as with most Irish party names, not completely clear. "Gael", the modernised spelling of Gaedheal, was clear enough, but "Fine" was an unfamiliar if not archaic term. Technically it denotes a small group of closely related families or a tribe but, suggests Coakley, when "Fine Ghaedheal" had been employed for an earlier nationalist movement it "was presumably intended to signify 'Irish nation' ".[25] The name is usually, if imprecisely, translated as "Tribe of Gaels", though of course the party is never known as such; "Tribe of Gaels" would be a rather inappropriate name for a twenty-first century party hoping to lead an increasingly multi-cultural, monoglot English-speaking population into an ever more integrated European Union. Coakley observes that the party journal in 1933 advised that the first word of the name should be pronounced "finna", but in practice pronunciation varies across the country; "fine" (rhyming with nine), and "fin" can both be widely heard.

The merger between the solid constitutionalists of Cumann na nGaedheal and the band of street fighters led by individuals who in some cases can accurately be described as fascists was an example of what in later decades came to be called "entryism". This refers to the process whereby a small group infiltrates a larger one and seeks to insinuate its members into positions of power, taking advantage of the popularity built up over the years by the larger group to win a level of popular support for its own members that they could never achieve on their own. Characteristically, the smaller group is a relatively "extreme" one and hopes to use the moderation of the larger one to cloak its own identity from the public until its takeover is complete. The National Guard's relationship with Cumann na nGaedheal has many of these features but differs from classic entryism in some respects. For one thing, Cumann na nGaedheal willingly allowed the National Guard to join its ranks. More strikingly, far from having to work their way up from the bottom like most entryists, the National Guard leaders were able to join right at the top.

Attempts at entryism usually end with the larger group, realising that it is being undermined from within, ejecting the newcomers, and essentially this is what happened within Fine Gael. The worst fears of those who had been wary of the Blueshirt merger were soon realised. O'Duffy lived down to his reputation for impulsiveness, a bellicose attitude towards ending partition, and a less than complete attachment to democracy. The Blueshirts were involved in many acts of violence around the country. A number of farmers refused to pay land annuities to the government, and attempts by state officials to move onto their land to seize cattle to the value of the annuities were resisted by Blueshirts, who also did their best to prevent the holding of markets where these cattle were to be sold; indeed, the Blueshirts attempted to disrupt road and rail traffic and the telephone network.[26] Tension between O'Duffy and the more constitutionally-minded members of the party grew, especially when O'Duffy failed to deliver the sweeping successes at the 1934 local elections that he had promised. He was eased out of the leadership in late summer 1934, and was succeeded by Cosgrave, so Fine Gael now took on the appearance of a slightly revamped Cumann na nGaedheal.

However tempting it might have seemed in the short term for Cumann na nGaedheal to link up with an energetic grouping such as the Blueshirts, there is no doubt that in the long term this alliance did the party much more harm than good. For a party that had demonstrated such a deep attachment to the institutions of democracy to merge with a body with paramilitary trappings that was only too willing to break the law when it suited it was clearly inconsistent, and undermined the party's reputation. It remains a moot point whether the Blueshirts were explicitly fascist. They are probably best seen as a specifically Irish response to a certain set of circumstances, but undoubtedly there were fascists within Blueshirt ranks, including O'Duffy himself, and anti-democratic sentiments were aired in speeches and in party journals.[27] This involvement with the Blueshirts made it difficult for the party to gain subsequent acceptance as anything other than a party of the right. Moreover, the alliance, while it lasted, was a full-blown marriage. Several former Cumann na nGaedheal ministers such as Richard Mulcahy and Ernest Blythe and the future minister Dr T. F. O'Higgins were deeply involved in the Blueshirts, while the future Fine Gael Taoiseach John A. Costello spoke warmly of them. Costello, indeed, informed the Dáil in February 1934 that just as the Blackshirts had been victorious in Italy and the "Hitler shirts" had been victorious in Germany, so would the Blueshirts be victorious in the Irish Free State.[28] Some Fine Gael deputies even took to attending the Dáil in their blue shirts.[29] In contrast, a few senior figures such as William T. Cosgrave, Patrick Hogan and Frank MacDermot kept their distance from the Blueshirts.

That is not to say that from 1934 all Fine Gael members regarded the Blueshirt episode as an embarrassment that they preferred not to be reminded of. Many members continued to see the Blueshirts as a necessary response to the tactics of the IRA – from March 1932 onwards – in harassing Cumann na nGaedheal members and trying to prevent them from speaking in public. In the eyes of many members of Cumann na nGaedheal and Fine Gael, the police, now under the direction of the Fianna Fáil government, did not provide adequate protection for those whom the IRA was trying to silence. As Maurice Manning observes, as of late 1933 the main opposition party found itself in the position of having its newspapers banned, its meetings disrupted, some of its leading members subjected to police harassment, and several of its ordinary members around the country killed.[30] As a result, there is no doubt that many members of Fine Gael in subsequent decades would have felt positively towards the Blueshirts, not out of sympathy with an anti-democratic philosophy but because of a belief, accurate or otherwise, that the Blueshirts had played a vital role in defending freedom of expression at a dark time in Ireland's history.

The 1999 Fine Gael membership survey did not, for reasons of space, ask current Fine Gael members about their feelings towards the Blueshirts, but it may well be that there is considerable variation. No doubt many members feel a sense of embarrassment about their party's involvement with O'Duffy's movement, while others, especially younger members, can be expected to see the whole episode as being so far in the past as to have no relevance to the party of today – though, as we shall see in chapter 4, the age structure of Fine Gael members is heavily skewed towards the older part of the spectrum and so there are a significant number of members who were alive in the early 1930s and who may retain some childhood memories of those days as well as having heard first-hand accounts from their parents. For some members – not necessarily the older ones, but perhaps especially these – the "myth" of the Blueshirts, in the sense in which we defined the term "myth" at the start of the chapter, is a positive one. The Blueshirts, in this vision, far from being an anti-democratic and partly fascist organisation, played a vital role in defending democracy and the right to free speech. It is not easy to estimate how widely held this perspective is held, but it is certainly held by some. In the mid-1990s, Tom O'Higgins (a senior figure on the liberal wing of the party during the 1960s, Fine Gael's presidential candidate in both 1966 and 1973, and Chief Justice from 1974 to 1985) wrote very supportively of the Blueshirts: "members of the ACA, wearing identifying blue shirts, rallied for the purpose of protecting the exercise of free speech, and did so successfully".[31] Similarly, Cronin found that the elderly former Blueshirts whom he interviewed in the 1990s were unrepentant about the organisation and their part in it.[32] Indeed, at a candidate selection convention attended by the authors in 2001, a speaker declared that his grandfather had been a party county councillor in the 1930s, "when wearing of the blue shirt was necessary to preserve democracy".

The Blueshirt episode was a long time ago, but it has left abiding traces. The flirtation of a significant section of the party with fascism was, understandably, an embarrassment in subsequent years even to those who were prepared to defend other elements of the Blueshirts' activities. At the level of street politics, "Blueshirt" became the insult thrown at an Fine Gael member by supporters of other parties; hecklers at Fine Gael election meetings, until these largely died out in the 1960s, would shout, "Ah, you're only a crowd of Blueshirts". John Waters, brought up in a Fine Gael-supporting family in County Roscommon, recalls watching a procession of celebrating Fianna Fáil supporters after that party had returned to power in March 1982:

> To the passing throng, Dermo and I were not merely Dermot Carroll, joiner's apprentice, soccer player and music fan, and John Waters, mailcar driver and part-time rock journalist. The pair of us, sitting in the green Hiace van opposite Flynn's public house in Main Street, were Blueshirts, and the sons of Blueshirts, to be smiled at as they passed.[33]

Blue remains the colour most closely identified with Fine Gael. In the early 1980s, when Fine Gael was planning a poster campaign to highlight what it saw as its dynamic, progressive proposals, focus groups were utilised to ascertain whether the posters could safely be blue, or whether this would instinctively be associated in voters' minds with the past, traditionalism and the Blueshirts. The focus group response suggested that blue would not trigger a negative response, and it was duly employed, without adverse consequences. As the title of this book – which is based on a phrase used by a Fine Gael branch secretary – suggests, members themselves are well aware of the significance of the colour blue in their party's history.

FINE GAEL FROM THE 1930s TO 1977

By comparison with the dramatic early years – forged from an independence struggle and a civil war, followed by a decade of single-party government in difficult circumstances and a merger with an unofficial militia tinged with fascism – the rest of Fine Gael's history might appear rather tame. Once the "old guard" had regained control of Fine Gael with the ousting of O'Duffy, and William T. Cosgrave was reinstated as leader, the party followed an electoral trajectory that went steadily downhill. The period from 1938 to 1948 has been described as "the most dismal in Fine Gael's history",[34] and by the mid-1940s it was in dire straits. When five by-elections arose in December 1945, the party was simply unable to find credible candidates in four of them and had to stand aside.[35] The party leader Richard Mulcahy, who had succeeded Cosgrave the previous year, told his parliamentary party in December 1945 that next year's ard-fheis was vital: "It is now more than ever essential that the Party should react in no uncertain manner against the suggestion that Fine Gael had no purpose". Consequently he requested each TD or Senator to undertake to bring ten members to the conference with them. In a discussion that is scarcely credible for the main opposition party of the day, several TDs said they would do their best (before in some cases leaving the meeting for more pressing engagements), and by the end of the meeting only six Oireachtas members had promised to bring the required number of delegates; five said they would bring ten while Senator Gerard Sweetman promised twenty from Kildare. Sweetman observed frankly that "the persons attending would not be essentially delegates representative of the Party Organisation so much as the personal followers of individual Deputies and Senators".[36] Photographs of ard-fheiseanna from this period show small numbers of delegates, well wrapped up in coats, sitting glumly (often underneath constituency signboards) in what appear to be cold and largely empty halls.

At the 1948 election Fine Gael actually fell below 20 per cent of the votes for the first and so far the only time (see Figure 2.1). Out of defeat came triumph, though, as Fianna Fáil lost its overall majority at this election, and against many expectations an alternative coalition (termed an "Inter-Party" government) was put together. Fine Gael took the initiative in constructing this government as well as receiving nearly half of the cabinet posts, and it was a Fine Gael TD, John A. Costello, who became Taoiseach. The very fact of being in government after 16 years during which the prospect had come to look further and further away gave an enormous boost to the morale of the party. In the minutes of the parliamentary party there is no longer talk of trying to justify the existence of the party; instead there are references to a rising tide of enthusiasm, a surge of support and a widespread demand around the country for meetings at which ministers would be in attendance.[37] (Unfortunately, the absence of membership records makes it impossible to tell whether it also led to an influx of members.) The experience of being in government with Labour for the first time also created a pattern of cooperation between the parties at local level that persists to this day, especially in some rural constituencies.

It led to a growth in the party's electoral support (briefly interrupted in 1957) so by the 1960s it consistently won about a third of the votes cast at elections (see Appendix D). However, the period 1957–73 proved to be another sixteen-year spell in the wilderness for Fine Gael. This was partly because Labour for most of this time was bent on establishing itself as a major party and consequently decided on an anti-coalition strategy, believing that its past participation in coalition governments had damaged it and hoping that by remaining in "principled opposition" it would attain the level of support enjoyed by the left in other European countries.

Fine Gael's leadership changed several times during this period. Costello, despite being Taoiseach in each of the two coalition governments of the 1948–57 period, was never party leader, and when it came to selecting the Fine Gael ministers to sit in government a major part was played by Richard Mulcahy, the party leader. Mulcahy was vetoed as a possible Taoiseach by Fine Gael's coalition partners, especially the neo-republican Clann na Poblachta, largely because of his record as Minister for Defence during the civil war. In 1959 Mulcahy resigned the leadership and the contest to succeed him was won by James Dillon, who defeated the former Minister for External Affairs Liam Cosgrave. Dillon's journey to this post had been a long one. He had been a TD since 1932, and, having been one of the leaders of the National Centre Party, became vice-president of Fine Gael when the party was founded in 1933. Unusually for a politician in any country, he resigned from high office in his party on a matter of policy, when in 1942 he left Fine Gael over the issue of Irish neutrality in the second world war. Whereas there was agreement across the political spectrum for this policy, pursued with success by de Valera's Fianna Fáil government, Dillon believed that the evil represented by the Nazis was so great that Ireland was morally bound to join in the struggle against them. When it became clear that his advocacy of this policy was incompatible with continuing to occupy a high position within Fine Gael he left the party and sat as an independent TD, with no signs of regret. He was Minister for Agriculture in the first Inter-Party government, and rejoined Fine Gael in 1952, holding office again in the second coalition government, although he felt more constrained in this administration precisely because he was now in a party.[38] He was a politician of vision whose horizons were far broader than Ireland alone, but critics said that his visions belonged to a bygone era and that his declamatory and orotund speaking style would have been more at home in the House of Commons in the 1860s than the Dáil of the 1960s.

As Fine Gael leader he was hardly a success, with no great interest in the details of policy, and he resigned immediately after the 1965 election. At this stage there was an uncharacteristic policy ferment within the party. Ever since 1959 a radical group, spearheaded by Declan Costello, son of the former Taoiseach and himself a TD since 1951, had been urging the party to move clearly to the left and to give priority to social justice and equality. In May 1964 he succeeded in persuading the parliamentary party to endorse an eight-point programme that became known as the "Just Society" programme. The document advocated full economic planning and government control of the banks' credit policies, and looked very radical by Fine Gael's standards. The May 1964 programme formed the basis of the party's 1965 election manifesto, which was titled *Towards a Just Society*. The party leadership, though, did not feign any enthusiasm for it and voters actually had to pay money to obtain a copy (see photograph later in book). Dillon introduced it to the press in whimsical manner and stressed throughout the campaign Fine Gael's attachment to private enterprise. Seán MacEntee, the most sharp-tongued of the Fianna Fáil ministers, described Declan Costello as "the cherubic Robespierre of the party, sitting tight-lipped", with Dillon as "the titular head bombinating about free enterprise".[39] Fine Gael gained no seats and Fianna Fáil remained in office. One internal party analysis of the "disappointing result" suggested that the party was taking the middle-class vote for granted and that it had given the impression that in the Just Society programme the only role for the middle class was as "a beast of burden for the rest of the community".[40]

The suddenness of Dillon's resignation, at the very first meeting of the parliamentary party after the election, took the party by surprise, and the same meeting unanimously elected Liam Cosgrave as his successor. The swift changeover was widely seen as a manoeuvre to ensure that the leadership remained safely in the hands of the conservative wing and out of the hands of Declan Costello in particular, though Dillon's biographer says there is no evidence to support this.[41] For the next few years there was evident tension within the party. This manifested itself openly at the 1968 annual conference, when a move to change the party's name to "Fine Gael – Social Democratic Party" received strong support from delegates but was prevented from being passed by the chairman, Gerard Sweetman, who persuaded conference to refer the matter to a postal ballot of all branches, in which it was heavily defeated.[42] Sweetman was a highly articulate right-winger, once described sarcastically as having "one of the keenest minds in the nineteenth century" and as being "so conservative that, if present at the creation of the world, he would have voted against it".[43] He was now seen as Cosgrave's strongest ally on the conservative side of the party, with the liberal wing, weakened by Costello's temporary retirement from active politics due to ill health, spearheaded by Tom O'Higgins and Senators Garret FitzGerald and James Dooge. This division, between a relatively conservative "old guard" and a more liberal or even radical wing, standing further to the left on economic issues and/or further towards the liberal end of the spectrum on church–state issues, is one that many observers of the party since the 1960s have identified. Whether it is at all evident among the Fine Gael membership today, and how far the left–right dimension and the liberal–conservative one coincide, are topics that we shall explore in later chapters.

Events of the next few years led to a fresh Fine Gael–Labour coalition. Labour's anti-coalition strategy had not brought the results the party had hoped, with growth being only modest – even at its peak in 1969 it was still less than half as strong as Fine Gael. An acceptance within Labour that the socialist millennium was not around the corner, coupled with the disarray within Fianna

Fáil engendered by the fallout from the Northern Ireland troubles in the early 1970s, brought Fine Gael and Labour closer together. This rapprochement survived a divergence between the parties on the important question of membership of the European Community, which was put to the people in a referendum in May 1972. Fine Gael supported entry, but Labour's line was one of opposition, though it was obvious that some of its parliamentarians were less than whole-hearted in their anti-EC campaign. Once Ireland joined the EC on 1 January 1973, the country received 12 seats in the European Parliament, and since MEPs sit by political bloc rather than by country, a decision had to be taken as to which of the parliament's groups to join. Fine Gael joined the European People's Party (the christian democratic group), thus offering an element of self-definition for the benefit of those who wish to categorise the party.

Labour and Fine Gael formed a government that remained in office from 1973 until June 1977, the longest-lasting and least fractious coalition the country had seen. Although by the standards of most later governments it performed well, at the time the rise in inflation and unemployment over which it presided was regarded as unacceptable by an electorate that believed that solving economic problems was well within the capacity of Irish governments. Cosgrave himself, although on the right of his party, was an effective chairman of the cabinet, treating Labour with due respect. His was a very distinctive prime ministerial style: he went home for lunch every day, did not disclose his home telephone number to any of his ministers, and would sometimes peruse the racing pages of the newspapers during cabinet discussions.[44] Despite this, or perhaps because of it, he was by no means the least effective Taoiseach the country has known. Only once, in May 1974, did he blot his copybook in the eyes of his ministers, when without warning he crossed the floor to vote against a government bill that would have legalised contraception, contributing to its defeat. He called the 1977 election, with the agreement of most of his ministers, before the government had received the results of opinion polls designed to assess its popularity; when these were received, it was apparent that Fianna Fáil would win the election in a landslide. Indeed, both Fine Gael and Labour lost heavily in the 1977 election. Liam Cosgrave immediately resigned the party leadership, and Garret FitzGerald was unanimously chosen to succeed him.

FINE GAEL FROM 1977 TO 1990

If Fine Gael members in 1999 were able to look back to a "golden age", that period would almost certainly be the first few years of FitzGerald's leadership. Organisationally there was an unprecedented energy and vitality, and until around 1983, when his second government started to lose popularity, the party's electoral fortunes soared. Fine Gael members could, perhaps for the first time, really believe that their party was poised to overtake Fianna Fáil. FitzGerald sought to invigorate the party. He launched a major membership drive and instigated an overhaul of the whole organisation.[45] Head office was professionalised and a new general secretary, Peter Prendergast, was appointed. The aim was to expand both the number and the activism of members, and to take control of constituency organisations out of the hands of incumbent TDs. The suspicion was that some TDs, who were termed "quota-squatters", were content to be continually re-elected as the sole Fine Gael TD in their constituency and were consequently opposed to the selection of a strong running mate, who might win a second seat for the party but who alternatively might simply oust them. FitzGerald toured the country tirelessly and was undoubtedly a very popular figure among the activists, though his changes seemed to be resented and resisted by some more traditional members.

At the 1981 election the dividends of this massive effort were apparent as the party's share of the vote rose to its highest level since the 1920s, and the party entered government with Labour, FitzGerald becoming Taoiseach. The coalition held only 80 of the 166 Dáil seats, but it displayed none of the caution that might be associated with minority governments. It introduced an emergency budget to try to contain a financial situation that was running out of control, and did not shrink from cutting spending and raising taxes to reduce the alarming budget deficit. During its short time in office it succeeded in changing the political climate, and within a few months fiscal rectitude, previously an obscure concept of interest only to economists, had become a matter of national concern. The government was able to persuade a significant section of the electorate that to continue spending at the present rate, without a large increase in taxes, would lead to economic disaster. It was brought down in January 1982 by a defeat on its budget; some of the independent TDs who had previously supported the government were unable to continue their backing, one issue being that children's shoes would be made subject to VAT.[46]

Nonetheless, the Fine Gael vote rose at the ensuing election, and even though the party lost office, Fianna Fáil, which had assumed that it would easily win an overall majority, was able only to form a minority government. This in turn lost a confidence motion in November of the same year, leading to a further election in which Fine Gael won over 39 per cent of the votes, the highest ever for either Fine Gael or Cumann na nGaedheal (see Figure 2.1). A second FitzGerald-led coalition government of Fine Gael and Labour was formed. This government proved far less successful than the first, though. There were constant tensions between the two participating parties – especially over how to close the gap in the public finances, with Fine Gael preferring to cut spending and Labour favouring the raising of taxes. The result was a strong element of deadlock, with economic policy producing sufficient austerity to cause resentment among Labour members and many voters but not enough to bring about improvement in the financial situation. FitzGerald was prepared to pay virtually any price to keep the government in office because of his concern at the possible consequences for the country if there were a return to office by a Fianna Fáil government led by Charles Haughey, given the misdemeanours of Haughey and his ministers in previous periods in power.[47]

One of this government's main achievements was persuading the British government to accept the Anglo–Irish agreement of 1985, under which the interest of the Irish government in the affairs of Northern Ireland was for the first time formally recognised as legitimate. This apart, not a lot went right for the government. Its attempt to introduce divorce (which required a constitutional amendment and hence a referendum) in 1986 failed when a large swing against divorce in the last two months of the campaign produced defeat by 63 per cent to 37 per cent.[48] An attempted reshuffle of the government in February 1986 went badly wrong when Labour's Barry Desmond refused to be moved out of the Department of Health and the Fine Gael Minister for Education, Gemma Hussey, accepted a new portfolio of European Affairs only to be told the next day that the portfolio would not after all be created and she was to become Minister for Social Welfare. FitzGerald's authority and judgement were both called into question by this debacle, and his own explanation that he had not sought to bring any fresh blood into the government because there was "no tradition" of dropping existing ministers indicates a conservatism that had not characterised his approach just a few years earlier.[49]

By the time the next election took place, in February 1987, Fine Gael was in difficult circumstances. The government had broken up the previous month when Labour had withdrawn because it could not accept the public spending cuts that Fine Gael was insisting upon. Worse, Fine Gael faced a significant challenge in its own electoral heartland. In December 1985 Des O'Malley and Mary Harney, who had both been elected in 1982 as Fianna Fáil TDs, formed the Progressive Democrats (PDs), whose outlook was firmly within the European liberal tradition of keeping taxes and spending low and separating church and state. In the months after their formation, the PDs achieved opinion poll ratings as high as 25 per cent, and Fine Gael's support plummeted. Other TDs defected to the PDs; these were mainly from Fianna Fáil, though one, Michael Keating, was a former Fine Gael junior minister. Yet, even though at the elite level the PDs seemed to be winning converts mainly from Fianna Fáil, among ordinary voters it was clear that most of their support was coming at the expense of Fine Gael, whose middle-class supporters in particular found much to attract them in the PDs.

Consequently, it was no surprise that Fine Gael's vote plunged when the election took place. It recorded its lowest vote since 1957 and lost 19 seats. Labour fared just as badly, but Labour was able to regain its strength at subsequent elections, whereas Fine Gael has remained in the doldrums ever since. FitzGerald immediately resigned the leadership of the party; despite having led it to unprecedented heights in the early 1980s, he left it electorally weaker (at just 27 per cent of the votes) than he had found it in 1977 (at 30 per cent). FitzGerald was regarded with great respect and affection within the party, and was instrumental in attracting many new young members in the late 1970s. He was both an intellectual and a university lecturer – the two characteristics do not necessarily coincide – who was able to impress a French president with his knowledge of the Catholic intellectual tradition in France, as he recalls in his autobiography.[50] While he was an outstanding Minister for Foreign Affairs in the 1973–77 government, and he made a consistently constructive input to the process of resolving the Northern Ireland problem, his overall record as Taoiseach perhaps did not live up to the high expectations many had held. Liam Cosgrave, like his father, was entirely practical in approach to questions, whereas it is said, perhaps apocryphally but entirely believably, that FitzGerald once responded to a proposal by saying "That's all very well in practice, but would it work in theory?" Cosgrave may have been seen as brisk and taciturn in cabinet; these allegations were never made about FitzGerald. In Brian Farrell's words, "his discursive style of chairing cabinet may have defused but did not resolve internal disagreements".[51] Cabinet meetings lasted for up to twelve hours, and FitzGerald was regarded as becoming too involved in the details of proposals – especially the statistics, which fascinated him.[52] Ministers reported that at times he seemed more interested in argument for its own sake, or for the sake of achieving consensus, than in reaching decisions. However, the tributes paid to him from all quarters upon his retirement were genuine and reflected not just affection but also widespread respect, and even his critics acknowledged that his leadership of the country had come at a period of exceptional difficulties.

There was a three-way contest to succeed him, in which the relative neophyte Alan Dukes defeated John Bruton and Peter Barry – in line with pre-2001 Fine Gael practice, the figures were not disclosed. Dukes, a TD representing Kildare, had been elected for the first time in 1981, and had joined a small and largely ill-fated band of deputies who have been made ministers immediately upon their election to the Dáil.[53] Dukes was aged 41 when he became party leader. Like most Fine Gael leaders, he did not follow the most common route to the Dáil, which entails getting elected to a county council. Instead his background was that of a technocrat; he was an agricultural economist who had worked in Brussels, first for the Irish Farmers' Association and then as part of the *cabinet* of Ireland's EC Commissioner, from 1973 to 1980. His rapid elevation to the cabinet in 1981 was testimony to his expertise and ability, but it was later suggested that a learning period as an ordinary backbencher might have helped him to avert some of the difficulties he was to encounter as leader.

Fianna Fáil formed a minority government after the 1987 election, and having bitterly criticised all of the coalition government's austerity measures it now proceeded to make even deeper cuts in public spending than the coalition had proposed, defying the opposition in the Dáil to defeat it. In September 1987 Dukes made a speech in Tallaght, a large satellite town to the south-west of Dublin, outlining what became known as the Tallaght strategy – indeed, the essence of the approach had been stated by FitzGerald on the night of the 1987 election count.[54] Essentially, this amounted to an undertaking that, in the national interest, Fine Gael would not bring the government down provided it pursued what Fine Gael regarded as a responsible economic policy. This was a remarkable departure from the confrontational norms of Irish political behaviour. Publicly, Fianna Fáil gave Fine Gael very little credit for what on the surface was a highly altruistic stance, stating that it would pursue whatever policies it thought best for the country and did not need Fine Gael or anyone else to keep it to a responsible line. Behind the scenes, though, Fianna Fáil ministers frequently met their Fine Gael counterparts and took on board Fine Gael requests for amendment of proposed legislation.[55] Not until 2000 did Charles Haughey acknowledge that Fine Gael's approach had been "enormously important" for his government's ability to pursue the economic policies it did.[56] Fine Gael certainly got very little credit from any quarter at the time. While some commentators praised what seemed to be a statesmanlike approach that was putting the national interest first, others suggested that Dukes's "Tallaght strategy" was simply an attempt to make the best of a bad position; Fine Gael was in no state to face an election in the near future, it was said, and was trying to put a positive gloss on its reluctance to pull the rug from under the government.[57] Fine Gael members seem to have been divided; even though many saw the strategy as further evidence of Fine Gael's determination to put the national interest first, others feared that Fine Gael was taking on a share of the responsibility for the government's actions without getting any of the power, and that an opposition party that declines to capitalise on a government's difficulties will get few thanks from the electorate.

At the next election, in 1989, the Fine Gael vote rose slightly, but not enough to secure Dukes's position as leader. Dukes was universally regarded as a politician of very high technical ability, but his handling of relations with party colleagues was not necessarily his strongest suit. His manner of dealing with party colleagues began to alienate a number of TDs. The blunt-speaking former Labour minister Barry Desmond says that when Alan Dukes became leader, "he treated his parliamentary colleagues as a senior psychiatrist treats a group of psychotic patients" and that he "could not resist portraying himself as the brightest boy in the class".[58] Dukes's position was fatally undermined by the outcome of the 1990 presidential election. Labour selected Mary Robinson as its candidate at an early stage, and by the time Fine Gael got down seriously to the business of finding a candidate she had already built up a strong base of support. The responsibility of finding a credible candidate rested with Dukes, and as a succession of big names declined what was looking like a poisoned chalice Fine Gael's anxiety levels rose. Finally the Dublin West TD Austin Currie agreed to take on the mantle, though by this stage Robinson clearly had most of the non-Fianna Fáil votes already sewn up. When Currie, despite a brave campaign, won only 17 per cent of the first preferences, this spelled the end for Dukes, who resigned a few days later just before a motion of no confidence that he was certain to lose.

THE BRUTON YEARS

Alan Dukes's successor, elected unopposed, was John Bruton, who was to spend an uneasy ten years as Fine Gael leader. Bruton had been elected to the Dáil in 1969 when just a month beyond his twenty-second birthday. Although he had law qualifications, he came from a prosperous farming family in Meath and was a reassuring figure for Fine Gael's sizeable agricultural support. He had worked his way up the party hierarchy, being a junior minister in the Cosgrave government from 1973 to 1977, and under FitzGerald had become one of the party's senior ministers. He was Minister for Finance in the first FitzGerald coalition, but his budget of January 1982 was the occasion of that government's collapse. In the second FitzGerald coalition he was seen as a strong advocate of cutting public spending, and in that capacity had become a bête noire to Labour, with FitzGerald frequently called upon to mediate in heated rows between Bruton and Labour leader Dick Spring. Throughout his career Bruton showed himself to have an enquiring mind and was always receptive to new ideas; for his supporters this was an asset, but his critics accused him of constantly taking up and then losing interest in what proved to be whims.

By the time Bruton became leader, the familiar political landscape had changed fundamentally as a result of Fianna Fáil's decision in 1989 to take part in a coalition government with the PDs. Previously Fianna Fáil had always opposed the idea of coalition in principle, which meant that if it failed to win sufficient seats to form a single-party majority or minority government, the only alternative was a government led by Fine Gael. Now that Fianna Fáil was "coalitionable", however, the rules of the game were very different. Fianna Fáil, it seemed, could remain in power almost indefinitely, by forming coalitions with either the PDs or Labour; given its famously or notoriously pragmatic nature, it would have no ideological hangups about making as many policy concessions to its coalition partners as they required. A route back to power for Fine Gael was difficult to identify, as Fine Gael and Labour together, with only 39 per cent of the votes at the 1989 election, did not look like a credible potential government. One political scientist outlined a future in which Fianna Fáil would be permanently in power, with Fine Gael able to enter government only in the extremely unlikely event of Fianna Fáil inviting Fine Gael to be its coalition partner.[59]

Faced with this unpromising scenario, it is perhaps surprising that Bruton lasted as long as he did as leader. At the first election into which he led the party, in 1992, Fine Gael slumped to a mere 24 per cent of the votes, its lowest since 1948. His attempts to put together a coalition with Labour and some other parties were brusquely rebuffed by Labour, whose leader Dick Spring had very unfavourable memories of Bruton's record in the 1982–87 coalition, when in Labour's view Bruton had been combatively right-wing with an excessive zeal for cutting public expenditure. Labour was also irritated that Bruton had seemed during the campaign to take Labour's participation in a post-election Fine Gael-led coalition for granted. As if to confirm Peter Mair's argument that all coalition options were now on the table, the government that emerged from this election was a coalition between Fianna Fáil and Labour, even though Labour had been extremely scathing during the election campaign about every aspect of Fianna Fáil. Fine Gael seemed indeed consigned to the wilderness.

With the party in the doldrums, speculation about Bruton's security of tenure was aired, and he had to deny more than once in 1993 that he was contemplating standing down as leader. Matters reached a crisis in February 1994, when the first, but not the last, challenge was mounted against Bruton's continued leadership of the party. Four front-benchers – Charles Flanagan, Jim Higgins, Jim O'Keeffe and Alan Shatter – went to Bruton and asked him to stand down; when he refused to do so, they resigned from the front bench. Bruton put down a motion of confidence in himself, and potential rivals for the leadership such as Alan Dukes and Michael Noonan indicated that they would oppose it and would stand in the resulting leadership contest if Bruton was ousted. However, after a lengthy discussion at the parliamentary party meeting, the motion of confidence was passed and Bruton remained in situ – partly, it was suspected, because there was no clear front-runner in the race to succeed him and some of the contenders preferred to let him continue rather than risk precipitating a leadership race which a rival might win. Bruton's winning margin was variously reported as 41–25 or 35–31; as usual, the party did not disclose the figures.

Bruton, and indeed Fine Gael as a whole, was thrown an unexpected lifeline in November of the same year when the Fianna Fáil–Labour government, which some observers had believed was virtually certain to remain in office for at least two full terms, collapsed. Fine Gael had little to do with the reasons for this, which resulted rather from tensions within the government, particularly between the two party leaders, Albert Reynolds of Fianna Fáil and Dick Spring of Labour.[60] During the days of crisis that followed Fine Gael did not shine, with the initiative in opposition being taken by the PD leader Mary Harney, whose Dáil performances overshadowed anything Fine Gael could offer. It did not seem that Fine Gael would benefit from developments, because once Reynolds had been forced to resign as Fianna Fáil leader Labour began negotiations for a fresh coalition administration with Fianna Fáil under that party's new leader Bertie Ahern. However, a fresh twist put an end to these talks and opened the door to a new possibility: a three-party "rainbow" coalition between Fine Gael, Labour and Democratic Left. This government duly took office in mid-December, with John Bruton as Taoiseach. Bruton gave ministerial posts to those senior Fine Gael TDs who had stood by him during the challenge ten months earlier, such as Enda Kenny, Michael Lowry and Nora Owen, but he also made a point of bringing his main rival Michael Noonan back into the fold as Minister for Health.

The government received consistently good ratings in the opinion polls, and in most policy areas was rated as reasonably successful.[61] However, Northern Ireland was an exception, as Bruton in particular seemed to lose the confidence of Sinn Féin without gaining the trust of unionists. Fianna Fáil repeatedly criticised Bruton for being insufficiently sensitive to the concerns of northern nationalists, thus confirming that nationalism remained a factor in defining the difference between Fianna Fáil and Fine Gael and moreover raising a theme that was to surface in Fine Gael's next leadership contest in 2001. The government, and in particular the Fine Gael element within it, was also hit by a number of difficulties, even if these never reached the scale of those by which Fianna Fáil was afflicted. Most were minor, but the most serious arose in November 1996 when Michael Lowry, the Minister for Transport, Energy and Communications and one of Bruton's right-hand men, resigned from the government after details of his private financial affairs emerged. It transpired that he had been secretly in receipt of money from a leading businessman, Ben Dunne, and "a web of off-shore accounts and convoluted transactions designed to avoid tax" was exposed.[62] Moreover, he had benefited from a previous tax amnesty without dis-closing this to the Taoiseach when he was first appointed to government. Lowry remained a member in good standing of Fine Gael until he resigned from the party in March 1997 and announced that he would be contesting the next election as an independent. When Fianna Fáil's image became seriously tar-nished by revelations about financial impropriety and allegations of corruption later in the 1990s, that party was quick to point to the Lowry case and to suggest that Fine Gael was in no position to criticise others.

The rainbow government operated efficiently and cohesively during its term, and it contested the following election as a coalition. This election took place in June 1997, a few months before the government would have been obliged to go to the country, and there were suggestions that the party leaders had allowed election speculation to get out of hand, leaving themselves in a position where the pressure to hold the election was irresistible even though the time was not ideal. The outcome seemed to confirm the analysis that the government might have done better by waiting a few months, since the three coalition parties between them dropped 7 seats on their 1992 standings. Fine Gael's own perfor-mance, though, marked some modest improvement; the party gained 9 seats, though its vote total, at 28 per cent, was a cause of relief rather than celebra-tion.[63] Fianna Fáil and the PDs were able to form a minority government with the support of several independent TDs, and Fine Gael returned to the opposi-tion benches.

The same pessimistic analyses that had been voiced between 1987 and 1994 now returned to the forefront. A road of endless opposition seemed to stretch ahead of Fine Gael. There were developments on the left: in January 1999 Democratic Left merged with Labour, but the merged party had no more sup-port than pre-merger Labour, bringing the prospect of an electoral majority for a Fine Gael–led government no nearer. John Bruton's leadership remained under continual threat, and the party's performance in various elections neither bolstered his position nor fatally undermined it. In November 1997 the party's presidential candidate, Mary Banotti, came a respectable but rather distant sec-ond to the winner, Mary McAleese.[64] Its vote in by-elections was generally down on the 1997 level, but it won the contest in Cork South-Central in October 1998 and came a close second in Tipperary South in June 2000. At the European

Parliament election in 1999, its vote was virtually unchanged since the previous contest in 1994 and it won the same four seats.

Matters came close to a head in November 2000, when the maverick back-bencher Austin Deasy placed a motion of no confidence before the parliamentary party. Bruton's heavyweight opponents were taken by surprise by this move and, uncertain which way the cat would jump, kept a low profile and generally did not support it. The motion was defeated, by a margin variously claimed to be 3–1 or 5–1. However, the end of Bruton's troubled reign was near. Following the publication of an opinion poll that showed that Fine Gael had the support of only 11 per cent of Dublin respondents and that only 37 per cent of respondents were satisfied with Bruton's performance as Fine Gael leader,[65] two of the party's senior figures, Michael Noonan and Jim Mitchell, announced in January 2001 that they would put down a motion of no confidence in Bruton. They stated that they were taking this step in response to pressure from ordinary members, who were conveying to them that "This can't go on". In a radio interview Noonan said:

> The demoralisation is palpable, the organisation is failing, the policy positions are not connecting and in terms of new politics being the ability to tell an alternative story, we haven't an alternative story to tell and the storyteller isn't convincing ... It's as clear as crystal to me now from talking to members of the public, from reading comment, and principally from consulting with my colleagues and with the party membership that Fine Gael is going to go and unless John Bruton stands down he'll close us down ... [Fine Gael is] failing to communicate its message properly and it's failing fundamentally to put forward an alternative vision.[66]

Bruton's opponents hoped that he would stand down quietly, but instead he came out fighting. Indeed, he showed a degree of combativeness during a number of media appearances that his critics said he should have shown earlier on the party's behalf. He was able to rally significant support, but on the eve of the parliamentary party meeting on 31 January the expectation was that he would narrowly lose the vote. This forecast proved correct, as the motion of no confidence was passed by 39 votes to 33 – the first time any Fine Gael leader had been voted out of office.

It was also, incidentally, the first time the party had released details from a leadership vote. Its previous practice had been to keep knowledge of the figures confined to those members of the parliamentary party who counted the votes, who were pledged never to reveal the figures. The curious rationale for this was that if the new leader turned out to have won only narrowly, his or her legitimacy might be weakened, while if one of the candidates had done very poorly, his or her subsequent standing in the party might be damaged.[67] It had been assumed that this was a party rule but now it was discovered that it was only a convention, one that the parliamentary party agreed to abandon, on this occasion at least.

Despite the criticisms made of Bruton's record, most of Fine Gael's difficulties were not his fault. He had inherited a party that was not in good shape internally and was in a weak position in the party system. Even his most dogged critics within the party invariably paid tribute to his integrity and decency, and most of them acknowledged that, however much responsibility Bruton bore for the party's uninspiring record during the 1990s, many other factors had also played a part. Bruton's defenders argued that the heave against him epitomised the way the political process was becoming trivialised, with integrity seen as only a minor counterbalance to the apparently more important factor of a disappointing opinion poll result. Those outside the party, and some within it, also pointed to a patchy performance by the party's spokespersons on various policy areas. Any realistic evaluation of Bruton's leadership has to take full account of the difficulty of making an impact as the leader of a party in opposition, at a time when there was little to choose between the policies of the various alternative governments and when the country was enjoying unprecedented levels of economic growth. He was party leader for over 10 years, which is by no means a bad tenure given the demands on politicians. If he was not able to inspire very much enthusiasm among the electorate, or transform the fortunes of his party, it has to be acknowledged that he is not the only party leader about whom this has been said.

Once Bruton had lost the confidence motion, the race began for the vote to fill the vacancy. The bookmakers offered prices about eight possible runners, but the odds for Michael Noonan (5 to 2 on) made it clear that the race was not perceived as wide open. Noonan was a former schoolteacher who had been a TD since 1981, representing Limerick East. After less than eighteen months in the Dáil he was appointed Minister for Justice in December 1982 by Garret FitzGerald, and he had been a fixture in Fine Gael governments since then. From about 1993 onwards, following Fine Gael's disastrous performance in the November 1992 election, he had been clearly identified as highly sceptical of the wisdom of John Bruton's continuation as party leader and as the front-runner to succeed or displace him. He was dropped from the front bench after his role in the unsuccessful heave against Bruton in February 1994, but when the party returned to government in December of that year he was appointed Minister for Health, and when the party reverted to opposition in 1997 he remained one of the most high-profile frontbenchers in the eyes of the public.

When the second favourite in the race, the Wexford TD Ivan Yates, announced that he would not be a candidate and indeed would retire from politics at the next election, the road was left clear for Noonan. Four candidates declared themselves, but two of these – Bernard Allen and Jim Mitchell – withdrew on the eve of the vote, acknowledging that their had not found the level of support that they had hoped for. Noonan was opposed by just one other candidate, the Mayo TD Enda Kenny, who had been one of Bruton's most loyal supporters during the 1990s; Kenny promised that if elected he would "electrify" the party. When the vote took place on 9 February, Noonan won 44–28; although the ballot was secret, many TDs declared their voting intentions to the media, and it was clear that, by and large, Kenny's support was drawn from those who had supported Bruton in the confidence motion. Michael Noonan thus became Fine Gael's eighth leader. At 57 he was the oldest person ever to become leader of the party,[68] and he took over the reins of a party facing into an uncertain future.

CONCLUSION

Fine Gael's record is one of qualified success. In electoral terms it has averaged around 30 per cent of votes at elections since 1932 (see Appendix D), which in many European countries would make it the largest party in the country. However, in Ireland it has trailed consistently behind Fianna Fáil, which has been the largest party at every election since 1932. Moreover, being consistently second has all too often earned it the position of being the country's leading opposition party; an honour of a sort, but not what any party aspires to. Over the twenty-five years between the elections of 1977 and 2002 Fianna Fáil spent about seventeen years and five months in government, Labour nine years and three months, the Progressive Democrats eight years and five months, and Fine Gael just seven years and six months. Not only is Fine Gael in government less than Fianna Fáil, which after all is larger; it also spends less time there than smaller parties do, since they have the option, which it does not, of going into coalition with Fianna Fáil. Too long a confinement to the opposition benches can undermine a party's morale, and this has been very apparent at times in Fine Gael's past, most notably the 1940s.

In our survey we did not ask Fine Gael members whether they are proud of their party's history, but if we had, we strongly suspect that the answer would have been a resounding yes. The party's image of itself is stated clearly in a booklet published in 1983 to mark sixty years of pro-Treaty organisation. Two quotes from it will convey a strong sense of the party's own perception of what it stands for and what its record has been. In a foreword, the then Taoiseach and party leader, Garret FitzGerald, wrote:

> Fine Gael has so many new members that we run a risk of forgetting what a proud tradition we are part of. Maurice Manning's work clearly demonstrates the courage, patriotism and real sense of duty which has been the strongest thread running through our history. It is very important that members of Fine Gael and non-members too, are aware of the way in which the first Cumann na nGaedheal government built up the new State. It took over a country divided by Civil War, with no machinery of administration and government and no international standing. It built up the economic and political structures of the country, based as this book demonstrates, on the independent, self-reliant policy of Arthur Griffith. We will continue as a party with that sense of service to the Community, courage and openness which is our greatest inheritance.[69]

The booklet finishes with the following paragraph:

> 60 years after the foundation of Cumann na nGaedheal, Fine Gael again finds itself in Government, leading and serving the Irish people. In the intervening years,

Fine Gael has shown itself to be a party with the ability to survive, to change, update and adapt to new circumstances, without ever losing sight of the values and philosophy and sense of nationhood, which permeated its founders, and which have inspired its leaders and its performance down through the decades. Today's Fine Gael party can look back on a lifetime of substantial and lasting achievement, proud of its contribution, sure in its identity, with the vigour, the vision and the courage to succeed.[70]

We will now move on to examine the role of ordinary members in Fine Gael over the years.

3 Membership and organisation in historical perspective

Since this book is concerned above all with the ordinary members of Fine Gael, in this chapter we examine the role members have played in the party over the years. On the whole, members have not occupied centre stage. As we shall see, Cumann na nGaedheal was created from the top down, by government ministers who were unconvinced about the need for any organisation at all and in some instances could hardly conceal their contempt for and indifference towards the party. It might be argued that the mould was set in these years. Certainly, up to the late 1970s the consistent picture is of a lacklustre, inactive party structure which occasionally a few individuals would try, usually unsuccessfully, to invigorate. Of course, a full examination of the party structure and of the power relations within Fine Gael is outside the scope of this book – in other words, while both in this chapter and in chapter 6 we will say something about how influential members feel themselves to be and how much notice they believe the upper echelons of the party take of them, we are not in a position to provide a rigorous assessment of how closely members' beliefs in this regard correspond to objective reality. Even so, in this chapter we will review the evidence available on Fine Gael's organisation.

CONTEMPORARY FINE GAEL ORGANISATIONAL STRUCTURE

The basic organisational structure of all of the main Irish parties is much the same,[1] and we outline the Fine Gael structure in Figure 3.1, which is reproduced from the party's *Branch Manual*. Party members join and belong to a local branch that covers a designated geographical area. In Fine Gael, each branch must have at least nine members. At the time of our survey in the autumn of 1999, Fine Gael had about 1,000 branches and 20,000 members. Each branch must have a minimum of nine members. Branches are required to hold an annual general meeting (AGM), and they are in fact supposed to meet quarterly, though the latter requirement is frequently not observed. There are nine officer posts (so in a minimum-size branch everyone can have one): a chairperson, a vice-chairperson, a secretary, two treasurers, a policy officer, a membership officer, an organiser and a public relations officer. Indeed, branches may elect other officer posts if they wish.[2] There is a 3-year term limit for the occupants of any specific post. There is considerable diversity in the observance of this. In some branches individuals simply disregard it and continue interminably, with no other member brave enough to point out that the incumbent is ineligible for the position – indeed, we

Figure 3.1: The organisational structure of Fine Gael

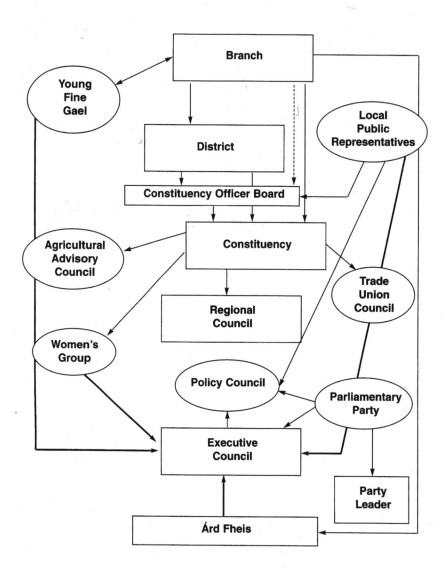

Source: Fine Gael, *Branch Manual*, p. 5.

found that branch secretaries had on average occupied their position for seven years at the time of the survey (see Appendix B). In others, a chairperson and a secretary might swap roles every three years, thus technically conforming to the rules but ensuring that control of the branch remains in their hands. In others again, the problem is not one of people trying to hold on to positions but of persuading anyone to volunteer for them in the first place. Analysis of the responses to our survey shows that the smaller the branch and the less frequently it meets, the longer the secretary is likely to have held that position.

Above the branch there may be a district organisation, covering groups of branches in the same area of a Dáil constituency, and above this is the constituency organisation. The constituency executive consists of all party members in the constituency and has ten officer positions of its own. This body oversees the activity of all the branches in the constituency, plans for elections, and performs a vital role in selecting parliamentary election candidates. Candidate selection, as in most countries, entails interplay between local and national party bodies. It is complicated in Ireland by the fact that under the PR-STV electoral system, the question of how many candidates to nominate can itself be an important strategic decision.[3] In Fine Gael the national executive decides how many candidates can be picked locally; members in the constituency, on the basis of one-member-one-vote (OMOV), then select this number of candidate(s); and the national executive (the executive council, as it is termed) may then add one or more names to those selected locally. The national executive might use this power to add the name of an aspirant who was defeated at the convention, so as to prevent party disunity in the constituency organisation, or it might deliberately from the start restrict the convention to picking one fewer than the number of candidates who will run so that it has a free hand to decide how to complete the ticket, perhaps adding someone who is not a party member. In 1997 the Fine Gael national executive added six names to those selected at constituency conventions.[4] OMOV, which we shall return to later, was first used in 1995; before then the local candidate selectors were branch delegates, with an estimated 40–50 per cent of members being directly involved.[5]

Before the introduction of OMOV there was an incentive to create "paper branches", ones that exist on paper but have no active members. This incentive, it is true, was a lot smaller than prior to the late 1970s, which is when the "model system" of candidate selection was introduced. Under this system, the number of votes that a branch could wield at a selection conference was linked to the size of the electorate in its "functional area" (thus removing the incentive to honeycomb a small area with branches), and this had gone some way towards dealing with the problem. The function of such branches was to boost support for aspiring election candidates; with candidates selected at conventions at which each branch had a fixed number of votes, it was in the interests of aspirants to create paper branches and pay the required membership fees themselves. The members in these branches, who did little or nothing within the party except vote as directed at the selection convention, were termed "ghost members". Under OMOV there is no point in creating paper branches, but ghost members are as valuable as ever. There is an incentive for aspiring candidates to sign their friends, relatives and neighbours up as members, even paying the small membership fee if need be, in order to guarantee a block of votes at the convention. The line between a ghost member and a genuine but not very active one is hard to define. In one case known to the authors, an aspiring candidate recruited large numbers of personal contacts into his own branch, which consequently was several times bigger than any other branch in the constituency. Other aspirants clearly regarded this as somewhat underhand behaviour and did not see the newcomers as "genuine" members.[6] In the candidate's own eyes, though, he had merely done what every member of the party should be trying to do, namely to boost membership, and had created a huge and enthusiastic branch in a constituency where the organisation generally was described as "moribund" – something that other aspirants should have been emulating rather than criticising.

The executive council is the most powerful body within the organisation. It contains the party leader and deputy leader, the two party vice-presidents, twelve members elected by the ard-fheis (annual conference), four members elected by the parliamentary party, two party trustees, and two members elected by each of four ancillary bodies: the council of local public representatives, the policy council, Young Fine Gael and the women's group. The executive council handles all disciplinary matters (including the question of withdrawing the whip from TDs). As we have seen, it also has some power over candidate selection: as well as being able to add a name to those selected at local level it may refuse to ratify a local selection. The ard-fheis is described in the party's constitution as "the governing body of the Party",[7] but although it discusses and passes policy motions no-one would suggest that it is a real decision-making arena. The constitution, indeed, does not bestow any particular power upon the ard-fheis.

Members do not have any role in the election of the party leader, although this idea was discussed in the 1990s, as we shall see in chapter 6. Instead, the leader is elected by the party's parliamentarians: the TDs, Senators and MEPs. As we saw in the previous chapter, two recent leaders, Alan Dukes and John Bruton, were ousted because they lost the confidence of the parliamentary party.

In all of the main Irish parties, including Fine Gael, there is no real pretence that ordinary members have a decisive voice in policy-making. With the sole exception of the power of Labour members to decide whether or not their party should go into coalition, party members simply do not decide policy. Even though on paper each party's annual conference may be the most important policy-making body within the organisation, in practice policy is decided by the party leader and by ministers (if the party is in government) or frontbenchers (if it is not). Most observers have the impression that members are satisfied with this; whether this is really true of Fine Gael members is something that we shall discuss in chapter 6 where we deal at length with members' views on the party organisation.

THE ROLE OF MEMBERSHIP IN FINE GAEL

On paper, the concept of membership of a party is pretty clear: someone is either a member of a party or they are not. In the USA, it is true, matters are not so straightforward, as people are termed "members" who would be seen only as "supporters" elsewhere. In Europe, though, there are usually some acid tests of membership: a member is someone who has paid a membership fee, has a party card, and belongs to a party branch. Certainly this has always been the case within Fine Gael.

Even so, in real life matters are not so clearcut. For one thing, there can be difficulties in defining who really is a Fine Gael member even given these apparently unambiguous criteria; people might register late, or only when there is some significant event such as a candidate selection convention coming up, yet remain on the rolls of their local branch. We will discuss these measurement issues in more detail in the next chapter.

More to the point, the very notion of membership, and Fine Gael's attitude to it, needs some exploration. One senior member of the party commented to the authors that "membership is a state of mind" and that many people around the country can and do consider themselves fully-fledged members of Fine Gael even if they have never paid a membership fee or at least are not currently paid up. John Waters comments that in his home town of Castlerea in County Roscommon, everyone was born into either Fianna Fáil or Fine Gael:

> Politics existed at different levels. There was a level of political activity in the town – people who took an active part in the organisation of one or other of the two main parties – but this, although related, was of a different order. Like the Church, which had its priests, sacristan and altar boys, so the political parties had their activists. These were the local guardians of the party's soul. But the spirit of the party in the constituency resided within the hearts of the people themselves, the people who had been "born into" the party, most of whom were neither activists nor members of the party in question. You did not simply "belong" to Fine Gael; you "were" Fine Gael.[8]

Indeed, as we shall see in the next chapter, some members, when asked when they had joined the party, said they had joined at birth.

The line between paid-up members and those who belong to the party in their own minds if not on paper is not always easy to discern. It has long been assumed that when the party needs workers, particularly at election time, many of those who come forward are not formal members at all; we will explore this further in chapter 6. More surprisingly, some leading Fine Gael figures have had at best an ambivalent attitude to the formal organisation of the party. Garret FitzGerald explains his first contact with it:

> It was indeed only the approach of a Presidential election, in May 1966, that brought me to a realisation of the curious fact that although by then I was a well-established member of the Fine Gael front bench I had never got around to *joining* the party itself. Clearly I had to find my local organisation, and through it join the

party. Accordingly I went to see my local TD, John A. Costello, to ask him how I should go about joining Fine Gael in Dublin. His response was, as usual, forceful, blunt, and idiosyncratic. "Forty years in politics; twice Taoiseach; never joined Fine Gael".[9]

Costello seemed to feel that FitzGerald need not bother joining either, but FitzGerald persisted and managed to persuade Costello to tell him where he could find a session of the local constituency executive, which proved to be "a small meeting, consisting mostly of fairly elderly people".

James Dillon, who succeeded Costello at the top of the party, was little different. He survived for ten years as an independent TD and clearly did not regard his departure from Fine Gael in 1942 as a high price to pay for standing by his principles. When he became party leader in 1959 he took some nominal steps to improve the organisation, which was in a run-down state, but in his own constituency of Monaghan he did not encourage the development of a strong organisation. He kept his distance from what organisation there was, and instead depended on a loose network of supporters for his local work.[10] Dillon was perhaps particularly unconvinced about the need for a strong party organisation. By the time he became party leader, he had been elected 10 times to the Dáil – but only five times as a party candidate, the other five times as an independent.[11] The idea of establishing a vibrant structured organisation peopled by members who might demand policy commitments in return for their labour would hardly have struck him as an attractive proposition. Other TDs, too, have been described as at best ambivalent towards the idea of strong local party organisation. For example, Oliver J. Flanagan represented Laois-Offaly as a Fine Gael TD from 1952 to 1987 (he had been an independent TD from 1943 to 1952), but an obituary suggested that he was "never a good party man" at local level and had often been in dispute with the local party organisation, which he had, perhaps not surprisingly, never tried to build up.[12]

This lack of commitment to, and indeed wariness of, organisation had been a feature of the pro-Treatyite camp from its earliest days. In the previous chapter we talked about the importance of "myths" that members might believe in – perceptions of the past that, regardless of whether they are accurate, play an important role in fostering a sense of identity. Many political parties appear to have a myth of a past golden age of high levels of activism, remembering a time a few decades ago when the local party branch was a hive of activity, when members participated enthusiastically in the social events it organised and discussed political affairs avidly. These glorious days of the past are contrasted with the current situation of declining levels of activism and organisational inertia. Admittedly, researchers who take the trouble to find out what really happened in the past often discover that the myths are almost completely inaccurate. Parties in both Britain and postwar Germany were never particularly active, and "some of the lamentations for formerly active constituency parties may be inspired by a nostalgic misperception of what members used to do".[13] Even so, the myth may at least serve a useful purpose in setting an ideal that the more committed members try to work towards.

In Fine Gael, there is no such myth – the only period that comes close to acquiring the status of a golden era was, as we have said, 1977 to 1983, after Garret FitzGerald became leader and before his second government started to lose popularity. Other than this, neither in reality nor in anyone's imagination was there a time when the party was characterised by organisational vitality. Part of the reason for the generally marginal role of ordinary members within the party lies in the way in which the party was created. The political scientist Maurice Duverger distinguishes between parties created "internally", in other words from the top down by existing parliamentarians, and those created "externally", by an extra-parliamentary body or movement. He believes that the way in which a party is formed will determine its subsequent nature: in internally-created parties, the parliamentary group will dominate, with members being peripheral.[14] While his thesis has caused some debate, there is no doubt that had he known about Cumann na nGaedheal when he wrote his book, he would have cited that party as an archetypal illustration of his point.

THE EARLY YEARS OF PRO-TREATY ORGANISATION

By the time the Cumann na nGaedheal party was set up in April 1923, the pro-Treaty government had in effect been in existence for over a year. Ministers had become accustomed to operating without any constraints from a membership-based organisation and, moreover, they had bad memories of the role played by the Sinn Féin organisation in the first half of 1922, when party congresses had to some extent tied the hands of the elite. Consequently, when Cumann na nGaedheal was established the organisational structure was one that deliberately downgraded the importance of the branch. The elite wasn't even sure that it wanted a national organisation, and if there had to be one, it must not be allowed to challenge the primacy of the parliamentarians.[15] When the party's founding convention took place in April 1923 a number of ministers ignored the event, as if the party had nothing to do with them. From the start the party relied on paid organisers rather than voluntary ones, and reports from around the country spoke of apathy, lethargy, and the difficulty in getting supporters to join the party or contribute time to it.[16] By the end of 1923 matters had if anything got worse. The party had only 247 branches compared with the anti-Treatyites' 729, in several constituencies the local organisation had run into debt and simply disappeared, and a member of its standing committee declared that Cumann na nGaedheal was "a shell not an organisation".[17]

Those within the party who wanted to strengthen the organisation tried to think of possible incentives that could be offered in order to attract members, but a suggestion that members should have the opportunity to be consulted on legislation was rejected by Kevin O'Higgins, who Tom Garvin concludes had "a positive contempt for the whole business of grass-roots organisation".[18] Membership numbers grew in 1924, not least because there were hints that when the untenanted lands were redistributed, party members would have preferment.[19]

There were signs that the organisation was becoming more assertive. There was criticism from members of the poor attendance in the Dáil of some wealthy Cumann na nGaedheal TDs, and when Ernest Blythe reduced old age pensions by a shilling the party's general secretary wrote to him in protest, urging him to take more account of the views of the party organisation. Blythe drafted a reply (in the event he sent a more restrained version) in which he could scarcely conceal his fury at this impertinence. He explained that the government and the Dáil had decided that his policy should become the law of the land, and went on:

> It is then surely the duty of a political organisation, by explaining to the people the reasons which have made this measure necessary, to endeavour to convince them of the need for it and to reconcile them to the acceptance of it. Instead of this I find that Cumann na nGaedheal and its Branches, so far from trying to realise the position and appreciating the needs of the case, has joined in the ignorant and irresponsible chorus of criticism.

Far from feeling it prudent to "keep the party on board", as politicians would nowadays, or thinking of himself as an organic part of the party, Blythe evidently regarded the party as having defaulted on its proper role as "a propaganda machine at the disposal of the Ministry", in Regan's words,[20] to become just another of the hostile and irresponsible forces by which the government was confronted. For Blythe, Cumann na nGaedheal was "you" rather than "we".

Later in 1924 the party organisation, through its standing committee (a kind of inner national executive) raised a different complaint, maintaining that the organisation was not receiving the level of patronage it expected. Being a Cumann na nGaedheal member, it argued, was more of a handicap than a help in receiving appointments and preferments – a perception that was to be echoed in our survey 75 years later. Patronage, it seemed, was needed since without it the organisation lacked numbers, enthusiasm and finance, and was described by the committee as "moribund" and "weak".[21] The business and professional classes for the most part kept their distance from politics, and it was hard to get money, support or candidates from them.[22] The organisation got a temporary lease of life in 1925 when J. J. Walsh secured the reinstatement of the old Sinn Féin rule that every branch could send two delegates to the ard-fheis (hitherto the number of delegates a constituency could send depended on how many TDs it returned), and the 1926 conference was a "more boisterous" affair. However, Walsh left Cumann na nGaedheal in 1927 owing mainly to his frustration at the refusal of the Cumann na nGaedheal elite to countenance economic protectionist measures (he was to become a Fianna Fáil supporter within a few years), and the stewardship of his successor as party chairman, John Marcus O'Sullivan, "was designed to neutralise the party as a departure point from which attacks on the elite could be launched".[23] Richard Mulcahy, writing many years later, traced the decline in organisational vitality to 1924, the year in which he left the government over his handling of the army mutiny. In his view, the Cumann na nGaedheal leadership, anticipating the views of some political scientists by over

MICHAEL COLLINS

GENERAL, COMMANDER-IN-CHIEF, NATIONAL ARMY   KILLED IN ACTION, AUGUST, 1922

Clockwise from top left: Michael Collins, pro-Treaty leader, Eoin O'Duffy, the first President of Fine Gael, W.T. Cosgrave who succeeded him and John A. Costello, the first Fine Gael Taoiseach.

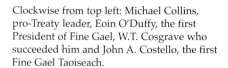

Clockwise from top left: General Richard Mulcahy, party president from 1944–59, James Dillon, leader 1959–65, Dillon and Mulcahy, following Dillon's election as leader and Dillon's successsor, Liam Cosgrave, who led the party until 1977.

Plate c

Clockwise from top: Garret FitzGerald, leader 1977–87 congratulates his successor, Alan Dukes (1987–90); Alan Dukes's successsor, John Bruton, who led the party until 2001 when he was replaced by Michael Noonan, who is pictured after his election by the parliamentary party.

Top: Fine Gael ministers in 1954–57 Inter-Party administration.
Front row: Gerard Sweetman, Seán MacEoin, Richard Mulcahy, John A. Costello, Liam Cosgrave, Pa O'Donnell. Second row: P. J. Crotty, John O'Donovan, Tom O'Higgins, Oliver J. Flanagan, Denis O'Sullivan.

Above: The National Coalition Government as it enters office, 1973. Front row: Mark Clinton, James Tully (Lab), Liam Cosgrave, Brendan Corish (Lab), Paddy Donegan, Richie Ryan.
Second row: Patrick Cooney, Tom Fitzpatrick, Tom O'Donnell, Peter Barry, Conor Cruise O'Brien (Lab), Dick Burke, Garret FitzGerald, Michael O'Leary (Lab), Declan Costello, Justin Keating (Lab).

Page right, top: Garret FitzGerald addresing an ard-fheis. Also pictured in two front rows are TDs John Bruton, Fergus O'Brien, John Boland, Paddy Donegan, Austin Deasy, Patrick Cooney, Peter Barry, Tom Fitzpatrick, Michael Begley, Eddie Collins, Michael Keating and Paddy Harte.

Above: Garret FitzGerald with members of his team in the early 1980s. Front row: Paddy O'Toole, Gemma Hussey, Tom Fitzpatrick, Austin Deasy and George Birmingham. Second row: Enda Kenny, Jim Mitchell, Eddie Collins, Paul Connaughton, Alan Dukes, Jim O'Keeffe, Michael Begley, Patrick Cooney, Nuala Fennell, John Boland, John Bruton and Michael Noonan.

Top: Paddy Donegan, Liam Cosgrave, Brendan Corish and Richie Ryan after receiving their seals of office from President Eamon de Valera, centre, in 1973.

Above: Fine Gael's front bench in February 1994. Front row: Richard Bruton, Seán Barrett, Gay Mitchell, Nora Owen, John Bruton, Bernard Allen, Bernard Durkan and Donal Carey. Back row: Maurice Manning, Jimmy Deenihan, Enda Kenny, Ivan Yates, Paul Bradford, Austin Currie, Avril Doyle and Paul McGrath. Back: Phil Hogan, Michael Creed and Michael Lowry.

Top: James Dillon speaking at an ard-fheis. The platform is flanked by pictures of Michael Collins and Arthur Griffith.
Above: The platform at the 1952 ard-fheis, with party luminaries displayed on a map of Ireland.

Top: Delegates at the 1953 ard-fheis, sitting under their county banners.
Above: Delegates in another meeting.

Plate i

Top: Tipperary, Louth and Meath delegations and a few journalists at an ard-fheis around 1950.

Above left: The candidate, Tom O'Higgins, addresses a party meeting during the 1966 presidential election campaign, and (above right) O'Higgins is welcomed by delegates.

Top: Limerick delegation at 1950 ard-fheis, including David Madden TD in the light overcoat.
Above: Delegates outside the 1956 ard-fheis. James Dillon is centre, second row, under the black hat.

Top: Fine Gael ard-fheis 1978, now at the RDS in Ballsbridge rather than the Mansion House.
Above: Delegates at an ard-fheis in the early 1980s listen to the speeches.

Plate I

Top: Delegates applaud the leader's speech, 1981 ard-fheis. The future TD P. J. Sheehan is second left.
Above: Garret FitzGerald is cheered by enthusiastic delegates after his leader's address.

Top: Fine Gael's nine women TDs, pictured in 1983: Gemma Hussey, Alice Glenn, Nuala Fennell, Mary Flaherty, Nora Owen, Avril Doyle, Madeleine Taylor-Quinn, Monica Barnes, Myra Barry.

Above left: John Bruton takes the applause on the platform at the 1996 ard-fheis and (above right) entering the hall with deputy leader, Nora Owen.

Top: Ann Flanagan, Deirdre
Cleary, Nuala Ryan and
others enjoying the Fine Gael
"Focus on Women"
conference in Dublin, 2000.

Left: John Bruton gets help
with his tie.

Above: Limerick delegates with Michael Noonan at the 1996 ard-fheis.
Bottom: Michael Noonan arriving to deliver address at special conference, 2001, following shortly after his election as leader.

Top: Members of Young Fine Gael in the idealistic early days. Future TDs Mary Flaherty and Phil Hogan can be seen near the centre of the picture. Ted Nealon, then the director of the party's press and information services, is third from the right.

Above: Young Fine Gael National Executive inside Leinster House in 1981 with the Taoiseach, Garret FitzGerald, who promised regular briefings in the future. Phil Hogan, future chairperson of the parliamentary party, is third from the left.

half a century, saw active members and branches as "a source of inconvenience and annoyance and demand on the government", so organisation was "damped down".[24]

From the perspective of the party leaders there were more congenial methods of organising than creating a mass organisation of potentially troublesome members. These methods consisted chiefly of making contact with "local notables" (usually these would be wealthy businessmen) in each constituency and using these as contact points.[25] The police commissioner Eoin O'Duffy claimed – admittedly in the context of a struggle to prevent the Cumann na nGaedheal government from cutting garda pay – that the gardaí were solidly behind Cumann na nGaedheal and with their local knowledge had played a vital role in pointing the party in the direction of influential people and in advising about the running of constituency campaigns.[26] In any case, the party's tactics produced disappointing results. Contemporary observers in Laois–Offaly in the late 1920s and early 1930s, for example, used such phrases as "not very strong", "practically inoperative", "quite supine" and "inertia" about the local Cumann na nGaedheal organisation, while remarking on the vitality and activity of its Fianna Fáil counterpart.[27]

A BRIEF HISTORY OF FINE GAEL ORGANISATION

Peter Mair writes that the main impression derived from analysis of Fine Gael and Cumann na nGaedheal organisation over a sixty-year period

> is of the long-term persistence of a poorly organised cadre-style party, continuing to lay organisational emphasis on key notables or individuals, while eschewing mass involvement and tolerating a lax and sometimes even non-existent branch network.[28]

The organisation was "generally debilitated", and in those years from the 1950s and 1960s for which the figures are available, it is clear that only about a quarter of the party's branches ever bothered even to register with head office.[29] Internal reports continued to emphasise the weakness of the organisation around the country, and when head office embarked on fund-raising exercises it saw constituency organisations as a rival rather than an ally.[30]

The minutes of the Fine Gael and Cumann na nGaedheal parliamentary parties show that the malaise reached all levels of the party. A continuous theme in these records from the 1920s to the 1940s is the poor attendance record of TDs, in Leinster House generally and in Dáil divisions specifically, and the reluctance of most TDs to be active participants in proceedings by, for example, putting down parliamentary questions.[31] The parliamentary party discussed the matter on a number of occasions but never managed to reach firm decisions, as in the last resort there seemed to be no sanctions it could deploy against the non-attending members. Expelling them from the parliamentary caucus would hurt the party more than the expellee. TDs knew that provided that their local supporters remained loyal to them, there was little the party's central organs could do to them. Fine Gael at this period corresponded closely to a party type outlined by Maurice Duverger, the "cadre party". Nineteenth-century cadre parties were dominated by parliamentarians, each of whom had his own local network of supporters and was sovereign within his own bailiwick, over which the national party had little or no control. The links between MPs were about the only ones that existed – there was effectively no national grass-roots organisation or powerful central body.[32] Although Duverger believed that such parties had largely disappeared from the scene by the start of the twentieth century – they had either died or had had to adopt a more organised form in order to compete with mass membership parties – Fine Gael conforms closely to the model. The party did hold national conferences at which members gathered but, as we saw in the previous chapter (see p. 26), the members who attended seem to have been primarily supporters of individual local politicians. Indeed, up to the late 1940s at least, conference delegates used to sit in blocks underneath a sign stating which constituency they were from.[33]

During his brief and unhappy spell as leader, Eoin O'Duffy mooted the idea of getting tougher with those TDs who were not pulling their weight. Addressing the parliamentary party, he began by expressing his disappointment at the low attendance and "complained that very little help had been given by deputies in some constituencies in the formation of branches and district executives". As for the absence of many deputies from Dáil divisions, he warned that he "would have to place the matter before the Constituency committees and make them understand that their organisation could be served only by their providing deputies who will do their work in the Dáil".[34] This unveiled hint that he would try to mobilise the party membership against the TDs and replace the existing TDs by more pliant personnel cannot have done much to boost O'Duffy's standing among the TDs – especially since O'Duffy was not himself an elected representative. Later in 1934 the parliamentary party decided that a record of TDs' attendance would be sent to every county executive meeting, but there is no indication as to whether this had any effect.[35]

Outside the Dáil matters were just as bad. In July 1934 the standing committee decided that due to the financial position the services of all the party's organisers would have to be dispensed with, and the following year the committee heard a report on "the apathetic condition of the organisation in Meath".[36] Meanwhile the parliamentary party was considering "the extent to which Constituency executives were in existence and properly functioning in each constituency" – although the minutes contain no more details, the clear implication was that many executives were not functioning or even in existence.[37] After Richard Mulcahy took over as leader in 1944 he identified the need to vitalise the extra-parliamentary organisation. He urged TDs to establish "closer contact with the Constituencies", and "explained the necessity of securing groups of persons who would form District Committees at pivotal places so as to stir up active thought and discussion locally".[38] TDs, it seems, were active neither in the Dáil nor in their own constituencies. However, as we saw in the previous chapter, the picture of almost unrelenting despondency was to be transformed in 1948, when Fine Gael entered government and the entire organisation took on something of a new lease of life. Even then, there were echoes of an earlier complaint – and, as we shall see later, of a complaint made by some members in 1999 – that Fine Gael did not "look after its own". At a parliamentary party meeting in 1949, two TDs, Seán Collins and John Esmonde, "protested that not enough favour was being shown by Departments to representations by our Deputies".[39]

In the 1950s and 1960s organisational deficiencies were still all too apparent. The parliamentary party continued to exude an air of amateurishness. Tom O'Higgins relates in his memoirs that on the day when the second inter-party government took office in 1954, both he and the incoming Taoiseach, John A. Costello (a fellow barrister), worked in court in the morning as usual; Costello told him only as he was leaving the law library that he would be appointed to government. After his spell as a minister was over, he took his place in Leinster House "after court", and being a TD for Laois–Offaly "necessitated visits over most weekends".[40] By his own account, O'Higgins was in effect a part-time politician between 1957 and 1973 – yet he was universally regarded as one of Fine Gael's most hard-working and effective politicians, which speaks volumes about the level of commitment of most other front-benchers.

At grassroots level the story was the same. When James Dillon became leader in 1959 he discovered that although on paper the organisation was extensive, "in many cases the branches had little more than a notional existence and no active role, coming to life generally only at elections to carry out the time-honoured rituals of canvassing, postering and manning the polling stations". He imposed a levy of £400 on each constituency organisation, not perhaps the most imaginative way of seeking to invigorate the membership or attract new members.[41] Towards the end of the 1960s Paul Sacks, an American academic who studied grass roots politics in County Donegal, contrasted the neatness, efficiency, centralisation and focus of the Fianna Fáil organisation with the more "diffuse" and loose style within Fine Gael.[42] At around the same time Basil Chubb wrote that in both Fine Gael and Fianna Fáil "many branches were almost inactive, and some were moribund", and that almost everywhere grass-roots organisation was "an uphill fight by a few enthusiasts in the face of considerable apathy".[43]

Incidents relating to the 1965 election bear this out. Liam Cosgrave, writing to the party's general secretary Colonel Dineen following the candidate selection convention in Kerry South, reported that "The Convention atmosphere was on the whole satisfactory, but I get the impression that the Organisation is rather loose and lax, and that a good deal of support could be tapped if a proper effort was made".[44] The laxness was apparent in a number of other constituency reports. The senator who had chaired the candidate selection convention in Galway East explained to Dineen that he had been reluctant to let matters go to a vote because there were doubts about the standing of some of the delegates present. Although he had been told that only 22 branches were affiliated, "I then asked all branch secretaries to put up their hands and about 150 hands went up".[45] The implication is that members of unaffiliated branches could have as much input as members of branches in good standing. This case may, though, have been exceptional because the Clann na Talmhan organisation in the constituency had recently come into Fine Gael.[46] As a rule, only delegates from affiliated branches could vote at selection conventions, and the result was that except when a convention was due many branches did not bother to register with head office.[47] Affiliation and indeed candidate recruitment could be rather informal processes. A member from a Munster constituency wrote to Dineen in the following terms: "It is some time now since you asked me ... if I could get you (F.G.) my son ... as a candidate. Thank God, it has come to pass – and both he and ... will probably be selected at our [convention] tonight ... I enclose £1 to affiliate the local branch – so that everything will be in order".[48] An unsigned analysis of the 1965 election outcome was withering about the state of the organisation and the attitude of members:

> Only 14 constituencies had selected their candidates before the election was announced. Directives and advice to have the candidates selected and in the field were ignored. Long delay in getting the election machine started in some constituencies because of poor organisation and slothful, negligent officials ... We must overcome overt attack as well as insidious propaganda through all media and also the cowardice and defeatism of some sections of our own supporters.[49]

Most Fine Gael leaders made at least a token gesture towards energising the organisation before giving up the struggle, but the first to make a serious and sustained effort was Garret FitzGerald. As we described in the previous chapter, as soon as he became leader in 1977 he embarked on a project to revive the organisation, involving a major recruitment drive (targeting young voters and women in particular) and an attempt to take constituency organisations out from under the thumb of the local Fine Gael TD.[50] In addition, he aimed to eliminate the paper branches. The "model system" of organisation that we described earlier in the chapter removed most of the incentive to create paper branches for candidate selection purposes.[51] In addition, the party insisted that branches had to affiliate to head office and supply it with details of their activities. A new, very professional and suitably ruthless general secretary, Peter Prendergast, was soon appointed – a break with the party's tradition of appointing retired military men to the position – and the number of members rose rapidly, from 20,000 in 1977 to 34,000 in 1982.[52] The impression at the time was that many of these new members were inspired by FitzGerald personally and shared his political agenda, one that was predominantly liberal on social issues, attached priority to peace and reconciliation within Northern Ireland, and was if anything slightly to the left of centre on socio-economic issues. Whether a discernible "FitzGerald generation" of members is still identifiable within the 1999 membership will be examined in later chapters.

The regeneration of the organisation in the late 1970s was followed by a large growth in electoral support for Fine Gael in the early 1980s, but of course we cannot be certain that it caused this growth. Perhaps the new image of the party under FitzGerald would have paid much the same electoral dividends even if no attention had been paid to the organisation – though our analysis in chapter 6 suggests that members do convey electoral benefits. In any case, during FitzGerald's second government, from 1982 to 1987, the number of members fell steadily and the party's electoral standing plummeted.[53]

Over the next few years the trend continued to be mainly downwards, and four months after Fine Gael's disastrous result in the November 1992 election, the party decided to conduct a full internal audit. It established the "Commission on Renewal of Fine Gael", which was also known as the Joyce Commission after its chairwoman, Gary Joyce. Although there were many good reasons for instigating this review, the exercise was seen by some as an effort by John Bruton to pre-empt a challenge to his leadership, with one senior member describing it as his "last chance to remain as leader".[54] Announcing its establishment, Joyce said that the party recognised that it had not "adequately responded to the needs of the Irish people in the recent past", and consequently its brief was to

> report and advise on the overhaul of Fine Gael as a party, in all its aspects (including its public image, the make-up of its membership, its organisation and its communications with the general public and the media) with a view to increasing significantly the electoral and parliamentary strength of the Party, to enable it to become established as the desired government of the country.[55]

To this end it would examine a number of areas, including some specifically concerned with the role of the membership. It wanted to ascertain the "image of Fine Gael held by its members, supporters, and voters" and compare this with the image held by those who did not vote for Fine Gael. In addition, it was to assess the continued relevance of the continued branch structure, the degree to which the party was successfully communicating with its own members and with the wider electorate, the selection of candidates (including the question of whether outsiders should be imposed on a constituency ticket) and the training of candidates.[56]

To this end the commission sought the views of a wide range of bodies, including Fine Gael members themselves. According to its report, meetings were held with party members in 28 different locations around the country, and a substantial number of written submissions were received.[57] The information gathered in this way is described as having "formed a valuable contribution to the Commission's work", but it is not presented directly in the report itself. The report, perhaps reflecting the fact that most of the commission's members were not party activists, was described by one analyst as not only longer but also less practical and definite than one drawn up by Fianna Fáil at around the same time, which was produced by "old party hands".[58] Even so, its analysis provides a significant insight into the state of the party in 1993, and some of its recommendations were implemented. Its conclusions about the state of the organisation were pessimistic, and it recommended radical change, though it emphasised that it did not believe that problems with the organisation were "at the core of Fine Gael's present difficulties".[59]

It found that the party organisation was interested more in itself than in the wider society; it was essentially "inward-looking", "internalised" and "literally talking to itself".[60] Consequently, it was innately discouraging to existing or potential members who were interested in ideas and issues. Branch meetings were all too often "fruitless" or "pointless".[61] (Our own survey data allow us to explore this, and we shall discuss our findings in chapter 5.) It felt that the existing branch structure seemed to work better in rural than in urban areas.

Its recommendations for change were sometimes far-reaching. It suggested rethinking the current organisational structure whose basic building block is the branch. For one thing, it urged that members should be able to join the party direct at head office without being attached to a branch. Regarding the organisational structure generally, it advocated pluralism: members in individual constituencies should be able to choose their own model. Some constituencies might decide, though only (it hoped) after a rigorous self-examination, to stick with the status quo, based on branches; this might be the case, the commission felt, in most rural constituencies. In other constituencies, though, something else might be better.

It explained that it had not had either the time or the resources to examine all the possible options and come up with a blueprint, but it made one main suggestion, namely that instead of geographical branches there might be "functional branches", such as a communications branch, an environment protection branch, a policy branch, a finance branch, a community enterprise branch, a community arts and education branch, and so on.[62] While the suggestion was understandable, party insiders did not regard it as very practical. In urban constituencies, especially in Dublin, the Fine Gael membership tends to be low: in 1997, for example, the party had about 2,200 members across all 11 constituencies, an average of 200 in each. There simply were not enough members to sustain a range of different functional branches, because many members would naturally be interested in several of the areas covered by branches and would thus be members of a number of different branches simultaneously. Indeed, different functional branches might end up as much the same group of people, i.e. the most active members, meeting under different names.

In addition, the commission recommended the establishment within each constituency of "single issue groups", which would be created by the local party organisation.[63] Their members would mainly be non-members of Fine Gael and would have no voting rights within the party; indeed, exactly why any non-member would join one, and what relationship they would have to the party, was not clear. At national level it suggested that the party set up "specialist groups" in a number of policy areas, with membership drawn mainly from outside party structures, in order to "generate debate and provide outlets for political expression". While it is clearly to any party's benefit to be able to draw on outside expertise, it appeared that the commission was thinking of the groups staging public meetings rather than playing the role of think tanks; the relationship between the groups and the party again seemed unclear.

The commission found evidence of disgruntlement among the Fine Gael membership:

There is a widespread sense within the Party that members are regarded as servants of the organisation whose role is limited to collecting funds and canvassing at election time.[64]

Our own survey asked members about their role within the organisation, and, as we shall see in chapter 6, this sense was as strong in 1999 as in 1993. To counter this the commission advocated that the members be given additional rights. First, the powers of the ard-fheis (which should take place every year) in policy-making would be enhanced. Second, the party leader would be elected by an electoral college in which the votes of the membership would count as 40 per cent of the total. Third, all members would have a direct vote in the selection of election candidates (the system known as one member one vote, or OMOV). The rationale of OMOV was that it would give members a stake in the party and might attract new members, and it was introduced on foot of the commission's report, as we have said. However (as was not pointed out by the commission), just as it provides an incentive to membership, so it provides a disincentive to activism, because now the most passive member would have just as much power in candidate selection as the most active one. More broadly, said the Joyce Commission, the members should be made to feel that they are appreciated. The Commission suggested that the party institute a system of awards nationally and within constituencies to allow recognition of members or branches that had made an exceptional contribution. How much has happened since 1993 to make members feel more appreciated is something that we shall discuss below in chapter 6.

CONCLUSION

Fine Gael's organisation has often been criticised from both within and without the party. Words such as inactive, inert and moribund abound in descriptions of the organisation, at least for the pre-1977 period. (We might note in passing that although this study is concerned only with Fine Gael, we suspect that many of the generalisations about Fine Gael's organisation would apply to other parties as well.) After Garret FitzGerald became leader a determined effort was made to vitalise the organisation, and since 1977 there has been a much greater degree of professionalism not only at head office but throughout the whole structure.

Even so, the scope for ordinary members to play a role within the party remains limited. The party leadership and the parliamentarians have generally been portrayed by commentators as taking the members for granted, relying on them to supply unpaid or cheap labour when election campaigns come around, appealing for money from them, often using them to pass on requests from constituents, but not being willing to give them many rights within the party. Indeed, it has appeared that members have not put the party under pressure to give them rights. Members, in this perception, have a basically marginal and supportive role within the party, and by and large are satisfied with this. How accurate this perception is will be explored in the remaining chapters of this book. We shall begin by examining the backgrounds of party members and finding out why they joined the party.

4 A profile of the membership

This chapter is the first of five in which we will present our analysis of the information provided by our surveys. In later chapters we will look at the activities and views of members, but here we will examine who the members are, how they come to be members of Fine Gael in the first place and what, if anything, are the differences between the party's members and its voters. We will start by examining membership in the aggregate, detailing how many members there are, and how much stability or turnover there seems to be.

MEMBERSHIP: STABILITY AND CHANGE

Party membership figures have been notoriously unreliable in the past, and not just in Ireland. There are a number of reasons for this. One is that many parties had no membership lists and could only estimate membership figures. Party central offices have been poorly equipped to keep accurate records even where these were deemed to be important. Another reason is that branches have had incentives to claim an inflated membership list, so as to obtain more delegates at selection meetings and party conferences. The branches themselves have been inclined to affiliate only sporadically to head office – as we observed in chapter 3, in the 1950s and 1960s almost three quarters of Fine Gael branches were not actually affiliated at any one time.[1] Hence estimates of individual membership could vary widely. Fine Gael began to regularise membership in the late 1970s as the then leader Garret FitzGerald sought to eliminate paper branches and weaken the influence of incumbent TDs within local party organisations. Affiliations became regularised. The professionalism and resources of the central party organisation increased and from the mid-1980s lists were kept in electronic form. Finally, Fine Gael was forced to further refine its national membership list when the one-member-one-vote (OMOV) system of candidate selection was introduced in 1994. Much better figures are now available than in the past, and these help us to see how Fine Gael has fared as a membership party over the past couple of decades.

Table 4.1 shows party membership figures back to the 1970s. It uses estimates published by previous researchers, and some more accurate figures compiled by Fine Gael and the authors. The data indicate a rise in the late 1970s and into the 1980s, followed by a decline over the 1986–88 and a subsequent stabilisation. At the time of our survey in late 1999 Fine Gael's register contained almost 20,000 members, a little over the official April figure recorded in the table. This total is fairly typical of the last decade or so

Table 4.1: Fine Gael membership figures 1967–2001

Year	Estimates of past researchers	Fine Gael figures
1977	20,000	
1978	20,000	
1979	27,000	28,529
1980	30,000	
1981	35,000	
1982	30,000	33,972
1983	31,000	
1984	30,000	
1985	36,000	30,002
1986	34,000	29,561
1987	25,000	24,923
1988	22,000	20,820
1989	20,242	19,533
1990	20,000	18,592
1991		23,456
1992		22,029
1993		18,715
1994		18,059
1995		17,132
1996		23,139
1997		16,972
1998		18,887
1999		19,232
2000		22,995
2001		23,315

Note: Estimates of past researchers taken from Farrell, "Ireland", p. 403; the party's own figures were supplied by Fine Gael or, in the case of 1985–87, calculated from information in Fine Gael party files.

although numbers do fluctuate, reaching a peak just before elections and then declining again. Chubb estimates Fine Gael membership at 12–15,000 in 1967, a figure that, if it is accurate, emphasises the increase in membership under the leadership of Garret FitzGerald.[2] Peter Mair's description of the rise in the numbers of registered branches, from between 200–400 in the 1950s and 1960s to 1,700 in the late 1970s underlines the change.[3] At its peak in the early 1980s Fine Gael had over 33,000 members, more if one includes those affiliated only to Young Fine Gael. The decline from those heady days puts membership in Fine Gael in line with the trend elsewhere in Europe where numbers have fallen in most countries over the past 10–20 years[4] but whereas some parties may be declining from a distant golden age, Fine Gael's high point is pretty recent and it still appears to be a more extensive member organisation now than it was thirty years ago.

The number of branches has also fallen from the 1,500 or so of the mid-1980s. There were 992 in 1999, the year of our study, a decline of about 33 per cent, paralleling the decline in member numbers. This suggests that the average size of a branch has not changed much. Indeed, in 1985, the last year in which membership exceeded 30,000, there were 1,569 registered branches, with an average size of almost 19 members. In 1999, the year of our survey, average size was only a little larger. Figure 4.1 shows the distribution of branch sizes based on information derived from our sample of secretaries. There are lots of small branches, few larger ones, and only a couple of very large branches with well over 100 members. The average figure (20.7) is somewhat distorted by the small number of very large branches. Two-thirds have no more than 20 members. Half actually have no more than 16 members. In other words, the party consists for the most part of numerous small branches, each of no more than 20 people, often no more than the bare 9 required for a legitimate branch. This is the setting into which new members come, and in which activities, such as they are, take place.

From the figures provided already it is clear that currently only a small proportion of those who vote for the party actually belong to it. In the 1997 general election Fine Gael won almost 500,000 votes, which means there were about 26 Fine Gael voters for every one Fine Gael member. Put another way, only 4 per cent of Fine Gael voters are party members.[5] This is low by European standards where the average level of membership is about 8 per cent of the electorate,[6] and thus about 10 per cent of those voting. Parties are more narrowly political in

Figure 4.1: Branch sizes in 1999

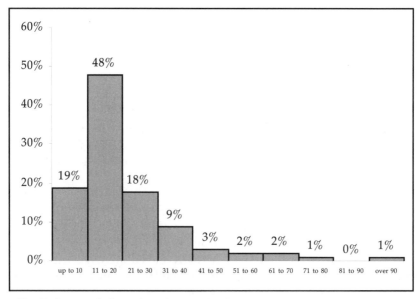

Source: Fine Gael secretaries' questionnaire, question 2.

Table 4.2: Fine Gael membership and votes per member in 1998–99, by European Parliament constituency

Constituency	Members (1999)	Votes (1997)	Voters per member
Dublin	2,017	104,119	52
Rest of Leinster	4,296	122,569	29
Connacht–Ulster	5,204	123,041	24
Munster	7,715	150,207	19
Ireland	19,232	499,936	26

Source: Calculations from Fine Gael figures and official election results.

Ireland than in some other parts of Europe; they are not rooted in social cleavages and therefore not underpinned by a network of organisations belonging to a particular segment of society. Some European social democratic and christian democratic parties once sought to provide organisations that catered for the whole of a member's social life from the cradle to the grave and while this era has passed, the linkages between parties and other organisations continue to help recruitment. By contrast, Irish parties, not least Fine Gael, have almost always appeared to be largely electoral organisations.

The membership level does vary across the country and is particularly low in Dublin (Table 4.2). In 1999 only about ten per cent of all members were affiliated in Dublin constituencies, although this area contains more than 30 per cent of all Dáil seats and more than 20 per cent of the Fine Gael vote. Electorally, Fine Gael's support is lowest in Dublin and highest in Munster. It has only about one member for every 50 votes in Dublin as against one for every 23 elsewhere. Arguably the weakness of the party in membership terms in Dublin helps explain its weakness in attracting votes. Certainly it is apparent that there is a significant relationship between the number of members and the party's electoral success, as we shall see in chapter 6.

The pattern of when people first joined reflects the overall decline described above. Most members have been there a long time, although the party continues to recruit new members. As Figure 4.2 shows, the average member claims to have joined between 1976 and 1985 and thus to have been a member for over 20 years.[7] Some members have been with the party for much longer, and a few apparently since before the first Inter-Party government, and almost a quarter of all members joined the party before Liam Cosgrave became leader in 1965. Only 14 per cent joined in the last five years. Taken together with the apparent stability of membership figures in the 1990s (as shown in Table 4.1), this evidence suggests there is little turnover in party membership. Very few members (7 per cent) report that their own involvement has been anything but continuous. The actual membership figures suggest a little more change than this, with increases or decreases of a few thousand from year to year. It is likely that many members

Figure 4.2: Year in which members first joined Fine Gael

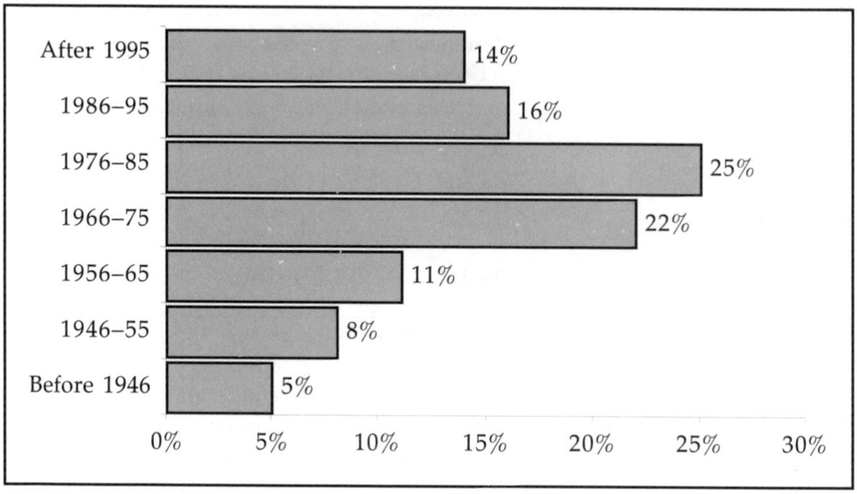

Year	Percentage
After 1995	14%
1986–95	16%
1976–85	25%
1966–75	22%
1956–65	11%
1946–55	8%
Before 1946	5%

Source: Fine Gael members' questionnaire, question 3.

simply don't realise they have moved off and back onto the register. It could also be that our survey was done at a relatively low point in the cycle. Membership tends to rise and fall, rising particularly when potential candidates mobilise their supporters prior to selection meetings. As has already been pointed out, membership did rise significantly in 1996, only to fall back following the 1997 election. Had our survey been carried out a year earlier we might have picked up much greater turnover. What we find here is perhaps closer to a hard-core membership. Even so, the picture is clearly one of stability rather than change. While the ability to retain members is good news for Fine Gael, its failure to attract significant numbers of new members should be more disturbing. Additional support may come and go, but current members are mostly in for the long haul.

For many, in fact, membership seems to have been an almost life-long commitment. Combining information on when people joined with their currently reported age[8] suggests that many members joined when they were relatively young, some of them very young indeed. Some members wrote comments emphasising this. One declared that he was "born Fine Gael", another had been a member "all my life", and a third said she had joined in 1929 and was now aged 88 and "no turncoat". By examining the different age profile of members according to when they joined we can get some idea of whether the party is indeed ageing. Reconstructing the party at any one time-point solely in terms of the survivors from those who joined at that time is something to be done with some caution. After all, if we use the sample of members who say they joined in, say, 1966–75 to generalise to all those who may have joined at that time we are assuming those who remain in the party are a typical cross-section of all who

Figure 4.3: Age at which members first joined Fine Gael, by cohort

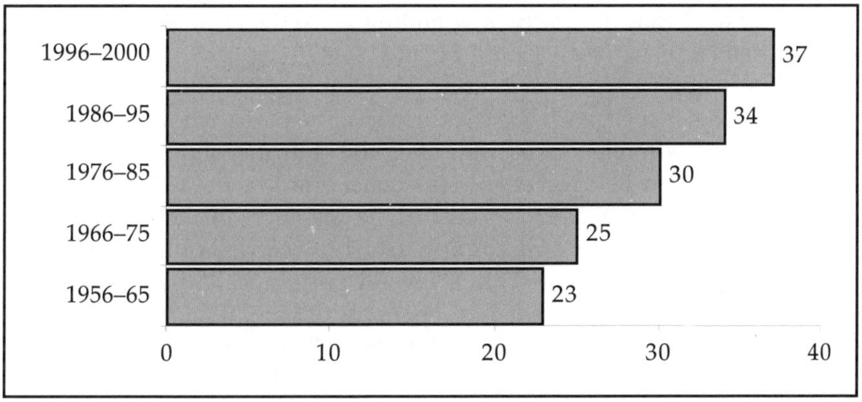

Source: Fine Gael members' questionnaire, questions 3 and 41.

joined at that time. This is a considerable and almost certainly false assumption. For instance, in this manner we can estimate the average age of those cohorts in 1966–75 to be 25 when they first joined. That group is, on average, 30 years older now and the older joiners of the time may well have passed on by now, or have dropped out due to old age or infirmity. If that has happened, we will have underestimated the age at which the average member joined. Obviously it would be much better to have made our estimates at the time, but since that was not done, and there are no national surveys prior to the current one,[9] we are forced either to say nothing about possible changes over time, or to examine the only available evidence and interpret with due regard for its possible bias.

Figure 4.3 shows our estimates of the average age of those who joined the party from the earliest years until the present day, using the same time periods used in Figure 4.2.[10] While the average age of joining is estimated at 28, the age at which people first enter the Fine Gael ranks *appears* to have changed over time, increasing steadily from 23 years old in the cohort joining between 1956 and 1965, to 37 years old for those joining after 1995. Each cohort is 2–4 years older than the previous one. However, this is the sort of regular increase in average age that we would expect from the selection bias of our contemporary sample[11] so we must be sceptical about the existence of any real trend in the age at which people join. New recruits may not be getting older. The absence of change over time contrasts with differences from place to place. Urban members tend to be a little older on joining and rural members a little younger. This holds for all cohorts and is probably linked to the lower tendency of urban members to have family links with the party (see below).

DEMOGRAPHIC PROFILE OF A FINE GAEL MEMBER

A Fianna Fáil party report painted a similar picture to that of Fine Gael described here, admitting that membership was "static" while the age profile of members showed that the party was getting collectively older.[12] The average Fine Gael member is between 45 and 54, and over 70 per cent of all members are over 45, with only 13 per cent under 35 (Table 4.3). Fine Gael compares favourably in this respect with the UK Conservative party, whose average member was recently estimated to be well over 60,[13] but this should not hide Fine Gael's essentially middle-aged character. Such a profile is not untypical of established parties. For instance, 88 per cent of the members of the Dutch christian democratic party were over 44 according to a study carried out in 1999, as were 79 per cent of members of the Dutch Liberal party and 75 per cent of Dutch Labour party members.[14] In Canada, 77 per cent of Liberal Party members were over 40, as were 70 per cent of Conservatives.[15] This tendency towards a disproportionately older membership profile is an inevitable characteristic affecting organisations, including stable democratic parties. Unless they are growing significantly, they must either shed experienced members, or become/remain dominated by them.

The typical Fine Gael member, then, is middle-aged. Table 4.3 demonstrates that other characteristics too are typical of a majority. Almost 70 per cent of members are male, although the gender balance is probably changing. Of those joining since 1995 only 58 per cent are male, compared with 65 per cent of those joining between 1976 and 1995. Every cohort is somewhat less male, and unless women are simply less likely to remain members, this points to a gradual feminisation of the party. The Commission on the Status of Women in 1972 reported that almost 25 per cent of members across all parties were women, but said that their membership was nominal for the most part. Yvonne Galligan and Rick Wilford claim Fine Gael changed in the 1980s as a result of high profile activists serving as role models combined with a concern by the party to attract more women: the Fine Gael Women's Group was established in 1985.[16] There are also some big urban–rural differences in relation to gender. In urban areas the gender balance is almost even (54 per cent male to 46 per cent female) but in rural areas the party remains very much a male-dominated organisation: only 27 per cent of all rural members are women.[17]

In terms of occupation the largest proportion, 32 per cent are farmers. Our data are insufficient to detail the relative numbers of larger and smaller farmers. However, relatively few report their farming as a part-time activity, which, given the difficulty of earning a living on smaller farms by farming alone, probably indicates the vast majority would fall into the category of "large farmers" (over 50 acres) rather than small ones. The remainder of the membership is predominantly middle or lower-middle class.[18] Only 10 per cent are skilled working class, and 12 per cent semi-skilled or unskilled working class.[19] Examining things in a little more detail, some of the more common occupations are teachers (3.3 per cent), secretaries (2.9 per cent), shop assistants (2.9 per cent) and nurses (2.5 per cent).

Table 4.3: Demographic profile of members

	%
Age group:	
Under 25	4
25–34	10
35–44	16
45–54	25
55–64	23
65 and over	23
Gender	
Male	69
Female	31
Class: Occupational grade of head of household	
AB (middle class)	15
C1 (lower middle class)	30
C2 (skilled working class)	10
DE (semi- or unskilled working class)	12
F (farmer)	32
Class: self assigned	
Upper/upper middle	14
Middle	56
Lower middle	8
Working	20
Other	2
Employment sector	
Self employed	43
Private sector	24
Public sector	23
Other	10
Educational qualifications:	
None	29
Inter/Junior only	21
Up to leaving	27
Up to technical qualification	2
Up to teaching cert/ degree	22
Church going:	
More than weekly	13
weekly	69
monthly	6
few times a year	8
rarely or never	4
Main newspaper read	
Irish Independent	52
Irish Examiner	19
Irish Times	17
Other	6
None	7

Source: Fine Gael members' questionnaire, questions 41, 35, 39, 38, 40, 43, 46 and 47.

There are, naturally, big differences between the profile in urban and rural areas, with more farmers and working-class members in rural areas. Among rural members 36 per cent are farmers with 39 per cent middle and lower-middle class (ABC1) and 25 per cent working class (C2DE). In contrast, 32 per cent of urban members are middle class and a further 41 per cent lower-middle class. Only 15 per cent are working class, a much smaller proportion than in rural areas despite the relative absence of farmers (12 per cent). The urban party is thus much more narrowly based on the middle class than the rural one. In a later section we will examine how this member profile compares with the party's electoral profile.

In response to a question (Q40) about the class members felt they belonged to, the vast majority said they think of themselves as middle class. Fifty-six per cent of members describe themselves as middle class, 14 per cent as upper or upper-middle and a further 8 per cent as lower-middle class. Only one-fifth see themselves as working class. Farmers tend to think of themselves as middle or upper-middle class, reinforcing the probability that Fine Gael farmers are generally "large" rather than "small". Fine Gael has always had the image of being a party of the middle-class and larger farmers[20] and this survey underlines the essential truth of that image.

Nearly half of members are self-employed, with the remainder fairly evenly spread between broadly public and private sector employment.[21] This preponderance is largely due to the substantial number of farmers, 80 per cent of whom are self-employed, but almost one third of the self-employed are not farmers but self-employed professionals (such as barristers), "company directors" and owners of small shops and service companies. Many members have little formal education, a characteristic that reflects the fact that the educational experience of many predates the modern era of widespread leaving certificate and third level participation. Younger members tend to have more qualifications than older ones. Twenty-nine per cent of members have no formal qualifications at all and another 21 per cent appear to have left school at 15 with no more than the inter mediate or junior certificate.[22] Twenty-six per cent have the leaving certificate and 24 per cent have either a degree (12 per cent) or a teaching or technical qualification, a figure that grows to 41 per cent amongst those under 35.

Almost all members (94 per cent) describe themselves as Catholic; only 4 per cent are Protestant and 2 per cent profess either some other religion or no religion at all. If Fine Gael has been the favoured home for Protestants, there are very few of them there now. Most members attend church regularly, with 69 per cent going weekly and a further 13 per cent going even more often. Eighty-three per cent own their own homes, with a further 12 per cent living on the family farm (which may be the same thing).

We also asked members what newspaper, if any, they read most. The *Irish Independent* was for a long time seen as the newspaper most inclined to support Fine Gael, and in view of that it is not surprising that 52 per cent read the *Irish Independent* compared with 19 per cent who generally read the *Irish Examiner*, 16 per cent the *Irish Times*, 6 per cent some other paper (mostly the *Herald* or the *Star*) and 7 per cent saying they do not read a paper at all. Only amongst the middle class AB group, 49 per cent of which tend to read the *Irish Times*, is the *Irish Independent* not the most popular paper. This popularity of the *Independent* might be seen as stemming from its traditional political leanings but in fact if we allow for their social class, the reading habits of members generally resemble those of the population at large.[23]

Most members, and particularly those members in rural areas, live in the constituency. Only 7 per cent live outside it (see Appendix B, Q11), a figure which rises to 17 per cent in urban areas. This is important in so far as members living in the constituency are best placed to provide the linkage between society and the party that we discussed in chapter 1 and which parties need if they are to respond to local problems and perspectives. As we will see in the next chapter, members do bring constituency problems to the attention of local representatives.

We also want to know something about the nature of members' other activities within society, given what we have already said about the linkage role played by political parties and the widespread view that parties are increasingly incapable of fulfilling this. Party membership is only one of many voluntary activities in which people might be involved. We were interested in whether members tended to be members of several organisations, which if true might help us understand their decision to be a party member. Overlapping membership is also important in that it tells us how a party can both pick messages up from, and disseminate messages to, a wider society. Members are generally seen as a channel through which communities and parties can be linked, with messages flowing through them. If members are active in other organisations this offers parties a way to stay in touch with a wider range of concerns, and perhaps demonstrate their interest to potential voters. Moreover, when members do join other organisations, what sort of pattern of overlapping membership is revealed?

Table 4.4: Members' links with other organisations

Organisational memberships	%
Farmers' associations	29
Gaelic Athletic Association	23
Community groups	19
Trade union	15
Residents' association	14
Irish Countrywomen's Association	5
Chamber of Commerce	3
Other	11
None	26

Source: Fine Gael members' questionnaire, question 34.

The data suggest that most are members not only of Fine Gael. Seventy-four per cent of members belong to at least one other organisation (see Table 4.4), and almost one-third of them belong to two or more. This is remarkably close to the findings from a study of Fine Gael and Fianna Fáil in Donegal in the 1960s which found 29 per cent belonging to no other organisation and 37 per cent belonging to two or more other organisations.[24] Most popular is the Irish Farmers' Association (IFA) or one of the other farming organisations such as the Irish Creamery Milk Suppliers' Association (ICMSA). Almost 30 per cent of all members, and 36 per cent of all rural members, belong to one of these, reinforcing the image of the party as one dependent upon farming interests. Given a Fine Gael membership of 20,000 at the time of our survey this suggests that some 6,000 members of a farming organisation are members of Fine Gael. The IFA is a very powerful sectoral interest group that represents about 85,000 farming families; the ICMSA is much smaller but is strong in particular areas of the country. Not all members of these organisation are farmers themselves: some are simply members of farming families, while others are involved in farming indirectly. Even so, the overlap between farming organisations and the party is striking.

Twenty-three per cent of members belong to the Gaelic Athletic Association (GAA). This is sometimes seen as an organisation closer in spirit to Fianna Fáil, but it is clear that a significant proportion of the Fine Gael membership is involved. The other most popular ones are community associations (19 per cent), residents' associations (14 per cent) and trade unions (15 per cent). Only 3 per cent belong to their local Chamber of Commerce, and, reflecting the relative paucity of Fine Gael women, only 5 per cent belonged to their local Irish Countrywomen's Association (ICA). Almost 9 per cent list a range of other organisations to which they belong, with some people citing several.[25] We have already pointed out that Irish parties are not linked strongly to any particular section of society. These data generally underline that assertion. There is a wide range of organisations whose membership overlaps somewhat with that of Fine Gael. With the exception of the IFA/ICMSA that overlap does not appear to be very large, but in some areas it would appear that party meetings might look a little like a sub-committee of the local farmers' association meeting.

MEMBERS AND SECRETARIES

Thus the typical Fine Gael member is middle-aged, male, middle-class, and living in his owner-occupied home. He is a regular church-goer, has modest educational qualifications, belongs to at least one other organisation and reads the *Irish Independent*. Some of these members may be relatively inactive, of course, and even where they attend meetings they may spend their time in the shadows at the back of the room. What of more active members? We will examine the nature and distribution of activism in more detail in Chapter 5 but here we will examine one activist role, that of the branch secretary. The secretary is a central person in the work of any branch who maintains the records of branch membership and meetings, serves as the main point of contact between different levels of the party and is probably the key person when it comes to whether the branch is active or not. Our sampling strategy was designed to ensure adequate representation of branch secretaries so that we could get a good picture of the typical holder of this vital position, as explained in Appendix A.

The average secretary reported that they had been in position for just over six-and-a-half years (see Appendix B). This is longer than the three years laid down in the party constitution but it could be that service has not been continuous. Many may even take up some other position and return to being secretary after a break. Even so, while half report that they have been in ofice only 4 years or less, 25 per cent report having been secretary for at least 10 years and 10 per cent for at least 15 years. This longevity is more characteristic of rural areas, where the average time in office is 7 years as opposed to 4 years in urban areas. This lack of turnover may reflect a general shortage of interest rather than show that many activists cling to power but as we shall see in chapter 6, members report both as problems.

Table 4.5 shows their demographic portrait, and compares the backgrounds of secretaries and other members.[26] On the whole these are very similar. The typical branch secretary is middle-aged, male, middle-class, self-employed, lives in his owner-occupied home, is a regular church-goer, belongs to at least one other organisation and also reads the *Irish Independent*! Only in a few respects are secretaries other than representative of the general membership. One marked difference is in terms of gender. Forty two per cent of branch secretaries are female as opposed to 30 per cent of other members. "Secretary" is a perhaps particularly gendered role in many organisations. Women are under-represented with respect to other offices within the party, and, as is well known, are drastically under-represented as candidates and elected representatives. In fact, leaving the role of branch secretary aside, only 25 per cent of women hold any office in the party organisation compared with 30 per cent of men. A second significant difference concerns age. True, most secretaries are middle aged: 47 per cent are aged between 45 and 64, as are 48 per cent of other members. But on average, secretaries are younger. Thirty-five per cent of them give their age as being between 25 and 44 compared with only 25 per cent of other members, and only 14 per cent are over 64 compared with 24 per cent of members generally.[27] Reflecting this difference, 58 per cent of secretaries joined between 1976 and 1995, compared with only 40 per cent of other members. There is little sign here that the observation made in previous studies, that members have to serve a long apprenticeship before obtaining office, is generally true nowadays.[28] Indeed, we would hardly expect this to be the case given that, as we pointed out in the previous chapter, each branch has nine officer positions. A third difference relates to education: 61 per cent of secretaries have at least a leaving certificate compared to only 49 per cent of members in general.

If in some respects, such as religious identification and observance, Fine Gael members (including secretaries) look like typical Irish citizens; in other respects,

Table 4.5: Characteristics of secretaries and other members

	Secretaries %	Others %	Difference %
Gender			
Male	58	70	-12
Female	42	30	+12
Class: Occupational grade of head of household			
AB	13	15	-2
C1	30	30	0
C2	7	11	-4
DE	17	12	+5
F	33	32	+1
Educational qualifications			
None	21	29	-8
Inter/Junior only	17	21	-4
Up to leaving cert	30	25	+5
Post-leaving cert	31	24	+7
Age			
Under 25	3	4	-1
25–34	14	9	+5
35–44	21	16	+5
45–54	26	25	+1
55–64	23	22	+1
65 and over	14	24	-10
Church going			
More than weekly	15	12	+3
Weekly	62	69	-7
Monthly	8	6	+2
A few times a year	9	8	+1
Rarely/never	5	4	+1
Member of other organisations			
Farmers' association	27	29	-2
GAA	19	23	-4
Community groups	23	19	+4
Trade union	19	15	+4
Residents' association	14	14	0
ICA	5	5	0
Chamber of Commerce	3	3	0
Other	16	10	+6
None	25	26	-1

Source: see Table 4.3 and 4.4.

such as their gender, age and educational profile, they do not. Of course there is no reason why they should resemble a cross section of Irish voters, but we might expect them to resemble Fine Gael voters, differing perhaps only in their greater commitment to the cause. In chapter 7 we will explore differences between members and voters when it comes to political opinions, but now we will compare the backgrounds of members and voters. Demographic differences may be important in as much as they might suggest some social distance between the members and voters, which may weaken the ability of members to help the party win electoral support.

WHO SUPPORTS FINE GAEL?

Since we want to know whether the Fine Gael members are a representative cross-section of those who support the party, we need first to establish who votes for Fine Gael. Fine Gael has long had the image of being the party of the better-off sections of Irish society: business people (especially those with long-established wealth rather than the nouveau riche), professionals, large farmers, and, in the early years at least, the church establishment. Is the image accurate? Testing it thoroughly would require data from opinion polls going back to the

Figure 4.4: Fine Gael's average support, by social class, at elections 1969–97

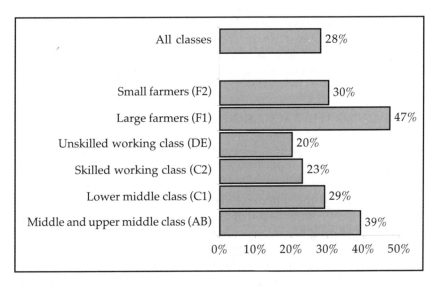

Note: The letters in brackets are the social class labels used in survey analysis. Large farmers are those with more than 50 acres of land, small farmers those with fewer than 50 acres. The figures for both categories of farmers apply to only seven of the nine elections, since in 1989 and 1997 farmers were not disaggregated as to farm size (Fine Gael received the support of 39 per cent of all farmers in both years). There are no figures from 1973.
Source: Calculated from Sinnott, *Irish Voters Decide*, p. 182; Marsh and Mitchell, *How Ireland Voted 1997*, p. 311.

foundation of the state, but of course polls were unknown in those happier days, and in fact the first survey data that we have were collected in 1969. For earlier years, and indeed for the modern period, we can employ techniques of aggregate data analysis, which in essence involve comparing the pattern of a party's support across the country with the socio-demographic nature of the constituencies, to see whether, for example, the party does best in poor or in rich constituencies, in the most industrialised or in the most agricultural constituencies.

In his comprehensive study of Irish voting behaviour, Richard Sinnott makes use of both these methods. Employing aggregate data analysis, he concludes that for most of the 1927–73 period the party's support was largely unstructured, though at some elections the party did significantly better in constituencies with a high proportion of employers and managers, and/or a high proportion of farmers, than in other constituencies. In the 1981–92 period, the party's support seemed to become more structured; the proportion of farmers became a strong predictor of how well Fine Gael would do in a constituency, with the proportion of middle class people also playing a role, albeit a less significant one.[29]

When the opinion poll evidence is examined, the same pattern emerges, as we would expect. At elections from 1969 to 1997 inclusive, the social group that gave strongest support to Fine Gael was consistently the large farmers, as Figure 4.4 shows. Fine Gael's next most supportive groups were middle class voters and small farmers, with working class voters giving it least support. Although the overall level of Fine Gael support varied from election to election, the pattern of support remains consistent. Fine Gael was usually slightly stronger than Fianna Fáil among large farmers and upper middle class voters; somewhat weaker than Fianna Fáil among lower middle class voters and small farmers; and much weaker than Fianna Fáil among working class voters.

COMPARING THE BACKGROUNDS OF MEMBERS AND VOTERS

Having established the pattern of Fine Gael support over the years, we shall now compare the profile of the 1999 membership with that of the party's voters, as measured in opinion polls from 1997 and 1999.[30] Table 4.6 profiles members, Fine Gael voters and the differences between the two. Several differences are apparent. Fine Gael voters are not disproportionately male, unlike the membership. Voters are also significantly younger. Fine Gael is relatively unsuccessful at getting support from younger voters; but the party is even more unsuccessful when it comes to attracting young members and it may be that each reinforces the other. There are also differences with respect to social class. Most striking is the over-representation of farmers and the under-representation of skilled and semi-skilled workers within the membership. Thirty-two percent of Fine Gael members but only 24 per cent of Fine Gael voters are farmers. This perhaps reflects the fact that membership is higher in rural areas but it once again underlines the importance of this interest group within the party organisation.

Table 4.6: Characteristics of Fine Gael voters and members

	Members %	Voters %	Difference
Gender			
Male	69	49	+20
Female	31	51	-20
Class: Occupational grade of head of household			
AB	15	14	+1
C1	30	24	+6
C2	10	18	-8
DE	12	20	-8
F	32	24	+8
Education qualifications:			
None	29	23	+6
Inter/Junior only	21	29	-8
Up to leaving	27	29	-2
Up to post-leaving cert	24	20	+4
Age			
Under 25	4	13	-9
25–34	10	18	-8
35–44	16	20	-4
45–64	48	32	+16
65 and over	23	17	+6
Church going:			
More than weekly	13	21	-8
Weekly	69	57	+12
Monthly	6	11	-5
Few times a year	8	9	-1
Rarely/never	4	3	+1
Associational memberships			
IFA/Professional groups	29	10	+19
Trade unions	15	8	+7
Community groups	19	6	+13
GAA/Sports	23	27	-4
ICA/Women's groups	5	4	+1
None	26	59	-33

Source: For members see Tables 4.3 and 4.4; voters, education, religion and membership from European Values Study 1999; class, gender and age from 1997 Lansdowne/RTE exit poll.

Members are more likely to be lower-middle class and less likely to be skilled working class than voters. Some care should be taken in interpreting these figures since, as explained above, the details given by respondents was sometimes less than adequate. If we contrast the percentage of members with that of voters we see members are 16 per cent less likely than voters to be working class, a bigger contrast than appears with respect to either farmers or the middle class. Members are more likely to have had no formal education but they are also more likely to possess third level qulaifications. This somewhat complex set of differences stems from the fact that members are older than voters, and more of them would have grown up at a time when second level education was much less widespread. However, the middle class bias in the membership comes out in the relatively high number with a degree.

An extensive survey of members and voters across Europe in the late 1980s discovered that, relative to a party's voters, members were more likely to be male, middle class and middle-aged.[31] Separate studies of British parties in the 1990s reached a similar conclusion. The British Labour Party was much more middle class than its voters as well as being more male and somewhat older.[32] The Conservative party was also much more middle class, and a lot more elderly although in gender terms members did not differ much from voters.[33]

This analysis demonstrates that Fine Gael's members differ from its voters in several demographic respects, but another contrast lies in their tendency to join things. Our own findings support this general conclusion, though comparison between members and voters is made difficult by differences in the data available. The 1999 European Values Study asked rather more general questions, for instance on membership of women's groups rather than the ICA, professional groups rather than farmers' organisations, and sports organisations rather than the GAA, but to the extent that comparisons can be made they seem to indicate that Fine Gael members are more likely to join other organisations than are Fine Gael voters.[34]

EXPLAINING MEMBERSHIP

This leads to an obvious question: what motivates people to join the party? The academic literature on this topic offers a number of explanations. One is that joiners have more of the resources necessary for some kind of political activism.[35] It is not really clear what resources are actually needed for party membership (as opposed to being needed for greater levels of activism, which we discuss in the next chapter), beyond some minimum amount of leisure time. More importantly, a resource-based explanation gives us little insight into why someone should choose to spend leisure time at a Fine Gael meeting rather than at some other pursuit. While a lack of resources may explain why some people do not join organisations, resource-based explanations give us little help in explaining who joins a party. A second set of explanations emphasise contact, suggesting that "joiners" are much more likely to have been exposed to contacts that "mobilise" them into the party.[36] A third set of explanations centre on the benefits people might derive from membership.[37] These are several. First there are the so-called "solidary" benefits that come from meeting and working with others. Next are "promotional" benefits, stemming from promoting certain policies or the parties and individuals who represent those policies. Last are "material" benefits, whether direct or indirect. The Joyce Report on Fine Gael, commissioned by the party in the early 1990s, argued that the party should ask itself about the benefits of membership and ensure that it could provide some positive answers. Unless people get something out of membership, it said, they would not join. The Joyce Report suggested that providing for greater member involvement in selecting candidates and even selecting the party leader would be a good start.

We asked our respondents a number of questions in an attempt to discover why they were Fine Gael members. First we asked them how they became members: was it on their own initiative, or did the party, or someone in the party, make the first move? Almost 50 per cent said they had approached the party, 39 per cent claimed to have been approached by the party and 11 per cent were unable to give a precise answer. By way of comparison, when asked the same question 33 per cent of British Conservatives said they approached the party, as did 79 per cent of British Labour Party members.[38] Fine Gael members are proactive, but not peculiarly so. While about half make the first move it is not clear from this whether or not such people may be prompted by a friend who is a party member, nor in what respect "the party" may have approached people. Informal contact may be the real source of both types of recruitment. All that is clear is that people do not typically join in response to any kind of formal membership drive. It has been argued that members brought in through recruitment drives tend to mirror those already in the organisation, as existing members approach those who are most likely to join.[39] However, we found little evidence of this although farmers, even allowing for the greater degree of such recruitment in rural areas, are more likely to say they were approached. It may be that the IFA and ICMSA are useful networks for such activity. In urban areas, it is the relatively uncharacteristic working class supporter who is more likely to say he or she was approached by the party. Perhaps most approaches are essentially personal ones, and, as such, idiosyncratic.

Next we asked members why they had joined, offering them a number of options including supporting Fine Gael policies, the influence of family and friends, interest in a political career, and a desire to put Fine Gael rather than Fianna Fáil in power. The largest group, almost 45 per cent, claim that they joined primarily for what we termed above "promotional" reasons, i.e. to work for Fine Gael policies, with a further 34 per cent saying they just wanted to help Fine Gael into office or (in 9 per cent of cases) to oppose Fianna Fáil. It is worth distinguishing the policy-motivated from the simply partisan here since as we will see they are rather different sorts of people. With fewer than 1 per cent claiming to be interested in a political career, or expecting any material rewards from membership, the remainder, 21 per cent, cited merely the wish to meet

Table 4.7: How and why members joined Fine Gael

	Approached party, %	Approached party, %	Total
Why joined Fine Gael			
Support/belief in Fine Gael policies	65	35	100
General support for Fine Gael			
put Fine Gael in power;			
oppose Fianna Fáil	54	46	100
Solidary motives			
meet interesting people;			
influence of family and friends	38	62	100

Source: Fine Gael members' questionnaire, questions 2 and 6.
Note: Don't knows from question 2 excluded.

interesting people and the influence of family and friends. Interestingly, there is a gender difference here. Women are more likely to cite solidary benefits (27 per cent as against 18 per cent of men) and less likely to cite partisan, non-policy, promotional motives (28 per cent as against 37 per cent of men). This would seem to indicate that more women might be attracted if there were more emphasis on the social side and less on the purely partisan (which does not include policy matters). Since we did not ask members about the size of their branch we are unable to identify any possible link between the size of branch people join and their motives, although we might expect larger branches to be more likely to be able to provide solidary benefits. There is a connection between why people join and how they join (Table 4.7). Of those who say that they joined because of the solidary benefits of membership, 62 per cent say the party approached them, perhaps through family or friends; but of those who say they were motivated primarily by policy concerns, only 35 per cent were approached by the party.

We should be cautious about accepting these reasons at face value. People take action for a variety of reasons, and sometimes for no conscious reason at all. They may only think about why they did something when someone asks them, and then provide an explanation which sounds good, but which may not be the right one, even if there is a right answer. We would not expect many people to say they joined for material benefit, even if they had done. Hence, the relatively small number of people mentioning policy factors is striking, as is the fairly high number mentioning what are essentially social rather than political factors. People who join Fine Gael, it would seem, are not all primarily interested in policy; many would appear to be motivated primarily by the social side of party membership rather than the more political element. Comparison with other parties in this regard is made difficult by the fact that the questions asked vary considerably but what evidence does exist suggests that Fine Gael is not unusual in the range and relative weight of members' motives. British studies show the importance of solidary and promotional incentives, both policy and partisan, with very few people admitting to materialistic motivations.[40] Dutch and

Norwegian studies seem to indicate solidary incentives are less important in both of those countries than promotional ones.[41] A recent study of Canadian parties highlighted the importance of supporting a specific candidate for leader or local nomination as a factor inducing people to join.[42] We did not include any reference to this motive in our question, but it is almost certainly important in the Irish context and, as we shall see in the next chapter, many people's activity seems to be focused on one candidate in particular.

Personal contact is a part of Irish political life and, as we have seen, many attribute their joining a party to the influence of family and friends. To explore the importance of contacts further we also asked members whether or not their parents belonged to, or supported Fine Gael. Sixty-two percent said that one or both of their parents belonged to the party (see Figure 4.5).[43] This is the most obvious way in which members are very different to the general population: they grew up in a household where party membership is part of normal life.[44] The comment of one party secretary in his seventies who "was born into a Fine Gael family and helped my father put up posters at election time for as long as I can remember" sounds as if it is not untypical. Another secretary detailed the family background in politics back to 1899. However, the urban party differs sharply from the rural one in this respect. Sixty-eight per cent of rural members followed parents into the party, but only 43 per cent of urban members have such a link. If we push this a little further, and ask whether members come from families with a long history of Fine Gael support, it is apparent that even fewer members come from outside this tradition. Seventy-five per cent of members say their families have a tradition of support for Fine Gael that goes back to the foundation of the state (see Figure 4.5). And fewer than half of the members without at least one parent in the party, meaning only 17 percent of all members, say their family has such a tradition, a fact which underlines the party's chronic inability to recruit members from outside traditional territory.

More surprisingly, secretaries are less likely to have followed a parent into the party, and are no more or less likely than other members to come from a traditional Fine Gael family. The difference is small: 46 per cent have no parents in Fine Gael compared to only 37 per cent of other members. But it is significant in suggesting that the sort of mobilising factors that aid recruitment into the party are not in any way necessary conditions for activism within the party. However, secretaries are hardly any more likely to cite a policy reason for joining. Forty-eight per cent of secretaries cite policy motives compared with 44 per cent of other members.

The importance of recruitment early in life is recognised by all organisations, and the establishment of Young Fine Gael in the late 1970s was a manifestation of that recognition in Fine Gael. The organisation, which is affiliated to but separate from the main party provides a forum in which younger people can participate with their peers and is intended to serve as a stepping stone to full party membership. As we shall see in chapter 6, many members see an active Young Fine Gael as the best way of attracting more young members into the party. Only twelve per cent of our sample reported that they had been in Young Fine

Figure 4.5: Extent of members' roots in the Fine Gael tradition

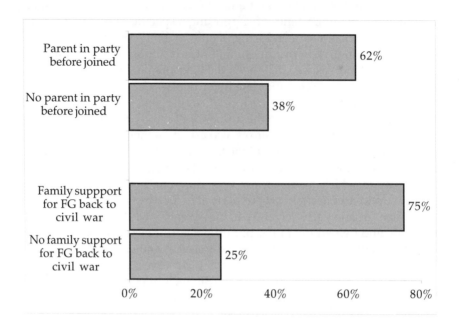

Source: Fine Gael members' questionnaire, questions 5 and 7.∴

Gael. Obviously many joined before the organsiation was established, although some who joined earlier, at a young age, could still have been in Young Fine Gael once it was set up. Amongst the cohorts joining in more recent years, 16 per cent have been Young Fine Gael members: 16 per cent (1976-85), 18 per cent (1986-95) and 15 per cent (1995-99). While Young Fine Gael does seem to be helping to get some people into the party, it is not becoming any more successful in doing so, and it is clear that most are not taking that route. It does appear to bring in members from outside the tradition but not very successfully. While 19 per cent of those from families with a tradition of support for support for Fine Gael reported a Young Fine Gael background, only 10 per cent of those from outside this tradition did so. Young Fine Gael appears a little stronger in rural areas than urban ones, with 18 per cent of rural members joining after 1976 having been in the organisation compared with only 12 per cent of urban members.

If we also look at the family related factors and motivations alongside information on when people joined the party we can get some indication of any changes that might be taking place in this respect. Perhaps policy is becoming more important and tradition less important in recent years. Once again, it should be said that this is a crude way to measure change over time, but in the absence of previous studies it is worth doing. Table 4.8 shows the results. Looking first at how people join, more and more seem to be approached by the party and fewer are joining on their own initiative, particularly in the last

Table 4.8: Changes in the methods of and reasons for joining Fine Gael

		When member joined Fine Gael				
	Pre-1955	56–65	66–75	76–85	86–95	Post-95
How joined Fine Gael						
Approached party	44	55	52	55	44	43
Approached by party	33	30	35	38	48	52
Family background						
Parent in party	82	70	67	52	58	54
Family has supported FG since						
20s	91	82	81	68	63	72
Family has supported FG since						
20s OR parent in party	95	84	87	75	74	79
Why joined Fine Gael						
General support for Fine Gael						
(put Fine Gael in power;						
oppose Fianna Fáil)	37	38	32	34	32	30
Support Fine Gael policies	51	49	49	47	37	31
Solidary motives						
(influence of family and friends)	12	12	19	18	30	38

Source: Fine Gael members' questionnaire, questions 2, 3, 5 and 7.

decade or so. This applies to about half of all members joining since 1986, compared to fewer than a third in the earlier decades. This does not of course establish that Fine Gael is becoming more pro-active, something that would be good news for Fine Gael. Nor does it tell us whether fewer members are wandering in by themselves or whether members who join on their own initiative drop out more quickly, either of which would be bad news for a party wanting to increase and broaden its membership. The relative decline in the proportion of members who have family links with the party is most marked in the change between 1966–75 and 1976–85, the latter coinciding with Garret FitzGerald's time as party leader (1977–87). This was an era of greater dynamism in the organisation and a much greater degree of electoral success. While the party appears to have become more open about 25 years ago, it has not become any more so since that time. The less exclusive pattern of membership has been sustained since but Fine Gael remains heavily dependent on family connections. Almost three quarters of all members joining after 1976 had either a parent in the party, or a long family tradition of support for Fine Gael. (Although the post-1995 period shows a slight increase in this figure, this is not large enough to be statistically significant.) Fine Gael's primary appeal is still to the children of the faithful.

Looking more broadly at reported reasons for joining, general support for Fine Gael and a wish to put Fine Gael into office remains a factor of constant strength but there is an apparent decline in the proportion stressing the importance of policy and an increase in those stressing social, solidary motives for membership. Once again, it could be that what we are seeing here is not a change in motive but simply the tendency of those who join for less political motives to move on to some other leisure activity rather more quickly: policy members stay, social members leave. Certainly there is a widespread view that parties suffer as alternative leisure options increase.[45] It is also plausible that, at a time when policy differences between the major parties are not always easily discernible, policy concerns are simply becoming less important as a factor in people's decision to join a party. Arguably, some of them join single issue groups instead. This is not to say that members see no party differences (we will explore the differences that members perceive between their own party and Fianna Fáil in chapter 8); only that they are perhaps less likely to emphasise that the major differences between parties are those of policy.

A classic feature of European political parties, as we noted in the opening chapter of this book, has been their role in recruiting candidates for election and thus members of parliamentary assemblies and even, indirectly, cabinet ministers. Those occupying the highest offices of the parliamentary party have tended to come from the ranks of the organisation that sponsors and supports them. This can be important in several respects. First, it provides an incentive for party membership. If parties control access to representative office, and use that control to the advantage of party members, aspiring politicians will have to join parties. Second, it provides cohesion both within the parliamentary party, in terms of shared experience, and between the party in parliament and outside it. Office holding, and the pressures and incentives associated with it, can distance deputies from their followers but perhaps a difference of views between members and deputies would be greater without the degree of common socialisation that party membership can bring. Of course, not every Fine Gael election candidate is a long-standing party member – in the past, indeed, John A. Costello could even become a Fine Gael Taoiseach without bothering to join the party, as we saw in the previous chapter. In the more professionally organised party of today that is unlikely to happen, but, even so, anecdotal evidence suggests that, in the current highly competitive market of electoral politics, central offices do not feel obliged to let the little matter of formal party membership stand between them and an attractive candidate. In chapter 6 we will see there is support for this approach amongst some members. Even so, it is also evident that the overwhelming majority of candidates do have a background of party membership and activity. The party provides at least one pool from which recruitment takes place. From that perspective it is instructive to look at the members who see themselves as aspiring candidates for a political career, at local or even national level. Do they differ from other members, and if so, in what ways?

We asked respondents if they hoped some day to be a TD or local councillor, or whether they had no interest in a political career. Two-and-a-half per cent had already taken the plunge and served as public representatives, and a further 10 per cent said they hoped to do so. Of these, a quarter had already sought an election nomination, and nearly as many had stood for a public office. The three groups – representatives (past and present), aspirants and the rest – differ from one another in a few respects. Aspirants are, perhaps not surprisingly, younger than the others. Sixty-three per cent of them are under 45, as against 25 per cent of representatives and other members. They are also more educated, 44 per cent having at least a leaving cert compared to 26 per cent of representatives and 31 per cent of other members, though this is no more than we would expect by virtue of their relative youth. Aspirants are also less likely to be female: 93 per cent of women members have no interest in a political career as opposed to 86 per cent of men. Interestingly, neither representatives nor aspirants are any more likely to say their parents were in Fine Gael. If anything, the opposite is true, although differences are too small to be significant statistically. Perhaps career motives help bring people into the party from outside the traditional fold.[46] We have no way of knowing, however, whether representatives became members long before they won nominations.

CONCLUSION

This chapter has profiled the Fine Gael membership, looking at when people joined, their background, and their motivations. It seems that while Fine Gael members resemble the wider population in many respects they differ in others, being disproportionately male, middle aged and, in broad terms, middle class. The party is by no means wholly a party of the well heeled, but the working class portion of the membership is relatively small, particularly in urban areas. Of course the party has more electoral support from the middle class, including farmers, than from the working class; judged as a representative group of party voters, members would pass muster in many respects, although not in terms of age and gender. Fine Gael is not unusual in this respect. It is a characteristic shared with many, if not most, other European parties.

Most members themselves cite either the desire to support the party and its policies as their reason for joining, or the influence of family and friends. This latter explanation taps the sort of social rewards many people get from their membership, but it also emphasises the importance of contacts in individual decisions to join. Most members come from families with a tradition of membership, and still more come from families with a tradition of support for Fine Gael. Members may be broadly representative of Irish people in demographic terms, but they are remarkably exclusive in their family political histories. Despite changes in the party organisation over the last 25 years, the party still fails to appeal to many outside its traditional orbit and where the family is less important, as it is in urban areas, membership overall is relatively low.

5 Activism within the party: what do members do?

Members are usually seen as vital to a political party – a perception that clearly implies that members actually do something. If members are completely inactive, then their value can be only symbolic, their contribution confined to whatever kudos the party obtains by being able to state that it has members. In reality, parties want members not just so that they can issue press statements saying that they have members – they want members primarily because of what these members can do for the party.

This contribution can take many forms, but we can start by distinguishing two main categories into which members' activity might fall: activity that takes place within the party organisation, and activity that entails engagement with the wider public. The first type of activity covers such behaviour as attending party meetings (these might be local branch meetings, or meetings at a constituency, regional or national level), giving money to the party, or standing for some position within the party organisation. The second type would mainly involve doing something for the party at elections (which could take many forms, such as door-to-door canvassing, putting up posters and so on), but is not necessarily confined to election activity, since ideally members will engage in inter-election activity designed to maintain the profile of the party in the public eye.

Looked at from the perspective of the party as a whole – if there is such a thing – it might seem that the most important activity consists of contact with the public. Activity that takes place purely within the party may, of course, be essential in order to create and maintain an organisation that is able to make the maximum impact upon the public and to operate efficiently when it's needed, especially at election times, but it is very much a means to an end rather than an end in itself. For a political party, public impact seems essential when we are judging activity, and internal activism is valuable only in as far as it contributes to enabling the party to make this public impact.

For example, if we came across a party that had lots of members who were very active in attending party meetings, donating money to the party, standing for positions within the party, reading the party newsletter and so on, we would not necessarily conclude that this was an active party *tout court*. We would want to know whether the wider society was aware of the party, and whether the party's members made any impression on their environment. A party whose members were very active within the organisation but were entirely inward-looking and focused on the organisation rather than on the broad electorate would be active in some sense but not in the sense that an outsider might think is most important, namely communicating with the public. Conversely, we might find a party whose internal organisation appears somnolent or shambolic and yet whose members manage to make an impact on the wider society. An

Top: Young Fine Gael members on a training course at the Vienna Woods Hotel in Cork, November 1980.

Don't sit on the fence

Get into action.
Get into Young Fine Gael.

Write or phone Dan Egan, Young Fine Gael, 51 Upper Mount Street, Dublin 2.
Tel. 761573.

Right: Newspaper advertisement seeking recruits for Young Fine Gael

FIANNA FAIL'S
"REMEDY"
FOR UNEMPLOYMENT

THEY WOULD APPLY IT!

By abolishing the Oath and tearing up the Treaty.

By repealing the recent Act passed by the Dail for the Public Safety.

By holding another General Election in a short time.

By setting up a "Constituent Assembly" to replace the Dail.

By settling down to revise the Constitution.

By starting more trouble with Britain and destroying the farmers' market.

By wasting three or four years haggling over the meaning of words.

By refusing to face facts and accept realities.

By attempting to put half-baked Socialist theories into practice.

By undoing the constructive work of the last ten years.

By destroying the trade and industry of the Country.

DON'T SWALLOW IT!
VOTE FOR THE
GOVERNMENT PARTY

PUBLISHED BY CUMANN na nGAEDHEAL, 5 PARNELL SQUARE, DUBLIN   Printed by TEMPLE PRESS, Temple Bar, Dublin

1932 election poster for Cumann na nGaedheal, then the "Government party".

FINE GAEL

NORTH MAYO CONSTITUENCY.

DILLON SPEAKS
BALLINA

WEDNESDAY, 31st MARCH, at 9.30 p.m.

with the Candidates,

M. BROWNE, P. J. LINDSAY and T. O'HARA.

BE WITH IT—VOTE FINE GAEL.

Issued by KEVIN LOFTUS, Election Agent for the Candidates, North Mayo.

1965 election poster for a rally in Ballina, County Mayo.

James Dillon, T.D.   Maurice E. Doekrell, T.D., T.C.
                       Lord Mayor 1960-'61.

£ FINANCE

Fine Gael the party which introduced the highly popular and successful Prize Bonds, the tax reliefs on exports ("the biggest factor in recent industrial progress" says Economics Professor Carter of Belfast University) will *extend its money reforms to income-tax.*

GROUND RENTS

Fine Gael will make a law to compel Ground Landlords to sell Ground Rents at fair prices to tenant occupiers who want to buy them and consider prohibiting the creation of new ground rents.

PEOPLE OF DUBLIN SOUTH-WEST—

There is *only one way* to get rid of Fianna Fail, *elect a FINE GAEL Government.* There is only one way to do that : vote for the Fine Gael Candidates 1, 2, 3 and 4 as you prefer them. In your area the Fine Gael men are :-

- for the Leadership which Ireland and Dublin want vote ▶ MACK - O'CONNOR - O'KEEFFE - RYAN

ARE YOU SATISFIED ?

In the last 30 years Fianna Fail has been 24 years in office with this result **which Fianna Fail find satisfactory.**

EMIGRATION

Over 210,000 emigrated since 1956—the fall in population in the past five years alone is greater than the total drop in population in the previous 30 years 1926-1956. That is how Fianna Fail fulfilled their last General Election promise to wives to get their "husbands out to work".

JOBS

Now 51,000 *less* than in 1956 (although 100,000 more were promised !).

HOUSES

Only 400 new Corporation houses in Dublin per year provided under Fianna Fail. Over 1,500 houses per year provided when Fine Gael was in office.

EDUCATION

Thousands of children are denied a full education because their parents cannot afford it. This State spends less on education than any country in the civilised world.

HEALTH

The public health service is hopelessly unfair and inefficient.

PENDING CRISIS

Industrial and Agricultural employment IS IN great danger because of Fianna Fail's absolute failure to negotiate with European countries in preparation for the Common Market.

FINE GAEL ARE NOT SATISFIED !

Dublin beat Fianna Fail in their attempt to abolish P.R. Use P.R. to beat them now.

★ **Don't waste YOUR vote**

ONLY FINE GAEL CAN BEAT FIANNA FAIL.

Therefore vote 1, 2, 3 and 4 in the order of YOUR choice for

MACK - O'CONNOR - O'KEEFFE - RYAN

but vote for ALL of them.

1961 election advertisement.

Above: Laois–Offaly candidate profiles of local candidates Frank Feery, Oliver J. Flanagan and Tom O'Higgins, and national reasons to vote Fine Gael, from the Leinster Express, 1961.

AN ACTIVE BRANCH

AN ACTIVE BRANCH IS ONE WHICH :

1. Meets at regular intervals — not less frequently than every two months.
2. Pays its affiliation fee in January each year.
3. Takes up the National Collection at the time appointed by the National Council.
4. Checks the draft Register of Electors and ensures that it is correct in all particulars.
5. Sends delegates to District and Constituency Executive Meetings as required.
6. Keeps in touch with Headquarters and Dail and Council Members and sends delegates to the Annual Ard Fheis.
7. Takes an interest in local affairs and keeps the Deputy and Senators and local representatives well informed on matters needing attention and of interest to the Party.
8. Informs the local press of its meetings, changes in Branch Officers, and local news favourable to Fine Gael.
9. Arranges for the holding of dances or other social functions in order to raise funds.
10. Orders from Headquarters, or at the Ard Fheis, copies of the Fine Gael Digest for circulation among members.

Left: The ideal branch, from the 1960 ard-fheis Digest.

Plate v

IT'S IN THE BAG!

THE FINE GAEL PLAN IS READY.* IT'S FOR YOU — AND IT'S YOURS FOR THE VOTING.

1. Introduction of Economic Planning.

2. New Health Services.

3. Modernised Social Welfare System.

4. Greater Investment in Agriculture.

5. Government co-operation with industry to meet the challenge of Free Trade.

6. New Housing Drive.

7. Equal opportunities in Education.

8. Radical reform of Local Government, and thereby reduction of Rates.

Read the details in the 32 page booklet "Towards a Just Society"—Fine Gael policy, available on request from Fine Gael Headquarters, 16, Hume Street, Dublin. (Price 2/- post free).

for your future VOTE

FINE GAEL

1965 election advertisement for the "Just Society" programme, available for a mere 2/- (about 13 cents) from party headquarters.

Devaluation of the National Spirit

Never was the sense of national pride, or the worth and importance of the Irish tradition, so abysmally weakened. The independence of our state was won by men who believed that Irishmen should run their own affairs because they had their own ideals and values — and their own culture. Yet after nearly half a century the Irish language is weaker than ever before. One Fianna Fail Minister who seems to **regret** *our freedom, has openly declared that "Independence isn't everything." What a comment on a party for whom at one time no one else was Irish enough — and who suspected everyone else of half-hearted patriotism! If the Irish language is now in desperate straits it is because the mixture of sham and hypocrisy at the top, and of compulsion and the jackboot at the bottom, has turned many Irishmen against it.*

And if a Fianna Fail Minister doubts the value of independence, **it is** *because the party — whose present leaders have no real national spirit — is empty of ideas on how to grasp the opportunities offered by independence.*

A revival of pride in Ireland and of a true National Spirit

Fine Gael will concentrate greater effort on developing our national resources and using our national talents.

Fine Gael will remove an important obstacle to genuine popular support for the Irish language by removing the forms of compulsion, in exams and in jobs.

Fine Gael will work to restore the vitality and self-confidence of Gaeltacht areas which have been sapped by government neglect.

Fine Gael will actively support the voluntary organisations working to preserve our physical and cultural heritage, and will introduce legislation necessary to ensure that historic buildings and scenic areas are preserved for the enjoyment of this and future generations.

Fine Gael will restore Irish prestige abroad by an active foreign policy — especially in Europe.

 VOTE

Published by the candidates.
Printed by the Elo Press Ltd.,
Dublin 8. Tel. 51257.

Vote for Cosgrave's Men

KELLY Prof. John M.

KELLY Paddy

McSHANE Michael

RYAN Richie, T.C.,

1, 2, 3 & 4 in order of your choice

1969 election advertisement outlining policy and calling a vote for Cosgrave's Men in Dublin South-Central.

Plate x

Left: Liam Cosgrave, centre, taking part in the traditional door-to-door canvass.

Below: Garret FitzGerald campaigning in County Laois. Also pictured on cart are Charles McDonald (left) and Oliver J. Flanagan.

Top: Garret FitzGerald campaigning in Borris, Co Carlow. His campaign bus is in the background.
Above: Garret FitzGerald in Charleville, Co Cork. To his left are his wife Joan, Frank Crowley TD for Cork NW (1981–97) and Dan Egan.

Top: Garret FitzGerald and his wife Joan coming from voting in the 1983 referendum on abortion.
Above: Austin Currie, the Fine Gael candidate for president, campaigning with John Bruton and
other supporters in Navan, Co Meath in 1990.

Above: John Bruton with Dick Spring (Labour) and Proinsias de Rossa (Democratic Left) as the three party leaders campaign in 1997 for a return of their rainbow coalition government.

Left: the ubiquitous election poster. The party leader in Drumcondra, 1997.

ꝼine Ꝺael

cuspoiꝛi.

Cun an béaloꝏeaꝛ náꝛiúnꝼa ꝏo buanú; aꝣuꝛ

Cun úꝛáiꝏ ꝏo bainꝼ aꝛ na coṁaꙍꝼaí ꝛialꝼaiꝛ aꝼá i láiṁ ṁuinꝼiꝛ na h-éiꝛeann aꝣuꝛ aꝛ coṁaꙍꝼaí eile an pobail i ꝏꝼꝛeo ꝣo ꝏꝛioꝼꝼaiꝏ an ꝼóꝛ iꝼ iomláine ꝛé oiꝣꝛeaꙍꝼ an náꝛꝛúin maꝏꝛiꝟ le polaiꝼíoꙍꝼ, culꝼúꝛ aꝣuꝛ co-ionṁaꝛ.

OBJECTS.

To carry on the National Tradition; and—To utilise the powers of Government in the hands of the Irish people as well as other forms of public activity for the fullest development of the Nation's heritage—political, cultural and economic.

ꝼine Ꝺael
United Ireland

CARD OF MEMBERSHIP

ꝼine Ꝺael
(UNITED IRELAND)

MEMBERSHIP FOR YEAR

Name..

Address...

....

was admitted a member of the

Link.........................Branch

of ꝼine Ꝺael (United Ireland)

on *27th Jan* 19 *49*

Signed *G. Brown*
Branch Secretary.

Annual Minimum Subscription. 1/-. First payment to be made on joining Branch.

AMOUNT OF SUBSCRIPTION

Paid *1/2*

on *27th Jan 49*

Signed *J. Carew*
Branch Treasurer.

Top and above: Outside (blue) and inside of a Fine Gael membership card from 1949. The minimum subscription was one shilling, or 6 cents.

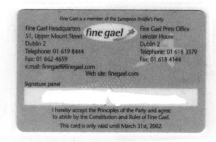

Top: Membership card 2001–2002. Now the back is blue, and the front is blue and green.
Above: Liam Cosgrave unveils a plaque to Donegal TD Micheal Og McFadden in Kilcar.
McFadden lost his seat in 1951, 8 years after Cosgrave and Oliver J. Flanagan (left) were first
elected to the Dáil.

Top: Michael Collins addresses a crowd.
Below: Michael Noonan giving the Michael Collins 2001 commemorative oration at Béal na mBláth, where Collins was killed in 1922.

Some of the Fine Gael general secretaries: the long-serving Colonel P. F. Dineen (top, centre of the front row), Peter Prendergast (1977–80, left) and the current (2002) incumbent, Tom Curran.

The funny side. Top: Liam Cosgrave enjoys a joke with Brendan Corish.
Above: John Bruton and former Fianna Fáil leader, Charles Haughey, at a race meeting in 1994.

objective observer might be more impressed by the second type of party, one that engages successfully with the public even if internally it seems weakly organised, than by the first type, one whose organisation functions smoothly in textbook fashion but doesn't seem to deliver an end product that anyone outside the organisation ever notices.

However, it is well known that any kind of organisation, once it comes into being, develops a life of its own, and maintaining the organisation becomes an end in itself for many members. This was pointed out by one of the earliest students of political parties, who wrote that "organization becomes the vital essence of the party".[1] In the worst case, recruits may themselves be predominantly organisation-oriented. Political parties, for whom communicating with the public is vital, will be especially concerned if this occurs – and there is evidence that it does. Alan Ware quotes from a study of British Conservative members that concluded, perhaps somewhat sweepingly, that "what all activists were interested in was not politics but organisation".[2] In the Netherlands, the social democratic party, the PvdA, engaged in some soul-searching in the late 1980s and early 1990s and concluded that the party suffered from a "meeting culture"; it demanded such high levels of participation that hardly anyone could reach them, so the organisation had become "introverted" and obsessed with organisational questions.[3]

Fine Gael itself has already identified this problem. Its Joyce commission, which we mentioned in chapter 3 and which was established to examine the party in the wake of some disappointing election results, reached similar conclusions to those of the PvdA:

> The Commission found that the constituency organisations have, in recent years, lost members who were motivated more by ideals or issues than political organisation. As a result, there is an imbalance in local organisations with the majority of activists being essentially organisation-oriented. This in turn has led to an increasingly inward-looking local organisation and a culture which is unattractive to people, particularly young people, who are primarily concerned with issues.

As a result, it said, the organisation

> does not relate adequately to the general public or to other campaigning organisations with which it should have an affinity. The organisation, in this sense, is literally talking to itself.[4]

Our data may not enable us to answer all of the questions that arise in this connection. We cannot pronounce definitively on whether the members of Fine Gael, or a significant proportion of them, are more interested in the party organisation for its own sake than in how that organisation communicates with the wider public. What we can and will examine in this chapter is just how active the members are in both spheres, the internal and the external. We can see whether, by and large, the same people who are most active within the party organisation are also those who are most active at spreading the party's message at election time, or whether those members who come to the fore at elections are among the least active between elections. Our data will also tell us whether members are generally becoming more active or less active, and what branches get up to when they meet. Finally, we shall address the question of whether many party members are supporters more of individual Fine Gael politicians than of Fine Gael itself and discuss the implications of the pattern that we find.

ACTIVITY LEVELS OF FINE GAEL MEMBERS

Anyone who has ever belonged to any kind of organisation knows that the level of activism displayed by members varies greatly. A few are very active; some are quite active; others, perhaps the majority, are not very active at all. It might be thought that this won't apply to political parties; after all, joining a party is entirely voluntary, and presumably no-one would join unless they had some interest in being active in some way. However, previous studies have shown that the general rule applies to parties just as much as to any other kind of organisation. As a broad generalisation, it has emerged from studies of party organisation in a number of countries that only about 10 per cent of party members can be considered to be activists in the sense that they are regular attenders at local branch meetings and participants in the party's internal affairs.[5] While this figure of 10 per cent is a useful and often-quoted benchmark, it is of course rather crude, and our data will enable us to go further than merely dividing Fine Gael members into "active" and "inactive" categories. We will take a close look at what exactly our respondents do in their capacity as party members, and at how much activism there is in a range of different contexts.

The overall picture that emerges from our survey is that Fine Gael members are rather more active than the typical member of parties in those other countries for which we have information – although we should not exaggerate the level of activism.[6] Our survey asked Fine Gael members about their frequency of attendance at branch meetings, how far they play a linkage role between politicians and the public, their record of donation to party funds, their activity at and between elections, and whether they feel they are becoming more active or less active over time.

Branch-level activity
The great majority of respondents, over 80 per cent, report that they had attended at least one branch meeting during the previous twelve months (Figure 5.1).[7] Only 18 per cent of respondents had not attended any branch meeting during that time, and about a seventh of these had the excellent excuse that their branch had not met at all in the past year! Nearly 40 per cent of respondents said that they had attended three or more meetings, and about the same number had attended one or two. This is quite an impressive record of attendance given that the average branch meets about three times a year, even allowing for the qualification made in note 7. Any experience of attendance at meetings of the European People's Party – the broad European grouping, to which Fine Gael

belongs, that embraces christian democratic parties from across the EU – is, not surprisingly, lower, but is still quite impressive, with nearly a fifth of members having been to such a meeting.

Comparative evidence is rather limited, as we have data from only two other countries. However, this evidence points to a clear conclusion: there are fewer completely inactive members in Fine Gael than in most other parties. Whereas only 18 per cent of Fine Gael members had attended no meetings during the previous year, the corresponding figure for the British Labour and Conservative parties were 36 per cent and 68 per cent respectively.[8] In Canada, only Liberal members were as active as their Fine Gael counterparts; there too 18 per cent had attended no meetings. In the other four parties the figures were higher: 29 per cent of Progressive Conservative members, 45 per cent of Alliance members, 56 per cent of Parti Québécois members and 59 per cent of New Democratic members had attended no meetings in the previous year.[9]

Just under a third (31 per cent) of our respondents held some position within the party organisation. There is something of a plethora of such offices, as we saw in chapter 3, and one might even suspect that some are created partly in order to give willing members something to do. As well as the large number of branch secretaries, members reported holding one of about ninety other positions. Some of these were branch offices, such as chairperson, president, vice-chairperson, joint treasurer, and public relations officer. In addition, a number of respondents reported that they held corresponding positions at constituency, regional, district or national level. We also received responses from members who held such diverse positions as press officer, committee member, district organiser, youth coordinator, youth officer, director of elections, ward chairman, organisation officer and correspondence secretary. As well as these current office-holders, a further 81 respondents (7 per cent) had either held or stood for a party office within the past three years. Holding office is not necessarily proof of activity – though, as we shall see later in the chapter, office-holders are in fact the most active members – but it does at least denote a willingness in principle

Figure 5.1: Branch meetings attended in last year

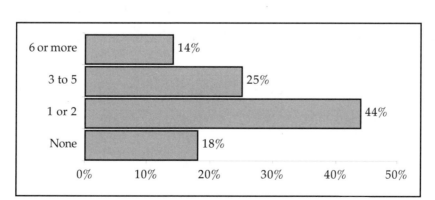

to take on responsibility and do some work.

Members may exaggerate their own activity, of course – though there is no reason why this is more likely to be true of Fine Gael members than of members of any other party – so we also asked branch secretaries to tell us about the pattern of activism in their branch. The secretaries' reports are in line with what the ordinary members say. According to the secretaries, each branch meeting is attended by about half of the membership of the branch (Table 5.1). The great majority (91 per cent) of secretaries said there was a core group in their branch that does most of the work between elections, and on average the size of this group was estimated at about six, with the number of "very active" members, who might be frequent attenders without doing as much of the work as the core group, seen as slightly larger. Extrapolating the figures in Table 5.1 to the national level, where in 1999 Fine Gael had about 20,000 members and 1,000 branches, would suggest that the party could count on approximately 7,000 genuinely active members.

We might expect to find a kind of "pyramid of activism", with a broad base of fairly or completely inactive members, a smaller number of quite active members, and even fewer highly active members. However, both the secretaries' reports, as we have seen, and members' own assessments suggest instead that the profile of activism resembles a cross-section of an oval more than a pyramid: the largest proportion of members seems to be in the middle (quite active) category, with smaller numbers at each end, representing those who are highly active or inactive. When members were asked how active they saw themselves as being, not in absolute terms but in relation to the average Fine Gael member, only 10 per cent described themselves as "not at all active", with just over a quarter seeing themselves as not very active and a fifth placing themselves in the most active category (Figure 5.2). The largest proportion, over 40 per cent, described themselves as fairly active. This contrasts strikingly with the pattern found by researchers who studied the British Conservative party, where over 80 per cent placed themselves in one of the two least active categories: 45 per cent described themselves as not at all active and 36 per cent as not very active.[10] Activity levels in the British Greens, too, took a pyramidal shape, with about 50 per cent being inactive, 30 per cent doing a little and the remaining 20 per cent

Table 5.1: Activism within Fine Gael branches, as reported by branch secretaries

	Average	Median	Maximum	Minimum
Branch members	21	16	156	5
Average attendance at branch meetings	11	10	60	3
Very active members	8	6	40	1
Core group	6	6	20	1

Source: Fine Gael secretaries' questionnaire, questions 2, 3, 8, 5.

Figure 5.2: Self-perceived activity level of members, relative to average member

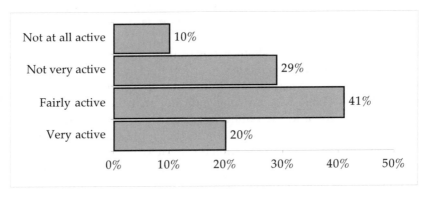

Source: Fine Gael members' questionnaire, question 13.

supplying the activists.[11]

Linkage role

One important role that parties have traditionally performed is what is termed a "linkage" role between civil society and the state. In the words of Kay Lawson, "Parties are seen, both by their members and by others, as agencies for forging links between citizens and policy-makers".[12] From the earliest days of political parties, as Richard Katz puts it, "the party organization served as the key linkage between candidates and elected officials on one side and the unorganized ... mass public on the other".[13] A lot of the academic literature on political parties in recent years has questioned the ability of parties to continue discharging this function. It is argued that for a variety of reasons – such as the rise of single-issue pressure groups, declining party membership, the use of television as a means of communication, and the introduction of public funding of parties – the political parties in many countries have moved closer to the state and further away from the ordinary people. "No longer simple brokers between civil society and the state, the parties now become absorbed by the state".[14]

However, in contrast to this general picture, studies of Irish politics frequently emphasise the notion of politicians providing "linkage" between citizens and the state. There are many accounts of the way in which people approach a TD for assistance in dealing with the bureaucracy, resulting in politicians' spending a lot of their time on constituency casework rather than discussing legislation.[15] Exactly what the causes of this phenomenon are, whether it is really as unique to Ireland as is sometimes supposed, and whether its advantages outweigh the disadvantages, are questions that we do not need to go into here. It does, though, suggest that politicians are very actively performing a linkage role, and our interest here lies in what part the party itself plays in this. The subject has not been systematically studied. Some politicians engage in a great deal of contact with the public at "clinics" (the politician arranges to be available every week in a certain location at a certain time) or in other ways, and virtually bypass the party organisation. Others might use the organisation extensively; for example, a constituency colleague of Liam Cosgrave said that Cosgrave never held clinics but relied instead on party councillors and support-ers to feed him with representations.[16]

We asked party members whether they sometimes pass on requests for assis-tance from people in the constituency to any of the Fine Gael TDs for the consti-tuency, a classic linkage activity. We found that about 60 per cent of Fine Gael members do this (Table 5.2), a strong indicator that the party organisation is actively linking people to the political system. Of course, this does not tell us how many cases reach TDs through some other route – in other words, it does not establish that the party organisation is central to this linkage – but at the very least it shows that the organisation is an important conduit for communication between politicians and people.

As we might expect, those who are most active in other ways (such as attend-ing branch meetings, devoting time to the party, and taking part in election cam-paigning) are also the most likely to pass on brokerage requests. In addition, members in rural areas are more likely than urban members to act as inter-mediaries in this manner. Belonging to another organisation also makes a Fine Gael member more likely to pass on requests to a TD (see Table 5.2); members in this category, who may be avid networkers, are likely to come into close con-tact with a wider range of people than members who don't belong to any other organisation, and probably receive more requests. It is also possible that some members actively solicit such requests in order to give a local Fine Gael TD an opportunity to display his or her problem-solving skills. Certainly, those mem-

Table 5.2: Fine Gael members as brokers between constituents and members of parliament

	Per cent of members who sometimes pass on to a local Fine Gael TD constituents' requests for assistance
All	61
Group membership	
Belongs to no other organisation	53
Belongs to 1 other organisation	59
Belongs to 2 other organisations	67
Belongs to 3 or more other organisations	79
When joined Fine Gael	
Pre-1985	69
1985–1999	47

Source: Fine Gael members' questionnaire, questions 32, 34 and 3.

bers who think of themselves as strong supporters of one of the party's local politicians are more likely to pass on constituents' requests (70 per cent of them do this) than members who support all the party's politicians equally (62 per cent of these members pass on constituents' requests).

While these figures may suggest that the Fine Gael organisation across the country is performing a function that justifies its existence, working to the benefit of both Fine Gael itself and the political system as a whole, there may be trouble ahead. Table 5.2 shows that the likelihood of a Fine Gael member acting as a broker between a TD and constituents is strongly related to the length of time he or she has been a member. By the same token, younger members are the least likely to pass on constituents' requests (only 45 per cent of those aged under 34 do this), with the over 65s the most likely to do so (65 per cent of them sometimes pass on requests). Of course, this may be essentially a "life cycle" phenomenon, with younger people, who perhaps have less strong roots in an area, being less likely to have the same breadth of contacts as older people or to be trusted by a constituent to pass on details of a personal difficulty to a TD. If that is the case, then there is no cause for concern, since today's young members, when they get older, will be just as active brokers as today's older members. On the other hand, there may be a "cohort" explanation for the pattern – it may be that older and longer-standing members were socialised into a pattern of behaviour in which acting as a link between TDs and constituents is one of the things that a party member does, and that younger members simply do not see their role in the same way. If that is the case, then Fine Gael will have a problem as its older members retire or die and the ties (at least, those supplied by the party organisation) binding its politicians to the citizenry grow weaker.

Financial donations
Giving money to the party is one form of activity, albeit a rather passive form, and it is one that some have suggested may be more to the liking of party members in the twenty-first century than traditional forms of activity. Some parties explicitly target new members, or "associate members", who they know will not be very active but who will at least make financial contributions to the party, simply because it is increasingly hard for parties to find people willing to be active between elections.[17] The archetypal member of Britain's short-lived Social Democratic Party (SDP) was described as "preferring to write out cheques for the party than to pound the pavements".[18] In Irish society generally, moreover, many charities are said to find these days that while people are more willing than ever to contribute money, it is increasingly difficult to get them to give up their time. Even members of the British Conservative party, who in general displayed remarkably low levels of activity when they were surveyed in 1992, were prepared to dip into their pockets for the sake of the party: of nine possible forms of activity, 75 per cent of members had donated money to party funds occasionally or frequently, and this was the only activity that as many as half of the respondents had performed.[19] Our data are not directly comparable with these figures, because instead of asking members how often they donated we

asked them how much they had given to the party each year.

As Figure 5.3 shows, virtually all members donate at least something – as indeed they should, given that the party imposed a membership fee of IR£8 (£3 for the unwaged) at the time of our survey.[20] What is striking is that the great majority of members give more than this required minimum; over 70 per cent give more than IR£10, and almost 30 per cent give more than IR£50. This may, of course, represent not so much an instinctive generosity on the part of members as simply their wilting in the face of what some of them feel is incessant pressure from party head office to squeeze money out of them, in the form of direct donations, donations to the constituency organisation to enable it to meet its target of payment to head office, and "invitations" to purchase tickets in the party lottery, the Superdraw. In our survey of branch secretaries, nearly half reported that members complain about the constant appeals for funds that come from the party. Some members to whom we spoke said that they gave several hundred pounds a year to the party, and saw this as part of the explanation for the party's lack of working-class members who, even if they joined, would find themselves embarrassed by their inability to meet expectations as to how much they would give to the party. Certainly in the past there have been suggestions that candidates without personal resources have been unable to afford to stand as Fine Gael candidates.[21] As we would expect, the size of donations was significantly class-related, with 37 per cent of middle-class members, but only 16 per cent of working-class members, giving at least £50. Making "best guesses" about the average amount donated by members within each of the bands in Figure 5.3 suggests that the party receives about £700,000 (890,000 euros) per year from its members, though of course in the case of the Superdraw lottery it has to pay some of this back in the form of prizes. This figure of 890,000 euros represents about half of what the party receives from the state each year.[22]

Figure 5.3: How much money donated to Fine Gael in last year

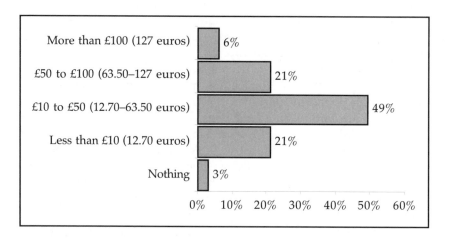

Source: Fine Gael members' questionnaire, question 16.

Candidate selection

Unlike most parties in Europe, Fine Gael now offers all of its members the opportunity to participate in what has often been seen as the most crucial area of internal party activity, namely the selection of election candidates, following the introduction of OMOV in the mid-1990s, as we saw in chapter 3. We could expect to find that all but the least active members will avail of this chance because, after all, selecting candidates amounts to real power, as the candidate selectors play a large part in determining the composition of the political elite, not only members of parliament but also cabinet ministers. Even members who cannot muster much enthusiasm for going to a branch meeting where there is nothing more exciting on the agenda than the reading of the minutes of the previous meeting might feel that taking part in the selection of candidates is an exercise worth engaging in. Candidate selection, after all, is a form of participation that produces high impact in exchange for little time, whereas attending branch meetings regularly might feel like a lot of time for very little impact.[23]

Sure enough, a clear majority of Fine Gael members have been active participants in recent candidate selections. Over 70 per cent of members who belonged to the party before the 1997 election (and 66 per cent of the current membership) had taken part in the selection of Fine Gael candidates for that election, which at the time of our survey was the most recent general election. Around 72 per cent of our respondents had taken part in the selection of candidates for the local elections that took place in June 1999, approximately four months before our questionnaire was mailed. In many ways we would expect those members who are most active generally to be most likely to take part in candidate selection, though there is also the opposite view, namely that the party's "ghost members" will be active in candidate selection and inactive everywhere else (since using their votes to ensure someone's selection is really the only reason they are in the party). Our findings show that activism in candidate selection is strongly related to activism in attending branch meetings; those

Table 5.3: Branch meetings attended in last year, by whether took part in candidate selection for 1997 general election

	Took part in 1997 candidate selection?		All
	Yes	No	members
	%	%	%
Meetings attended			
None	37	63	100
1 or 2	62	38	100
3, 4 or 5	81	19	100
6 or more	87	13	100
Total	66	34	100

Source: Fine Gael secretaries' questionnaire, questions 9, 23a.

who did not take part in one were less likely to take part in the other, suggesting that there may not be as many ghost members as sometimes believed. The more frequently a member had attended a branch meeting over the past twelve months, the more likely they were to have taken part in the candidate selection process (Table 5.3). The implication is clear: when members are given the opportunity to participate meaningfully at low cost in terms of time, most of them will take it.

Changes over time: declining activism?

One of the most widely held beliefs about political parties is that both the number of members and the activism of those members who remain is declining over time. This may be merely an unsupported generalisation, and, as we noted in chapter 3, some writers have observed that when a long-term perspective is taken, perhaps not a great deal has changed. Scarrow, for example, comments that when she tried to assess the level of party activity in Britain and Germany in past decades, the available records showed a remarkably low level of activity in the 1950s and 1960s, contrary to some suggestions that this was a "golden age" for vibrancy within political parties. In addition, the general impression of membership decline can be misleading in that the point of comparison is usually the third quarter of the twentieth century, when membership levels were atypically high.[24] Maor also points out that the British Labour Party had low levels of individual membership before the second world war, and that the decline in its membership since the 1970s has merely taken the party back to pre-war levels.[25] However, there is no doubt that membership of most European parties has been falling in recent decades.[26] We discussed Fine Gael membership trends in chapter 4; here we look at the evidence for decline in activism.

A snapshot survey such as the one that we carried out cannot definitively tell us about trends over time, but we can and did ask members whether they felt that they were now more active or less active than they had been four years ago. The results are shown in Table 5.4. Fine Gael is by no means suffering complete membership burn-out, yet the level of activism is evidently declining, since there are rather more members (31 per cent) who say that they have become less active than say that they have become more active (20 per cent). By comparison with the major British parties – the only others for which data are available – Fine Gael might seem to have done not too badly in retaining most of the commitment of its members over the past few years. This would provide little comfort, of course, if those Fine Gael members whose commitment to the party was wavering had simply left the party rather than becoming less active while remaining as members. However, as we saw in chapter 4, it does not seem that the party has lost members over this period. There are marked class differences in the backgrounds of those who have become less active; 39 per cent of middle-class (ABC1) members have become less active, compared with 28 per cent of working-class (C2DE) members and 24 per cent of farmers.

In addition to simply asking whether members had become more active or less active, we invited members to tell us in their own words why their activity

Table 5.4: Members' level of activity compared with four years ago, compared with British parties

	Fine Gael %	British Labour %	British Conservative %	British Liberal Democrats %
Change in activity				
More active	20	20	8	20
About the same	48	37	57	50
Less active	32	43	25	30
Total	100	100	100	100

Source: Fine Gael members' questionnaire, question 14; Seyd and Whiteley, *Labour's Grass Roots*, p. 89; Whiteley, Seyd and Richardson, *True Blues*, p. 68; Bennie et al., "Party members", p. 140.
Note: British party members were asked to compare their current levels of activity with those of five (not four) years ago.

levels had changed, and then we grouped their responses into a small number of categories. Those who had become more active gave a variety of reasons for the change (see Table 5.5). As we mentioned in chapter 1, although most of the questions in our survey were "closed", confining respondents to the options we presented, a few were "open", meaning that respondents could write in their own answer in their own words. Responses to the open questions are thus a particularly rich resource, representing the authentic voice of the members, and in the rest of this chapter and in subsequent chapters we shall present verbatim quotes from the members' replies to these questions.

Among those who say they have become more active, a plurality (35 per cent) identify national developments as the main cause. The tribunal revelations about certain leading Fianna Fáil politicians had evidently galvanised a number of members:

- I am more active because I believe Fianna Fáil are not fit to govern this country
- I'm more concerned with what goes on in this country now than before
- Because Fianna Fáil are such a pack of crooks and PDs as well
- John Bruton is the most honest leader
- To get Fine Gael into government.

Some members have become more active because they have moved into positions of responsibility within the party, such as branch secretary, or because in some way there is more demand for their contribution. In some cases, it is clear that the commitment has increased. In others, though, Fine Gael can take only limited consolation from the increased activity of some of these members, because they explain that they have had to become more active simply because of the decline in others' activity:

- Others nominated to do jobs refused to take them
- More work to be done, less people to share the work with

Table 5.5: Reasons given by members who have become more active

	%
Response to national political events	35
Have acquired position of responsibility	26
Response to local political events	13
More demand for my party work	11
I have more free time	10
Step in building a political career	1
Other	4
Total	100

Source: Fine Gael members' questionnaire, question 15.
Note: Responses were received from 19 per cent of members (weighted). Since question 15 was completely open, the categories used are devised by the authors.

- Because if I didn't do the work no-one else would
- I have no choice: the few depend on me, no-one wants to do anything.

We saw earlier that for some members developments at local level had had the effect of diminishing their enthusiasm. For others, though, some local event has had an invigorating effect; for example, a friend or relative has contested an election, or an energetic politician has inspired the local organisation:

- My brother was elected as a member of [local] County Council last June for Fine Gael
- I am more active because I personally know our local TD
- A young friend has joined the council
- More active new local candidate in the area who is promising in terms of his potential
- Satisfaction gained from introducing constituents to helpful politicians, i.e. Michael Noonan
- Because we have a new TD representing us and he is holding monthly clinics in our parish, the first Fine Gael TD to do this in years. His name is Michael Ring. A gift from God to Fine Gael
- A person who was going for local election, I backed them all the way and worked hard for her because she was the best person for the job. If we don't get it right at the bottom how can they get it right at the top?

Finally, there are members whose life circumstances have changed in such a way as to allow them to devote more time to the party:

- I have more time, business is going well, that's why I'm more active
- Joined when I was 17, now older and more interested in the political world around me
- Retired, more free time, tired of Fianna Fáil government
- The longer I have been in, the more contacts I have made, and I have self belief in helping Fine Gael.

The reasons given by those members who had become less active are shown in Table 5.6. Given the age profile of members that we discussed in chapter 4, it is no surprise to find that age and poor health, sometimes both, are the largest factor in leading to reduced activism. Examples of responses from members who said that they have become less active due to old age or ill health are:

- I am retired from farming, I am 77 years old, I no longer drive a car
- Getting old, the only reason I'm involved now is that there are no young people joining
- Not as young as I used to be, prefer gardening nowadays
- I have been working for the party for 45 years and I think the young people should take over.

A close second to age and ill health is that many members have less free time due to changes in their life circumstances:

- Busy in work, haven't got much time
- I was single when I joined and for some time after, now I'm married with children
- Pressure of work but very active at election times.

Taking these two factors together, just over half of the members can be said to have become less active due to changes in their own situation, which would be likely to have led to their becoming less active in any organisation that they might belong to, rather than to specifically political factors. Fine Gael might take some comfort from this, in that most of the decline in activism does not result from discontent with anything it has done or failed to do. The remaining reasons given by members for becoming less active are all related to politics. Foremost among these is a reduction in political commitment or interest, or in many cases a simple disillusionment with politics. As we saw above, the plethora of

Table 5.6: Reasons given by members who have become less active

	%
Old age or ill health	29
I have less free time	27
Reduced political commitment	12
Behaviour of FG at national level	10
Behaviour of FG at local level	9
Less demand for my party work	7
Have given up position of responsibility	4
Other	2
Total	100

Source: Fine Gael members' questionnaire, question 15.
Note: Responses were received from 31 per cent of members (weighted). Since question 15 was completely open, the categories used are devised by the authors.

tribunals enquiring into and discovering strong evidence of corruption was a spur for some members to become more active and increased their determination to get Fianna Fáil out of power. For other members, though, the effect was the opposite:

- I have lost trust in most politicians, in what has been revealed over the past twelve months
- Disgusted with the carry on of all politicians
- I have become somewhat disillusioned, less enthusiastic about politics, due to all the negative publicity regarding politics in general, tribunals etc
- No great interest; most politicians seem full of empty promises and soft talk
- Loss of faith in effectiveness of party membership in changing anything really significant in life
- I was approached by the party and only joined the party to help a good friend
- I have no interest in politics except alone to vote.

A further twenty per cent have become less active because of something that Fine Gael specifically has done. Sometimes it is an aspect of the party at national level that has displeased them, in other cases a local matter has been responsible. Looking first at those who cite a national reason, examples are:

- It is very hard to be active when nobody listens to grassroots
- Can't abide John Bruton, especially his views on the North
- I am completely fed up with the leader John Bruton and I consider he is a very bad leader of Fine Gael
- Feel that women are not treated as potential candidates; great on organisation and executive but not given other chance
- I am not happy with the way the party is being led, the liberal wing and Young Fine Gael policies are given too much freedom and the older generation of members are fed up. The party lost its soul in recent times with weak leaders
- They have no time for people only when there is an election.

For others, the problems are much closer to home. Some are turned off by the internal conflict and the way politicians in the constituency behave:

- Have lost interest, don't find it stimulating. Discouraged by attitude and bitchiness of more seasoned members
- Less active on account of the way the party treated [names former TD], as are a lot of members
- Because of the way the local elections went and because of the way our TD was not given a portfolio in opposition
- In-party fighting
- Disillusioned with constituency organisation, totally controlled by TD – not to the benefit of Fine Gael.

Others in this category find local party activity, at least between elections, tedious and uninteresting:

- Same boring topics always from some people
- The local party seemed to frown upon new younger members upsetting

traditional old and boring meetings with new ideas
- Not involved in Young Fine Gael any more. Local constituency very inactive, uninteresting, members much older than myself, lacks ideas, motivation
- Hate local meetings, a waste of time; always canvass and help during election times.

And for others again the explanation seems to be a lack of appreciation:

- Other parties bring tea, food and drinks to the party workers on election day, all I get from Fine Gael is a shake hands
- Very disappointed at the performance of local TD and County Councillors when asked for favours
- Local problems not given enough attention by TD.

Finally, around 7 per cent of members are less active because there is less demand for their activity; in some cases, in fact, there seems to be no demand at all:

- No meetings in my area, only for that I would be more active
- Local branch rarely meets and despite a strong desire on my part to contribute the opportunities to do so are virtually non-existent
- Lack of branch meetings and not being informed of branch activities; I am unaware of the branch officers' names
- Would prefer to be told when meetings are
- Poor attendance at meetings, lack of interest, no new members
- Matters have seemed to die down in [constituency] in recent years whereas it was very active when I first joined
- Young Fine Gael branch has disbanded. The local senior Fine Gael are less active, that I am in now
- The general apathy of fellow members to politics and politicians have made me and my branch less active
- Not much activity unless election looming.

Although the members of the party organisation seem to be reasonably active when it comes to maintaining the organisation, it is clear that working at elections is the main occasion for activity. In between elections, it seems, there is not really a great deal to do other than attend the occasional branch meeting, and many respondents evidently feel that this alone does not really amount to being "actively involved". Indeed, when we asked branch secretaries whether there is a core group that does most of the work between elections, one secretary replied "I'd say no work was done between elections" – though this is untypical. Most members (57 per cent) report that over the past four years they have tended to get actively involved in the party only at election times, much the same proportion as was found among the notoriously inactive members of Britain's Conservative party.[27] Similarly, when asked how much time they devote to party activities in the average month, just over half (55 per cent) said "None", with 37 per cent reporting that they spent up to five hours and 9 per cent saying they devoted more than five hours. This resembles the pattern in the British Labour and Liberal parties, where about 50 per cent of members said they spent no time on party activities in the average month, and is better than the Conservatives' position (the figure here was 76 per cent), but, even so, it is still clear that many Fine Gael members keep a low profile between elections.[28]

Activity at elections

There is little doubt that for Fine Gael, as for virtually every other modern European party, elections are the focal point of activity. To a certain extent, indeed, the work done between elections is valuable only in as far as it produces an organisation that can fight elections effectively. So, taking up the point we made at the beginning of this section, we have established that the Fine Gael organisation ticks over reasonably satisfactorily between elections; now we need to ask how much it engages with the electorate when it matters, during election campaigns. In chapter 6 we will take this a step further and try to assess the electoral impact of the organisation.

Fortunately for Fine Gael, it is clear that most of its members do indeed rise to the challenge at election time. Just under three-quarters report that they have been active in recent Fine Gael campaigns (see Table 5.7). By far the most common form of election campaign activity was door-to-door canvassing, which 58 per cent of members said they had taken part in. This is a very prominent aspect of election campaigning in Ireland, though it is employed in very few other countries (Britain and Hong Kong are two others where it is used). Members themselves strongly believe that door-to-door canvassing, along with other forms of campaigning that involve direct personal contact with voters, is the most effective at increasing the party's vote.

Table 5.7: Activity in recent Fine Gael election campaigns, in per cent

Active	73
Not active	27
Active in	
door-to-door canvassing	58
other canvassing	1
distributing literature	25
putting up posters	4
fund-raising	3
local campaign planning	3
local campaign support	2
personation on election day	1
driving voters to polls	1
persuading friends or family	1
other	3

Source: Fine Gael members' questionnaire, questions 18a, 18b.
Note: Multiple responses were possible. Responses to question 18b were received from 19 per cent of respondents (weighted).

A significant number of members, nearly a quarter, helped out by mailing or distributing campaign literature, and indeed members contributed in a whole range of other ways. The most common of these involved putting up posters, fund-raising, organising part or all of the local campaign, acting as personation agents on polling day, driving voters to the polls on election day, and telephone canvassing. The role of "ambassador to the community" on behalf of the party is only occasionally mentioned explicitly, with just 1 per cent of members describing activities that would come under this heading; examples from respondents include:

- Socially putting the message across
- Coffee mornings, invitations to neighbours etc to Fine Gael functions
- Advised members of my family to vote for Fine Gael party
- Word of mouth, encouraging friends to vote Fine Gael
- Indicating to colleagues and friends that I'm a Fine Gael supporter.

We have already made the point that activism has two components. One, which we could describe as concerned with the internal affairs of the party, entails activity within the organisation, attendance at branch meetings and so on; the kind of activity that, though no doubt essential from the perspective of the organisation, is quite unseen by the public generally. The other, which could be described as the external relations of the party, entails above all election campaigning, showing the party's face to the outside world and attempting to promote a positive image of it. Now that we have measured the extent of both types of activity, we can ask whether different people are to the fore in different spheres of activity, or whether those members who are most active in one are also most active in the other.

Table 5.8: Activity in recent election campaigns, by other activity

	Per cent of members who took an active part in any Fine Gael election campaigns in previous four years
All	73
Branch meetings attended in past year	
None	41
1 or 2	70
3 to 5	88
6 or more	95
Active in candidate selection at 1997 election?	
Did not take part	50
Took part	85

Source: Fine Gael members' questionnaire, questions 18a, 9 and 23a.

The answer, beyond doubt, is the latter: activists are active wherever their services are called upon, and those who are inactive in the party's internal affairs are also inactive when it comes to external relations. Table 5.8 shows a strong relationship between attendance at branch meetings over the past year and activity in election campaigns: the more branch meetings a member attended, the more likely he or she was to have taken part in the most recent general election campaign. Similarly, those who had taken part in the candidate selection process were much more likely to have been active election campaigners. Within the ranks of the Fine Gael membership there is a highly inactive substratum that neither attends branch meetings nor helps out at election time and, at the other end of the scale, a group that is highly active in both internal affairs and external relations. Fortunately for Fine Gael, the latter group far outnumbers the former; fewer than 10 per cent of our respondents are inactive on both counts, whereas over a third both attended at least three branch meetings over the previous year and took part in recent election campaigns.

WHO ARE THE ACTIVISTS?

We have looked at the overall levels of activism within Fine Gael; now it is time to examine the degree of activism among different categories of members, to see whether there is any systematic variation. In later chapters we shall explore some of the consequences of activism, considering whether activism seems to make a difference electorally and whether the most active members tend to hold different political views from those of less active members. In this section, we will try to identify the factors that could be seen as causes of activism, or at least are associated with it. Of course, the distinction between causes and consequences of activism is not always easy to draw. If the most active members are found to hold strong views on a particular issue, then this may well have consequences for the party, as there will be pressure from within party ranks for it to adopt policy positions that may not represent the views of members as a whole, let alone voters. At the same time, these strong views could also be a cause of activism, in that those members with a firm point of view may become highly active precisely in order to promote their viewpoint within the party. In any case, without denying that political views may well be a cause of activism, we shall defer discussion of the links between views and activism until chapter 7. Here, we shall concentrate on the backgrounds of members, which we discussed broadly in chapter 4, to see whether these are related to activism.

In order to measure activism we constructed a scale, as detailed in Appendix C. In essence we employed four different indicators of activism – whether a member has been active in any recent party campaigns, how much time a member devotes to the party in the average month, whether a member took part in candidate selection for the 1999 local elections, and how active a member considers himself or herself to be relative to the average member – and awarded a "score" for activity on each indicator. These scores were added, giving an overall activism score that, being based on four different indicators, is more reliable than a score based on just one indicator. Respondents were then divided into four categories, those with the highest scores being termed "very active", those in the second category termed "quite active", those in the third category "a little active", and those with the lowest scores "inactive". How, if at all, do the backgrounds of the most active members differ from the backgrounds of the least active?

Given the weak relationship between socio-demographic factors and voting behaviour in Ireland,[29] we would not expect to find that these factors have much bearing on levels of activism among Fine Gael members. Sure enough, there is little sign that they do (see Table 5.9). The standard set of factors that are conventionally used to try to explain political behaviour seem to have absolutely no bearing on how active a member of Fine Gael is. Each of the following "usual suspects" is not significantly related to the degree of activism among Fine Gael members: social class, age, education level, housing tenure, religiosity, and whether the member's branch is in an urban or rural constituency. These factors may have a bearing on the decision to join Fine Gael in the first place, as we saw in chapter 4, but they don't seem to be related to how active someone is once they are a member. On the whole, this is not so very different from what was found by studies of the main parties in both Britain and the Netherlands, where socio-demographic factors play a much larger part in structuring voting behaviour. These studies found some patterns, but the patterns were weak and in any case were not the same for all parties.[30]

There are two factors that do show up as related to activism within Fine Gael: gender and length of membership. Men are a little more active than women: 40 per cent of men are in one of our top two categories of activism, compared with only 32 per cent of women. What is more interesting, as it could have implications for Fine Gael in the years ahead, is that those who have been members for a long time are noticeably more active than recent arrivals. Of those who joined before 1985 – and, as we saw in chapter 4, this applies to most of the membership – 45 per cent are in one of the two most active categories (very active or quite active); of those who have joined since then, only 27 per cent are in one of these categories. It is important to bear in mind that this is not a matter of age; older members are hardly any more active than younger ones. Middle-aged members who joined the party twenty years ago are likely, other things being equal, to be more active than older members who joined more recently. To some extent the explanation is due to a process of self-selection: those members who remain within the party for a long period of time can be expected to be the keenest and most committed, so it is not surprising that they show relatively high levels of activism. Likewise, we can reasonably assume that most of those who joined in earlier decades and who were relatively less committed have left rather than lingering on as inactive members. However, this does not really explain why, for example, members who joined in the late 1980s should today be less active than those who joined in the 1960s or 1970s, unless the latter are occupying the branch officerships and preventing more recent recruits from playing as

Table 5.9: The relationship between activism within Fine Gael and social characteristics

	Inactive %	A little active %	Quite active %	Very active %	Total %
All	27	35	21	17	100
Social class					
AB	34	29	19	18	100
C1	26	36	19	18	100
C2	21	35	27	17	100
DE	27	35	15	23	100
Farmer	25	36	25	14	100
Self-assigned social class					
Upper or upper middle	26	34	21	19	100
Middle	25	35	22	18	100
Lower middle	35	35	20	11	100
Working	29	35	17	19	100
Age					
Less than 25	36	39	17	7	100
25–34	30	32	23	14	100
35–44	25	38	17	20	100
45–54	29	32	22	17	100
55–64	24	35	23	18	100
Over 64	27	35	19	19	100
Education level					
National school	24	34	25	17	100
Second level	26	33	22	19	100
RTC or VEC	27	39	24	10	100
University	30	31	19	20	100
Other	35	38	12	15	100
Religiosity					
Low	27	33	19	21	100
Medium	28	35	21	16	100
High	23	35	22	19	100
Location					
Urban constituency	26	34	19	21	100
Rural constituency	28	35	21	16	100
Gender					
Male	26	33	22	19	100
Female	31	37	17	14	100
When joined Fine Gael					
Pre-1985	21	35	24	21	100
1985–99	39	34	16	11	100

Source: For activism categories, see Appendix C. For other variables, Fine Gael members' questionnaire, questions 35–46, 3.

large a role as they would like to play.

As we noted in chapter 4, when we remarked upon the surprisingly high proportion of the party's current membership who joined a long time ago, the glass could be seen as either half full or half empty. It is good for Fine Gael that it has been able to retain so many long-standing members, and that so many of these are still active after all these years, but at the same time it is disturbing that so few of its members have joined it recently, and that, moreover, those who have joined in the 1990s in particular display the lowest activity levels of all. The glass may still be half full, but unless something changes, all the signs are that it will become steadily emptier in the years ahead.

The most active members of the party stand out in other ways that we would expect. They are to be found especially among those who hold some office in the party – 33 per cent of secretaries are in the very active category and only 9 per cent are inactive – and among those who have contact with other members through their work or social life. Those who donate most money to the party are the most active generally: among those who donate more than £50 a year to Fine Gael 60 per cent are in one of the two most active categories, compared with 34 per cent of those who donate between £10 and £50 and a mere 20 per cent of those who give less than £10. (£1 is equal to 1.27 euro.) We might have expected some kind of trade-off between giving time and giving money, with some members giving a little of one but a lot of the other, but this is not the case; those who give least of one also tend to give least of the other. Fine Gael activists are more active people generally; they are more likely to have campaigned in the 1995 divorce referendum on one side or the other (especially on the Yes side) than the less active members, and they are also more likely to belong to other groups (those members who belong to residents' associations or local community associations, as opposed to a sectional group such as a farmers' organisation or a trade union, are especially likely to be highly active members of Fine Gael).

Activism is also linked, again not surprisingly, to a general attachment to Fine Gael. Among those who, when asked how strongly they support Fine Gael, describe themselves as "very strong" supporters (Q1 of the questionnaire), 54 per cent are in one of the top two categories of activism, compared with a mere 21 per cent among members who describe themselves as less strong supporters. Consistent with that, we find that inactive members are most likely to see no difference between Fine Gael and Fianna Fáil, to be ready to welcome a merger between Fine Gael and Fianna Fáil, and to expect Fine Gael to fall behind the Labour party at some election before 2020 – all topics that we shall discuss at greater length in chapter 8. In other words, those who are most pessimistic about Fine Gael's future, and least convinced that there is anything distinctive about Fine Gael, are the least active – pretty much as we would expect. In a similar vein, those who entered the party via Young Fine Gael are especially active. Those whose recruitment involved some enterprise on their part are marginally more active than those who were more passive: among those who joined by approaching the party 43 per cent are in one of the two most active categories, compared with 38 per cent of those who were approached by the party and 19 per cent of those who can't remember exactly how they joined. Similarly, those whose most important reason for joining was the influence of family and friends, which may be seen as a passive acceptance of the advice or request of others, are markedly less active (only 24 per cent are in one of the two most active categories) than other members. In contrast, those who have political ambitions are especially active: of those members who already are, or hope to be in future, a councillor or a TD 66 per cent are to be found in one of the two most active categories, compared with only 35 per cent of other members.

Might members' degree of activism have something to do with their experience of party life and the extent to which they think the party cares about them? There is some evidence of this, but it is not very strong. For example, in answer to the question (Q66) as to whether ordinary members of Fine Gael have enough say in determining party policy, there is no difference in activism levels between those who are satisfied with their input and those who are dissatisfied. On other measures, which we discuss in greater detail in chapter 6, there is some statistical relationship with activism: those who believe that Fine Gael does not make the best use of its members' energy and commitment are a little more active than those who are satisfied with the status quo, those who believe that the only way to be really educated about politics is to be a party activist are a little more active than those who are unconvinced by this statement, and those who believe that Fine Gael would be more successful if more people like themselves were elected to the Dáil were more active than other members. In addition, those who agree that "Attending party meetings can be pretty tiring after a hard day's work" are rather less active than those who disagree with this. This could mean that relatively inactive members have scaled down their activities after finding them tiring, and indeed it is true that 76 per cent of those in the two least active categories say that they have become less active in the last four years. More cynically, one could note that those who are most likely to pronounce branch meetings tiring are those who go to fewest of them, and their conclusion, or assumption, may not always be based on first-hand evidence.

BRANCH ACTIVITY

As we saw in chapter 3, the branch is the basic building block of party organisation in Ireland. All members belong to a local branch, and members' life within the party revolves around the branch. The place of the branch within the hierarchical structure of the party organisation is clear enough on paper. But what do branches actually do?

The number of occasions on which branches meet seems to vary quite markedly. Some schedule meetings approximately monthly (though there is usually a break between June and September), while others hold very few meetings (see Table 5.10). Indeed, 6 per cent of secretaries said that their branch had not met at all in the past year. While this may well be a sign of a dormant or paper branch, the idea of an active branch that meets only once or twice a year is not necessarily a contradiction in terms. It is clear that a certain amount of important activity takes place outside the formal organisational structure. One branch secretary reported that although the branch held only one formal meeting each year, there would also be a number of "informal meetings". Table 5.10 shows that urban branches tend to meet more frequently than rural ones and, in addition, in rural areas (though not in urban ones) the frequency of meetings is related to size, with larger branches meeting more often. One reason for urban–rural differences may be that in rural areas members are more likely to keep in contact with each other in their daily lives. A lot of writing about Irish politics has seen it as characterised by informal networks of relationships in which personal contacts between people who have some kind of link – which could be based on kinship, locality or friendship – are often more important than formal structures.[31] This phenomenon is usually seen as strongest in rural areas, where a given set of relationships is more likely to be stable than in towns or cities.

Consequently, we asked Fine Gael members whether they were in frequent contact with a number of other branch members through their work and social life. The results showed that there are strong ties binding Fine Gael members: nearly three-quarters replied that they were in such contact. As we expected, this tendency was strongest in rural constituencies: there, 78 per cent experience frequent contact with other members, compared with 60 per cent in urban areas, with middle-class (AB) members being least likely to have such contact. We shall return to this theme of the personal links of Fine Gael members later in the chapter.

We know, then, that on average branches meet about three times a year, and the average attendance, according to branch secretaries, is about 11 (see Table 5.1 above). But what do branches actually do when they meet? Branch meetings of political parties do not have a great image in the public eye, it must be said. The picture they conjure up is of a Ballymagash-style gathering of a small group of people sitting disconsolately in the back room of a pub while the meeting grinds through such items as the minutes of the last meeting, report of the correspondence secretary, and the branch's response to head office's latest scheme to raise

Table 5.10: Frequency of branch meetings, by location of branch

	Urban %	Rural %	All %
0–2 per year	38	57	54
3–5 per year	29	28	28
5+ per year	33	16	18
Total	100	100	100

Source: Fine Gael members' questionnaire, question 8 – based on responses of branch secretaries only.
Note: For detail of urban / rural coding, see chapter 4, note 17 (p. 265).

money from members, before to general relief the meeting is brought to a close and members can go home or adjourn to the bar. While this is of course a stereotype, it may not be such a long way from the reality. The authors were told after a session with one branch to pilot the questionnaire that it had been the most interesting meeting for years, partly because there had been some genuine political discussion. The Joyce commission was blunt, stating unequivocally that "meetings at constituency and lower levels are tedious and uninteresting" and describing them as "fruitless" and "pointless". It said that it had found widespread agreement among members that "the conduct of meetings leaves a lot to be desired", adding pointedly that if the organisation is going to be truly useful, "it follows that it cannot, for instance, have an agenda that is packed with administrative matters".[32]

We asked respondents to tell us what branch meetings spent their time on (for the detailed results, see Appendix B, Q12). Possibly the displeasure of the Joyce commission has had some impact, since internal organisational matters do not dominate. Instead, local political matters – a term that could embrace everything from reacting to a local factory closure to discussing some of the proverbial potholes in the roads – occupy the lion's share of the time. Over forty per cent of respondents said that most of the time was spent this way, with only 16 per cent – perhaps still an undesirably high proportion – saying that most of the time was spent on internal organisational matters. These internal organisational matters ranked about equally with fund raising (also, of course, essentially a matter of interest only to the organisation) and national political matters, with in each case a small majority of respondents agreeing that "some time" had been spent on them. These figures are quite similar to those found by a 1992 study of British Conservative members, except that local issues loom larger in Ireland than in Britain.[33] While the sight of an agenda packed with items concerning organisation may not be exactly inspiring to anyone except lovers of organisation, perhaps it is inevitable that branch meetings have to deal with these issues, however uninteresting they may be to those not involved. We should also note that since the membership was conducted, Fine Gael has issued a manual to all its branches, setting out a suggested agenda (which lasts just over an hour). Even though this agenda is still dominated by organisational matters, the manual points out that "Branch meetings rarely result in more votes for the Party" and suggests that the meeting be preceded by a walkabout, survey or door-to-door canvass with a public representative.[34]

Although we did not explicitly ask members to tell us in their own words about their experiences of branch meetings, we invited branch secretaries to give us any general thoughts on the party, and several gave their impressions of branch meetings. The comments were invariably negative.[35] Some echoed the Joyce Commission by stressing the tedium of meetings that were dominated by organisational matters to the exclusion of policy discussions:

- Branch meetings are pretty boring and disappointing ... We have failed to attract young people. Fund raising on the agenda is turning people off
- Fundraising details put a lot of people off coming to meetings. They feel they are

constantly coughing up for the party
- Since I joined the branch here I have never heard anything discussed other than fund raising. Now that I have been appointed Secretary I have asked the Chairman to consider having quarterly meetings – I have not had a reply since
- Not enough is done to keep members motivated, interested, encouraged. Too many activities are just about raising funds (what for?) instead of geared towards political issues
- Most meetings lack direction and are badly chaired
- Branch activity non-existent between elections and conventions. Meetings seem irrelevant and boring. Would be embarrassed to introduce new members to above. No social element.

Other secretaries were even more pessimistic, seeing little point in branches discussing political issues since it appeared that no-one would be listening anyway:

- Meetings are completely unproductive – a tiny worthless talking shop
- There is a perception in rural branches that HQ take no notice of opinions or suggestions made by them even with the nominally democratic notion of one member one vote
- Most rural branches are not viable units. Too few members and same people
- Attendance at meetings is becoming a serious consideration. It is very difficult to interest and recruit new members.

Clearly this is something of a problem for Fine Gael, and indeed for all parties. If branches concentrate on fund-raising and other organisational topics, the result will be a major turnoff to all but those who are interested in organisation for its own sake or are extremely dedicated to the party. Keeping existing members will be difficult enough, never mind attracting the lively new members that all levels of the party say they want. On the other hand, if branches make a point of having discussions on burning political issues, this may not solve the drain of members either. For many members, clearly, it requires a leap of faith to imagine that anything said at a branch meeting is ever going to be heard, let alone taken heed of, outside the branch. That being so, talking about politics in a branch meeting achieves no more than talking about politics with one's friends at home or in the pub – and it may be less enjoyable. Aware of this, quite a number of secretaries suggested that the branch structure is itself obsolete, and that the main emphasis now should be on district or constituency meetings, where prominent national speakers could be invited and a sizeable attendance could be expected. We shall say more about the implications of our findings for the present Fine Gael organisational structure in chapter 6.

The branch secretaries' questionnaire also asked respondents to tell us what they saw as the most important role of their branch, giving them five options and asking them to rank these (see Table 5.11). There is a clear consensus that the two most important are those relating to election campaigning and to supporting the work of the local Fine Gael politician; indeed, no doubt the second is important partly because of the electoral payoff of this work. Discussing policy matters clearly ranks low, bearing out the Joyce commission's observation that the agenda of branch meetings holds little to capture the interest of

Table 5.11: Branch secretaries' rankings of roles of branch

	Most important role %	Second most important role %
Election campaigning and campaign planning	41	22
Support work for the TD or Dáil candidate	26	31
Recruiting new members	19	14
Discussing policy matters	9	10
Fund-raising for Fine Gael	5	16
No second preference	—	7
Total	100	100

Source: Fine Gael secretaries' questionnaire, question 6.

policy-oriented members. The views of branch secretaries, then, lend support to the widespread view among political scientists concerning the centrality of elections in political parties' view of the world. The organisation exists primarily to fight elections; whether things were ever really any different we cannot tell, given the lack of comparable data for earlier decades. Certainly a study of Donegal politics in the 1960s concluded that the primary function of the Fine Gael branches then was "the provision of support on election day".[36] Secretaries do not believe, contrary to some views, that the role of the local branch in election campaigning has diminished over time, swept aside by the prominence of television and by the focus on national political issues and the image of the party leaders. When they were asked whether the role of the local branch in election campaigning has changed, almost half (50 per cent) said it had not, with slightly more (29 per cent) feeling that it had become more important than the number (22 per cent) who thought it had become less important.

MEMBERS AND INDIVIDUAL POLITICIANS

In chapter 3 we outlined the organisational structure of Fine Gael, but some writers on Irish politics have expressed scepticism about how seriously we should take the parties' formal organisational structures when we want to understand what's really going on. Some suggest that personal links count for much more than people's nominal position within an organisation, and it has been argued that personalism is especially prominent in Ireland. Personalism, as John Coakley explains, "implies a tendency to evaluate and respond to persons in positions of power (such as the President, the Taoiseach or a local Dáil deputy) in terms of their personal character rather than in terms of the authority associated with their office".[37] Sacks, in his study of grass roots politics in

Donegal, identified personalism as a key component of Irish political culture, asserting that, especially in rural Ireland, "face-to-face transactions are the basic mode of political participation", while Chubb argued that the values of the "dying peasant society" led to "great emphasis on the personal and local in politics".[38] Some institutions that look from the outside to be run along impersonal and bureaucratic lines may, on closer examination, be based primarily on personal links. For example, Samuel Decalo, writing about the military in Africa, says: "Many African armies bear little resemblance to the Western organizational prototype and are instead a coterie of distinct armed camps owing primary clientelist allegiance to a handful of mutually competitive officers of different ranks". He describes them as riddled with "mutual-advancement loyalty pyramids" that are "only nominally beholden to military discipline and hierarchical command".[39]

The research of the Canadian political scientist Ken Carty would suggest that this statement – once we take arms out of the equation, of course – would apply equally well to Irish political parties. Having studied grassroots party activity in Kildare in the 1970s and looked at the activities of "parochial politicians", he concludes that "the parties are, after all, really little more than these same parochial politicians with their personal networks (formal and informal) of supporters". TDs, he said, aim to build a machine whose aim is to support them personally rather than the party as a whole, so "wherever possible, personally loyal supporters, including astonishing numbers of relatives, are installed as local branch officers to solidify control". As a result, "the degree to which many TDs are able to transform nominally party organizations into purely personal machines is quite remarkable".[40] It is generally assumed, not always on the basis of firm evidence, that this personalistic style of politics is more pronounced in rural areas than in towns and cities. The party, in this perception, is not so much an organisation in its own right as a shell that provides the arena within which political entrepreneurs compete for support, which is how American parties are sometimes perceived.[41]

Partisans of a person or of a party?

How far, then, are Fine Gael members not really partisans of Fine Gael as such but simply supporters of individual politicians – politicians who, perhaps, just so happen to belong to Fine Gael? We asked members whether they regarded themselves as being a strong supporter of one of the party's leading politicians in the constituency or whether they supported all of the party's politicians equally. The results (see Table 5.12) show quite strikingly that nearly half of Fine Gael members are oriented primarily towards a specific politician, which, at first sight at least, lends strong support to Carty's conclusions. Other questions designed to measure the same phenomenon produced comparable results. Members were asked whether, at the 1997 general election and the 1999 local election, they had worked equally for all the party's candidates or primarily to secure the election of one particular candidate. In each case, more members had been working for the election of one specific candidate than for the party ticket as a whole (Table 5.12).

**Table 5.12: Members' orientations to individual politicians and to the Fine
Gael party as a whole**

	%
Strong supporter of one local FG politician	45
Support all local FG politicians equally	55
At 1997 general election:	
worked primarily for one FG candidate	40
worked equally for all FG candidates	32
At 1999 local election:	
worked primarily for one FG candidate	40
worked equally for all FG candidates	31

Source: Fine Gael members' questionnaire, questions 33, 19a, 19c.
Note: Regarding the 1997 general election, a further 28 per cent of respondents did not indicate that
they had worked at all; for the 1999 local election, too, this applied to 28 per cent of respondents.

It is true that there are some constituencies where Fine Gael does not run
more than one candidate, and in these cases campaign workers did not have
the opportunity to work "equally for all the Fine Gael candidates". This
applies only to a small minority of constituencies, though – to just five of the
41 constituencies at the 1997 general election, for example, and to an even
smaller proportion of constituencies at the 1999 local election – and the picture
hardly changes if we exclude these cases. Moreover, of those who had been
working for one candidate in particular, the overwhelming majority had
known that candidate personally before the campaign began: 93 per cent of
those who had worked for one candidate during the 1997 election, and 95 per
cent of those who had worked for one candidate in 1999. This was not, then, a
case of election workers finding an affinity with a candidate during the course
of a campaign, but, rather, of people who already knew a particular individual
campaigning for him or her.

The personal connection is manifested in other ways as well. Three-quarters
of members have had personal contact during the past year with a local Fine
Gael TD; an even higher proportion have had contact with a councillor (Table
5.13). If we compare the figures in Table 5.13 with those relating to attendance
at branch meetings (Figure 5.1), we can see that concentrating solely on the latter would give a rather misleading picture of the activity of the Fine Gael
party. Although most Fine Gael members went to fewer than three branch
meetings in the twelve months before the survey, that does not mean that they
were doing nothing. It is true that, by and large, those who attended most
branch meetings were also most likely to have had contact with the party's
elected representatives and to have passed on constituents' requests to a party
TD, but even many of those whose attendance at branch meetings was low or
non-existent did the same: 40 per cent of those who hadn't attended any

Table 5.13: Urban–rural differences in extent of personal networks among Fine Gael members

	Urban %	Rural %	All %
Strong supporter of one particular local FG politician	40	46	45
Worked for one particular candidate in 1997 general election	50	57	56
Worked for one particular candidate in 1999 local election	59	55	56
Contact with local FG TD in last year	76	75	75
Contact with local FG councillor in last year	81	88	86
Ever pass on to TD constituents' requests for assistance	52	64	61
Frequent work or social contact with other branch members	59	78	74

Source: Fine Gael members' questionnaire, questions 33, 19a, 19c, 30, 31, 32, 10.
Note: For definition of urban see chapter 4, note 17 (p. 265).

meetings in the past year, and 62 per cent of those who had attended only 1 or 2 meetings, had acted as brokers between TDs and constituents in this manner. Moreover, we noted earlier in the chapter that nearly three-quarters of members are in frequent contact with other branch members through their work or social life.

The impression, then, is that the Fine Gael organisation operates in some senses on two planes: on a formal and official plane, where members attend a rather low number of branch meetings, and on an informal and unofficial plane, where members interact frequently with each other and with their party's elected representatives. The indicators of activity on the formal plane are perhaps modest, but those relating to the informal plane seem altogether healthier. The existence of this parallel network of contact between party members outside the formal structures of the organisation might raise the question of whether Fine Gael, or indeed any other party, really requires a formal branch structure any more. In an era of email and mobile phones, is there any longer any need for an organisational structure that was devised when communications were far less developed? As we shall see in chapter 6, some members of the party doubt whether the branch structure is relevant any more.

It is often assumed that the personal connection looms larger in rural than in urban areas. However, when we examine urban–rural differences carefully, they turn out not to be particularly significant (see Table 5.13). On most measures, it is true, members in rural areas are more likely to participate in personal networks than their urban counterparts, but the differences in nearly every case are fairly small. Only when it comes to work or social contact with other party members does the urban–rural gap reach ten percentage points, and even here it is still true that a majority of urban members report that they have such extra-organisational contact with fellow members. Nor is there any urban–rural difference in the likelihood (not shown in the table) that members knew personally the candidates for whom they worked during an election campaign.

Implications for party cohesion

A party might well be concerned by the presence of so many members whose loyalty seems to be to one particular politician rather than to the party per se. It might mean, for example, that within the party ranks there is a sizeable dead-weight of nominal members who have little interest in the well-being of the party, see no reason to participate in its activities except when this is of direct benefit to the politician whom they support, and perhaps have little interest in political issues. Such people may be a great resource for the politician in ques-tion, but they might seem to be of dubious benefit to the party as a whole. They could have a detrimental effect on party unity and on the cohesion of the par-liamentary group, encouraging TDs to follow their own course in policy matters and in Dáil votes secure in the knowledge that many party members and cam-paign workers will back them through thick and thin – even if they were to break away from the party. How serious a problem is this for Fine Gael and, by extension, for other political parties?

It is, of course, true that there are members of the party who do contribute very little, partly because they were recruited in the first place by and specifi-cally for the benefit of a specific politician. We pointed out in chapter 3 that Fine Gael, like all the parties in Ireland (and no doubt in many other countries too) has "paper branches" with "ghost members": rolls of members who may pay a membership fee (or, at least, on whose behalf a membership fee is paid) but who don't seem to do much else. When head office, or a politician from outside the constituency, tries to make contact with the organisation in an area riddled with paper branches, it may be very difficult to get any response. The nominal mem-bers will do what they are required to do – that is, use their votes to secure the selection of their champion or patron as a party candidate, and then campaign for him or her at election time – but they have no interest in doing anything more. In the worst case, the apathy of such members towards the well-being of the party per se may create a sub-culture of inertia, having an enervating effect on other members, sapping the enthusiasm of existing members and discourag-ing the recruitment of policy-oriented people.

However, we should not overstate the apparent conflict between personality and party. The PR-STV electoral system, as we explained in chapter 1, both per-mits and promotes this dual focus on parties and individual candidates. While there is always the potential for tension between individual politicians pursuing their own interests and the interests of the party as a whole, Irish parties would have long since fallen apart if they were not capable of managing this tension. Indeed, as far as possible they do not merely manage but positively harness these tensions for the benefit of the party. When individual politicians work hard at building up a network of active supporters and cementing an appeal to the electorate at large, the benefits for the party outweigh the difficulties. The personal retinue of a politician could, after all, go elsewhere; better in most cases to have it, and the politician at its head, within Fine Gael than working for another party or operating under an independent label. Certainly there could be no automatic assumption that if the politician at the top of his or her personal machine did not exist, all those party members who currently work so actively on his or behalf would still be party members, working equally enthusiastically for some other individual or for the abstract entity that is "the party as a whole". Personal loyalties, whether of members or of voters under PR-STV, do not preclude party loyalties, and it would be a mistake to interpret Table 5.12 as meaning that 45 per cent of Fine Gael members have no loyalty to Fine Gael per se. Some, perhaps many, of these members are loyal to the politician only because he or she is a Fine Gael politician – this is supported by the stability of membership figures in the party over the years and the longevity of members (something that implies fairly low turnover). Likewise, some members live in a constituency where there is only one leading Fine Gael politician, and these members may feel that the option of "supporting all the party's politicians equally" is unrealistic in their case; moreover, even if they support one politician especially, they may still be basically supportive of the party's other candidates as well.

This is not to say that there is no inherent tension between individual politicians looking above all to secure their own (re-)election and party leaders who prioritise the total number of seats that the party will win.[42] If constituency politicians try to boost their own position by undercutting the position of internal party rivals, securing a seat for themselves at the cost of destroying any chance of the party's winning an extra seat, then clearly their behaviour is dysfunctional for the party as a whole – and undoubtedly this sometimes happens. Internal competition, and the existence of networks of personal loyalty within the organisation, seem "healthy" when they have the effect of boosting the organisational strength and electoral support of the party as a whole, and "pathological" when they result in a party that is unable to act in a unified and coherent manner and whose whole is considerably less than the sum of its parts. Do the attachments of so many Fine Gael members to a specific politician work to the benefit or the detriment of the party generally?

To answer this question fully would require another study, but our survey can throw some light on the matter. We can compare those members who, in answer to question 33 of the questionnaire, say that they think of themselves as a strong supporter of one of the party's leading politicians in the constituency with those who responded that they support all the party's politicians equally. If the former are less active, less interested in politics and political issues, and less loyal to Fine Gael per se than the latter, then the networks of personal loyalty are likely to have some implications, many of them negative ones, that need to be teased out. On the other hand, if the two types of party member seem to be almost indistinguishable with regard to their behaviour and their attitudes, there appears to be little cause for concern.

When we compare the two groups of supporters, the main impression is the lack of difference between them, both demographically and attitudinally. Those who are strong supporters of one local politician in particular are neither older nor younger than other members, and nor is there any difference between men and women, between new and long-standing members, or between those employed in different sectors of the economy or belonging to different social groups. Nor, as we have seen, is there any significant difference between urban and rural constituencies. There is some relationship with the number of Fine Gael TDs in the constituency; thus where Fine Gael had 3 TDs elected in 1997 52 per cent of members saw themselves as supporters of one politician in particular, and this figure dropped to 47 per cent where it had 2 TDs, 45 per cent where it had 1 TD, and 36 per cent where it had no TD. Interestingly, one of the lowest figures of all, 25 per cent, occurred in the Tipperary North constituency, where the party organisation had been badly hit by the defection of the former Fine Gael TD Michael Lowry, who headed the poll in 1997 as an independent. There can be little doubt that if the survey had been done while he was still in the Fine Gael ranks the figure for Tipperary North would have been much higher.

However, when it comes to attitudes to the Fine Gael party, we find that there is effectively no difference between the two groups (Table 5.14). It is simply not the case, as some might expect and Fine Gael might fear, that those who are strong supporters of one particular politician see themselves as significantly less strong supporters of Fine Gael itself. For the most part, loyalty to a person and to the party seem to be perfectly compatible. Looking at the other things that the two kinds of Fine Gael members do, there is not a lot of support for the idea that those who are primarily attached to one particular politician form a kind of apolitical deadweight within party ranks. They are no less likely to be interested in national political issues, and, in fact, are slightly *more* likely than other members to have voted and campaigned on one side or the other in the 1995 divorce referendum. They are no less likely to be content with the role of members within the Fine Gael party; it is not the case, as we might have expected, that these members care little about policy matters and thus have relatively little interest in participating in the internal decision-making of Fine Gael. Members who are strong supporters of one particular local Fine Gael politician are a little more likely than other members to be in

Table 5.14: Strength of support for Fine Gael, by support for local Fine Gael politicians

| | Support for local FG politicians | | All members |
| | One in particular | All | |
	%	%	%
Strength of support for FG			
Very strong	44	56	100
Fairly strong	46	54	100
Not very strong	41	59	100
Not at all strong	52	48	100
Total	45	55	100

Source: Fine Gael members' questionnaire, questions 1, 33.

frequent contact with other branch members and to have been active in recent election campaigns; not surprisingly, they are much more likely to have campaigned for one candidate in particular (61 per cent of these people are strong supporters of one particular politician) than to have campaigned for all Fine Gael candidates equally (only 31 per cent of these people are strong supporters of one particular politician). When it comes to rates of participation in recent candidate selections, there is no difference at all between the two types of member.

At the same time, there are some signs of a different, more personalistic and locally-oriented style and approach to politics among those members who think of themselves primarily as strong supporters of one of the local politicians. These members are more likely than other members to be in personal contact with a local Fine Gael TD, to pass on to a Fine Gael TD constituents' requests for assistance, and to see the most important role of a TD as being the local one rather than the national one. Members with a strong personal attachment to one politician are also more likely than other members to say that they are actively involved only at election times, and less likely to devote more than 5 hours per month to party activities. Their route into the party, too, is slightly different. They are less likely to have been members of Young Fine Gael than other members, and more likely to have joined for what in chapter 3 we termed "solidary" reasons, essentially non-political reasons such as meeting people or the influence of family and friends. In nearly all these cases, though, the differences are not great, and only barely achieve a level of statistical significance.

All in all, then, it is clear that many Fine Gael members do see themselves primarily as supporters of one particular politician in the constituency, but this is not as damaging for the party as it might at first seem to be. Loyalty to an individual within the party does not usually, let alone necessarily, come into conflict with loyalty to the party per se. It might, of course, and when this happens – for example, when a TD breaks away or is expelled from the party, either to join another party or to become an independent – these members will find themselves cross-pressured. As we have already mentioned, there was a high profile example of this in Tipperary North before the 1997 election, when the former Fine Gael cabinet minister Michael Lowry (under something of a cloud) left the party and took a significant section of the local Fine Gael organisation with him. In normal circumstances, though, the existence of so many members whose loyalty is primarily to an individual Fine Gael politician does not pose a problem for Fine Gael as a whole. Indeed, it brings many benefits, because for the most part the party is able to manage and harness the desire of individual politicians to build up personal electoral and organisational support so that this results in additional support for the party as a whole. Given that members with a strong loyalty to one politician account for about half the total, Fine Gael might be in dire straits without them. These members are no less active than other members, no less interested in political issues, and no less valuable to the party.

CONCLUSION

The Fine Gael members' survey suggests that activism within the party is reasonably high, especially for a party that was seen around the time of our survey as being "in crisis" and whose organisation had been the subject of a highly critical report six years earlier. There is a respectable level of attendance at branch meetings, and, in any case, it is clear that many members are in frequent contact with each other outside the formal structure and that there could be a lively organisation even where a branch meets infrequently. There is no disjunction between activity within the organisation and activity within the wider society: on the whole, those who are most active in one way are also most active in others. In other ways too the picture seems rosy. Most members participate in election campaigning and in candidate selection, and donate money to the party. The Fine Gael organisation performs a significant linkage role between the political system and ordinary citizens, with most members acting as a channel of communication between constituents and TDs. Many members see themselves as supporters primarily of one specific Fine Gael politician in the constituency, but these members are no less active or attached to the party than other members, and on balance the party benefits from their presence.

Comparing Fine Gael with the few other parties for which we have similar data also leads to encouraging conclusions. The decline of activism in Fine Gael is noticeably smaller than that experienced by the British parties. Fine Gael members attend branch meetings more than their British or Canadian counterparts. In other ways they appear little different, with many members inclined to get involved only at election time.

Not all the news is good for Fine Gael, however. The level of activism, as reported by members themselves, is declining, and it is little consolation that some parties in other countries are faring worse. Although many of the indicators are reasonably good, it is noticeable that long-serving members are markedly more active than newer recruits on virtually all dimensions: attending branch meetings, campaigning at elections, and acting as a link between TDs and constituents. There is a real danger that levels of activism and linkage will decline in the years ahead. Many branch secretaries are concerned that their branch is on its last legs, and indeed quite a few question the relevance of the branch structure itself in an era of email and mobile phones, as we shall see in the next chapter. Internal organisational matters still loom large on the agenda of branch meetings, something that was heavily criticised by the Joyce commission in 1993. As we said earlier in the chapter, the glass can be still be seen as half full rather than half empty, but it looks likely to become emptier in the years ahead.

6 The impact of members

We have so far described the party's membership, discussed the reasons why people belong to the party, and outlined the sort of things members do and how often they do them. Here we will review some evidence on what contribution members make to the party – what impact do their activities have? Opinion is quite divided in the academic literature on this subject.[1] Some, such as Katz, have argued that party members are of declining importance today.[2] Campaigns are nationally organised and implemented; the emphasis is on party leaders, while party images are channelled through national media, particularly television. Moreover, while this campaigning style is costly, parties have more sources of cash independent of members' contributions. Admittedly, parties still need bodies around at the right time, cheering the leader at set piece speeches, forming a guard of honour when he or she is on walkabouts, and so on. But such people can be shipped in for the day. The lifelong, committed, involved partisan, according to this argument, is a political dinosaur. In addition, members are liable to make demands on parties that parties may not want to meet. In their absence, party leaderships are freer to seek electoral favour without the ties that have bound some parties to a particular political–ideological territory.

This view is descriptively flawed and analytically somewhat naive. Despite the signs of membership decline, few would see Irish parties as fitting comfortably into this new mould. The concerns, often parochial ones, of Irish voters compel parties to campaign locally, and the importance of personal contact requires the presence of locals "on the ground". In addition, parties have always needed the funds coming in from members, even if for some politicians they have been far outweighed by bundles of notes from well-heeled supporters. Nevertheless, the sort of "electoralist" party characterised above is not so unreal, and arguably trends in this direction have both followed from and reinforced the decline in party membership seen in many nations.[3] How important, then, is the presence in the constituency of hundreds of members? We consider two sorts of evidence here. First, we will look at the views of the members themselves on the subject of membership. Their assessment of their own role has implications for the future of membership. In addition, their views as to how membership might be increased tell us something about how members see the costs and rewards of belonging to a party, and we will go in particular depth into the opinions of branch secretaries as to whether the present organisational structure has a future. We also report on how members see their role in candidate selection, which is a very significant arena for grass-roots influence. Second, we will analyse the party's electoral record and see how this ties in with patterns of membership. Does the party do better where it has more members, and, if so, what does that tell us about the role of members in the party?

MEMBERS AND THE PARTY

A general view

We asked members to indicate whether they believed that the Fine Gael organisation makes the best use of the energy and commitment of its existing members
(Q79a). Opinion was fairly evenly divided, with 48 per cent saying it does and
52 per cent saying it does not. Dissatisfaction is greater amongst the activists,
with 64 per cent of the most active group (these members are defined in chapter
5 and Appendix C) expressing the feeling that members are under-utilised.
Below that level of activity there is little difference of opinion. Dissatisfaction is
also greater amongst women and among members with more education,
although these differences are generally small. Perhaps significantly, those
claiming to be less active than they were four years ago are also more dissatisfied, although again the difference is relatively small. The key point here is that,
regardless of the type of member, a substantial proportion feel members have
more to contribute and this is particularly so amongst those currently most
active.

We asked a couple of other questions in a similar vein. Respondents were
invited to say whether they agreed or disagreed with the statement "The Fine
Gael party leadership doesn't pay a lot of attention to the views of ordinary
party members" (Q80.1), and were asked also if ordinary members of Fine Gael
have enough say in determining party policy (Q66). In both cases the majority
response was again negative. Fifty-five per cent agreed that the leadership paid
little attention to members (36 per cent of them strongly), 22 per cent disagreed
(only 10 per cent of them strongly), while 23 per cent sat on the fence. On policy,
75 per cent said members had insufficient say. On each of these items, it is the
activists who are most likely to express dissatisfaction although there is little difference between the most and least active on the extent of members' policy
input.

Not all of the dissatisfaction with the role of the member is linked to policy,
although that is clearly a significant element. Of those who complain both about
their lack of say on policy and the inattentiveness of the leadership, 67 per cent
say members are under-utilised. Amongst those with no complaint on either
score, only 34 per cent feel under-utilised. If the complaint is only about policy
or only about inattentiveness, then 42 per cent and 46 per cent respectively feel
under-utilised. Apparently, at least some members have things in mind other
than policy, or just being "listened to", when they say members could contribute
more.

All this suggests clearly that Fine Gael's members do not accept that membership should now mean very little, even if there has been a decline in the numbers taking it up. Many say that members could and should contribute rather
more. If membership parties such as Fine Gael now offer members a reduced
role it does not appear that this is simply due to member apathy. Certainly there
are members, both passive and active ones, who are satisfied with their contribution to the party but for many the judgement is essentially: could do better.

Concerning the lack of input on policy we asked people what they would suggest to improve matters, offering them the choice of regular meetings between local TDs and members, making ard-fheis resolutions binding, and holding regional conferences to discuss policy. Sixty-three per cent (of those dissatisfied) indicated that regular meetings with local TDs would help. This would allow views to be channelled upwards as well as providing a chance for TDs to explain current thinking. The second most favoured option was the regular regional conference (something that has in fact been recently introduced), which was endorsed by 54 per cent. Least favoured was the idea of binding conference resolutions, favoured by only 33 per cent. This has been promoted within many parties, in particular those on the left, but full internal democracy has never been a strong element of Fine Gael's practice or self-image, as we saw in chapter 3. Members want a say in policy; they are not asking for control.

This is emphasised in what members wrote when invited to indicate how the party might make better use of them. More than a third of our respondents put pen to paper on this issue. It is not easy to summarise all of the detailed points they made, although at a general level almost all are singing from the same hymn sheet in calling on the party to value their efforts more. Our classification and summary of the spread of answers is given in Table 6.1. The most common themes were a need for more communication downwards, more listening by those in office, and the provision of more opportunities for member involvement. Just over a quarter demanded better communication with members, particularly from the centre: members need to be told what is going on. Here are some illustrative responses, again presented verbatim:

- Existing members would work harder if their value was recognised at times other than election; clique element is not appreciated by grassroots
- TDs should attend more meetings and meet Fine Gael's supporters regularly, not just at election time. They may then be more encouraged to be committed
- There seems to be a lack of communication between branches and districts

Table 6.1: Most important ways to make more use of members

	%
More communication within party	26
Give members more influence on policy	24
Involve members more	21
More meetings, activities, socials	10
Improve national image of party	8
Create data base of members and their expertise	8
Other	2
Total	100

Source: Fine Gael members' questionnaire, question 79b.
Note: Responses were obtained from 70 per cent of dissatisfied members (weighted). Since question 79b was completely open, the categories used are devised by the authors.

- Letting members like myself know what is going on such as when the leader Mr. Bruton is in town and not have to read about it in the local paper. Also we should know what happens at Board of Officers meetings
- Difficult to get the message through in HQ. Could argue for a head of Fine Gael in each constituency to allow more contact between branches and leadership
- More district and constituency meetings.

Members can contribute, even as ambassadors, and sometimes even only as cheerleaders, only if they know what is going on. But many members clearly want more than this. Twenty-four per cent want their voice to be heard in discussion of party policy, something that they think does not happen at the moment. For instance, members suggest:

- Policy workshops open to all members, held locally (e.g. select six topics), chairperson for each topic, round table discussions – members select two topics to discuss
- Meeting the constituency on a regular basis and get the views of the members
- Fine Gael could survey members on policy, e.g. ask serving teachers about education policy
- Give [members] a say in the policy making decisions at regional meetings where their voices could be heard
- Each TD should have advisory committees dealing with different areas of government. They would examine bills and propose amendments and also give views and ideas on various areas of policy
- All party members should have voting rights on policy formation at a full two-day annual Ard Fheis
- Listen better to what is being said at branch meetings
- Just listen.

The first two types of comment are essentially for communication up and down the party. Another 21 per cent of members demand that the party listens and call for more involvement of members. This encompasses a wide range of ideas, including a say in the selection of the leader, training for members, and generally making wider use of the skills and resources of ordinary members.

- Voluntary manning of the office during an election; utilise members' skills
- Running training programmes similar to those for people who have a message or product to sell
- In the event of the election of new leader the party members should have 20% of the vote. The party's TDs and senators are not listening to membership. The party constitution needs urgent amendment to give more power to members
- Members who have special attributes should be encouraged
- Eliminate inner circles, encourage members to have an equal say. Practise what we preach: everybody counts. When Fine Gael was in government members received no [special treatment] contrary to how other parties treat their supporters
- The party has lost the skill of establishing and using expert committees
- Give members a real function within the structure of the party other than that of canvassing at election. Connect all the layers of the party from the top to the bottom

- By involving members more in decision making
- Give them positions within the party structures which are already held and dominated by older members
- Give members some responsibility, a job to do and appreciate the work done; also tease out their private views on matters.

Eight per cent even suggest something like a member database, so that the party will know what members can contribute.[4] Another 10 per cent seek to improve the quality and frequency of local activity. For some this means more meetings, for others it means more social activities, for still others it means using members as activists in the community. All such people seem to feel there is not enough going on. For example:

- In our own area district branches only meet once a year for the AGM, I feel it should be regular with more input from HQ and respective TDs
- Less frequent but more interesting meetings
- Fine Gael should get more people involved with local organisations, associations and clubs
- Forget boring meetings. Do something youthful – a weekend away in a big hotel with Brendan Grace.[5] Wake up!
- Putting on social activities and getting members to mix and socialise
- By visiting schools, colleges, promoting debates on local issues
- More meetings; meetings are very badly attended; only at election time will you see a big crowd.

Finally, 8 per cent feel that change must start with the leadership: a better image for the party, more work by frontbenchers and TDs and even a change of leader. It is not clear why this will make better use of members, but presumably such people feel that until things are right at the top there is little those on the ground can do to help the party.[6] For most members, though, at least for most of those expressing a view, the ordinary member is undervalued and under-involved.

What is not said here is as significant as what is said. There are no complaints that members are inadequately used as fundraisers, no complaints about not being used for canvassing, and no complaints about being asked to take on too much responsibility. As the Joyce Commission pointed out, members are used as sources of income and as foot soldiers on the canvass but are given insufficiently attractive opportunities for influence within the party. This survey bears out that contention very well. And as we saw in chapter 5, many members are becoming less active for just the sort of reasons indicated here as they feel undervalued by the party.

Not surprisingly, more active members were much more likely to respond to this question. Those we have described as "very active" were almost twice as likely to have something to say compared with those who are "inactive". Hence, these comments might be thought to reflect the ideas of the more active members to a very disproportionate extent, though differences between the type of response given by the most and least active members are relatively small. More active members are a little more likely to stress the need for more "involvement" while the least active members are more likely to blame those at the top and complain that no one tells them what's going on. There are also few differences between members who may have joined for policy, solidary or what we term partisan promotional reasons. All cite much the same range of complaints: the need for more involvement, more influence and more communication.

In general it seems safe to say that most members have complaints: they do not have the impact they feel they should. They do not know enough about what is going on, and are allowed too little say in, and involvement with, party decisions. Some members expressed the view that they were required for fundraising and canvassing but given little enough in return. This raises the question again not so much as to why parties have members, but why people become and remain members of parties. Since party membership is in decline, it seems that fewer people are finding a positive answer to that question.

Recruitment and the role of members

Given this problem, which is widely recognised, we asked our respondents whether they thought the party was doing enough to recruit new members and what they themselves thought was the way forward on this (Q78a and Q78b). Fine Gael members certainly seem to think that more could be done. Eighty-nine per cent say the organisation could take more steps and only 11 per cent think that enough, or at least as much as possible, is done already. But what more could be done? Answers, provided by over half of our respondents, are classified and summarised in Table 6.2.

Many focused on who should be recruited, with the absence of youth and, to a lesser extent, women in the party of most concern. However, the issue is really *how* this should be done. As with many such matters, some felt it was a matter for the party leadership, while others want the grassroots to do more. Either way, the answers frequently reveal something about members' views of what motivates other members to join a party, something that we discussed in chapters 4 and 5. Social, organisational and policy rewards all feature. Meetings should be made more interesting; there should be more contact with elected representatives; more opportunities for involvement in decision-making; the party itself should have an image and project a message that more people support. All these of course featured strongly in answer to the previous question about how members were (not) used. Members also stressed the need to contact people, both personally and through sub-units of the party, putting the emphasis on mobilisation.

The largest number, 46 per cent, thought recruitment a task for central direction. Central action covers a multitude of strategies. Most common was a demand for more action by public representatives and improved centre–branch links. Councillors, TDs and Senators were seen by many to have a role to play at a personal level in bringing members into the party, although no-one made explicit the bases that might underlie the special appeal of such people, whether it was prestige, glamour or the promise of privileged access to power. In

Table 6.2: Steps the organisation could take to get more members

	%
Central action and central organisational solutions	46
Listen to and involve members, make membership more attractive	19
Local-level action	12
New policies	9
Other	15
Total	100

Source: Fine Gael members' questionnaire, question 78b.
Note: Responses were obtained from 64 per cent of members (weighted). Since question 78b was completely open, the categories used are devised by the authors.

addition, there were calls for better PR in general (a less "fuddy-duddy", less "snobbish" or more "visionary" image), using Young Fine Gael more and targeting schools and colleges, getting the leadership to be more active and mounting membership drives. Some examples:

- Improve public relations, nationally and locally
- Get more branches of Young Fine Gael up and running
- Stimulate members' interest by closer contact and giving information and encouragement
- Have public representatives who work
- Emphasise Fine Gael's values and core principles more. Try to show where it is different from other parties
- Publicising activity in opposition, constituency seminars/strategic planning etc
- More involvement by constituency TDs to attract new members.

A different line of thought, expressed by 19 per cent, is to make party membership itself more attractive, in particular by giving members a greater say. Comments made already about listening to members and becoming more "people oriented" point in this direction. The point is made here about the need to involve members more at both branch and national level. Drawing, it may be assumed, on their own experience and interests, members themselves think this would attract more volunteers, and help to keep existing members in the party. We shall return to this in the next section when we examine the views of branch secretaries specifically. The appeal of membership may also be increased by making meetings less mundane and having more social events:

- Less collusion between so-called established members
- Get young people involved; cut down on length of meetings
- Make participation in the party more interesting. New members are easily attracted, holding on to them is the problem
- Good recruitment, some branches are a closed shop
- Interesting meetings. Speakers invited on certain topics

- Get rid of branches and have larger central units which would have more interesting meetings, with TDs / councillors attending
- More power and involvement of members of branches in determining policy.

The 12 per cent who argue for a local solution include those wanting more public meetings, the reorganisation and revitalisation of local parties, greater involvement in local concerns, canvassing, and the use of personal contacts. Significantly, only 3 per cent of all respondents argued for this last position, namely that members themselves have a personal responsibility for attracting new members – even though the party's branch manual fixes the responsibility for finding new members firmly on the shoulders of existing ones.[7] Comments included:

- Actively canvass members of the public, especially young people
- Get active in the community organisations, local issues, items in newspapers, local activists
- Members of branches should be more active in attracting members, talking to friends and contacts asking them to join party
- Get involved in more issues on the ground. Fianna Fáil county councillors and TDs always seem to be in first on local issues
- Invite people who are already interested in political issues (masts, dumps, poverty, environmental issues etc) to join the party
- Current members should try and get at least 2 new members each year.

It is striking that such suggestions were made by relatively few people. Arguably, this sort of approach has been adopted with some success by "new" parties such as Sinn Féin. Perhaps this campaigning element appears inappropriate to a well-established party but the relative absence of a feeling by grassroots members that they have some responsibility cannot help recruitment.[8] According to secretaries, recruitment is of only middling priority on their agenda. Only 17 per cent said it was the top priority, and on average it was only third of five – above fundraising and discussing policy, but below campaigning and supporting local representatives.[9] Given the members' comments it is surprising that it rates as highly as it does.

Nine per cent suggest that better policies, targeted at particular groups, are the way forward, and 14 per cent give some other response, in many cases simply reiterating the need to attract more members. In all this there is the recognition that membership of Fine Gael does not confer the benefits that it might, and that in any case far more could be done by the party and its members to raise levels of support. It is recognised that key groups, notably youth and women, are underrepresented in the party. This point comes out again in relation to candidate selection, which we discuss later.

Since a concern about membership numbers is neither a new nor a specifically Irish phenomenon, it is interesting to look at these responses against the background of the proposals made within the party in the past – notably by the Joyce Commission as outlined in chapter 3 – and those measures proposed or adopted in other countries such as Britain, Germany and Norway.[10] The main suggestions, from Joyce and from elsewhere, fall into four categories. First, an increase in direct democracy within the party. Second, better communication within the party, between and even across levels. Third, more attention to the world outside the party than to internal, organisational matters. And lastly, a softening of the boundaries between members and supporters. The first and second were mentioned by a combined 19 per cent although members were relatively unspecific in their answers. A few mentioned the need to involve members directly in the election of the leader, a suggestion made by the Joyce Commission, but the idea did not apparently strike many as the key to future growth. Norwegian parties have started to experiment more with electronic communication to members, a medium which might make possible rapid and extensive consultations within a party, but this too is not at the forefront of members' minds. The suggestion that the party spend more time on outreach activities is made only by the 12 per cent stressing the need for more involvement in community activity. The last item got little or no mention. Notwithstanding the call by some to change the party's image, which might open it up to the young or the less well off, the prevailing impression is that Fine Gael members are inward looking. Some parties have sought a less exclusive version of membership, providing for different levels of involvement with fewer distinctions between members and supporters, but we found little indication that Fine Gael members were thinking along these lines.

The party hierarchy has gone some way to following up the recommendations of the Joyce Commission and addressing the problems it identified. In 1995 a party committee produced a report entitled *Renewing the Party*, which certainly took on some of Joyce's proposals.[11] Most notably it proposed the one-member-one-vote system of candidate selection. However, it was much more cautious about the idea of giving members a direct role in the election of party leader. While recognising the case made by Joyce in terms of the desirability of widespread participation, and the impact of such a process on the mandate of the leader and intra-party activity, it nonetheless voiced what it saw as "strong arguments" against the change. The first was that since the party leader could become Taoiseach, the current situation, in which the leader is elected by those with a direct mandate from the electorate, was more democratic.[12] The second point was that members of the parliamentary party had firsthand knowledge of the candidates and were thus better equipped than the ordinary members to judge who could best do the job. The third objection was practical: a mass ballot and a campaign would take too much time when there could be a demand for a quick result. A fourth was that such an election would entail publishing the results, and the practice in Fine Gael at that time was to keep them secret, known only to the party chairman and teller. (This practice, as we noted in chapter 2, was dropped in 2001.) There is of course nothing new in the arguments on either side. What is significant is that more and more European parties are coming down in favour of giving the party leader a broader mandate within the party, and are putting aside the practical arguments. Not so Fine Gael. In the end, the decision was made to stick with the current system but it was clear in any case that there was little support for the idea of change in the upper echelons of the party.

The Joyce Commission also made recommendations about giving members more say on policy. It suggested the party establish specialist groups of members, and even supporters, with particular interests and skills, and link these at a high level into a new policy council, a body which would be "capable of defining the position of the party across the whole range of broad political issues" (p. 60). This council would also encourage a link between itself and constituencies through constituency policy officers. The party committee was rather happier about that, and proposed that such a committee be established, although integrating it into the party rather than allowing it to be free standing.[13] All in all, wrote the then party secretary Ivan Doherty in a one-page circular to members in January 1995 that amongst other things reported the adoption of OMOV and a fee increase from £5 to £8:

> In a gradual way Party members will play a more meaningful role in the running of the party at every level...[with] greater communication between party members at local level and the Party at national level and this will result in a better informed membership.

The view of our respondents less than four years later suggests that the party still had some way to go to meet members' demands. In general it must be said the party's implementation of the Joyce proposals was piecemeal rather than wholehearted. It extended participation where it already existed, but maintained the more oligarchical system of leader selection which had served the party to date. It also retained the basic branch structure, notwithstanding the move to OMOV, which might be held to weaken this structure by investing power in individuals and not branch delegates. The party underwent a makeover, but it was a modification rather than a transformation. Many members feel something rather more dramatic is required, even if there is little consensus about exactly what such a transformation might entail.

After they had completed the full questionnaire our respondents were asked to identify the main issues that Fine Gael needs to face up to (Q114). Responses are shown in Table 6.3. Most people answered and a majority of respondents, just over 50 per cent, wrote something about policy, usually indicating a specific policy, or set of specific policies that were required. Agriculture, Northern Ireland, taxation and single mothers were the most common, with many mentioning several policy areas, such as "Taxation, agriculture, roads (country), waste management (water/refuse), finance control" or "Reduce taxation, help farmers, traffic and road casualties, Northern Ireland". Others demanded the party adopt "more relevant" policies, or find out what the people want (and give it to them).

A second theme, expressed by 28 per cent, is the need for some overhaul of the organisation itself. Some of these comments simply indicated that "the organisation" was a problem; others reiterated the sort of complaints about "not listening" already described above, and still others demanded the party find better candidates. One member covered most of it in a string of comments:

Table 6.3: What Fine Gael should do now

	%
New / better policies	51
Better organisation	28
Better public relations	17
Better leadership	12
Other	6

Source: Fine Gael members' questionnaire, question 114.
Note: Responses were obtained from 82 per cent of members (weighted). Since question 114 was completely open, the categories used are devised by the authors. Column sums to greater than 100 per cent because of multiple responses

- Fine Gael is a mess organisationally. HQ staff need to visit branches and listen to members, apathy [is] rampant, older members cling to power, [there is] no training for new members.

Sixteen per cent stressed the need for "better public relations". Many complain that Fine Gael does not make best use of the media, others that the party image needs improving and selling, with more appeal to young people, the disadvantaged, and women. Typical comments are:

- Try to get the message across more effectively in the media
- Fine Gael need a better public relations system. The party seldom have TDs' statements etc. published in the press – I would like to see Fine Gael being mentioned in press releases a lot more often and lesser known TDs getting more publicity
- Policies are fine but need to focus on getting their points across to the public – especially to the youth of the country
- Fine Gael comes across as the party of the middle class
- Fine Gael need to get a good PR firm to promote their policies because they have good policies
- Make Fine Gael more attractive to the young voters
- They should be able at the moment to cash in on all the dirt that is around Fianna Fáil and try to get on TV more and get people to listen.

Only twelve per cent called for changes in the leadership, a surprisingly small figure given the fact that John Bruton was made the scapegoat for his party's poor poll ratings a year later and replaced as leader. In fact, while many among this 12 per cent thought Bruton should be replaced immediately, some limited their criticism to saying that his image needed improvement. Also widespread were criticisms of front-benchers and ordinary TDs, members saying they needed to be more dynamic and visible, both on the local and national stages. For example:

- Get rid of John Bruton. Speak out more against Fianna Fáil in the Dáil
- Elect a better leader and front bench spokesperson

- A good shake up in the leadership and front bench also has to be done to bring in the youth
- Wouldn't know where to start as I feel the party is a mess. New leadership might help and would be a starting point
- A change of leadership. Be more effective in opposition
- A new dynamic leader required
- I think that the Fine Gael leader John Bruton will have to come across more to the people and hit the government harder in the future and take a firm stand on his issues so that the people of this country will get behind him.

Members generally, then, have a number of ideas as to what should be done. They feel that they have a significant role to play in the party, and that the party's success requires the commitment, if not just of them, then of them and others. Before we move on to look at one area where members are relatively satisfied, namely candidate selection, we will consider the views of a key subsection of the membership, the branch secretaries, and examine their views on the future of the organisation.

The future of the organisation: branch secretaries' views

Having looked at what members generally have to suggest about the way forward, let us now examine the opinions of branch secretaries, who occupy a vital role in the party organisation. Given the rather downbeat reports on the current state of the organisation that we received from a number of secretaries and reported in the previous chapter, it is no surprise to find that some secretaries now wonder whether the current organisational structure, based as it is on the branch, has any future or whether it persists simply because of the structural inertia that tends to characterise all large organisations. As we noted in chapter 3, the Joyce Commission in 1993 expressed serious doubts as to whether the existing organisational scheme, based on the branch, makes sense any more, especially in urban areas.

Many secretaries expressed concern, in some cases about the survival prospects of their own branch and in others about the point of having branches at all. To give a few examples of the first category:

- It has taken a very committed effort by a few dedicated souls to keep this branch alive. At the moment morale is pretty low and could do with an injection of new members to keep it going. There was a drive approximately 2 years ago to bring in new members but this bore no fruit
- The branch has too many older members and not enough new members for the area covered ... In other words the [local] Branch is "dying" sad to say
- Why can Fine Gael not encourage young people to join? We are now an ageing branch slowly getting smaller through ill health and death
- There is a fear that because of a lack of interest among the younger folk, that local branches will disappear in the very near future
- The Fine Gael members are getting older as young people will not join. Public reps ignore the grass roots supporters but expect them to work to elect them
- Is our branch similar to many others in that the effort is mainly to affiliate and fly a (sagging) flag?

- Something needs to be done to get the youth involved in Fine Gael. The people that are there are all getting on and we need young blood if we are to continue
- The age profile in the branch is high, c60–63 years. The branch will not survive the next 15 years if young blood is not brought in. I feel it is imperative that young people are encouraged and recruited to join Fine Gael. Perhaps on each election panel at future elections (national and local) one candidate should be under 35 years of age.

Others linked the problems they were experiencing to the need for a general re-think of the rationale of the branch structure:

- The days of the branch (all branches) are finished – caput; we used to meet at least 6 times a year – now mostly once a year
- Local branches decline as few people are interested in officer posts. With the telephone we can always communicate. In almost 30 years' membership I found people find politics boring and drop out early. They sometimes appear to help out at elections. Parties like the Greens or Sinn Féin are more exciting
- It is hard to see the relevance of branch meetings other than to keep a "hard core" of activists in social contact with one another. Support at election time is alto-gether more important
- The age structure of the branch is getting older. The party has lost many members in recent times due to an image problem and disillusionment with lack of clout of constituency TDs. Traditional political allegiances are no longer applicable with people under 30 years of age. Radical political approaches are needed to attract new members. Party meetings are no longer relevant if aims of people are to be obtained. Pressure groups are the only way to change minds
- For Fine Gael especially is the structure of branch and members relevant to mod-ern politics which for our type of supporter are fought on media. Policy and par-ties are now consensus and dictated by so-called market research. The branch / membership function is in the main to raise funds and provide an election machine of sorts. Modern urban society, especially middle-class Fine Gael baili-wick, doesn't need a local mediator / contact. But what is the alternative? Society needs democracy, democracy needs parties who need activists to control TDs etc
- Most rural branches are not viable units. Too few members and same people. Would (party) be better facilitated by creating a District unit that would meet reg-ularly to discuss all party business?
- Too many small branches (paper branches) that never meet. Should be more regional / constituency meetings. Very little new blood
- Believe that branches are no longer relevant or necessary
- I get the impression that local branches are treated as non-essential items in the party. However it is refreshing that a survey is being undertaken and hopefully this will convey the endemic apathy I sense in meeting other party members and organisations
- Time to revitalise branch structure – members will need to receive something more tangible for their membership. Days of blue loyalty over
- It's harder to [get] people interested and to get them to come to meetings.

However, it was not all bad news. Some secretaries reported that things were picking up, or that even members who were not to be seen much at meetings were nonetheless there when they were needed, notably at election times:

- My branch is a small rural one. If all branches around the 26 counties were 60% as good Fine Gael would be in government most of the last 20 years
- It is very hard in a rural area to get people to come to meetings, but many are helping when election time comes up. They give of their time late and early and spend some of their own money
- In the history of local government the [names town] area has never had a local representative until my success in June 1999 local elections. During this election I concentrated on having as many young people (18 to 30 years) as possible on my canvass. This has revitalised interest in Fine Gael in the area and I'm confident that the coming year's membership will grow considerably
- We are a small branch but very strong. We would have elderly members who are now unable to participate in many campaigns. The younger of us would do most of the work especially at election time when it necessitates walking miles.

Clearly, the future of the branch structure is an issue that all parties will have to grapple with in the years ahead. Small rural branches often simply do not have the critical mass to do much more than meet once a year in order to hold their AGM and thus fulfil their obligations under the party constitution. The case for merging small branches into larger units, which could hold policy discussion meetings with guest speakers, is obvious. And yet, at the same time, there would no doubt be a cost in doing this; some members who are prepared to attend a meeting of a branch close at hand might be less willing to travel some distance to a meeting. The implication of some of the responses is that the structure might not matter much: as long as there is a network of party supporters, and these people come out to help at election time, how much does it really matter what they do between elections?

CANDIDATE SELECTION

While members feel they have insufficient say with respect to some aspects of party activity, the relatively open process of candidate selection gives them a chance to determine the sort of politician who promotes the party's message. Candidate selection is also an area in which members have been given more rather than less formal power in recent years with the introduction of the OMOV system of candidate selection. As we saw in the previous chapter, most members have taken that opportunity. We asked members for their views on the process. What did they think of the calibre of Dáil candidate on offer? Sixty-eight per cent thought existing procedures ensure that the best candidates are put forward. In contrast to other measures of satisfaction with the party discussed above, this is strikingly high and is perhaps a result of involving more members in the process. Once again, however, those most dissatisfied are those most actively involved in the party, but even 62 per cent of the most active group approved selection methods.

We asked members how the quality of candidates selected could be improved and responses are set out in Table 6.4. The most common response, made by 34 per cent, was to point to a relative absence of certain types of can-

Table 6.4: Steps to be taken to attract better candidates

	Percent
Improve the selection pool, get particular types of candidate	34
Improve the appeal of the party	20
Better selection: targeting, grooming, selecting outsiders	15
More decentralised selection	14
Improve the job of a public representative	4
More centralised selection	4
Other change	6
Current situation is fine, no change needed	2

Source: Fine Gael members' questionnaire, question 72.
Note: Responses were obtained from 58 per cent of members (weighted). Since question 72 was completely open, the categories used are devised by the authors.

didate, thus indicating either what the respondents thought a "better" candidate might look like, or at least what might be required for a better slate of candidates.[14] Young candidates were mentioned by 16 per cent, with women candidates, better educated candidates and candidates from the local area all getting some mention by 1–2 per cent. Many argued simply that the party should seek to increase the number of members from a particular category so as to have more potential candidates of this background available.

A second response, given by 20 per cent, was for the need to make the party more attractive to "better" candidates. While a few cynics suggested that winning office would provide the most potent lure, others stressed the need to improve the party image or change the leadership, or to make the party more open and democratic. For example:

- The image of the party will have to be improved. It should be a policy driven party rather than just chasing Fianna Fáil down and reminding them of their many sins
- The party should take a clear honest stand on important issues
- Improve front bench profile in opposition
- Have a leader with charisma
- A Taoiseach of integrity and a degree in Commerce and let the younger generation see there is a challenge in this government for them instead of having rubber stamps in Leinster House, doddering men with little brains.

In contrast to calls for general action, 33 per cent stressed the need for specific changes to the selection process. Fourteen per cent wanted *less* central interference in candidate selection; 4 per cent wanted *more* such interference, and a further 15 per cent just wanted better decisions to be made without being specific as to whether this required action by the centre or the constituency.

Those wanting an even more decentralised selection process tended to say the leadership should listen to the grass roots rather than impose candidates on them. This would be aided by better organisation at local level, to involve local

members more. Although the process might seem to be completely decentralised already, given the OMOV system, in fact the centre still has power since
it can add names to those selected locally, as we pointed out in chapter 3. The
implication, rarely explicit, is that imposed candidates often turn out anyway to
be unsuitable, having no aptitude for the job and being unsatisfactory in their
dealings with local people. Some representative comments along these lines:

- Better organisation at Cumann [sic] level
- Generally we do not attract quality candidates but sometimes through lack of
  research the wrong one is marketed. Pros and cons of all potential candidates
  should be listened to before a decision is made, not just high profile members as
  they do
- Dublin should not push candidates where the local people do not have their say
  as to who is put forward
- There has to be more transparency [and] less dictation from so-called big-wigs
  from Dublin and Galway etc
- HQ should listen more to party workers in the different constituencies who know
  the candidates
- Give the ordinary members more say
- Hard working TDs who come up from local government and are ambitious will
  keep the party vote high in their area. They are preferable to high profile or high
  academic people who neglect the voters and frequently drop out when they find
  they have no flair for it
- No imposition of candidates by headquarters
- Party strategists should pay more heed to local members. They are likely to be
  more au fait with the candidates' credentials. A good actor can play a blinder for
  the higher executives but may not be quite so shiny at local level
- Pressure should never be exerted on candidates to "step-down" from being
  elected. This only results in the party's favourite candidate being selected and
  elected
- Improve local branch meetings and make it more attractive for people with interesting topics etc, in the hope of attracting more people out of which it would be
  hoped to get better calibre of people.

A smaller group (4 per cent) wants more centralisation. This can take place
through the head hunting of candidates by the leadership, or making use of the
executive's powers for imposing candidates on the constituency. The move to
the one-member-one-vote (OMOV) system of selection has been seen as making
more difficult the oblique efforts at central influence that used to operate
through the convention,[15] so the task of the party leadership is obviously not a
simple one.

A further 15 per cent simply call for better decision making and suggest targeting and grooming candidates without saying who should do it; or stress the
need to recruit good candidates regardless of whether they hold party membership; or suggest changing the selection rules; or complain about the disproportionate influence exercised by local notables. Many of these members are probably thinking of giving more of a role to the centre. There is also some dissatisfaction with the OMOV system, which can certainly be manipulated by aspiring

candidates to their advantage. They are able to sign up supporters as members and these can then all vote at conventions, something that could not be done so effectively under the old system. In general there seems to be a fair degree of support for Fine Gael to seek out and develop good candidates, despite the fact that this may increase the degree of centralisation in the party. The following indicate the sort of concerns:

- Identify and target possible candidates, encourage them to become active at grass roots level with a view to firstly becoming involved in local government
- Head-hunt young people in constituencies who are actively involved in community organisations and who have the interest in a political career
- Approach high profile people
- One member one vote system open to abuse – a candidate could potentially add extra members to local branches to ensure he passed convention
- Try to see that new candidates are not blocked by those already elected for fear of losing their own seat
- All candidates should be carefully screened
- Do not need to be long-time party members, high profile candidates such as those active in community/sport/music/art.

For 4 per cent the answer lies in making the job of a TD itself more attractive. Most mention better salaries here, but a few highlight the insecurity of the job, the poor status and the general requirements of the job.

Most of these comments leave aside the question of what actually makes a good candidate and what members – who after all represent the "selectorate" in the process – should be looking out for at the conventions. As we have pointed out, it is clear that for some "better" means, for instance, more young people or more women, but most respondents directed their comments to the process rather than the outcome. Assuming candidates are judged as potential TDs, there are several different conceptions of what a TD should do. One role is essentially a legislative one, and requires a TD to spend a lot of time in and around the Dáil, contributing to legislation. The growing time and resources given to parliamentary committees has provided an outlet that has been lacking in the past for TDs wanting to fulfil this sort of role. Very different to this largely national function is the rather less glamorous "errand-boy" or brokerage role so memorably described as "going about persecuting civil servants".[16] TDs link the state with individuals and groups in the constituency, and this requires them to hold clinics and follow up voters' complaints with ministers and civil servants. A third role is a partisan one, defending party policy as necessary and accepting party discipline in the Dáil. For most deputies life consists of achieving a balance between all three, but for those who choose candidates, one role may be more important than another. We asked members how important were each of these for a TD to be doing his or her job properly, by ranking each in order of importance.

Opinion is pretty evenly divided between the 43 per cent who rank legislator over broker or partisan, and the 49 per cent who rank broker over legislator or partisan (see Figure 6.1). Only 8 per cent ranked the partisan role first. If we

Figure 6.1: Members' views regarding most important role of TDs

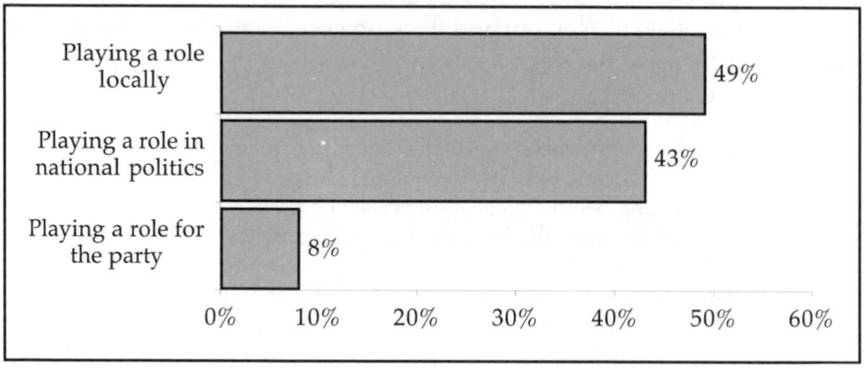

Source: Fine Gael members' questionnaire, question 81.

concentrate just on the two most widely selected roles, legislator and broker, we find that 46 per cent give priority to the role of legislator and 52 per cent to that of broker, with 2 per cent undecided or not known. Those looking for legislators are most likely to be disappointed by the existing system, although there is only a 10 per cent difference in satisfaction between those looking primarily for legislators and those looking for brokers. Who favours legislators? Older members, those with more education, those from urban areas, those recruited from outside the traditional family network and readers of the *Irish Times* are all more likely to be looking for legislators although none of the differences is large. Perhaps the relationship with age is surprising but the dividing line is really between those over and under 35 so only the "young" minority favouring brokers disproportionately is very different to the norm. An urban–rural contrast is particularly marked, with urban members almost twice as likely to prefer a legislator while rural members are evenly divided. Those favouring brokers are essentially the mirror image of the former group. Party secretaries also prefer brokers, but the difference between secretaries and other members is small.

Absence of female candidates
In addition to thinking about these roles, some thought may also be given to finding candidates and deputies who represent their constituents by sharing their social characteristics, thus bringing about "microcosmic" representation of the electorate. Arguably, those groups not so represented will be ignored.[17] One obvious problem with candidate selection in this respect is the party's failure to nominate many women candidates, a point made by some respondents. Only 13 women were nominated by Fine Gael to stand in the 1997 general election, the same number as in 1992.[18] We asked respondents why the party nominated so few women. Drawing on what is now a substantial literature on this issue[19] we offered members four possible explanations and invited them to indicate the extent to which they agreed or disagreed with each of them. One possible factor

is that there is a lack of ambition amongst women themselves, and so relatively few come forward. Another explanation is that women have too many family commitments to allow them to follow a political career. Both of these are "supply-side" explanations, implying that the main reason why more women are not selected is that women simply don't come forward in sufficient numbers. An alternative set of arguments deal with the demand for women as candidates. Two such explanations were provided to members. The first puts the blame on the voters, suggesting that the electorate is wary of women candidates, and the second locates responsibility within the party itself, suggesting that "attitudes within the party" discourage women from coming forward. Responses are displayed in Table 6.5.

This table shows the responses of the sample as a whole, and also indicates the mean score on each agree–disagree scale for both men and women, who differed somewhat in their responses to these items. Nearly half the members disagree with the first of the two supply-side explanations, that women are less ambitious than men. Women are particularly prone to dismiss this argument. However, a majority (52 per cent) accept the second supply-side argument, that family commitments inhibit more women from coming forward. Women are more likely to be convinced of this. Moving on to the demand–side arguments, there is substantial consensus against the argument that women lose votes, with 80 per cent rejecting it. Finally, there is a lack of much agreement about whether responsibility lies with the party itself. Forty-two per cent feel women don't get an equal opportunity, and 38 per cent feel they do. Again, women are rather more likely than men to feel they do not. There are some small differences between urban and rural members here with rural members more conscious of discrimination. Members longest in the party also seem to be more critical of attitudes in the party than the most recent members. These differences are quite small but perhaps this indicates that attitudes are changing, particularly in urban areas. The strongest finding here is the rejection of the argument that voters don't like women candidates.[20] But equally important is the widespread

Table 6.5: Why does Fine Gael have so few women candidates?

	Strongly agree 1	2	3	4	Strongly disagree 5	*Mean score for* Men	*Mean score for* Women
Because:							
Women are not as politically ambitious as men	19	17	16	13	36	3.2	3.5
Most women have too many family commitments	33	20	19	11	19	2.7	2.5
Women candidates lose votes for the party and so are not chosen	6	5	9	16	64	4.2	4.4
Attitudes within the party mean that women don't get an equal opportunity	27	14	20	13	25	3.2	2.7

Source: Fine Gael members' questionnaire, questions 73, 76, 74 and 75.

recognition, and not only amongst women, that there are those within the party who have blocked greater equality. While most accept that there is a problem of supply, few locate the problem only in that area and many accept there that there are structural impediments to the political equality of women. This was a recognition conspicuous by its absence from the outlook of party spokespersons summarised by the Commission on the Status of Women in 1972.[21]

One answer is quotas, a measure introduced by many parties in other countries to ensure the selection of a certain number of women. Fine Gael has never embraced this as policy, although it has accepted the need for affirmative action to increase women's role in decision-making within the party.[22] There is substantial, but not majority support for the idea amongst members. Forty-one per cent find quotas acceptable, at least at the one-third level suggested in our question. Interestingly, although women are more likely to favour quotas than men (52 per cent to 40 per cent) the margin is not large. Nor are there are many other marked demographic differences with respect to the approval of quotas – although most of the small number of members under 25 are in favour. More significantly, perhaps, there is no disproportionate support from amongst more active members. Those who blame attitudes within the party are particularly attracted to the idea of quotas. Sixty-three per cent of those agreeing strongly that women are treated unequally support the measure, compared with 44 per cent of those simply agreeing, and only 29 per cent of those strongly disagreeing that women get unequal treatment (Table 6.6). This is the only "reason" of the four that serves to underpin the case for quotas in the minds of members. In the case of the other three, it is those who disagree who are most in favour of quotas. Thus people are more likely to support quotas if they reject both supply-side explanations, or the demand-side explanation blaming the voters. However, many see a case for quotas even if, for instance, they believe that women are less ambitious.

Table 6.6: Support for gender quotas, related to views on why there are so few women candidates

	Strongly agree				Strongly disagree
	1	2	3	4	5
Women are not as politically ambitious as men	32	30	37	37	52
Most women have too many family commitments	40	32	42	32	52
Women candidates lose votes for the party and so are not chosen	29	26	32	36	44
Attitudes within the party mean that women don't get an equal opportunity	63	44	32	29	29

Source: Fine Gael members' questionnaire, questions 73 to 77.
Note: Cell entries are percentage supporting a one-third gender quota.

MEMBERS AND ELECTORAL SUCCESS

What difference do members make to a party's ability to win votes? We saw in chapter 5 that in the eyes of branch secretaries, the electoral role is the primary one of branches these days. We have also pointed out that some observers have expressed some scepticism about the importance of members to electoral success these days. For instance, Peter Mair suggests that "a capital-intensive marketing-oriented party can make substantial advances ... almost regardless of the strength and coherence of its local machine".[23] Yet members themselves see local, personal contacts as the best way to mobilise support. When asked to choose between local personal contact, local posters and national activities, members plumped in overwhelming numbers for local personal contact as the best way to maximise the Fine Gael vote (Q111–113). Despite the emphasis on national activity in the media, members see campaigns as necessarily local and personal. Nearly eighty per cent put local contacts in first place, with almost all the remainder opting for national activities. Local posters, for all their visibility, come in a poor third. The party itself exhorts branches to play an active role in election campaigns. The 43-page Fine Gael *Branch Manual* explains that "the work done before, and particularly during elections is of the utmost importance" to the aim of maximising the number of seats obtained. Each branch is exhorted to canvass its functional area during the campaign, distribute election literature and record full details of findings for those planning the campaign. The party offers a video giving tips on canvassing, and the Manual also offers advice on running local surveys. Members are given detailed advice on how to get the vote out on election day and each branch is recommended to draw up a plan to ensure the vote is maximised in every box.[24]

This all places the emphasis on what individual party members and supporters actually do and suggests that, other things being equal, the activities of members will be crucial to the success of the party's effort. At one candidate selection meeting attended by the authors, one candidate's proposer declared that in the local branch there were "153 battle-hardened activists" ready to work in support of the party's efforts at the next election. He obviously saw this as a strong card. If old-fashioned door-to-door canvassing and the efforts of partisans to win the votes of people they know, either through conversion or confirmation, are going to make a big difference, then local parties with more members will do best. In the absence of information on other parties, we must confine our analysis to Fine Gael, but what we can do is compare level of membership and activity across the country and measure the association between these and election success.

Figure 6.2 graphs the numbers of members in 1997–98 against the percentage of the electorate supporting Fine Gael in the 1997 general election in each constituency. The link is pretty clear, and is summarised quite well by the straight line running up through the scatter of points that show each constituency's rating on the two quantities. Where there are more members there are more votes. In fact, the line indicates that, on average, every extra 100 members seems to be worth over just over 1.5 extra points on the Fine Gael vote as a percentage of the electorate.[25] This appears to be a constant increase – the gain does not level off at high levels of membership, or decrease at low levels. However, it does suggest that Fine Gael would win about 9 per cent even where it has hardly any members. This might be thought of as the product of the national campaign, or as a core vote that is independent of local electoral efforts.

There are some constituencies that appear exceptional. Tipperary North is particularly so, as the party won many fewer votes than might have been expected. Kerry South and Wicklow also showed relatively low votes for the party, while Cork North West and Cork South West saw performances that exceeded expectations from this analysis. However, in general the scatter of points remains reasonably close to the line. A further feature of this chart is that

Figure 6.2: Constituency-level relationship between Fine Gael support 1997 and the number of Fine Gael members 1997–98

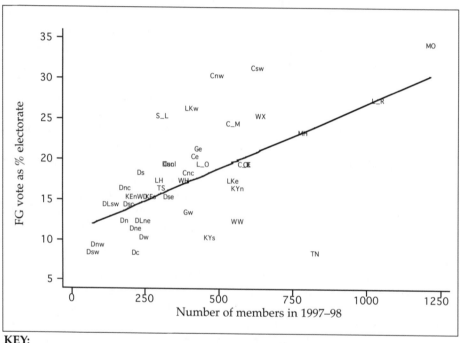

KEY:

C_K: Carlow–Kilkenny	Dn: Dublin N	Gw: Galway W	MH: Meath
CE: Clare	Dnc: Dublin NC	KEn: Kildare N	S_L: Sligo–Leitrim
C_M: Cavan–Monaghan	Dne: Dublin NE	KEs: Kildare S	TN: Tipp N
Ce: Cork E	Dnw: Dublin NW	KYn; Kerry N	TS: Tipp S
Csc: Cork SC	Dw: Dublin W	KYs: Kerry S	W: Waterford
Cnc: Cork NC	Dse: Dublin SE	L_O: LaoisOffaly	WX: Wexford
Csw: Cork SW	Dsc: Dublin SC	LKe:Limerick E	WH: Westmeath
Cnw: Cork NW	Dsw: Dublin W	LKw: Limerick W	WW: Wicklow
Dlne; Donegal NE	Ds: Dublin S	L_R: Longford–Roscommon	
DLsw: Donegal SW	Dunl: Dun Laoghaire	LH: Louth	
Dc: Dublin Central	Ge: Galway E	MO:Mayo	

the Dublin constituencies in general are not at all exceptional. Certainly Fine Gael does relatively poorly there, but no worse than we might expect from the low level of membership in the capital.

The figure of 1.5 per cent per 100 members is based on several assumptions, some of which are of dubious validity. The first is that membership is the only factor underpinning Fine Gael support. While membership is important, we certainly would not want to claim that nothing else matters. If we knew what the additional causes were, and could factor them in to our calculations, however, our estimate of the importance of members would be more accurate. In the absence of any firm knowledge of what these factors might be, let alone data on them, we have to fill in with something else. One way to do this is to use some other variable that predicts support quite well. One such has typically been the social class composition in a constituency. The argument here is that where farmers or professional people are prevalent, Fine Gael is relatively strong. The percentages of farmers and of professional people in a constituency go a good way towards predicting the Fine Gael vote in 1992.[26] Unfortunately, no comparable data is available for 1997 but using the social class composition from 1992 still enables us to predict the Fine Gael vote percentage moderately well.[27] Including these factors, and using the statistical technique of multiple regression – which is analogous to the simple line drawn in Figure 6.2 – gives us a different estimate of the impact of 100 Fine Gael members, putting it a little lower at 1.3 per cent of the electorate.[28] If we could identify and measure the variety of other factors more accurately this might decline further. Nonetheless, the impact in this formulation remains highly significant.

A second assumption is that it is members who generate voters. Yet it could be that members are attracted to the party in greater numbers where it wins more votes. It is likely that this happens, at least to some degree. Where the party has more TDs and councillors membership may well seem more relevant, although it is implausible to suggest that seats have a stronger effect on membership than does membership on vote. Moreover, these sorts of cause and effect sequences are impossible to establish in the absence of much longer series of data, on membership and vote success. However, it is worth recalling (see Table 4.1) that the rise in Fine Gael membership between 1977 and 1981 preceded electoral success rather than following it. Membership figures are available for 1996–97, 1997–98 and 1998–99. The 1997–98 figures, which also indicate the highest membership, are more closely related to the Fine Gael vote in 1997 than are the figures for 1996–97,[29] but those for 1998–99 indicate a relationship as strong as that for 1997–98. We might see that as indicating that party membership in the year prior to the election is a weaker guide to the real strength of the party than membership in the following years, when there are no Dáil candidates to be selected. Certainly membership typically peaks at the time when candidates are selected, probably as fringe members are pulled back into the party.

There are a couple of other pieces of evidence to support the argument that members matter. The first comes from examining the impact of active members specifically. We can use our survey of secretaries to estimate member numbers and levels of activism in each constituency and use these to predict electoral success in 1997. If membership matters, the number of *active* members should be more closely related to the Fine Gael vote than the number of *inactive* members. This is what we find (Table 6.7). We use the technique of multiple regression to estimate the relationship between members and Fine Gael's vote as a percentage of the electorate. The coefficients in the table indicate the impact of an additional 100 very active and 100 inactive members on the Fine Gael vote (expressed as a percentage of the electorate). The results are clear: active members are what matters, 100 more being worth an extra 5.6 per cent on the vote. Translating this into terms of actual votes, on average another 10 members should be worth another 100 votes. (It should be said that most constituencies do not have even 100 very active members to begin with: the average per constituency is only 119 with a minimum of 8 and a maximum of 322.) Inactive members by contrast matter very little, if at all. Table 6.7 suggests that inactive members actually *lose* votes (every additional 100 inactive members costing 1.1 per cent of the vote), though this is not a large enough effect to be statistically significant, meaning we cannot be at all certain that the actual impact is not zero. Members matter but only active members, not nominal ones. This result is in line with a similar analysis by Seyd and Whiteley of the impact of Labour party membership in the UK that also found activism was important rather than simply membership.[30] We also examined the relationship between active members and the Fine Gael vote controlling once again for the percentage of farmers. Once again, the conclusion that members matter is supported, although again the impact is a little weaker when we control for the social composition of the constituency.

Campaign support is not limited to party members. We might expect friends and relatives of the candidates to help out, even if they were not members of the party. But if the party machine functions in the manner in which it is supposed

Table 6.7: Constituency-level relationship between active and other members and Fine Gael vote as a percentage of the electorate in 1997 Dáil election

	Dáil election 1997	
Number of very active members (in 100s)	+5.6	+3.7
	1.6	1.2
Number of inactive members (in 100s)	-1.1	
	2.1	
Percentage of farmers		0.15
		0.10
Constant	+12.8	+12.0
	1.6	1.5
R^2	0.38	0.41
N	38	38

Source: Active and inactive measures from Fine Gael secretaries' questionnaire, question 8; percentage of farmers supplied by Richard Sinnott, calculated from 1991 census.

to, such people should be in the minority. Where it is relatively moribund, we might expect such personal supporters to predominate. We asked secretaries to tell us how important supporters who are not fully paid up members were to election campaigns in their area. Not all such people would be friends and relations of the candidates, of course. Some might be simply supporters who were not currently members but who were at some stage in the past. The secretaries reported that non-members were pretty important. In 21 per cent of cases they did most of the work, and in another 24 per cent they did as much as paid up members. In 23 per cent of cases they did a minor fraction of the work and in only 33 per cent of instances were such supporters almost completely irrelevant. This set of judgements indicates that the boundaries of what constitutes the party are fairly fluid, especially at election time. Whether it is the candidates themselves or other people within the party who mobilise such support is not known, but we might expect, given the highly personal support given by members themselves to candidates (see chapter 5), that the candidates play a significant role. There is little difference between urban and rural branches in terms of the importance of non members. Nor is the importance of non-members linked significantly to the Fine Gael vote but the association between the strength of non-member support as defined above and the strength of the organisation is, if anything, a positive one. Non-members are more important where there are more active members. In particular, those branches where "supporters" are not important have fewer members, meet less often and have fewer active members than other branches. It appears that local organisations that can mobilise members can also mobilise non-members at election times. In addition, secretaries of branches that rely more on such supporters are also likely to more likely to say that the branch has become more important over time. This all goes to suggest that while non-members are important at election time, this is a positive rather than a negative development for local parties. Rather than being a replacement for a moribund local party, the use of local supporters serves to indicate the more vibrant organisations and complement what they are doing.

CONCLUSION

Members themselves feel they have little impact internally. While they may fulfil important roles, for instance in financing the party, they feel they should be listened to more and be accorded more influence. This comes through when they are asked how more members can be recruited. While many members point to the need for more young members and more women, they also indicate how the party needs to change to bring this about. And that change means giving more say to members, giving them more information, *involving* them more in the life of the party. While some would obviously like real power – binding ard-fheis resolutions, for example – the majority want something much less.

Members do have more say in candidate selection, and dissatisfaction is lower in this area. Where members expressed dissatisfaction with the locus of decision making with respect to candidate selection, it tended to be directed at too much central control rather than too little, although there is a degree of support for some kind of screening and head-hunting, which might effectively be an argument for more central control.

When it comes to the external impact of members, our evidence suggests strongly that the party performs better where it has more members, and particularly so where it has more active members. The implication of this is that if the party could attract many more members, this would bring electoral benefits. The initial "cost" would appear to be the need to give members greater involvement. Of course it has been argued that giving members more say may actually damages a party's electoral fortunes, by making it more difficult for parties to target centre-ground voters. In the case of Fine Gael this argument would only hold any water if members' views were very different from those of the party's potential voters. This topic is the next to be explored, in chapter 7.

7 The political views of Fine Gael members

In this chapter we will explore the political opinions of Fine Gael members. How important party members' views are depends partly upon the role of members within a party. If a party attaches high priority to internal party democracy, such that the approval of members is needed for each major policy statement and decisions of the democratically-elected party conference are binding on the whole party, then the views of members matter a lot. Early studies of parties often focused on conflict between a party's parliamentarians, who were seen as keen to adopt pretty much whatever policies would maximise the party's vote, and ordinary members, who were portrayed as being determined that the party should not abandon its core principles even if this meant losing votes and government office.[1]

While the theme of tension between vote-hungry politicians and policy-hungry party activists has not entirely disappeared from studies of political parties, it is no longer dominant. Most analyses of power within parties these days paint a picture of an altogether more marginal role for members, whose views, to put it bluntly, don't matter a great deal one way or the other. Members are seen as being valued by the party leadership and MPs for their role in legitimising the party, acting as "cheerleaders" on behalf of the party top brass, and doing a lot of the donkey work in election campaigns, but they are not usually seen as being in any position to dictate the policy line that the party must follow.[2] Indeed, as we saw in the previous chapter, members of Fine Gael don't even seem to want control over party policy, though they might like rather more input than they have at present.

WHY MIGHT THE VIEWS OF PARTY MEMBERS MATTER?

Before we dismiss the significance of members' political views altogether, though, we should bear in mind that these views might still matter in various ways. One famous theory in the study of political parties is the "special law of curvilinear disparity" formulated by John May.[3] In essence, the theory May outlined is that party members tend to be policy "radicals" or "extremists" while the voters are moderate and centrist, so the party's MPs and leaders end up placed uneasily between the two: they want to move to the centre to win as many votes as possible, but they are constrained by the party's members who, one way or another, can prevent them moving as close to the centre as they otherwise would. The implications of this are not very benign for a party. First, it implies that there will be inherent tension between the party's MPs and its members, with the two groups constantly trying to pull the party in different directions. Second, it implies that party members are not very typical of party voters; they cannot be used as a reliable sounding board by the MPs, and the effect of their views is to force the parties to offer policy platforms that are further from the centre than the voters really want. May's law is perfectly plausible, though opinions differ on whether it is actually true. To test it empirically requires larger resources than most studies (including this one) possess, since such a test needs data, gathered at around the same time, relating to the political views of party voters, party members and MPs.

Studies that have been able to test May's law find that the evidence is mixed. When Seyd and Whiteley examined the main British parties, they found that the pattern varied from issue to issue. In the Labour party, there were no real differences between members and voters on most issues, but when it came to nationalisation and unilateral disarmament Labour members were well to the left of the party's voters, just as May predicted.[4] Among Conservative members things were much the same: little difference on most issues, but clear signs of greater member extremism on two issues, namely reintroducing capital punishment and reducing the power of trade unions.[5] Other studies in Britain, Sweden and Norway, though, have concluded that while party members are generally more extreme than party voters, MPs are quite likely to be more extreme than members rather than closer to the centre as May suggests.[6]

Few people would instinctively expect May's law to apply to the main Irish parties. The picture of fire-breathing policy-obsessed party activists certainly does not correspond to the common view of both Fianna Fáil and Fine Gael, which is that they are parties with very few policy hang-ups at all, whose members are prepared to accept virtually any kind of vote-winning approach and who have little interest in details of policy. The evidence we have presented so far in this book does nothing to dispel this view. One reason why May expects members to be relative "extremists" is that he expects them to have joined the party to achieve certain policy goals but, as we saw in chapter 4, many members did not join for policy reasons. Indeed, contrary to a pattern predicted by writers such as Kaare Strøm and Alan Ware, the proportion of Fine Gael members joining for policy reasons is decreasing over time while the proportion joining for solidary reasons seems to be increasing, as we showed in chapter 4 (see in particular Table 4.8).[7] Even so, the members' views might still make an impact.

First, it is clearly unrealistic to imagine that members care so little about policy that they simply hand the leadership a blank cheque. If the leaders of either major party in Ireland decided off their own bat to write Irish withdrawal from the European Union, support for paramilitary violence in Northern Ireland or the introduction of unrestricted abortion into the party manifesto, they could expect a membership revolt.

Second, it is not quite true that members can't do anything even if they don't really like the policies that the leadership espouses. They can adopt the strategies sometimes termed "voice" or "exit". They could voice protest at the party's annual conference or through other channels of communication with the parliamentary group and the leadership, at least letting the party elite know that they are unhappy with the policy line being taken even if they don't have the formal power to block it. If nothing changes as a result of these protests, they can "exit", in other words leave the party, withdrawing the free labour that they supply in keeping the party's TDs in touch with their constituents and in working at election time.

Third, members' opinions might impinge on the party during the process of candidate selection, when members might make a point of favouring candidates whose views resemble their own. If they do this, it will in time feed through into the parliamentary party and indeed the party's group of ministers in government, all of whom need to be selected and reselected as Dáil election candidates by ordinary party members. Over the long term, then, if the membership was, say, considerably more "liberal" than the TDs, members might pick candidates whose views were similar to their own, and the composition of the parliamentary group would move in a more liberal direction. Even if power in a party rests mainly at the top, those who decide who gets to the top – a process in which the candidate selectors play a large part – can have a significant role in shaping the policy stance of the party.

Fourth, the views of party members can be expected to "rub off" onto TDs to some extent, given that TDs keep in close contact with the organisational grass roots. As we saw in chapter 5, three-quarters of members have had contact with a local Fine Gael TD during the previous twelve months, and over sixty per cent say they often pass constituents' requests along to TDs. If members have particular policy views, TDs will, at the very least, find it hard to avoid knowing what these are, and they may well play a part in shaping the TD's own opinion, which in turn will have some impact when the parliamentary party discusses policy matters. Even if a TD does not feel under any pressure to conform to local members' views, he or she may well be persuaded by them. Both in this way, and by putting down motions at a party conference, members can act as policy innovators.[8]

Fifth, another reason why it is important to know about the views of ordinary members is that the public's impression of the party is based partly on what it sees of these members. It is true that the party leader, and after that other TDs, will have the greatest impact in shaping the public's sense of what the party stands for, but ordinary members still play some part in this. Members, as we pointed out in chapter 1, can be seen as "ambassadors to the community", and in this capacity what they say makes an impact. If members were to be strong proponents among their friends and neighbours of unpopular views, this would not do the party much good, even if its leadership was espousing a more mainstream line. Conversely, if a party is portrayed by sections of the media as holding extreme or maverick opinions, the presence on the ground of level-headed members who don't resemble the media stereotype will be to the party's benefit. Moreover, the public's perception of members' political views does not come solely through personal contact and local interaction. Party conferences receive a certain amount of media coverage, and the views expressed by ordinary delegates thus get some exposure, especially if these views are in conflict with those of the party leadership. The leadership may try to ensure the defeat of motions advocating policies that it does not agree with, or to reassure the public that when the party is in power the views of members will not be allowed to determine government policy, but it can take these steps only at the cost of leaving the public with the impression of a disunited party, something that is almost certain to cost votes.

In short, party members' political opinions do matter and they are worth studying. These opinions may shape or constrain party (and hence government) policy, and may affect the composition of the party elite. Any major difference between the views of members and voters may lower the popular appeal of the party; such difference between members and elected representatives may create the appearance of a party suffering from internal conflict and thus reduce the party's electability.

In this chapter, then, we will explore the political views of Fine Gael members. In the penultimate section of the chapter, we will try to assess the implications of our findings in the light of May's law, examining the extent to which the views of members coincide or conflict with those of Fine Gael voters and Fine Gael TDs. Are Fine Gael members more extreme in their views than TDs or Fine Gael voters and, if so, does this apply on all issues or only a few? Are there consequences for Fine Gael's ability to represent its voters? In the last section of the chapter we shall consider the implications of our findings for the unity and cohesion of Fine Gael, and try to identify the issues that could cause internal discord.

HOW IMPORTANT IS POLICY FOR MEMBERS?

We stated above that if Fine Gael members hold views that differ markedly from those of the party's TDs or voters, this could have some serious implications. However, this is really only likely to be true if members actually care about these views, and many observers of Irish politics would be sceptical about that. Conventional wisdom would suggest that policy is not central to competition between the Irish parties: that there are few if any major policy differences between the parties, that many people's voting behaviour is determined by factors other than policy, and that even many party members are not especially interested in policy matters. If this wisdom is true, our findings might tell us little about conflict or consensus within Fine Gael, because the views expressed by members in answer to our questionnaire would not shed much light on their behaviour. If an issue, or policy generally, is of very low salience to a member, then it may not really matter what their views on it are, because these views will never affect what they do: they won't hold forth on the issue in their local pub, they won't be in the slightest degree affected by aspirants' views on the issue when it comes to selecting Fine Gael parliamentary candidates, and they won't care one way or the other what policy line the party leadership adopts on the issue.

Clearly, we did not want to risk testing our respondents' patience beyond breaking point by asking them how important each individual issue was to them personally, but in order to get some sense of how prominently policy matters loomed in their thoughts we asked them how interested they were in national political issues. Some people might assume that anyone who joins a political party must by definition be very interested in such issues, but, as we saw in chapter 4, quite a number of members joined for essentially social reasons. Our question asked about interest not in "politics", which many people might follow avidly as a long-running soap opera or horse race without necessarily having any interest in policy matters, but specifically in "national political issues". The results seem to bear out the suspicion of the sceptics (see Table 7.1). Only half of our respondents (see bottom row of table) can muster enough enthusiasm to declare themselves "very interested" in national political issues; nearly as many describe themselves as merely "quite interested"; and about 5 per cent, or one in twenty of the membership, say bluntly that they are not at all interested.

We might be tempted, then, to infer that the views of members don't matter a great deal, since half the membership describes itself as something less than "very" interested in national political issues. That would be too hasty. Table 7.1 also shows that there is a very strong relationship between activism and interest in political issues; only 37 per cent of the least active group are very interested in these issues, whereas 79 per cent of the most active group are very interested (see Appendix C and chapter 5 for definition and discussion of activism categories). In other words, those members who participate most are also, as we would expect, the ones who care most about political issues. Even if a bare majority (50.2 per cent) of Fine Gael members describe themselves as less than very interested in national political issues, these members form something of a silent and inactive majority. Among those who actually do things – attend branch meetings, campaign at elections, donate money to the party, devote time every month to party work, or participate in candidate selection conventions – a majority describe themselves as "very interested". Those who are most interested in national political issues are also those most likely to describe themselves as very strong supporters of Fine Gael (in Q1). These, then, are the people whom the party leadership and the TDs cannot afford to alienate, because they are the life blood of the organisation.

Moreover, these are the members whose voice both the public and the TDs are likely to hear. They are the ones whose views are most likely to rub off on TDs; 81 per cent of those who are very interested in national political issues had had contact with a local Fine Gael TD in the previous twelve months, compared with 72 per cent of those who are quite interested and 38 per cent of those who are not at all interested. They are especially likely to have close contact with a TD: we found that 73 per cent of those who are very interested in national political issues sometimes pass constituents' requests on to one of the local Fine Gael

Table 7.1: Interest in national political issues, by activity levels

	How interested in national political issues			All
	Very	Quite	Not at all	members
Very active	79	21	0	100
Fairly active	53	46	1	100
Not very active	44	53	3	100
Not at all active	37	50	13	100
All members	50	46	5	100

Source: Fine Gael members' questionnaire, question 24.

TDs, compared with 52 per cent of those who are quite interested and 23 per cent of those who are not at all interested. Although we did not ask a question about this, we would strongly suspect too that the members who are most interested in these issues are the most likely to attend and speak up at party conferences. Certainly they are the most inclined to hold opinions, one way or the other, on the particular issues that our survey asked about and, moreover, when our questions asked about the intensity of opinions, they were most likely to feel strongly on an issue. Since they have a higher rate of attendance at candidate selection meetings than members who are less interested in political issues, their views, whatever these may be, are the ones that have the greatest potential to shape the outlook of the Dáil group.

In some respects, the background of the "very interested" members stands out from the rest. The more education a member has, the more likely he or she is to be very interested in national political issues. Similarly, those who describe themselves as middle, upper middle or upper class are more likely to be high in interest than those who see themselves as working or lower middle class. Newspaper readership, too, is related to political interest: among *Irish Times* readers 67 per cent are very interested, among those who read the *Irish Independent* or the *Examiner* the figure is 50 per cent, and among those who don't read any of these papers it is only 29 per cent. No doubt there is scope for argument here as to whether those who are most interested in political issues make a point of reading the *Irish Times*, or whether reading the *Irish Times* makes one more interested in political issues. Members in urban constituencies are much more likely to describe themselves as very interested in these issues: 64 per cent of them say this, compared with 46 per cent of members in rural constituencies.

As we have found – rather to our surprise – in other areas of the survey, the oldest and longest-serving members stand out, not for apathy and inactivity but the reverse. These members are more likely to describe themselves as very interested than are younger and newer members. Likewise, those who joined the party on their own personal initiative express more interest than those who were approached – which might suggest that the people whom existing members are approaching are not necessarily the people most likely to have a policy contribution to make. And, when we asked about motives for joining, those who joined for solidary reasons (to enhance their social life, or due to the influence of family and friends) were much less likely to have an interest in national political issues. Among these members only 33 per cent are very interested in national political issues, with 10 per cent being not at all interested; among the other members, 54 per cent are very interested and only 3 per cent are not at all interested.

We have established, then, that members' views are worth exploring. The most active members are both the most interested in national political issues and the most likely to hold strong opinions. For all the reasons we outlined earlier, members' views have the potential to make their mark on the party, to constrain the leadership, to influence the opinions of TDs, and to affect public perceptions of the party. We will now examine the views of the Fine Gael membership in some detail.

LEFT AND RIGHT

It is a familiar observation that politics revolves around the conflict between left and right in every country across Europe – in every country, that is, except Ireland. As we discussed at greater length in chapter 2, the Irish party system has never reflected a clear left–right cleavage. It has, it is true, always had a left, in the form of the Labour party; but this left has been weaker and, certainly until the mid-1960s, much less left-wing than the left in all other European countries.[9] The largest two parties, Fianna Fáil and Fine Gael, are routinely described or dismissed by the left as "right-wing parties", yet they themselves shun this label. The available survey evidence suggests that many voters do not see the party system in terms of left and right, and that the ones who do see it this way perceive Fianna Fáil and Fine Gael as occupying virtually identical positions on the centre-right of the spectrum.[10]

Placement of self and of Fine Gael
We asked Fine Gael members to place themselves and the largest four parties on a left–right scale running from 1 (furthest left) to 10 (furthest right). The results are shown in Table 7.2. They bear a strong resemblance to those reported by public opinion surveys; the average Fine Gael member places himself or herself on the centre-right of the political spectrum and sees the two main parties as occupying virtually identical positions slightly to the right of their own. The number of respondents unable to place themselves or the parties on the left–right spectrum is lower than that found among the public as a whole – which we would expect, given that we were after all surveying party members – but is still quite high, with up to a fifth of Fine Gael members leaving these questions blank, as if, to use Richard Sinnott's words, a sizeable section of the Fine Gael membership "could make no use at all of a left–right dimension in differentiating between the parties".[11] Those who did not respond to the question of where they

would place themselves on the spectrum are not greatly different from members as a whole, but the elderly, those with relatively little interest in political issues, and – especially – those with only national school education are more likely than other members not to have answered this question.

In broad terms, the ratings of Fine Gael members make sense; or at least, they are in line with the assessment of politicians and political commentators. Comparing the placings given by Fine Gael members in 1999 with those of Fine Gael TDs sixteen years earlier, we can see that the TDs placed themselves further to the left and Fianna Fáil further to the right than members did – but their scores for Fine Gael and for Labour were virtually identical. Irish political scientists, when asked in 1997 to place the parties on an economic policy scale, came up with very similar scores, as Table 7.2 shows. This does not prove that any of these groups is "correct", but it suggests that they are all looking at and reading the political world in much the same way.[12] We might wonder about just how the political world is viewed (or the terms "left" and "right" are interpreted) by the 9 per cent of Fine Gael members who regard Labour as a right-wing party and the 15 per cent who feel that the PDs are a left-wing party – not to mention the 5 per cent who place Fine Gael, and the 6 per cent who place Fianna Fáil, on the extreme left of the spectrum (at position 1 on the scale). Overall, though, it is clear that the majority of the Fine Gael membership is comfortable and familiar with the idea of thinking about the parties in terms of the left–right spectrum.

For the most part, we don't find any strong relationship between the background characteristics of members and where they place themselves on this spectrum, with two exceptions. The first is class: farmers place themselves furthest to the right, with an average placement of 6.6 compared with 5.9 for all

Table 7.2: Placement of self and parties on left–right spectrum

| | Mean score | Per cent placing themselves or party on | | | Percent non-response | Political scientists' placement of parties (1997) | Fine Gael TDs (1983) |
		Left (1–4)	Centre (5–6)	Right (7–10)			
Self	6.1	19	40	41	19	–	5.1
Fine Gael	6.4	13	40	47	13	6.4	6.3
Fianna Fáil	6.4	19	32	49	19	6.2	7.4
Labour	3.7	73	18	9	18	4.2	3.7
PDs	7.1	15	22	63	20	8.7	–

Source: Fine Gael members' questionnaire, questions 62, 63, 64, 64.1, 65; Laver, "Party policy in Ireland, 1997", p. 166; Gallagher, *Political Parties in the Republic of Ireland*, p. 144.
Note: The penultimate column refers to the judgements of 30 political scientists surveyed in mid-1997 who were asked to place the parties on an economic policy scale, with "Increase public services even if this means increasing taxes" at the low end of the scale and "Cut taxes even if this means cutting level of public services" at the high end. The scores have been recalculated to match the 1–10 scale used in the Fine Gael members' survey. The last column is based on a mail survey of TDs.

other members. The second is gender: it turns out that gender makes a difference to where someone places themselves on the left–right spectrum, but it does not make people either more left-wing or more right-wing; rather, it is related to whether someone places themselves in the middle of the scale as opposed to either at the right or the left. Among women, 47 per cent place themselves in the centre (at either points 5 or 6 on the scale), while only 36 per cent of men situate themselves here. Men are more likely to place themselves either on the left (21 per cent of them, compared with 16 per cent of women) or on the right (42 per cent of them, compared with 38 per cent of women). In a rather similar fashion, education is related to members' inclination to place Fine Gael in the centre of the spectrum. Among members with national school education only, 30 per cent place the party in the centre, with 20 per cent on the left and 50 per cent on the right. At the other end of the educational scale, those with university education are much more likely to see Fine Gael as a party of the centre: 51 per cent place it here, with only 9 per cent seeing it as standing on the left and 41 per cent placing it on the right.

Members were asked whether Fine Gael should move on the left–right spectrum, and a clear majority, 72 per cent, want the party to remain pretty much where it is. Perhaps surprisingly, it is the middle-class professional members (the AB group) who are most likely to want it to move to the left, while the only social group among whom more members want it to move to the right than want it to move to the left are farmers. Which way, if any, members want Fine Gael to move also depends on where they stand. Members who place themselves on the left are most likely to want the party to move to the left (38 per cent of them say this, as opposed to only 4 per cent of them who want the party to move to the right), while members who place themselves on the right are most likely to want the party to move right (17 per cent of them say this, as opposed to only 11 per cent of them who want Fine Gael to move to the left), while 73 per cent of those who place themselves in the centre feel that Fine Gael should stay exactly where it is. This is not surprising, but it does bear out the points we made at the start of the chapter about the importance of members' views. These views *do* matter, because members of different outlooks actively want the party to move in their direction.

Placement of other parties
Where respondents place themselves also has a bearing on how they see the rest of the political world. Put simply, there is a tendency for them to see Fine Gael as close to their own position and Fianna Fáil as further from them. Thus, as table 7.3 shows, those members who place themselves on the left of the spectrum are much more likely than other members to see Fine Gael too as being on the left; those who place themselves in the centre are the most likely to see Fine Gael as being in the centre; and right-wing members are by far the most likely to see Fine Gael as being on the right (74 per cent of them feel this, compared with only 22 per cent of left-wing members). The overall correlation between where a member places himself or herself and where they place Fine Gael is

Table 7.3: Fine Gael members' self-placement on the left–right spectrum by their placement of Fine Gael

| | Placement of Fine Gael | | | All |
	Left (1–4)	Centre (5–6)	Right (7–10)	members
Placement of self				
Left (1–4)	39	39	22	100
Centre (5–6)	8	63	29	100
Right (7–10)	4	22	74	100
All members	12	41	46	100

Source: Fine Gael members' questionnaire, questions 62, 63.

0.61.[13] In contrast, there is a tendency, though a rather weak one, for members to place Fianna Fáil at the opposite end of the spectrum from themselves (reflected in a negative correlation, with a coefficient of -0.08, between self-placement and placement of Fianna Fáil).

Thus even though Table 7.2 might suggest that Fine Gael members feel just as close on the left–right spectrum to Fianna Fáil as to Fine Gael, this is not the case. When we calculate the distance between respondents and each of the other parties, we find that on average each member feels himself or herself closer to Fine Gael than to Fianna Fáil, as we can see in Table 7.4. On average each member *individually* places Fianna Fáil 2.5 points away from himself or herself; the reason why Fine Gael members *collectively* seem to place Fianna Fáil very close to their own position, as Table 7.2 suggested, is that some members place Fianna Fáil well to the left of themselves and others place it well to the right of themselves, so overall the differences largely cancel out. Table 7.4 shows that members collectively have a very clear sense that Labour stands to the left of both their own position and Fine Gael's position, and they are fairly clear in their minds that the PDs are to the right of themselves and of Fine Gael. Members are more likely to feel themselves to be to the left of both Fine Gael and Fianna Fáil than to the right of these parties. When it comes to the relative placing of Fine Gael and Fianna Fáil, though, the lack of certainty is apparent. One of the first questions usually asked about Irish politics by those looking at it from overseas is whether Fianna Fáil is to the left of Fine Gael or vice versa, and our survey cannot provide an answer to this mystery (though in chapter 8 we will explore in greater depth the differences between the two parties). Virtually the same number of Fine Gael members see their party as being to the left of Fianna Fáil as see it as being to Fianna Fáil's right.

The implication of Table 7.4 might seem to be that Fine Gael members see Fianna Fáil as the closest party to their own, with the PDs further away and Labour as the most distant. Historically, though, Fine Gael has often been in coalition with Labour, it has considered though never entered coalition with the PDs, while coalition with Fianna Fáil has never been contemplated. This sug-

Table 7.4: Distance on left–right spectrum between Fine Gael members and each of the four main parties

	Average distance between placing of self and placing of party	Where is party in relation to self (%)			Where is party in relation to Fine Gael (%)		
		Left	Same	Right	Left	Same	Right
Fine Gael	1.2	25	39	36	—	—	—
Fianna Fáil	2.5	37	16	47	37	24	39
Labour	3.2	77	10	13	83	8	9
Prog Democrats	2.8	26	14	60	28	15	57

Source: Fine Gael members' questionnaire, questions 62, 63, 64, 64.1, 65.

gests either that positioning on the left–right spectrum is not the main criterion when it comes to looking for a coalition partner, or that the preferences of Fine Gael members are systematically disregarded by the party leadership when it comes to doing coalition deals. We shall explore this in chapter 8 when we discuss members' views on Fine Gael's place within the Irish party system.

Wealth redistribution and trade union power
Our survey asked two further questions related to the traditional left–right spectrum. One concerned redistribution of wealth; we asked whether the government should intervene more decisively so as to transfer wealth and resources to the less well off (Q48.1). It seems that the wording of this question may have been too "bland", because even though it appears to call for a radical change of policy it produced relatively little opposition. Altogether two-thirds of members agreed with the statement (51 per cent strongly agreed), with only 13 per cent disagreeing. Secondly, we asked whether trade unions have too much power (Q48.4); even though the question of trade union power has never become a central issue in Irish politics in the way that it did in Britain in the 1970s and 1980s, this question did at least produce more division among Fine Gael members. Just over a third agreed (22 per cent agreed strongly), and 38 per cent disagreed (24 per cent disagreed strongly).

Given that both of these are economic left–right issues, we would expect a member's attitude to these questions to be strongly related to where he or she stands on the left–right spectrum. After all, evidence from across Europe shows that among the mass public self-placement on the left–right scale is correlated with a person's attitude to economic left–right issues and indeed also with attitudes to church–state issues and to what are termed post-materialist issues, both of which we shall discuss further later in the chapter. Correlations tend, though, to be weaker in Ireland than in other countries.[14] Table 7.5 shows that among Fine Gael members there is indeed a relationship, but it is not especially strong, especially when it comes to the redistribution of wealth: 11 per cent of those

Table 7.5: Left–right self-placement and attitudes to wealth redistribution and trade unions

	Left-wing members (1–4)	Centre members (5–6)	Right-wing members (7–10)	All members
Wealth should be redistributed				
Agree	72	59	62	67
Neutral	17	28	21	20
Disagree	11	13	18	13
Total	100	100	100	100
Trade unions have too much power				
Agree	24	27	41	34
Neutral	27	34	29	28
Disagree	49	39	30	38
Total	100	100	100	100

Source: Fine Gael members' questionnaire, questions 62, 48.1, 48.4.

who designated themselves as left-wing manage to disagree with this while 62 per cent of self-designated right-wing members agree with it. The pattern of attitudes to trade union power is more clear-cut, with left-wing members markedly less likely than right-wing ones to agree with the statement. Even so, it is apparent that where a member places himself or herself on the left–right spectrum does not by any means determine what view he or she will take even on what seem to be archetypal left versus right issues. We shall see later in the chapter that left–right self-placement is also only weakly related to attitudes to other issues. All of this bears out the general belief that Irish politics is not underpinned by a significant left–right dimension. Even though most Fine Gael members are willing to place themselves on the left–right spectrum, this does not provide them with a worldview or ideology that determines their view of the political world as a whole.

CHURCH AND STATE

Irish politics has never seen a strong left versus right conflict, and for many voters the cleavage involving the role of the Catholic church and Catholic values in Irish society may be more meaningful than the left–right cleavage. Whereas in earlier decades there was a virtual consensus across the political spectrum on matters relating to church and state, and little inclination to challenge the powerful position of the church in various spheres of Irish life, society and public policy, things began to change from the late 1960s. Arguments for the liberalisation of laws on contraception and divorce in particular, for the "deconfessionalisation" of the constitution, and for complete separation of church and state were heard with increasing frequency.[15] These developments highlighted divisions both within and among the parties. Labour was the most liberal of the three main parties, and Fine Gael, at least after Garret FitzGerald became its leader in 1977, was seen as being in the centre, with Fianna Fáil the most conservative. However, it was apparent that all the parties had major internal divisions on the issues – not surprisingly, since these questions cut across the lines of cleavage that structure the Irish party system.

In the Fine Gael membership survey we asked five questions designed to tell us where our respondents stand on the liberal–conservative spectrum and the role of the church. Two of these questions related to the November 1995 referendum on divorce, one related to abortion, one to the place of the church in the education system, and one to Fine Gael's own positioning on this spectrum.

Our questions on divorce asked how (if at all) respondents had voted in the referendum (Q28), and whether they had taken an active part in the campaign on either side (Q29). It is well known in survey research that voting recall questions, which ask people how they voted on some past occasion, do not always provide reliable answers. For many people, voting is simply not very important, and they may just forget how they voted. Others may remember but deliberately give a false response, either to make their past behaviour appear consistent with their present attitudes, or because their past behaviour now seems somehow discreditable – for example, polls carried out in the aftermath of the assassination of John F. Kennedy found relatively few people who admitted having voted against him in the presidential election three years earlier compared with the actual percentage vote cast against him then. In addition, some respondents will be too young to have had a chance to vote in a past election.

Our judgement, though, was that questions about the divorce referendum, which took place about four years before our survey was conducted, would nonetheless be valid. For one thing, the questions would be put not to the mass public but to paid up members of a political party, most of whom, as we have just seen, are very or at least fairly interested in political issues. Divorce had been a major issue in Irish politics for over a decade, and the referendum had generated a turnout of 62 per cent which, leaving aside those referendums held on the same day as a general election, was the highest referendum turnout since 1972. We thought it unlikely, therefore, that many respondents would have forgotten which way they voted. Nor did we think that deliberate misrepresentation would be a problem. The proposal to legalise divorce was carried by a very narrow margin in the referendum (by 50.3 per cent to 49.7 per cent), so having taken the minority view hardly carries any stigma. And, while it is true that no-one under 21 at the time of our survey could have voted in the 1995 referendum, the very small number of young members in Fine Gael (only 4 per cent are younger than 25) means that the great majority of members were eligible to vote in 1995.

On abortion, we asked which of four positions most accurately represented the respondent's position (Q53). These options ranged from abortion on demand to a complete ban on abortion in all circumstances. The intermediate options were that it should be allowed "in special circumstances" and that it should be allowed only where there is a threat to the mother's life. Three of these options are unambiguous both in their meaning and in their position on the liberal–conservative spectrum. The exception is the option of permitting abortion "in special circumstances", which could be seen as vague, since there is no definition of these circumstances; two respondents could agree with the statement while having very different ideas as to what would constitute the "special circumstances" in which abortion should be permitted.

We also asked how the respondents evaluated the role – a very central one in the past, and still exceptionally high by comparative standards – of the Catholic church in the education system. Education has become a key battleground between confessional and secularising forces in a number of Catholic countries, such as France and Spain, and the same may happen in Ireland, although it is also possible that the conflict may be forestalled by an effective withdrawal by the church simply through declining manpower. We asked respondents whether they felt the church had too much or too little power in this area (Q52). Finally, we asked whether Fine Gael should in the future become more liberal or less liberal on social issues (Q69).

Attitudes to church–state issues

The results (see Appendix B for full details) show that the Fine Gael membership leans towards the liberal rather than the conservative end of the spectrum. Most members (59 per cent) voted Yes in the 1995 referendum, against 33 per cent who voted No. Twice as many members (17 per cent) had campaigned for a Yes as for a No (8 per cent). It is noticeable, though, that the great majority of members (75 per cent of them) did not campaign at all. This is presumably a reflection of the relatively low salience of the issue to a majority of the membership, but points to a certain marginalisation of the party organisation during this intense campaign.[16] Even though Fine Gael was the main party in the government that was promoting the proposal to introduce divorce, the membership remained detached from the fray, and the organisation definitely did not play a political leadership role on this occasion.

On abortion, opinions were fairly evenly divided, with most respondents selecting one of the two central options and only a minority choosing one of the end points (14 per cent said it should be available to any woman who wants an abortion and 12 per cent said it should never be allowed). On the role of the church, many more believed the church had too much influence in the education system (34 per cent) than thought it had too little (8 per cent), while a majority felt that the status quo was about right. Similarly, in response to the question as to whether Fine Gael should change its position on the liberal–conservative spectrum, a majority opted for no change, with far more (33 per cent) wanting it to become more liberal than wanting it to become more conservative (9 per cent).

As we would expect, attitudes on these five separate items run together. Those who are relatively liberal on one issue also tend to be relatively liberal on the others. The technique known as factor analysis confirms that each of these items can be seen as an aspect of one underlying factor, namely the liberal–conservative dimension.[17] Thus those who campaigned for the liberalisation of divorce in 1995 also tend to have voted for divorce, to favour one of the more liberal options on abortion, and to believe that the church has too great a role in the education system. They also believe that Fine Gael itself should become more liberal and, conversely, those who are most conservative are the most likely to believe that Fine Gael should become more conservative.

Who are the liberals?
Who are the liberals among the Fine Gael membership? Several characteristics have a bearing on the attitudes of Fine Gael members on the moral issues that we are examining, but there are two that, perhaps surprisingly, do not. Let us deal with the latter first. We are referring here to gender and to a respondent's position on the left–right spectrum. Gender is often a strong determinant of an individual's stance on moral issues in Ireland, with women, at least in the past, expressing markedly more conservative attitudes than men.[18] In the 1986 divorce referendum there was a very large gender gap; the last poll before the referendum showed that women were opposed to divorce by a two to one margin, while men were evenly divided.[19] In the 1992 referendums on abortion, women were once again more conservative than men, even when it came to the question of protecting the rights of the mother.[20] In the 1995 divorce referendum there was again a gender gap, but this time it was far smaller than in 1986, with men only about 5 percentage points more likely than women to vote for divorce. Our survey shows no sign of a gender gap. It remains true that, as in most other countries, women are more religious than men; for example, 21 per cent of female Fine Gael members, compared with only 10 per cent of their male counterparts, attend church more often than once a week. However, there is absolutely no sign of a gender gap when it comes to attitudes to the moral issue questions that we asked.

The other factor that, contrary to our expectations, has no bearing on these attitudes is where a respondent places him- or herself on the left–right spectrum. Conceptually, of course, this spectrum is quite distinct from the liberal–conservative spectrum; it is perfectly possible to envisage an economic right-winger who is liberal on social issues, or a believer in social justice and equality who is conservative on social issues. Nonetheless, many would expect these two dimensions to run parallel to each other, with those on the left of the spectrum being most likely to be anti-clerical – especially given that a study of party activists in the early 1970s found that self-placement on the left–right scale corresponded more closely to positions on the liberal–conservative dimension than to positions on a socio-economic dimension.[21] However, this is not the case. There is little relationship between where a Fine Gael member places himself or herself on the left–right spectrum and how he or she feels about moral issues. On some specific issues, there is some sign of a relationship: for example, it is true that those on the left of the spectrum are rather more likely to have voted for divorce in 1995 (68 per cent of them did so) than are those on the right (56 per cent of whom did so).[22] Yet when it comes to the place of the church in education, a rallying point for the left in many countries, the pattern is so weak as to be virtually non-existent: 38 per cent of those on the left, 34 per cent of those in the centre, and 34 per cent of those on the right believe that the church has too much influence in the education system.[23]

The lack of correlation between opinions on the left–right spectrum and on the liberal–conservative moral issue spectrum supports the view of those who see Irish politics as operating along these two dimensions.[24] Laver concludes, drawing on the assessments of Irish political scientists, that the Northern Ireland dimension correlates strongly with the moral issue dimension. There are indeed signs of this among Fine Gael members: on the whole those who are most nationalist on the question of Northern Ireland also tend to be the least liberal on social issues. We asked respondents whether they felt the Irish government should have special regard for northern nationalists, whether it should be even-handed between northern nationalists and northern unionists, or whether it should have special regard for northern unionists (we will discuss this issue more fully later on). Among those who believe the government should care particularly for northern nationalists, 52 per cent had voted for divorce in 1995, compared with 62 per cent of those who wanted the government to be even-handed and 73 per cent of those who wanted it to have special regard for northern unionists. Similarly, those who want the government to have special regard for northern nationalists are the most likely to feel that the church should have greater influence in the Irish education system, and those (very few) Fine Gael members who want the government to have special regard for northern unionists are the most likely to feel that the church's influence should be reduced. However, while attitudes on these two issues are evidently related, they are a long way from coinciding.

What factors, then, do help to predict a Fine Gael member's views on moral issues? As we might expect, religion is one: Catholics are more conservative on every issue than the small number of non-Catholics. For example, whereas only 31 per cent of Catholic members believe that the Catholic church has too much influence in the education system, 75 per cent of other members (a small group, to be sure) hold this view. Similarly, religiosity is strongly related to conservatism, with those who attend church more than once a week consistently holding the most conservative attitudes and those who attend less than once a week the most liberal, weekly attenders being in the middle. On divorce, for example, 44 per cent of the first group voted Yes in 1995, compared with 57 of weekly attenders and 76 per cent of those with the lowest church attendance. On abortion, 25 per cent of the most frequent attenders believe it can never be justified, compared with figures of 12 per cent among weekly attenders and 3 per cent among the least frequent attenders. On the church's influence in the education system, among the most frequent attenders 18 per cent feel it has too little influence and 16 say it has too much; among the least frequent attenders the respective figures are 2 per cent and 65 per cent.

It is no surprise, either, to find that age is strongly related to attitudes on moral issues: just as among the public as a whole, as opinion polls consistently testify, the older a person is, the more conservative he or she tends to be. To give just one example, 48 per cent of those under 35 believe the Catholic church has too much influence in the education system, compared with 39 per cent among the 35–54 age group and only 26 per cent among those aged 55 or more. Other socio-demographic factors are more weakly related to attitudes. Education is related to voting behaviour in the divorce referendum (41 per cent of those with only national school education voted No, compared with only 21 per cent of those with university education), but not to attitudes towards the church's role in the education system. Occupation, too, plays a role: middle-class members are the most likely to have voted for divorce in 1995 and farmers are the least likely. Indeed, more farmers worked actively for a No vote than worked for a Yes vote, in contrast to the pattern among all other social groups. Similarly, *Irish Times* readers are more likely than readers of other papers to have voted Yes to divorce in 1995, but, contrary to some perceptions of the stereotypical *Irish Times* reader, they were no more anti-clerical than other members on the other church-related issues. Whether the respondent is in an urban or a rural constituency is even more weakly related to attitudes. It is not related to which way a member voted in the 1995 divorce referendum (rather surprisingly given that urban areas were much more pro-divorce than rural ones) or to views on church influence in education, but it is related to activism on the Yes side during the divorce referendum, with 28 per cent of urban members, but only 14 per cent of rural members, having worked actively for a Yes. Fine Gael's urban members, then, were not noticeably more pro-divorce than their rural counterparts, but the ones who were pro-divorce were more committed than the rural pro-divorce members, which is in line with our earlier observation that urban members are more interested in political issues than rural ones.

To sum up, Fine Gael members can be seen as having quite a liberal set of attitudes, in the sense that on each of the moral issues that we asked them about, liberals outnumber conservatives – although quite often defenders of the status quo outnumber those who want a move in either a liberal or a conservative direction. Although we did not ask directly about the salience of these issues to Fine Gael members, we can draw some conclusions from the fact that only 25 per cent of the party's membership campaigned actively on either side in the 1995 divorce referendum. Fine Gael members are in some respects more liberal than party supporters, as shown by their voting behaviour in this referendum and in their attitudes to abortion – we shall return to this in the penultimate section of the chapter. Among the Fine Gael membership, Catholics, those who attend church most often, the elderly and those with least education tend to be the most conservative. Attitudes on moral issues are related, albeit weakly, to attitudes towards Northern Ireland, but they are not at all related to where members place themselves on the left–right spectrum. With young members being most liberal, we can expect Fine Gael, like society generally, to become steadily more liberal in the years ahead.

ATTITUDES TO EUROPE AND THE WIDER WORLD

Like the church–state issues that we just discussed, the question of European integration is one that causes divisions within parties as much as between them. All parties in Ireland are basically pro-EU, but as the scope of integration deepens and as Ireland's increasing relative wealth is beginning to turn the country from a net recipient of EU funds into a net donor, enthusiasm may be cooling. The pattern of support for continued European integration has been one of steady decline, from 83 per cent in the 1972 referendum on joining the EC to 70 per cent on ratifying the Single European Act in 1987, 69 per cent in the Maastricht referendum in 1992, 62 per cent in the Amsterdam treaty referendum of 1998, and a mere 46 per cent in the Nice treaty vote of June 2001. Relations with the EU now form the centrepiece of Irish foreign policy,[25] but other issues are also important. The subject of neutrality has been a central feature of Irish foreign policy since the 1930s, but there has been increasing discussion since the 1980s about whether it should be abandoned explicitly and about how far Ireland can become involved with international organisations without stretching the concept of neutrality beyond breaking point. In more recent years, Ireland, traditionally a country of emigration, has for the first time experienced significant levels of immigration, mainly from eastern Europe and Africa. Some have welcomed this and the potential that it brings for a move towards multiculturalism, arguing that in any case Ireland is morally and legally obliged to give haven to asylum-seekers. Others maintain that many immigrants are economic migrants rather than "genuine" asylum-seekers and feel that Ireland should adopt a more selective policy towards admittance of foreigners. Although this issue has not openly become a point of contention between the parties, there are reasons for supposing that public opinion is quite divided on the subject.

Accordingly, in our survey we asked three questions on attitudes towards the wider world. On European integration specifically, we asked whether Fine Gael members felt it should be pushed further or whether it has already gone too far (Q49). We asked whether Ireland should drop its policy of neutrality in order to take part in a common EU defence policy (Q50). And we asked respondents whether they agreed or disagreed with the statement that "There are too many immigrants being let into this country" (Q48.3).

European integration

When it comes to European integration, party members are quite evenly divided between those who want to see further integration (38 per cent) and those who feel the integration process has already gone too far (31 per cent) – the rest answered "don't know", but it can be assumed that some of these were in fact supporters of the status quo, an option not on the questionnaire. The fact that nearly a third of the membership of Fine Gael, which is generally seen as the most pro-integration of the Irish parties, believe that integration has already gone too far is surprising.

When we look in detail at who is in favour of and who is against further integration, we find some striking variation (see Table 7.6). There is a clear gender gap, with men markedly more pro-integration than women. Rather surprisingly, support for further integration is strongest in Dublin and in urban constituencies generally and is weakest in rural constituencies, even though it is generally assumed that the financial benefits of EU membership have been felt most directly in rural areas, and even though support in Dublin for European integration has been below the national average in every referendum held to date. The Dublin membership of Fine Gael is much more integrationist in its views than Dubliners generally are.

Religiosity is related to attitudes, though not in a straightforward way: those who attend least are the most supportive of further European integration, but the least supportive are weekly attenders at church, not those who attend more often than weekly. Generally, the more clericalist a member's attitudes are, the less enthusiastic he or she is about the prospect of further integration. On all measures of clericalism, those who are most clerical are the most likely to feel that European integration has already gone too far. Although our survey did not ask members about their reasons for supporting or opposing further integration, the implication here is that many of the more clericalist members of Fine Gael, and no doubt of society generally, see the EU as a secularising force that has been partly responsible for the liberalising trend within Irish society in recent years.

Occupation and education, which of course are strongly related to each other, are both related to attitudes towards integration. The occupational differences are sharp, with a 58–22 balance in favour of further integration among middle-class members at one end of the scale and a 27–37 balance against it among farmers at the other end. Similarly, those with university education are more strongly in favour of further European integration than any other sub-group in our sample, while those whose education ended at national school are less in favour than any other sub-group. Age, in contrast, is only weakly related: younger members are a little more in favour than older members, but the relationship is not statistically significant. *Irish Times* readers are also strongly supportive of the integration process, readers of the *Irish Independent* are less strongly in favour, while among members who read neither of these papers more feel that integration has already gone too far than want to see it carried further.

In addition, we can see that those who have attended a European People's Party conference and met members of Fine Gael's allied parties are far more strongly in favour of further integration than those who have not done so. We cannot tell, of course, which way the causal link runs – whether pro-integration members are more likely to go to such conferences in the first place, or whether attending such conferences makes members more pro-integration, or perhaps both. Indeed, activism generally, not just when it comes to attending European conferences, is related to attitudes to the EU, as Table 7.6 shows; the more active a member is, the more favourable he or she is towards the idea of further integration. One implication of this is that the views expressed by those members

Table 7.6: Socio-demographic background and attitudes to European integration

| | European integration | | | |
	should be pushed further	has already gone too far	don't know	All members
All members	38	31	31	100
Male	41	29	30	100
Female	31	34	35	100
Dublin	55	22	24	100
Rest of Leinster	42	26	32	100
Munster	33	36	31	100
Connacht–Ulster	32	32	36	100
Urban constituency	51	25	24	100
Rural constituency	34	32	34	100
Attend church more than weekly	41	30	29	100
Attend church weekly	32	33	35	100
Attend church less than weekly	57	23	20	100
AB social group	58	22	20	100
C1 social group	44	31	25	100
C2 social group	38	31	31	100
DE social group	33	28	39	100
Farmer	27	37	36	100
University education	58	25	17	100
National school education only	26	33	41	100
Other educational background	39	32	30	100
Aged 54 or below	41	29	30	100
Aged 55 or more	34	33	33	100
Irish Times reader	57	23	20	100
Irish Independent reader	37	31	32	100
Reader of other paper or no paper	30	34	36	100
Have attended EPP conference	50	27	23	100
Have not attended EPP conference	35	31	33	100
Very active FG member	52	26	21	100
Moderately active FG member	44	28	28	100
Moderately inactive FG member	34	31	35	100
Very inactive FG member	30	34	36	100

Source: Fine Gael members' questionnaire, questions 49, 35, 46, 42, 41, 47, 23b.

who attend and speak at party meetings may not be typical of the entire membership, as there exists a "silent majority" of members who are markedly less enthusiastic than the activists. Finally, we should mention one factor that does not show any relationship with members' views on European integration: where members place themselves on the left–right spectrum has no bearing on their attitudes towards integration.

Putting these findings together, then, we can construct profiles of the ideal-type pro- and anti-integration members of Fine Gael. The archetypal pro-integration member is a youngish university-educated man who lives in Dublin and rarely attends church, believes that the church still has too much influence in the country, travels to work with a copy of the *Irish Times* under his arm, has attended a meeting of the European People's Party, and takes an active part in the affairs of Fine Gael. The archetypal opponent of integration is a elderly woman from a rural constituency who attends church weekly, regrets that the power of the church has declined, did not proceed to second-level education, does not read either the *Irish Times* or the *Irish Independent*, has never attended a European party conference, and is not a particularly active member of the Fine Gael party.

Neutrality
When we move on to examine attitudes towards Irish neutrality, we find a very similar picture. Members are on balance in favour of keeping neutrality: 40 per cent are in favour of dropping it, 44 per cent oppose dropping it, and the other 16 per cent offer no opinion. When we analyse the pattern of support and opposition we come up with exactly the same findings as for European integration. Dublin members are in favour of dropping neutrality, members in the rest of Leinster are evenly divided, and those from Munster or Connacht–Ulster are against the idea. Men are in favour of dropping it (44 per cent say this, compared with 41 per cent who want to keep it), while women are opposed (30 per cent want to drop it and 50 per cent do not). Those in the AB social category, those with university education, and those who read the *Irish Times*, are in favour of dropping neutrality; all other groups would prefer to keep it. Those who have been to a European party conference are much more likely to favour dropping neutrality than those who have not. In one respect there is a different pattern: whereas younger members tended to be more pro-European integration than older ones, when it comes to neutrality the pattern is the other way round.

As the above discussion suggests, there is a strong relationship between attitudes towards further European integration and towards neutrality. This is confirmed in Table 7.7, which shows clear evidence of an integrationist tendency and an isolationist tendency. Those who are most in favour of European integration are most in favour of dropping neutrality; those who are against one are the most likely to be against the other.

Immigration
In addition, this integrationist–isolationist spectrum extends (albeit more

Table 7.7: Attitudes to European integration, by attitudes to neutrality and immigration

| | European integration | | | |
	should be pushed further	has already gone too far	don't know	All members
All members	38	31	31	100
Neutrality should be dropped				
for common EU defence policy				
Agree	58	24	18	100
Don't know	17	19	64	100
Disagree	27	42	31	100
Too many immigrants				
Agree	28	39	33	100
Neutral	38	30	32	100
Disagree	47	25	27	100

Source: Fine Gael members' questionnaire, questions 49, 50, 48.3.

weakly) to the issue of immigration, as Table 7.7 also shows. Those who are against European integration are the most likely to feel that Ireland is allowing too many immigrants into the country; those who favour European integration are the most likely to disagree with this. Overall, Fine Gael members are quite evenly divided on the question of immigration. About 37 per cent agree that there are too many immigrants (29 per cent strongly agree), while a further 36 per cent disagree with the statement (23 per cent strongly disagree), the other 27 per cent placing themselves at the mid-point between agreeing and disagreeing.

Attitudes towards immigration, then, are related to attitudes towards European integration and neutrality, though the pattern is not quite the same. Some of the factors that have a strong bearing on a member's attitude to the last two items, such as gender, urban/rural base, or attendance at a European party conference, are not related to attitude towards immigration. The location of a member's constituency is not significantly related to members' views on immigration, but this itself is notable, given that the impact of immigration has been greatest in Dublin; indeed, Dublin members are slightly less hostile to immigration than are members elsewhere. This could be taken as a sign that contact with immigrants is likely to dispel suspicion and that reservations held by members elsewhere will fade as they too come to know incomers with a different cultural background; less optimistically, it may simply be that most Dublin Fine Gael members are liberals who live in the wealthier parts of the city and who are glad to welcome immigrants to the country knowing that they themselves will be little affected by this. That the latter explanation may be nearer the mark is suggested by the detailed breakdown of attitudes within Dublin. Of members in the constituencies where most recent immigrants live (Dublin Central, Mid-West, South-Central, South-West and West) 42 per cent agree that too many immigrants are being let into the country; in the more prosperous constituencies (Dublin North, South-East, South and Dun Laoghaire) only 21 per cent agree.

Age is related to attitudes towards immigration, with older members being least enthusiastic, and self-placement on the left–right scale is also a factor, with those placing themselves on the right being more inclined to agree that the number of immigrants is excessive. Education, too, is significant. Among those with national school education only (a quarter of the whole sample), 45 per cent agree that there are too many immigrants, while at the other end of the scale only 23 per cent of those with university education feel the same. Working-class members and farmers are the most likely to agree that there is too much immigration. And, as with other aspects of the integrationist–isolationist dimension, we find that *Irish Times* readers are distinctive: only 25 per cent of them feel there is too much immigration, compared with 38 per cent of *Examiner* readers and 40 per cent of those members who read the *Irish Independent*.

Let us sum up where Fine Gael members stand on the isolationist–integrationist dimension. We are entitled to speak of a dimension because, by and large, those members who favour greater European integration also favour the dropping of Irish neutrality and disagree with the idea that too many immigrants are being allowed into Ireland. Likewise, by and large those who feel that European integration has already gone too far also want Irish neutrality retained and are likely to feel that immigration into Ireland is excessive. The number of members in the first group is much the same as the number in the second; the Fine Gael membership is evenly divided on these issues. Those in the first group are usually younger, with higher education, more likely to be men and resident in Dublin, not clericalist in their attitudes to church–state issues, and *Irish Times* readers. Those in the second group have the opposite characteristics. Activists are more likely to be found in the first group, and it is their voice that is more likely to be heard in party forums.

NORTHERN IRELAND

Although Fine Gael and Fianna Fáil are often seen as virtually identical in policy terms, few would dispute that the issue of Northern Ireland still distinguishes them. Fianna Fáil's traditions in the anti-Treaty movement have always led to a sharper anti-partitionist approach, with the emphasis on a united Ireland as the only possible long-term "solution" to the Northern Ireland question. Fine Gael, in contrast, has been associated with a less irredentist approach and, especially after Garret FitzGerald became leader in 1977, with an emphasis on improved relations between the communities within the north as a first priority. It may reasonably be argued that by the time of our survey in late 1999 the differences between the parties were simply nuances; with all the southern parties whole-heartedly supporting the Good Friday Agreement of April 1998, policy differences between them are very minor. However, it may still be that at the level of party activists differences remain, with Fianna Fáil members more likely to take a traditional nationalist view of the north and Fine Gael members more likely to feel that Irish governments should take account of the interests of both communities. Moreover, as we shall see in chapter 8, a significant number of Fine Gael members are inclined to cite Northern Ireland as the main policy issue distinguishing the two parties. Our survey could not, of course, reveal the feelings of Fianna Fáil members, but we were at least able to gauge the views of Fine Gael members.

We asked just one question on Northern Ireland, which was designed to identify the cleavage that we believe underlies southern attitudes towards the state's Northern Ireland policy. This question (Q51) asked members whether they felt that the Irish government of the day should have special regard for northern nationalists, special regard for northern unionists, or adopt an even-handed approach between the two communities. This issue was to surface during Fine Gael's 2001 leadership contest. Following the vote of no confidence in John Bruton, the eventual winner, Michael Noonan, gave as one of his reasons for challenging the leader his concern that Bruton had not paid sufficient attention to northern nationalist opinion specifically. He suggested that Fine Gael should return to what he described as its "pro-nationalist" position of the 1980s, and implied that under Bruton the party had become misperceived as being neutral as between nationalism and unionism.[26]

However, we found a perhaps surprising degree of consensus among Fine Gael members that governments should be even-handed: 76 per cent of members felt this, with only 14 per cent wanting the government to have special regard for northern nationalists (see Figure 7.1). There is no evidence here that many Fine Gael members were looking for a more nationalist line from the party, although undoubtedly a minority of members were very unhappy with Bruton's approach, regarding it as insufficiently nationalist, as we shall see in the next chapter when we discuss the differences between Fine Gael and Fianna Fáil. Very few members (just 3 per cent) wanted Fine Gael to have special regard for northern unionists.

With such a high degree of consensus among members – that is, with so little variation to explain – it is hardly surprising that few factors seem to have much bearing on members' attitudes towards Northern Ireland. Although we saw in the previous chapter that not many members (only about 14 per cent) believe that Irish governments should have special regard for northern nationalists, some evidently felt in 1999 that the party's stance was becoming unduly skewed in favour of northern unionists. Such members, then, wanted Fine Gael to become more nationalist, but in their eyes this would have redressed the existing pro-unionist leaning and made the party's stance more balanced rather than necessarily pro-nationalist. Rural members generally, members with unskilled working-class occupations, and men as opposed to women, are more inclined to favour special regard for northern nationalists, though these relationships are not strong. Those who are most opposed to immigration are the most inclined to

Figure 7.1: Preferred policy of Irish governments towards Northern Ireland

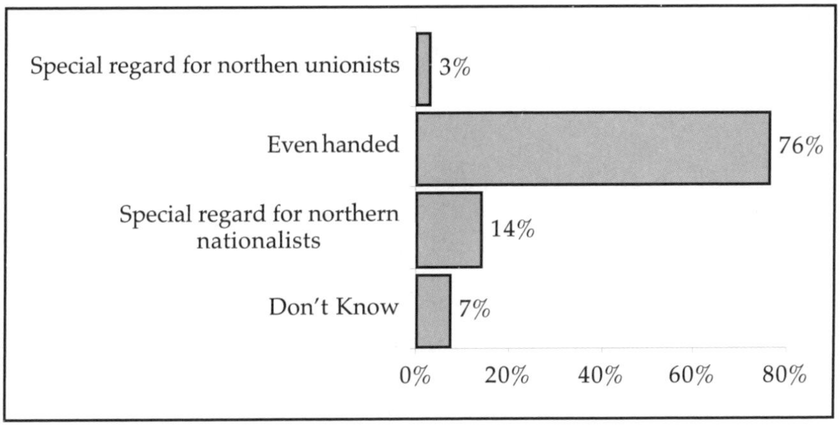

Source: Fine Gael members' questionnaire, question 51.

favour a policy of special regard for northern nationalists; such a group in the wider Irish society, combining strong nationalist views with opposition to immigration, could potentially form the basis for a far-right party were one ever to develop in Ireland, since such views characterise these parties' supporters in other European countries.[27] However, attitudes towards Northern Ireland are not clearly related to respondents' self-placement on the left–right spectrum, because members both on the left and on the right are somewhat more inclined to favour the government having special regard for northern nationalists, with only members in the centre having an above-average preference for an even-handed approach.

As we have already pointed out, there is a relationship between attitudes towards Northern Ireland and attitudes to church–state issues. The greater the influence a member feels the Catholic church should have in the education system, the more likely he or she is to want the government to have special regard for northern nationalists specifically. Even so, it is clear that there is a broad consensus on an even-handed approach even among the most clericalist group of members. With this limited exception, members' attitudes towards Northern Ireland are not significantly related to their attitudes towards other issues.

POST-MATERIALIST ISSUES: THE ENVIRONMENT AND MARIJUANA

As well as traditional left–right and bread and butter issues, what are sometimes termed "post-materialist" or "quality of life" issues have surfaced in a number of European countries. As the material needs of many Europeans have been satisfied, some have been inclined to give greater priority to issues such as the environment or freedom of the individual, and these issues were termed "post-materialist" by Ronald Inglehart, who has outlined his arguments in a number of books.[28]

We sought evidence of attitudes to some of these questions among Fine Gael members by asking three questions. Two concerned the environment. We asked, firstly, whether respondents agreed or disagreed with the statement that "Job creation should be a top priority even when this means some damage to the environment" (Q48.5). Secondly, we put the proposition that "There should be tighter controls on farming practices so as to prevent harm to the environment" (Q48.6). In addition, we asked members whether they were in favour of legalising the use of marijuana (Q48.2), which in many European countries has become a prominent freedom-of-the-individual issue and has the potential to attain this status in Ireland now that legislation in the area of sexual morality has been liberalised.

Attitudes to the jobs-versus-environment question were fairly evenly divided, with 35 per cent giving priority to jobs and 45 per cent to the environment (see Appendix B for full details). Views were related to some socio-demographic variables: men, those who attend church most often, people in rural areas and older members are most likely to put jobs first even if this means damage to the environment. Perhaps not surprisingly, those few Fine Gael members who are registered unemployed express particularly strong support for the statement (54 per cent of them strongly agreed with it and a further 4 per cent agreed). Members who place themselves on the left are more inclined to disagree with the statement, as are readers of the *Irish Times* and Dublin members. Education is particularly strongly related to the issue: those with most education, either because of an innate concern for the environment or simply because they feel confident of secure employment whatever happens, are most likely to disagree with the statement, exactly as theories of post-materialism would predict. As Table 7.8 shows, most members with university education disagree that jobs should be given priority over the environment, whereas most members with only national school education take the opposite point of view.

Views on this issue are not related to views on church–state issues and nor, perhaps surprisingly, are they significantly related to the question of whether

Table 7.8: Attitudes to jobs versus environment, by level of education

	National school education only	University education	Other education	All members
Jobs should take priority over environment				
Agree	51	18	31	35
Neutral	16	21	21	20
Disagree	33	61	48	45
Total	100	100	100	100

Source: Fine Gael members' questionnaire, questions 48.5, 42.

there should be tighter controls on farming so as to prevent damage to the environment. On this last question, there was broad agreement right across the board within Fine Gael, with 60 per cent agreeing (45 per cent strongly agree) and only 24 per cent disagreeing. Agreement is slightly higher than average in Dublin, but in all provinces a majority of members agree with the statement. Farmers, hardly surprisingly, are the least likely to agree with the idea of tighter controls on farming, yet even among farmers there is widespread agreement, with 42 per cent agreeing and only 40 per cent disagreeing.

We also asked about the idea of legalising the use of marijuana, and we found that this is a prospect that Fine Gael members evidently regard with something approaching horror.[29] A massive 74 per cent declare that they strongly disagree with the idea and a further 6 per cent disagree (though not strongly), leaving just 10 per cent favouring legalisation – even though legalisation is a policy that has highly respectable advocates in many countries. The usual liberal suspects do, it is true, produce the expected relationships: that is, young people, those who place themselves on the left-hand side of the left–right spectrum, those with university education, members from urban constituencies and especially from Dublin, those who are least clericalist both in behaviour and in attitude, and *Irish Times* readers are all more likely than other members to favour legalisation. However, it is worth noting that in *every one* of the sub-groups we have just mentioned, a majority of members still strongly disagrees with legalisation, as Table 7.9 shows. The party is evidently in a state of inner peace, harmony and tranquillity on this issue. Subject to the qualification that we don't know how salient this issue is for Fine Gael members – and in fact we might suspect that it is not of huge importance to them – this consensus is strong enough to make a real impact. Any future Fine Gael minister who wishes to set jaws dropping at a Fine Gael conference could probably achieve this by declaring that he or she has

Table 7.9: Attitudes to the legalisation of marijuana use, by various socio-economic factors

	Strongly disagree that marijuana use should be legalised
All members	74
View of the sub-group most favourable to legalisation:	
Age: under 35	60
Education: university	59
Province: Dublin	62
Left–right self-placement: left	57
Religious practice: attends church less than weekly	52
Newspaper read: *Irish Times*	57

Source: Fine Gael members' questionnaire, questions 48.2, 41, 42, 62, 46, 47.

decided to introduce legislation legalising marijuana use. Similarly, individuals who favour legalising marijuana would be well advised to keep their views to themselves if they are seeking to be selected as a Fine Gael election candidate, and TDs are unlikely to have their ears bent by members suggesting that legalisation of marijuana would be a good idea.

THE POLITICAL VIEWS OF MEMBERS, VOTERS AND POLITICIANS

We explained in the opening section of the chapter why it is important to make comparisons between the views of members and voters, and between members and public representatives. Making such comparisons is easier said than done, though, because data are limited, and in particular it is not possible to make comparisons at exactly the same points in time. However, enough evidence exists to suggest that there is little difference between Fine Gael members and those who vote for the party. There may perhaps be a little more difference between members and public representatives, although data are even more limited here.

Positions on the left–right spectrum

The most extensive data comes from questions asking respondents to place themselves on the left–right spectrum. As we have seen already, Fine Gael members tend to put themselves on the centre or the right, and to put the party in much the same place. Voters polled in 1999, at around the same time as our survey was conducted, did not different very greatly from members, although the differences are large enough to be statistically significant. Voters have a stronger

Table 7.10: Placement of self and of Fine Gael on left–right spectrum by Fine Gael members, voters and politicians

	Fine Gael members		Fine Gael voters		Fine Gael TDs and MEPs	
	Self %	Fine Gael %	Self %	Fine Gael %	Self %	Fine Gael %
Left (1–4)	20	12	16	13	42	13
Centre (5–6)	40	41	49	31	38	67
Right (7–10)	41	46	35	56	21	21
Total	100	100	100	100	100	100
N	914	914	147	133	24	24

Source: Fine Gael members' questionnaire, questions 62, 63; voters from European Election Study 1999 (base is all those who voted or intended to vote for Fine Gael at the previous general election, the next general election, or the European Parliament election); TDs and MEPs calculated by authors from original data of the European Representation Study 1995–96; see Katz and Wessels, *The European Parliament* for details and analysis of this.

Table 7.11: Support for divorce in the 1995 referendum among Fine Gael members and voters

	Fine Gael members 1999 %	Fine Gael voters 18 Nov 1995 %	Fine Gael voters 15 Nov 1995 %
Yes	59	44	51
No	33	43	38
Did not vote / no opinion	8	13	10
Total	100	100	100
N	1106	206	211

Source: Fine Gael members' questionnaire, question 28; MRBI poll 18 November 1995; IMS poll 15 November 1995.
Note: Among all voters, the Yes–No balance was 45–42 in the 18 November 1995 poll and 47–39 in the 15 November 1995 poll. MRBI asked "If the referendum were held today would you vote yes ... or no ..." while IMS asked "If you do vote ...".

tendency to place themselves in the centre, as Table 7.10 shows.[30] On the placement of Fine Gael, voters are more likely than members to place the party on the right. In contrast, the TDs and MEPs sampled a few years earlier (in 1995–96) tend to see themselves as left of centre and the party as centre, just like those TDs surveyed in 1983, as we saw in Table 7.2. Differences between politicians and the others are much greater than those between members and voters. With only 24 deputies in our sample there is more room for error but these are still quite large differences. There is certainly no sign here that the members are in any sense "extreme". In fact, their perceptions of their own position and of the party are closer to those of the voters than are those of Fine Gael deputies.

Church and state
Turning to the issues on the so-called "liberal agenda", such as attitudes to abortion and divorce, the picture is much the same. When we compare the views of members and voters, even allowing for the fact that the data are not contemporaneous, there are again no huge differences. As Table 7.11 shows, on divorce members appear to be more liberal than voters; members (as they recalled their behaviour when asked in 1999) were more supportive of divorce in the 1995 referendum than voters had been in 1995. The most recent data relating to voters' views on abortion are from 1992, when the question asked offered the same options as in Q53 of the members' survey; comparing the Fine Gael voters in these polls with the members of 1999 shows a remarkably similar set of attitudes.[31]

Europe and neutrality
On Europe, the views of members and voters again seem to be very close. Here data is almost contemporaneous but the response categories offered to members

Table 7.12: Attitudes of Fine Gael members and voters to European integration

	Fine Gael members %	Fine Gael voters %
Push further / 1–4	38	34
Don't know / 5–6	31	34
Gone far enough / 7–10	31	32
Total	100	100
N	1131	155

Source: Fine Gael members' questionnaire, question 49; European Election Study 1999.
Note: The question asked was whether European unification should be pushed further or has already gone too far. Voters were asked to respond using a 10-point scale.

and voters were different. Members were asked to say if integration should be pushed further or had gone far enough. Voters were provided with a 1–10 scale with "pushed further" at one end and "gone far enough" at the other. Quite probably, many who were uncertain or who had no opinion opted for a middle position. Table 7.12 equates 1–4 with those who say integration should be pushed further, 5–6 with those who don't know, and 7–10 with those who say it has gone far enough. This produces a remarkable match between the two sets of responses.

The contrast between members and voters looks sharper on neutrality, though we should note the time difference here. Table 7.13 compares the members' responses in 1999 with those of Fine Gael voters in 1991. It suggests that the Fine Gael membership is about evenly balanced on whether to abandon "neutrality" in favour of a common EU policy but that Fine Gael voters in 1991 were definitely against the idea. Once again, the lack of clearly comparable data makes it difficult to tell whether opinion has shifted since 1991, although it may well have done given Ireland's closer involvement in the EU's foreign and security policy and its membership of the Partnership for Peace (PfP).

Members and votes: a summary

This somewhat scattered and limited evidence can be no more than suggestive of differences between the separate layers of the Fine Gael party. Our interest is primarily in assessing the extent to which Fine Gael members might hold positions that are very different from those held by the party's voters, which as we pointed out earlier in the chapter is the prediction of one theory about the internal functioning of political parties, summed up in May's "law of curvilinear disparity". The evidence indicates very little support for such a view; there are very few disparities of any sort. Only on neutrality is there any apparent marked difference, and even there we have argued that the difference may well be more apparent than real. One implication of our findings is that if the existing Fine

Table 7.13: Attitudes of Fine Gael members and voters to Irish neutrality

	Fine Gael members 1999 %	Fine Gael voters 1991 %
Drop neutrality	40	34
Don't drop neutrality	44	55
Don't know	17	10
Total	100	100
N	1106	195

Source: Fine Gael members' questionnaire, question 50; MRBI poll 3 January 1991.
Note: The question asked in 1991 was "Should Ireland drop its neutrality to take part in a common defence policy in the EU?"

Gael members were allowed a significantly increased say on party policy, there is no reason to believe that they would drag the party away from the bulk of its normal supporters – though of course giving members the right to determine party policy could attract new members whose views might not coincide with those of the existing ones. Moreover, even where gaps between members and voters might be relatively large, on divorce and neutrality, party policy as voiced would seem to be closer to the position of members. The party did campaign for a Yes vote in 1995, and has not made a big issue of neutrality in its EU policy.

If this conclusion appears to paint a fairly rosy picture of political representation in Ireland – with voters and members united on policy platforms – it would be a little misleading. On most of the measures of voter opinion shown here, Fianna Fáil voters could stand in for those of Fine Gael without the switch being noticed. Fine Gael members may closely resemble Fine Gael voters, but they also resemble voters in general, and particularly those who support the more established parties.

A UNITED PARTY?

Finally, we may ask, on the basis of our findings, whether Fine Gael is basically a united party or whether there are certain issues that have the potential to divide it. In Table 7.14 we present the political issues that we have discussed in this chapter and show how opinion is distributed on these questions. Deciding how much support is needed before we can declare the existence of a consensus is a matter of subjective judgement; Crewe and King, in their study of Britain's SDP, suggested that a party can be regarded as divided if neither of the two options commands the support of at least 60 per cent of the members.[32] On the issues placed in the top band of Table 7.14, there appears to be strong agreement within the ranks of Fine Gael members; when it comes to not legalising marijuana, the fundamental principle underlying Northern Ireland policy, the redistribution of wealth, and greater controls on farming so as to protect the environment, at least 60 per cent of members are of one mind

On the other issues, support for one side or the other is less than this, but in several cases this is because of the large number of members who place themselves in the middle or on the fence. In the case of the three issues in the middle of the list in Table 7.14, the number of members who are in favour of retaining the status quo rather than moving in one direction or the other approaches or exceeds 60 per cent. None of these issues – the influence of the church in the education system, and whether Fine Gael should move on either the left–right or the liberal–conservative spectrums – seems to have the potential to cause ructions within the party.

That leaves five issues, those in the bottom group in the table, that do bear such potential. Of these, we might discount two as unlikely ever to cause real discord within the party. The question of whether job creation should take

Table 7.14: The extent of unity among Fine Gael members on political issues

	Majority / plurality view	Neutral position	Minority view	Total
Consensus on one side				
Policy on Northern Ireland	84		16	100
Do not legalise marijuana	80	9	10	100
Redistribute wealth	67	20	13	100
More controls on farming to protect environment	60	16	24	100
Consensus for status quo				
Church influence on education too great	34	58	8	100
FG should move on liberal– conservative spectrum	33	59	9	100
FG should move on left–right spectrum	18	72	10	100
Division				
Jobs priority over environment	45	20	35	100
Drop neutrality	44	17	40	100
Trade unions too powerful	38	28	34	100
More European integration	38	31	31	100
Too many immigrants	37	28	36	100

Source: Appendix B; further details are in tables in this chapter.
Note: In the case of policy on Northern Ireland, the figures refer to those who favour a policy of even-handedness between nationalists and unionists versus those who favour a policy of having special regard for northern nationalists. "Majority / plurality view" is the larger of the for-or-against options.

priority even when this entails damage to the environment is a rather abstract one, and it is not obvious that a tangible issue will arise in day-to-day politics that will require a decision by the party one way or the other. In addition, the question of whether trade unions have too much power is not a particularly live issue in Irish politics and it shows no sign of becoming one.

There are, then, just three issues that seem to have the potential to cause real discord within the Fine Gael party, and all three concern what we have termed attitudes to Europe and the wider world, or an integrationist–isolationist spectrum. These issues – whether neutrality should be dropped, whether European integration should be extended, and whether Ireland is allowing too many immigrants into the country – tend to evoke similar responses from the members, as we have seen, in that members who adopt an integrationist position on one issue are more likely to adopt an integrationist position on the others. Those members who favour further European integration also have an above-average tendency to favour the dropping of Irish neutrality and to disagree that too many immigrants are being allowed into the country.

Something else that these issues have in common is that they are all topical and at times are close to the top of the political agenda. Decisions have to be taken, especially on specific treaties within the EU, such as the Nice treaty. On the whole, the Fine Gael party's policies are much more in line with the integrationist side of the arguments, in that the party is generally perceived as the most integrationist of the main parties and as the most willing to drop neutrality, and it has criticised the treatment of refugees by the Fianna Fáil–Progressive Democrat government. Our survey shows that the activists among the membership are also on the integrationist side. However, there is a large body of members, a silent significant minority albeit not quite a majority, who do not subscribe to the integrationist perspective. They may not be the kind of members who will make eloquent speeches at party conferences in support of their views, but there is certainly the possibility that they will become less active or drift away from the party if Fine Gael policy remains firmly integrationist.

CONCLUSION

In this chapter we have examined the views of Fine Gael party members. Although some might be inclined to dismiss the views of party members as of little account, we have argued that these views have the potential to make a difference both to the policies the party adopts and to the way the electorate perceives the party. In the case of Fine Gael specifically, while it emerges that many members don't have any great interest in political issues, interest is highest among the most active members, whose impact on the party and the public is likely to be the greatest.

When we explored members' views, we found that the left–right spectrum evidently has some meaning for most of them, despite suggestions that this dimension is pretty much absent from Irish politics. Fine Gael members place themselves on the centre-right and in addition see both their own party and Fianna Fáil as being centre-right. Although it seems at first sight that they see Fianna Fáil as being as close to them as Fine Gael is, when we look at the data at individual level we find that members feel that they are closer to their own party than to Fianna Fáil on this dimension. Labour is generally perceived as being on the left and the PDs are placed furthest to the right. The judgements of Fine Gael members correlate closely with those of Irish political scientists – this does not prove that either group is correct, but the judgement of each to some extent validates the judgement of the other. However, even though members are willing to place themselves on the left–right dimension, this dimension does not seem to provide them with an ideology, because their views on most policy issues, even those that in most countries would distinguish left from right, are not strongly related to where they place themselves on this dimension.

On church–state issues, Fine Gael members emerge as relatively liberal, although the party organisation was largely absent from the battlefield when the divorce referendum was held in November 1995. Some members are consistently more liberal than others; factors that are related to liberalism include youth, high education, and infrequent attendance at church. Looking to the wider world, we were able to identify an isolationist–integrationist dimension. Some members want greater European integration and the dropping of Irish neutrality, and also do not agree that too many immigrants are coming into Ireland; others feel that European integration has already gone too far, want to keep neutrality, and feel that too many immigrants are being allowed into the country. The two groups are about equal in size. Those in the former group tend to be younger, highly educated, Dublin resident, non-clerical or anti-clerical, and *Irish Times* readers; they are also more active within the party than those in the latter group. These issues, uniquely, have the real potential to divide the party, given the even balance between opposing views among the members and the inherent salience of the issues.

We have compared the views of TDs, members and voters on different issues, as far as the data permit this. Even allowing for the patchy nature of our data, it seems clear that there are no great differences between members and voters, or indeed between members and TDs. The membership does not give the party a negative and extremist image in the eyes of ordinary voters, and it is not spreading a message locally that is at odds with what the party leadership stands for or with what the voters want to hear. If existing members were given much more power in policy-making there is no reason to believe that the nature of party policies would change much. The membership, precisely because its views seem to be so mainstream, is not going to be pressing for any radical new departures in party policy. This makes for internal party harmony, at least on policy matters, though it also means that the membership may not be a significant source of policy innovation.

Do the views of members matter? The opinions analysed in this chapter cannot answer this question, but it is clear that the views of party members have the potential to make an impact in the various ways we have outlined. If party leaders deviate too far from the views of members, they run the risk of weakening the commitment of those members or even of losing them completely from the party. The membership is quite divided on left–right issues, European integration and jobs-versus-the-environment, which could be seen as giving the leaders reasonable freedom of manoeuvre though at the same time it presents them with the risk of facing considerable resistance whatever they do. On church–state issues, though, there would clearly be little enthusiasm for a leader or a front bench who tried to turn the clock back and take Fine Gael in a more conservative direction. And on some issues, notably pursuing a policy of even-handedness to the two communities in Northern Ireland and not legalising marijuana use, the consensus among party members is so strong that there is the potential for serious consequences if the party were to change its position.

8 Fine Gael and the Irish political system

In the previous chapter we looked at the views of Fine Gael members on a range of current political issues. Among other things, we examined how party members place Fine Gael and the other parties on the left–right spectrum, which gives us some idea of the way in which they visualise the Irish party system. In this chapter we will explore this in more detail, analysing Fine Gael members' preferences when it comes to coalition partners and relating this to how warmly they feel towards the other parties. We will be able to ascertain whether there is significant disagreement among the membership over coalition strategy, and, if so, whether this is related to other differences within the party, such as those distinguishing more left-wing from more right-wing members or more liberal from more conservative members. More generally, we will assess members' expectations regarding Fine Gael's future prospects – are members upbeat or demoralised? We also examine their opinions as to whether Fine Gael should consider merging with any other party, and their views on one of the thorniest questions about Irish politics: just what is the difference between Fine Gael and Fianna Fáil? We look at Fine Gael members' assessments of a range of current and past political figures from north and south of the border. Lastly, we discuss Fine Gael members' views on how well the political system as a whole is functioning and how, if at all, it could be improved.

MEMBERS' FEELINGS TOWARDS THE IRISH POLITICAL PARTIES

We wished to explore the way Fine Gael members perceive the Irish party system – by this term, we mean the individual parties along with the way in which these parties relate to and interact with each other. In order to do this, we asked a number of questions concerning several different topics. One of these was coalition, which we discuss in greater depth in the next section. In this section we shall focus on the extent to which Fine Gael members feel close to or distant from the various political parties. We shall then go on to examine the way members identify the difference between Fine Gael and Fianna Fáil.

Fine Gael and the Irish party system

To assess how Fine Gael members felt about the various parties, we asked them to tell us where they would place the parties on a "thermometer" scale running from 0 to 99. We explained that if they felt warm and sympathetic toward a party they should give it a score of over 50; if they felt cold and unsympathetic they should give a score of less than 50; and if they felt neither cold nor warm they should give a score of precisely 50.

The results, which are shown in Table 8.1, contain a number of notable features. We could feel completely confident even without conducting a survey that Fine Gael would prove to be the favourite party of Fine Gael members, and so it is, but the rankings of the other parties were less predictable. As we saw in the previous chapter, Fine Gael members place Fianna Fáil closest to themselves on the left–right spectrum, with the PDs next closest and Labour furthest away. However, when it comes to political alliances, Labour has been a frequent coalition partner and Fianna Fáil has always been on the opposite side. The PDs stand somewhere in between: pre-election allies, implicit or explicit, on occasion but never coalition partners and, at the time of our survey, in coalition with Fianna Fáil while Fine Gael was in opposition. Hence if members' feelings of warmth or coolness were determined primarily by the left–right spectrum we would expect them to rank Fianna Fáil above the PDs and the PDs above Labour, while if these feelings were determined primarily by the pattern of party competition, we would expect Labour to be ranked ahead of the PDs, who in turn would be ranked ahead of Fianna Fáil.

Table 8.1 shows that the lines of battle count for more than the left–right spectrum. Fine Gael members' second favourite party is Labour, whose average score was 50, just about the mid-point of the scale. The PDs came next, and Fianna Fáil was only fourth, with most Fine Gael members giving it a score of 40 or less. It is striking that these three parties all scored higher than the minor parties about which we asked. It is no surprise that Fine Gael members rated Sinn Féin very low (in fact 58 per cent gave it a score of 10 or below, with 17 per cent giving it a score of zero, indicating complete rejection of the party and what it is perceived to stand for). Less foreseeably, Fine Gael members had a negative view of the Greens, who were rated less favourably than Fianna Fáil. This is especially surprising given that, first, the Greens were widely seen at the time as a likely coalition partner in any Fine Gael-led coalition government that might

Table 8.1: Fine Gael members' warmth or coldness towards the political parties

Party	Average score	% of FG members who give party a score of				
		0–19	20–39	40–59	60–79	80–99
Fine Gael	76	4	1	8	29	57
Labour	50	8	10	42	34	6
Progressive Democrats	40	19	20	37	19	5
Fianna Fáil	34	28	22	37	11	3
Green Party	31	35	23	28	12	2
Sinn Féin	19	60	20	15	5	1

Source: Fine Gael members' questionnaire, questions 98 to 103.
Note: The maximum score is 99, denoting a very positive feeling, and the minimum is 0, indicating a very negative feeling.

be formed after the next election, and, second, that the worst thing usually said about the Greens by their critics is that they are well-meaning but rather utopian and not always realistic. We would not, therefore, have expected the Greens to engender the strongly negative reaction that we found within Fine Gael ranks. We will note in passing that the researchers who surveyed members of the British Conservative Party were similarly puzzled to discover that Conservative members felt even more hostile to the British Greens than to the Labour Party.[1]

This implies that the left–right dimension of politics does not determine the degree of warmth that Fine Gael members feel towards the various parties, and this conclusion is strikingly confirmed when we look at members' ratings of the parties in the light of their placement of themselves on the left–right spectrum. There is, quite simply, no significant relationship between the two: how far to the left or to the right members see themselves as being has effectively no bearing on how they evaluate the parties. For example, we might expect that the further to the left a member places himself or herself on the left–right spectrum, the more warmly disposed he or she will be towards Labour. As Table 8.2 shows, there is indeed a very slight tendency for those who place themselves further to the left to evaluate Labour more favourably than those who place themselves on the right,[2] and, conversely, for right-wing members to feel more warmly towards the PDs than left-wing members do. But the tendency in each case is very weak, and it is apparent that attitudes to the parties are not determined by how right-wing or left-wing a member is. Clearly, the general warmth among Fine Gael members towards Labour is based on the perception of that party as Fine Gael's traditional ally in the battle against Fianna Fáil rather than on a liking for its left-wing policy positions.

When we look in more detail at the factors that are related to members' attitudes to the various parties, we find that the degree of warmth a member feels toward the parties is related to how strongly he or she supports Fine Gael. Obviously, this is true of members' rating of Fine Gael itself, but when it comes

Table 8.2: Fine Gael members' ratings of the political parties, by members' self-placement on left–right spectrum

Party	Average score from all members	Average score from members placing themselves		
		Left (1–4)	Centre (5–6)	Right (7–10)
Fine Gael	76	74	75	76
Labour	50	54	50	49
Progressive Democrats	40	39	41	42
Fianna Fáil	34	34	33	34
Green Party	31	36	32	29
Sinn Féin	19	25	18	17

Source: Fine Gael members' questionnaire, questions 98, 99, 100, 101, 102, 103, 62.
Note: The maximum score is 99, denoting a very positive feeling, and the minimum is 0, indicating a very negative feeling.

to the other parties we notice an interesting pattern (see Table 8.3). In the case of all the parties except Labour, the more strongly someone supports Fine Gael, the *less* warm he or she feels towards that party; in the case of Labour the relationship is (albeit weakly) in the other direction. The clear impression is that, at an instinctive level, Fine Gael members think of Labour as a party that is "on our side", or at least not an opponent, and they think of all the other parties as "on the other side".

Other than this, when we look at the way in which the thermometer scores are affected by other characteristics of members, we find that attitudes to Fine Gael itself do not vary a great deal; as we would expect, virtually all members, whatever their views on particular policy issues, feel favourably disposed to their own party. Attitudes towards Labour also seem to vary little, with nearly all categories of members giving Labour a score of close to 50, which is the neutral mid-point of the scale. Predictably, those Fine Gael members who want Fine Gael to move to the left have a more favourable attitude towards Labour (they give it an average score of 54) than those members who want Fine Gael to move to the right (they give Labour an average score of 46).

When it comes to Fine Gael members' feelings about the other four parties, all of which receive negative ratings (that is, average scores of less than 50), there are some common patterns, but there are also other patterns that are specific to particular parties. One common trait is that the more active a member is in Fine Gael, the less warm he or she feels towards Fianna Fáil, the PDs, the Greens and Sinn Féin. Active members, then, have the most positive feelings towards their own party and the most hostile feelings towards other parties (except Labour); inactive members are least enthusiastic about their own party and least antipathetic to the other parties. This is much as we would expect. Likewise, those who come from families with a tradition of support for Fine Gael going back to the 1920s feel more hostile to Fianna Fáil, the Greens and Sinn Féin than other members do.

Table 8.3: Average thermometer scores given by Fine Gael members to the political parties, by strength of support for Fine Gael

| | | *Strength of support for Fine Gael* | | | |
| | All | Very | Fairly | Not very | Not at all |
Party	members	strong	strong	strong	strong
Fine Gael	76	78	75	69	61
Labour	50	51	50	49	39
Progressive Democrats	40	38	42	43	45
Fianna Fáil	34	31	34	38	48
Greens	31	29	32	38	36
Sinn Féin	19	17	20	25	37

Source: Fine Gael members' questionnaire, questions 98 to 103, 1.
Note: The maximum score is 99, denoting a very positive feeling, and the minimum is 0, indicating a very negative feeling.

Attitudes to the other parties partly reflect the perceived policy stances of those parties – perhaps smaller parties are more strongly associated with specific policies in the minds of voters generally than larger parties are. For example, rural Fine Gael members do not like the Greens, and this undoubtedly has a lot to do with perceptions of the Greens as a party that puts the environment ahead of both job creation and the rights of property owners, especially farmers. The average score given to the Greens by the farmers among the Fine Gael membership was only 25, compared with an average of 34 among all other members. One of our questions (Q48.5) asked members whether they agreed that job creation should take top priority even when this means damage to the environment, and we found that those who strongly agree with this take a markedly less favourable view of the Greens (they give the party an average score of 25) than those who strongly disagree (they give the Greens an average score of 37). There is some tendency for younger members, members with most education, and women to rate the Greens more highly than other members.

Attitudes towards Sinn Féin do not vary significantly, with all sections of the party displaying strongly negative feelings towards the party. The least hostile group consists of those members who believe that the Irish government of the day, when framing its Northern Ireland policy, should have special regard for northern nationalists. These members give Sinn Féin an average score of 32, while other members give it an average score of just 17.

FINE GAEL AND FIANNA FÁIL

The difference between the two main parties is, as we have said before, one of the most intriguing mysteries of Irish politics. Barry Desmond quotes a Cork Fianna Fáil perspective on this puzzle: "Dem dat know don't need to ask and dem dat don't know don't need to know".[3] Given that so many people claim that there is little or no policy difference between these two parties, we wondered what differences Fine Gael members themselves perceived, and whether certain categories of Fine Gael members were less hostile than others to Fianna Fáil. We found that when it came to members' ratings of Fianna Fáil, those members who were least active and least interested in political issues were the least hostile to Fianna Fáil; not, we suspect, because these members have a particularly positive view of that party, but because they care less about the political battle and about politics generally, or because they don't think there is much difference between Fianna Fáil and Fine Gael: warmth towards Fianna Fáil was inversely related to interest in national political issues; those members who are most interested give Fianna Fáil a score of 32, while those who are least interested give it a score of 41 (see Table 8.4). Similarly, those who see no real policy differences between Fine Gael and Fianna Fáil are the least hostile to Fianna Fáil, and those members who would welcome a merger between their party and Fianna Fáil are, hardly surprisingly, more favourably disposed towards Fianna Fáil than are other members.

Table 8.4: Fine Gael members' ratings of Fianna Fáil, by selected variables

	Average thermometer score awarded to FF by FG members
All members	34
Interested in political issues?	
Very	32
Quite	35
Not at all	41
Main FF–FG policy difference	
Some policy area cited	31
Response given: "None"	39
Would you welcome a FG–FF merger?	
Yes	43
No	31

Source: Fine Gael members' questionnaire, questions 98, 24, 6, 86, 85.
Note: The maximum score is 99, denoting a very positive feeling, and the minimum is 0, indicating a very negative feeling.

It is also no surprise that those who joined the party for what we have termed "solidary" reasons – for example, to meet people, or due to the influence of their family and friends – have less strong anti-Fianna Fáil feelings than other members; as we noted in previous chapters, these members tend to be relatively apolitical. In contrast, those who joined to get Fine Gael into government, or joined out of opposition to Fianna Fáil, give Fianna Fáil a lower score than other members do. As with attitudes to the other parties, we find that policy perceptions do play some part, and Fianna Fáil's image as a relatively clericalist and nationalist party has a bearing on members' attitudes. Fianna Fáil is most highly regarded by those Fine Gael members who attend church most often and, in addition, it receives above-average scores from those members who want Fine Gael to become more conservative and who favour a line of having special regard for nationalists when it comes to the government's Northern Ireland policy.

We asked two questions designed to discover the key factor that Fine Gael members would identify as distinguishing the two parties. First, we asked which of a short list of policy areas was the one where the parties differed most, and then we invited members to tell us in their own words what they saw as the main difference. Of the four main policy areas presented in the first question, Northern Ireland was most often cited, and this was followed by taxation and then agriculture, with only 5 per cent seeing the EU as the policy area where differences were greatest (Figure 8.1). However, a plurality of members answered that they did not see *any* real policy differences between the two major parties, a pattern that we would not expect to find in any other European country.

Figure 8.1: Policy area in which Fianna Fail and Fine Gael differ most

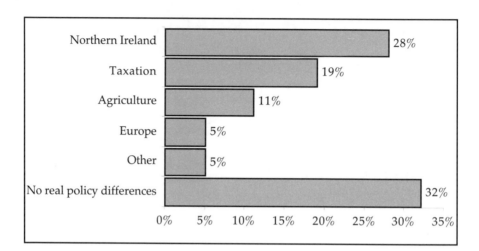

Source: Fine Gael members' questionnaire, question 86

Members' own situation had an impact on their perception: for example, 20 per cent of farmers identified agriculture as the main issue that divided the parties while only 4 per cent of middle-class members gave this response. The categories are broad, and from this question alone we cannot be sure what the responses mean: for example, two members answering "taxation" might have different specific issues in mind, and two members answering "Northern Ireland" might have different views as to which party's policy is better.

Our second question was designed to overcome this problem by giving members the chance to express their views in their own way. The responses, shown in Table 8.5, show that the great majority of members, when asked about the main difference between their party and Fianna Fáil, do not cite a policy area at all.

Far and away the most common factor mentioned is something to do with honesty and integrity, which has often been cited as the Achilles heel of Fianna Fáil; as the former Fianna Fáil government press secretary Seán Duignan puts it, the high moral ground is "traditionally treacherous terrain for Fianna Fáil".[4] Examples of members' responses in this category are:

- Fine Gael are honest, Fianna Fáil are completely dishonest
- Fine Gael are a much more honest party, otherwise not much difference
- Fine Gael are decent people and are generally seen as such, Fianna Fáil are very definitely not
- I regard Fine Gael as an honourable party and Fianna Fáil as a crowd of chancers! That is why I joined Fine Gael
- Fianna Fáil are a crowd of crooks and Fine Gael are honest men [sic]
- Fine Gael set the wheels of the new state in motion, we founded the state, we are a party of the highest integrity and standards

Table 8.5: Fine Gael members' perception of main differences between Fianna Fáil and Fine Gael

	Percentage citing as main difference
Integrity, honesty	48
No difference	12
Fianna Fáil is more active, better organised	10
Civil war legacy / Northern Ireland	9
Fine Gael puts country first, Fianna Fáil populist and will do anything to get votes	6
Position on left–right dimension	3
Position on liberal–conservative dimension	1
Fine Gael modern and progressive, Fianna Fáil is backward-looking	1
EU / neutrality	1
Other policy area	2
Miscellaneous other	8
Total	100

Source: Fine Gael members' questionnaire, question 87: "Now please tell us in your own words what you feel is the main difference between Fianna Fáil and Fine Gael today".
Note: Responses were received from 75 per cent of members (weighted). Since question 87 was completely open, the categories used are devised by the authors.

- Fine Gael has members with breeding and intelligence and ethics, in Fianna Fáil these are extreme rarities and it seems not to be found in the Dáil
- The type of people in Fine Gael are generally a more honourable sort than the sleaze types in Fianna Fáil.

It is tempting to ascribe these views to the variety of enquiries under way at the time of our survey into allegations of corruption or impropriety on the part of leading Fianna Fáil figures such as Charles Haughey and Ray Burke. However, it may well be that this pattern was by no means specific to 1999. When Tom Garvin undertook a small-scale survey of party activists in Dublin South-Central in 1972–73 and asked members of each party what they liked or disliked about the main parties, he found that the activist layer of Fine Gael "tended to emphasise the virtue of its leaders and prided itself on its honesty and integrity, sometimes contrasting this integrity with the alleged corruption of Fianna Fáil. Fine Gael was the party of justice and honour, and it had a stated policy programme to which it would adhere if it were to come to office". He summarises the party's sub-culture as "moralist".[5]

What was striking in our 1999 survey was the number of Fine Gael members who, even while citing integrity as the most important factor distinguishing the two parties, felt that their own party was only marginally better than Fianna Fáil, or expressed hope rather than confidence that the two parties really were significantly different:

- I would like to think that in Fine Gael we have a party we can trust
- Most of Fine Gael TDs are honest
- Fine Gael appear to be more honest
- Fine Gael are hopefully more honest
- Fine Gael are honest (with a few exceptions)
- Leadership of Fine Gael more honest and decent (can't say the same for all Fine Gael TDs)
- Fianna Fáil have hidden a lot under the carpet, Fine Gael are a small bit more honest about it
- I would like to hope that Fine Gael is a more moral party than Fianna Fáil
- Some semblance of decency and honesty appears to still exist in Fine Gael, whereas Fianna Fáil seems to be totally riddled with corruption and deceit
- Crooks versus half-honest crooks
- The Fine Gael party appears to be more honest than Fianna Fáil but maybe that is because they haven't been in power as long as Fianna Fáil.

After those members who see integrity as the main distinguishing factor, the second most common response (given by 12 per cent) to the question as to the main difference between the parties was simply that there is no difference. Many of the comments in this category are ones that we might expect to come from disaffected non-partisans rather than from paid-up members of one of the two parties:

- I really could not say as I have lost faith in both parties, I think it is all about themselves
- I think both are nearly the same and I see no reason why they would not get together and form a government
- I asked my own branch that very question – they couldn't give me an answer
- Very little really, as both are not doing much for PAYE and poverty at the moment
- Don't know
- None – they all do the same thing when in power
- There is not a lot of difference. I would not know enough about the policies of either party to make a judgement call on this issue
- There is no real difference apart from they all feather their own nest
- In essence very little difference, just the type of person / people attracted to the different parties
- To be really honest not a big difference, it was a sad day when this split came in our country
- I really don't have an opinion, I go more for personalities; local Fine Gael rep is superb and always has been
- There probably isn't a lot of difference, when are they ever going to do anything for the ordinary person like me?
- None whatsoever.

The third most common response (given by 10 per cent) to the question, perhaps surprisingly, was provided by those members who contrasted Fianna Fáil favourably with their own party and suggested that Fine Gael had a lot to learn from its larger rival. Some members suggested that Fianna Fáil communicates better with the public than Fine Gael does:

- Very little difference except Fianna Fáil more pushy, speak out more, appear in local radio and local meetings, always making their presence felt
- Just to say Fianna Fáil appear to be the better of the two today. The country seems to be fine at the moment
- When Fianna Fáil make dodgy policies they seem to escape criticism. When Fine Gael do similar they lose out which is an area for improvement
- No difference except Fianna Fáil has a leader and Fine Gael has none
- Fianna Fáil is more professional in appealing to the wider audience while Fine Gael seem only capable of appealing to the professional and wealthy classes
- Fine Gael appears inactive – says little, silent on issues including scandals, no mention of Fine Gael policy position
- Fianna Fáil have much stronger candidates than Fine Gael in every area
- Fianna Fáil very involved in local committees and often seem to have access to money to pay activists
- Fianna Fáil make it happen, Fine Gael let it happen. Fianna Fáil want to be in power all the time
- Fianna Fáil are more in touch with the ordinary folk
- Fianna Fáil are much more conservative in expressing their views, unlike Fine Gael they do not show their hand and think afterwards, some Fine Gael pronouncements over the years have been disastrous
- Fianna Fáil have the best organisation machine for winning elections
- Fianna Fáil better able to communicate with public, Fine Gael needs to be more approachable to ordinary voters
- Fianna Fáil are more in touch with grassroots politics, their leader is on top of the world, after all the scandal. What does that say about Fine Gael?
- Fianna Fáil are better at getting their message across and their TDs are better at working at local level
- Fianna Fáil was and is inherently corrupt. However, it is better organised and appeals to more people. Its policies are basically the same as Fine Gael on most issues yet Fine Gael is seen as aloof to voters and party members alike
- Fine Gael honest and ineffective, Fianna Fáil still corrupt but effective.

Many of the members in this category speak about a lack of contact with party TDs (there are echoes here of the kind of complaint heard in earlier decades, which we mentioned in chapters 3 and 6) and sometimes draw a contrast with what they believe the situation to be in Fianna Fáil. In Fine Gael, some respondents feel, members are less appreciated and, perhaps in consequence, less committed:

- Fine Gael not much good at standing up to Fianna Fáil. Fianna Fáil listen to members better
- If Fine Gael gave as much support and attention to its members (and not just the chosen few) as Fianna Fáil do we would be as strong if not stronger than Fianna Fáil
- Fianna Fáil party machine is much better than ours, we are lacking in commitment – with Fianna Fáil the party always comes first, not so with Fine Gael. Some older members get angry when ministers do not get them favours and can be very disruptive at election time when branch members are trying to

hold the seat for TD

- All Fianna Fáil I know seem to be well looked after by the party
- Fianna Fáil TDs are far closer and more involved with their local cumainn than Fine Gael TDs
- Fianna Fáil are more confident, lots of Fine Gael people are afraid to say that they are Fine Gael
- The Fianna Fáil public reps seem to keep in contact with party members more
- Fianna Fáil are more professional at winning votes and its supporters are more outspoken while Fine Gael supporters seem to be less active
- Fianna Fáil is essentially a party of government for most of its existence and has an insatiable appetite for power at almost any price. Fine Gael is essentially a party of opposition where most of its parliamentarians seem quite happy to remain
- The main difference is the commitment, Fianna Fáil are professional whereas we are not, everything is haphazard
- Being a member of Fianna Fáil seems to be more of a commitment than being a member of Fine Gael
- Fine Gael members tend to be more reserved and almost secretive about membership
- Fianna Fáil look after their members over the years much better than Fine Gael.

The area of policy most often cited is Northern Ireland (the response given by 9 per cent of members), although a few of the responses that we have categorised under this heading tended to point to the Treaty split of eighty years ago rather than to current policy as the main difference. Examples of these responses are:

- The only difference I can see is that some people are still bitter over the civil war
- The main difference is in feelings of party members at branch level. There is still a lot of belief in the causes of the Irish civil war
- Fianna Fáil is still fighting the civil war and Fine Gael is not
- No difference only civil war hatred.

Among those members who identify the parties' current policies on Northern Ireland as the main difference between Fianna Fáil and Fine Gael, there is a sharp division between those who favour Fine Gael's approach and those who see Northern Ireland as the least acceptable aspect of Fine Gael. Some members are supportive of their party and critical of Fianna Fáil:

- Fianna Fáil are only able to see one side of the equation as regards Northern Ireland (nationalist). Fine Gael has always put forward a more equal approach and have always been more stern in their condemnation of terrorism
- Fianna Fáil are out and out republicans, Fine Gael are a more moderate party, the Irish SDLP
- Fine Gael more likely to see the broad picture, Fianna Fáil still caught up in nationalist politics and reactive policies
- Fine Gael treat Northern Ireland even-handedly
- I feel on Northern Ireland Fine Gael have a more balanced view, Fianna Fáil are

too close to Sinn Féin and the IRA
- The Fianna Fáil leadership pays too much attention to their grassroots members, the ones who think the British never left and who are still anxious to fight the fights their fathers fought
- Fine Gael has a social conscience, are an open and receptive party in pluralist mode. Fianna Fáil still has and indeed at times prides itself with its pseudo republicanism and baggage from its foundation days
- The continued Fianna Fáil belief that the Unionists can be bullied into a united Ireland.

Other members, though, are clearly more in sympathy with Fianna Fáil's stance on Northern Ireland. Although we saw in the previous chapter that not many members (only about 14 per cent) believe that Irish governments should have special regard for northern nationalists, some evidently felt in 1999 that the party's stance was becoming unduly skewed in favour of northern unionists. Such members, then, wanted Fine Gael to become more nationalist, but in their eyes this would have redressed the existing pro-unionist leaning and made the party's stance more balanced rather than necessarily pro-nationalist.

- Northern Ireland: Fianna Fáil appear to have a more balanced view. Whereas Fine Gael very pro-Unionist (my biggest problem with Fine Gael)
- Fianna Fáil seem to listen to what the people want, Fine Gael don't have the same contact with the party grassroots. Fine Gael statements on Northern Ireland at times are out of touch with the 26 counties thinking. Fianna Fáil have a clearer policy on Northern Ireland
- Fine Gael appears Unionist, Fianna Fáil appears Nationalist
- Fine Gael seem to be more pro-Unionist
- I back Fianna Fáil policy on Northern Ireland and wholeheartedly disagree with Fine Gael especially Bruton's
- On Northern Ireland Fine Gael are too right wing
- Don't be afraid to be Irish and proud, stop appeasing the Unionists
- Fianna Fáil are more republican and better at solving Northern Ireland, Fine Gael are too pro-Unionist.

For around 6 per cent of the Fine Gael membership, the main difference between their party and Fianna Fáil is that the latter is unprincipled, opportunistic and essentially guided only by its perception of its own self-interest. Again this is very much in line with Garvin's findings from the early 1970s (see p. 183 above).

- Fine Gael is a party which puts the interests of the country and people first. Fianna Fáil have only one aim and that is to stay in power with no regard for the future of the country
- Fianna Fáil are the party of low standards, u-turns, a catchall party. The poor man's party and the rich man's party. Fine Gael are a party you could be proud of for leadership and vision
- Fianna Fáil much more cunning and devious. Good of country fairly low in Fianna Fáil's list of priorities. It is party first and foremost

- Fianna Fáil will always put the interest of Fianna Fáil before the country, eg Northern Ireland peace talks would not have gone so smoothly if Fianna Fáil were in opposition
- Fine Gael is a party of principle whose principles are frequently out of line with majority opinion eg the North, Europe, certain taxation matters, agricultural policy. Fianna Fáil are a party of pragmatists who will always move in line with majority opinion
- I think Fine Gael attempts to operate to a political philosophy – broadly the framework offered by the ideology of "social" Christian Democracy. I have no sense of Fianna Fáil being anchored by anything other than pragmatic short term political gain
- Fianna Fáil always take care of their own, Fine Gael always put the country first eg Tallaght Strategy in 87–89
- The main difference is a cultural one, Fianna Fáil have a cute hoor culture always with the hand out, will always attempt to play to the gallery, with no thought given to the consequences of such actions
- Our desire, however misplaced or unpopular, to do the right thing
- Fine Gael is more policy driven and is loyal to its principles, whereas Fianna Fáil will change its policies at the whim of the electorate
- Fine Gael's basic mind frame is to do the right thing at all costs, Fianna Fáil's is to count the cost first then do what is most suitable for Fianna Fáil.

A number of other responses were given, but, as Table 8.5 shows, no other policy area was cited by more than a small number of members. A few said that the main difference was that Fine Gael was more liberal than Fianna Fáil. Others (though very few) identified the main difference in terms relating to the left–right dimension of politics, sometimes alleging that Fianna Fáil's supporters are better off than Fine Gael supporters – an opinion that, as we saw in chapter 4, is not borne out by the evidence:

- Fine Gael is for an equal society, not, like Fianna Fáil, for the rich in society
- Fine Gael party is for the working man and Fianna Fáil is for the big farmer and big business
- Fianna Fáil are for the rich people in our country, they proved it in the budget. I think Fine Gael are for the ordinary person on the street or in the country
- Fianna Fáil look after wealthy and Fine Gael look after the ordinary person
- Unfortunately people still see Fianna Fáil as leaning more towards the working class and Fine Gael as middle to upper class
- Fianna Fáil are more for farmers and Fine Gael are more for business
- Fine Gael are more in touch with need of professionals and businessmen
- Fine Gael is more for middle class people, Fianna Fáil attracts lower class people. Fine Gael members are more conservative
- I believe Fine Gael is better than Fianna Fáil party and they are more for the low pay working class
- Fine Gael more interested in the welfare of low pay workers, agri sector and elderly
- The perception seems to be that Fianna Fáil would represent the working class and Fine Gael would be more middle class
- Main difference is that Fine Gael are more representative of all sections of the community and more conscious of the needs of the underprivileged sections

- I see Fianna Fáil as more right-wing than Fine Gael.

Finally, there is a miscellaneous group of responses that defy categorisation; a few of these believe that Fine Gael's personnel are of higher quality than their Fianna Fáil counterparts:

- Fine Gael TDs slightly more intelligent
- Fine Gael seem to have a much higher calibre of candidate
- Fianna Fáil will never match Fine Gael, they don't have the calibre of members from their party leader down to the ordinary branch member at grassroots
- Fine Gael appear to be anti-Fianna Fáil rather than stating a policy of their own
- The main difference being Fianna Fáil treat politics like a religion, Fine Gael however can see both sides, more tolerant of people and their views.

Summing up these findings, it is striking that most members define the difference between the two parties in terms of style or ethos rather than in policy terms. Fine Gael is seen as a party of greater integrity, one that is true to its principles even when these are not popular. Some members, indeed, wish it would bend a little more to the wishes of the public on occasion – a theme that, as we saw in chapter 2, goes right back to the days of Cumann na nGaedheal. A significant number of members see no real difference at all between the parties. Only a minority of members, around 16 per cent, cite a policy area as marking the main difference between the parties, and the area most often mentioned is Northern Ireland. Even here, some members say that in the policy area where the two parties differ most, they actually prefer Fianna Fáil's policy. Only a few members give an answer that relates to the left–right dimension of politics, and the parties' positions on the "liberal agenda" issues are also not seen as important in distinguishing them. Fine Gael members do not quite share the view of many critics of the two main parties, that they are identical twins with nothing to distinguish them, but many members do seem to see the relationship as one between an honest and principled Tweedledee that always puts the country first and an unprincipled and self-interested Tweedledum that is tainted by corruption.

In mid-1960, nearly forty years before our survey was conducted, there was a discussion between two Fine Gael TDs: the radical reformer Declan Costello and the party leader James Dillon. During the course of this, Costello said that he had asked at a recent parliamentary party meeting what exactly were the differences between Fianna Fáil and Fine Gael. The replies he received are rather reminiscent of some of those offered by Fine Gael members in late 1999. One senior colleague had said he could not identify the policy differences since he didn't know what Fine Gael's policy was on any issue; another said that there was no difference between the parties; a third had agreed but said that this didn't matter; and a fourth, Maurice Dockrell, a patrician Protestant representing Dublin South-Central, said that "the main thing was that we were decent fellows and our opponents weren't".[6] For many Fine Gael members in 1999, Dockrell's assessment still gets to the heart of the matter.

FINE GAEL AND COALITION

As we elaborated in chapter 2, up to the time of our survey in 1999 Fine Gael had taken part in coalition governments on six occasions, each time with Labour (for details see Appendix D). Up to 1989, indeed, the lines of political battle seemed very clear-cut, with Fianna Fáil on one side and Fine Gael with Labour on the other. Fianna Fáil's decision in that year to take part for the first time in a coalition government changed the ground rules; in 1989 it formed an administration with the PDs, in 1993 it took Labour as its partner, and in 1997 once again the PDs were the party with which it formed a government.[7] The coalition options seemed to have become much more open than prior to the 1990s, and accordingly we asked Fine Gael members to rank order three options.

The first was a coalition between Fianna Fáil and Fine Gael, which has long been advocated by many outside those two parties. The policy differences between them do not seem great – even, as we have just seen, to Fine Gael members themselves. As we saw in the previous chapter, Fine Gael members see Fianna Fáil as the closest party to them on the left–right spectrum, while from 1987 to 1989, Fine Gael's "Tallaght Strategy" entailed supporting a Fianna Fáil minority government, as we saw in chapter 2. For all these reasons, then, one might in theory expect Fine Gael members to be reasonably open to the prospect of a coalition with Fianna Fáil. The second option was a three-party coalition involving Fine Gael along with both Labour and the PDs, and the third consisted of just Fine Gael and Labour. We reasoned that although many members might prefer Fine Gael to have to share power with only one other party, which would point to the Fine Gael–Labour option, others would prefer to have the PDs in government as well, since Fine Gael would then be the centre party in the coalition and could expect all the government's policy decisions to be very close to its own preferred position. We did not offer members the option of a coalition with the PDs alone, even though this was offered to the electorate by both parties jointly in 1989, since the combined strength of the two parties was nowhere near enough to make this a realistic possibility.[8]

Fine Gael members were very clear in their preference (see Table 8.6). Over two-thirds of them would prefer to go into government with Labour alone, and over three-quarters of the rest opt for Labour plus the PDs as Fine Gael's partners, with a mere 7 per cent favouring the option of a link-up with Fianna Fáil. The idea of a coalition between Fine Gael and Fianna Fáil appears to be a complete non-runner, and this impression is reinforced when we look at respondents' second preferences. Among those whose first choice is Fine Gael plus Labour, most opt for Fine Gael, Labour and the PDs as their second choice, with nearly all of the rest expressing no second preference and only 4 per cent opting for Fine Gael plus Fianna Fáil. Similarly, among those whose first choice is the three-party coalition of Fine Gael, Labour and the PDs, most indicate Fine Gael plus Labour as their second choice and nearly all of the rest

Table 8.6: Fine Gael members' coalition preferences

	All members	FG and Labour	*Second preference* FG, Labour and PDs	FG and FF	No second preference	Total
First preference						
FG and Labour	69	—	56	4	40	100
FG, Labour and PDs	24	51	—	5	44	100
FG and FF	7	28	37	—	35	100
Total	100	—	—	—	—	

Source: Fine Gael members' questionnaire, questions 70.1, 70.2, 70.3.

have no second preference, with only 5 per cent going for the Fine Gael–Fianna Fáil option. Hardly any Fine Gael members can countenance the prospect of a coalition with Fianna Fáil, even as a second choice.

There is not a lot of variation between sub-groups of the membership on this question, though some sub-groups are less hostile than others to the idea of a historic grand coalition with the traditional enemy. Those members who would welcome a merger with Fianna Fáil (an idea that we will discuss in the next section), or who see no policy differences between Fine Gael and Fianna Fáil, or who want Fine Gael to move to the right on the left–right spectrum, are more likely than other members to favour a Fine Gael–Fianna Fáil coalition. In addition, those who have joined the party since 1985 are a little more likely to favour a coalition with Fianna Fáil (this is the first choice of 11 per cent of these members) than those who joined before 1985 (among whom it is the first choice of only 5 per cent).

The three-party option that would see Fine Gael in coalition with both Labour and the PDs is favoured especially by those who would welcome a merger between Fine Gael and the PDs, and by those members who feel that Irish neutrality should be dropped. Finally, the Fine Gael plus Labour option is especially strongly supported by those who place themselves on the left of the political spectrum, and by those who would like Fine Gael itself to move to the left.

THE FUTURE OF FINE GAEL

Fine Gael's electoral prospects

How optimistic are Fine Gael members about the future of their party? A recurring theme in analysis of the party at the time of its leadership change early in 2001 was that the membership was "demoralised", seeing little ahead but the prospect of a long period in opposition. Our survey did not directly ask about the morale of members, but we did ask members whether they thought Fine

Gael would continue to be the second largest party in the Irish political system in the years ahead. Specifically, we asked two questions. First, we asked whether they believed Fine Gael would overtake Fianna Fáil at any election in the next twenty years; only an optimistic member would expect this, given that Fianna Fáil has been stronger than Fine Gael at every election since 1932 and that Fine Gael had won only 54 seats at the 1997 election (the most recent when our survey was conducted) compared with Fianna Fáil's 77. The narrowest gap between the parties had come in November 1982, when Fianna Fáil won 75 seats and Fine Gael won 70. Second, we asked whether Fine Gael would be overtaken by Labour at any election in the next twenty years. This was a question designed to bring out the pessimists among the membership. Labour has never won more seats than Fine Gael, and Fine Gael held about three times as many when our survey was conducted; the closest it had ever come to Fine Gael was in 1992, when it won 33 compared with Fine Gael's 45.

Fine Gael members do not seem to be demoralised; most of them, indeed, were optimistic about the future. Almost half can foresee Fine Gael overtaking Fianna Fáil in an election before 2020, and the great majority of the rest envisage Fine Gael retaining its traditional second-party status (see Table 8.7). Only 7 per cent take the pessimistic view that Fine Gael will be pushed down to third place by Labour at some stage. A further 4 per cent expect considerable upheaval in the party system, with Fine Gael both overtaking Fianna Fáil and being overtaken by Labour, though not necessarily in the same election. This scenario is not logically impossible, though it would require an unprecedented degree of electoral volatility to bring it about.

The most optimistic members, those who expect to see Fine Gael overtake Fianna Fáil at some stage, in many ways have the characteristics that we would expect. That is, they tend to express the strongest support for Fine Gael (in response to Q1) and they are also the most active members; naturally enough, those who have the strongest faith in the eventual success of an enterprise are the most willing to devote time and energy to it. We also found that those who are happiest with the way things are at the moment, and particularly with the political status quo, are the most optimistic about Fine Gael's future, while the pessimists are the most likely to be dissatisfied. Thus optimists are to be found especially among those who feel that the PR electoral system produces good quality candidates, that Fine Gael's existing methods of candidate selection produce candidates of as high a calibre as possible, that Fine Gael makes the best use of the energy and commitment of its existing members, and that Fine Gael should move neither to right nor left, neither in a more liberal nor in a more conservative direction. In contrast, pessimists – those who expect Fine Gael to be overtaken by Labour at some stage – are to be found especially among those who do not feel the political system is working well, who want Fine Gael to move to the left, who agree that attending party meetings can be tiring after a hard day's work, or who would welcome a merger between Fine Gael and Fianna Fáil (something that we discuss below). There is no particular relationship between optimism / pessimism and the current electoral strength of Fine

Table 8.7: Fine Gael members' assessment of party's prospects in the next twenty years

	Percentage agreeing
Fine Gael will overtake Fianna Fáil in at least one election ("optimists")	49
Fine Gael will neither overtake Fianna Fáil nor be overtaken by Labour	40
Fine Gael will be overtaken by Labour in at least one election ("pessimists")	7
Fine Gael will overtake Fianna Fáil in at least one election and will also be overtaken by Labour in at least one election	4
Total	100

Source: Fine Gael members' questionnaire, questions 82, 83.

Gael in each member's constituency.

Some other characteristics of the most optimistic members are less predictable. In terms of their social profile, they are disproportionately older than other members, with only a national school education, and, occupationally, retired people or home makers. The longest-serving members – those who have been in the party for 25 years or more – are the most optimistic. There seems to be a sense in which these members are expressing their confidence that the future is bright for Fine Gael, even if they themselves may not be around to see it. Younger members, and those with a university education, are the most likely to be pessimists. In addition, there is a significant though unexpected relationship with the local or national orientations of members. Locally oriented members – those who prioritise a local role for a TD (Q81.2), those who believe that the most effective campaigning methods are those involving personal contact with the voters (Q111), and those who have had personal contact with a Fine Gael councillor in the last twelve months[9] – are the most likely to be optimists. In contrast, the more nationally oriented members – those who prioritise a national role for TDs, who believe that the most effective campaigning methods are those involving national activity (Q113), and who have not had contact with a local Fine Gael councillor – are the most likely to be pessimistic. For example, of those who have had contact with a Fine Gael councillor, 51 per cent are optimists and 6 per cent are pessimists; of those who haven't had such contact, 36 per cent are optimists and 14 per cent are pessimists. It seems that those who believe in and are active at the grass roots are the most likely to feel that their hard local work will eventually pay dividends, while those whose focus is on national-level activities and who believe that the party's future is determined primarily by what it does at national level have less confidence that Fine Gael's future is bright.

The possibility of a merger

One way in which Fine Gael could transform its position is by merging with another party. We asked members whether they would favour Fine Gael merging with Fianna Fáil and whether they would favour its merging with the PDs. Of these, the second is by far the more realistic prospect. The PDs are a small party whose policy differences with Fine Gael appear minor and who, having been founded as recently as 1985, do not carry very much historical baggage that would stand in the way of a merger. From Fine Gael's point of view, a merger would have a lot of advantages; given the difference in size between the two parties, it would really be more of a takeover than a merger. It would result in the elimination of a rival for the support of the kind of voters that Fine Gael particularly appeals to: urban, middle class, socially liberal and economically right-wing. In addition, it would damage Fianna Fáil, for whom the PDs had at the time of our survey twice (in 1989 and 1997) been a crucial coalition ally. If the PDs could be absorbed into Fine Gael, Fianna Fáil's ability to stay in government and thus exclude Fine Gael from power would be greatly reduced. A merger between the two parties was under discussion for several months in 1993 until the PD leader Des O'Malley ruled it out. It would, then, be perfectly rational for Fine Gael members to welcome the PDs should that party seek to merge with Fine Gael.

In contrast, the chances of a merger between the country's largest two parties are slim; not only are their historical traditions antithetical to one another, but, from a Fine Gael point of view, such a move would mean the effective end of the party given Fianna Fáil's larger size. In addition, given what unkind critics have characterised as the Tweedledee–Tweedledum relationship between the two parties, a merger might seem to deprive Fine Gael (and indeed Fianna Fáil) of a significant part of its raison d'être. However, we deemed the idea worth testing among the membership since, as we have remarked before, not only commentators but also, as our survey shows, many Fine Gael members themselves are unable to identify any policy differences between the two parties these days.

Our findings on this were rather surprising, with much more support for the idea of a merger than we had expected.[10] A clear majority of Fine Gael members, 61 per cent of them, are in favour of a merger with another party (see Table 8.8). Most members (55 per cent) would welcome a merger with the PDs, and a remarkable 19 per cent are in favour of merging with Fianna Fáil (this is especially surprising given the low support for a coalition with that party that we discussed earlier). Even more extraordinarily, 11 per cent are zealous proponents of a major rationalisation of the centre-right of the Irish party system who would like Fine Gael to merge with *both* Fianna Fáil and the PDs!

We did not ask any open questions on this subject, so we cannot be certain why nearly a fifth of the Fine Gael membership would be willing to see the party merge with its traditional opponent. It may be that many of those saying that they would welcome a merger reasoned that the idea could become realistic only if both parties lost significant support, and in that context it would make sense for them to bury the hatchet and bring the centrist forces together under

Table 8.8: Fine Gael members' attitudes to a merger between Fine Gael and another party, by change in activity level over past four years

| | Percentage in favour | Activity level compared with four years ago | | | |
		More active	No change	Less active	Total
No merger	39	24	45	31	100
Merge with PDs alone	43	19	51	29	100
Merge with FF alone	7	19	50	31	100
Merge with both FF and PDs	11	15	44	41	100
Total	100	—	—	—

Source: Fine Gael members' questionnaire, questions 14, 84, 85.

one label, rather than remain fragmented and leave themselves open to being dominated (in policy terms) in coalition by parties to their right or their left, or being compelled to dance to the tune of independents holding the balance of power. On paper, a merger of Fianna Fáil and Fine Gael would create a virtually unbeatable combination, a giant centre party that could be ousted only by an unholy and unstable alliance of right and left. The idea of a merger or a coalition between the parties has been mooted occasionally by figures within one or other party, but most observers of the Irish political scene would regard the prospect of a merger as extremely remote in the foreseeable future, and it is remarkable that so many Fine Gael members said they would welcome the idea.

Although the question of a merger does not bear directly on the degree of demoralisation among the Fine Gael membership, the fact that almost one in five members would welcome a merger with Fine Gael's larger rival suggests a disturbing lack of confidence on the part of some members in Fine Gael's future as a stand-alone party. Certainly, attitudes to a possible merger do seem to be related to enthusiasm for Fine Gael and optimism about its future. Generally, those whose professed support for Fine Gael is strongest, and those who are most active, are the most likely to say that Fine Gael should not merge with either Fianna Fáil or the PDs. Members who report that they have become more active are least keen on a merger, while those who have recently become less active are the most likely to favour a merger with both Fianna Fáil and the PDs (Table 8.8). Given the passive nature of the question (Q85 asked members not whether they positively wanted a merger to come about but whether they would welcome one if it occurred), plus the fact that the least active members are the most likely to welcome a merger, we can infer that there are not many Fine Gael members who are actively pressing or calling for a merger.

Naturally enough, those who show support for either of the prospective partners are more likely to favour a merger with that party. Thus those giving high thermometer scores to the PDs and to its leader Mary Harney (we discuss the scores of individual politicians later in the chapter), and whose first choice of government is a coalition with the PDs and Labour, are the most likely to favour a merger with the PDs; those who give high thermometer scores to Fianna Fáil, to its leader and to past Fianna Fáil Taoisigh, and those who would choose a coalition with Fianna Fáil ahead of the alternatives, are the most likely to favour a merger with Fianna Fáil. Those giving a high thermometer score to Fine Gael and to its past Taoisigh are the least likely to favour merger with Fianna Fáil.

Taking first the more realistic possibility, that of a merger with the PDs, attitudes are clearly affected by perceptions of the PDs' policy positions. Thus members who are against decisive government action to redistribute wealth, are for further European integration, or are for the dropping of Irish neutrality, are all especially strongly in favour of a merger with the PDs. Members who place themselves on the right-hand side of the left–right scale are the most likely to favour this merger, as are *Irish Times* readers, those who are or have been in Young Fine Gael, members in urban areas (where the PDs have nearly all their strength) and older members. Home owners are more likely than those living in rented accommodation to favour merging with the PDs, yet, surprisingly, there is no sign of a relationship with private / public sector employment. The PDs' critics argue that the party is hostile to the state sector, and during the 1997 election campaign the party had "attracted much criticism" by proposing to make significant cuts in public sector employment.[11] Nevertheless, among those members employed in the public sector (in the state sector, the semi-state sector, by a local authority or by a health board) the proportion favouring merger with the PDs, at 55 per cent, was just the same as the proportion among other members. Attitudes to a possible merger with the PDs are not related to optimism or pessimism about Fine Gael's future.

In contrast, those whom we have dubbed the pessimists, who expect Fine Gael to be overtaken by Labour at an election in the next twenty years, are the most likely to be in favour of a merger with Fianna Fáil (29 per cent of the pessimists want this, compared with only 17 per cent of other members). Not only those who are most active, but also those who are most interested in national political issues, are the most likely to oppose a possible merger with Fianna Fáil. Those who joined Fine Gael for "solidary" or "material" reasons are the least opposed to the prospect of a merger; those who joined to put Fine Gael into government, or out of opposition to Fianna Fáil, are the least in favour. Interestingly, there is no sign that historical antagonism is a crucial factor; for example, there is no relationship between attitudes to a merger on the one hand, and whether or not the member comes from a family with a tradition of supporting Fine Gael and Cumann na nGaedheal back to the civil war on the other. When we relate attitudes to merger with Fianna Fáil with what members identify as the main policy differences between Fine Gael and Fianna Fáil (Q86), members identifying Northern Ireland as the key policy difference between the two parties are hardly any less likely to favour a merger with Fianna Fáil than members generally (see Table 8.9). Those who see Europe, agriculture or taxation as the main bones of contention are the least likely to want Fine Gael to throw in its lot with Fianna Fáil; those who cannot think of any policy differences are, not

Table 8.9: Fine Gael members' attitudes to a possible merger with Fianna Fáil, by perceptions of the main policy difference between Fine Gael and Fianna Fáil

| | Attitude to possible future merger with Fianna Fáil | | |
	In favour	Against	Total
Main policy difference			
Europe	9	91	100
Agriculture	9	91	100
Other	12	88	100
Taxation	13	87	100
Northern Ireland	18	82	100
No real policy differences	28	72	100
All members	19	81	100

Source: Fine Gael members' questionnaire, questions 85, 86.

surprisingly, the least resistant to the suggestion.

When we relate attitudes to a merger with responses to our open question about how Fine Gael differs from Fianna Fáil (Q87), we find, once again, that those who see no difference are the most likely to welcome a merger, as we would expect; over a third of these people would be happy with such a development (see Table 8.10).[12] Among those who believe that the main difference between the parties is something relating to nationalism (either the civil war legacy or Northern Ireland), over a quarter would welcome a merger, as would nearly as many among those who have a grudging admiration for Fianna Fáil and regard it as better organised and more active. The strongest opposition comes from those who regard the main difference between the two parties as consisting not of policy but of ethos. There is overwhelming opposition from these members, i.e. from those who believe that the most important difference is that Fine Gael is a party of greater integrity and honesty than Fianna Fáil and/or feel that Fine Gael is motivated primarily by patriotism while Fianna Fáil's sole ideology is self-interest.

In summary, most Fine Gael members do not seem to be demoralised. Most of them expect that the party will leave the first division – if we can describe the party's current status in that way – at some stage over the next twenty years, with far more expecting promotion to the premier division than relegation to division two. The most active members, and those who are most satisfied with the way things are at the moment both within the party and in the political system generally, are the most likely to believe that the future is bright. Most members are in favour of a merger with the PDs, a step that can be advocated in purely tactical terms since it would most probably strengthen Fine Gael's position in post-election bargaining and would weaken Fianna Fáil's position. However, there is an undercurrent of pessimism within the party. There is a relatively dispirited, low-morale group of members, somewhere between 7 and

Table 8.10: Fine Gael members' attitudes to a possible merger with Fianna Fáil, by perceptions of the main difference between Fine Gael and Fianna Fáil

| | Attitude to possible future merger with Fianna Fáil | | |
	In favour	Against	Total
Main difference			
No difference	38	62	100
Civil war legacy / Northern Ireland	28	72	100
Fianna Fáil is more active, better organised	26	74	100
Integrity, honesty	12	88	100
Fine Gael puts country first, Fianna Fáil populist and will do anything to get votes	9	91	100
Total	19	81	100

Source: Fine Gael members' questionnaire, questions 85, 87.

19 per cent of the total depending on exactly which measure is used, who do not see a bright future for Fine Gael. Members in this category are the most likely to predict that Fine Gael will be overtaken by Labour at an election before 2019, and are the most willing to welcome a merger between Fine Gael and Fianna Fáil, which would effectively signal the end of Fine Gael. These members are already "voting with their feet"; they are low in both activity and enthusiasm for the party, and we suspect that they are the most likely to leave Fine Gael. As Table 8.8 shows, activism levels have dropped most among those who want Fine Gael to merge with both other parties and have dropped least among those who oppose any merger. Disturbingly for the party, older members are the most optimistic, while young members (who have no memory of the glory days of 1977–83) with a university education are the most likely to be pessimists

EVALUATIONS OF INDIVIDUAL POLITICIANS

Past Taoisigh

As well as asking Fine Gael members how they rated the political parties (as we saw in an earlier section of this chapter) and how they rate some current prominent politicians (as we shall see in the next sub-section), we sought their views on the ten individuals who had held the position of Taoiseach (prime minister) in the past (see Appendix D for biographical notes on these individuals). The results confirm that Fine Gael Taoisigh are the more popular, as we would expect, averaging 67 on the thermometer compared with 40 for the Fianna Fáil Taoisigh (see Figure 8.2). However, there is considerable variation among each party's champions. Of the five Fine Gael former Taoisigh, Garret FitzGerald is clearly the most popular; FitzGerald is still seen as the leader who modernised the party after becoming leader in 1977 and took it to new electoral heights in the 1980s. Cosgrave *père* and *fils* and John Bruton all lag some way behind FitzGerald; the relatively low rating of Bruton compared with other Fine Gael leaders emphasises the lack of enthusiasm for his leadership that was to result in his ousting sixteen months after our survey started. The fifth Fine Gael Taoiseach, John A. Costello, is the least popular, marginally below the top-rated Fianna Fáil Taoiseach. There is no particular reason why Costello should be unpopular with Fine Gael members, and his relatively low score may simply reflect the fact that many Fine Gael members have little knowledge of him and his record.

Among the five Fianna Fáil former Taoisigh, the extent of variation is greater. Both Jack Lynch and Seán Lemass are evaluated positively (i.e their average scores are above 50), reflecting the conventional wisdom that their popularity extended beyond the ranks of Fianna Fáil supporters, partly because they were seen as somewhat detached from some of the perceived traditions of their party that Fine Gael members are least enthusiastic about. Lemass was a moderniser who is generally credited with giving priority to economic growth when he became Taoiseach after decades of stagnation and for downplaying the traditional nationalism of his party regarding Northern Ireland.[13] Lynch would be remembered by many Fine Gael members for having stood up to the hardliners within his party on the Northern Ireland issue during the 1970s, and for the "immense popularity" that he enjoyed among voters across the political spectrum due to "his sporting background (in Gaelic football and hurling) and personable character".[14] Albert Reynolds is evaluated less favourably – he was, after all, a fairly recent rival and was seen as much more combative towards other parties than Lynch was – and Eamon de Valera, whom some Fine Gael members in earlier decades would have regarded as close to being the devil incarnate, was less popular still. By some way the least highly regarded former Taoiseach is Charles Haughey, who was not highly thought of by other parties' supporters even in his heyday, and whose stock had fallen even lower by the time of our survey due to revelations about the large scale on which he had been receiving money from business interests and then spending it on a champagne lifestyle.[15]

There are certain common patterns. In the case of all five Fine Gael former Taoisigh, the more strongly a member supports Fine Gael and the more active he or she is within the party, the more highly he or she evaluates the Taoiseach. Those who are the most optimistic about the party's future are likely to give Fine Gael former Taoisigh higher scores than the pessimists award. In addition, those who come from a family with a tradition of supporting Fine Gael right back to the civil war of 1922–23 (Q7) evaluate these Taoisigh more highly than other members. This is particularly marked in the case of the first prime minister, William T. Cosgrave; members with such a family background give him an average score of 69, while other members rate him at 60. Evidently the family back-

Figure 8.2: Fine Gael members' evaluations of past Taoisigh

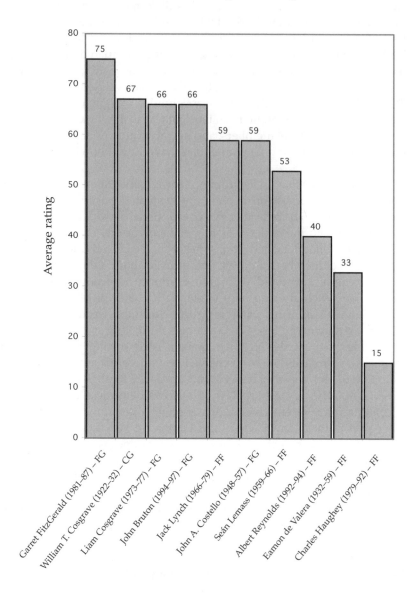

Source: Fine Gael members' questionnaire, questions 88 to 97.
Note: The maximum score is 99, denoting a very positive feeling, and the minimum is 0, indicating a very negative feeling. The dates are the years when the individual first became Taoiseach and last held that office. The office of prime minister was known as President of the Executive Council before 1937.

ground of members has played a part in socialising them into a set of attitudes that is broadly supportive of the party's traditions and its former leaders. Older members are more enthusiastic than younger ones about four of the leaders, the exception being FitzGerald, who is strongest among middle-aged members. Length of membership is positively related to rating of William T. Cosgrave, John A. Costello and Liam Cosgrave, but is unrelated to rating of John Bruton.

FitzGerald scores highly among members of all backgrounds and is especially highly rated by those who joined Fine Gael during the period when he was at his most popular nationally, between approximately 1973 and 1983. He is also very slightly more highly rated among readers of the *Irish Times* than among members who read other (or no) newspapers – it would be worrying if it were otherwise, given that he writes a weekly column for that newspaper!

To some extent members' political views affect their evaluations. Those who go to church most often, and who feel the church has too little influence in the education system, tend to give relatively high scores to both Cosgraves and to Costello, each of whom held what would now be seen as very conservative views on church-related matters. In contrast, FitzGerald, whose last government promoted the unsuccessful divorce referendum in 1986, scores more highly among those members who voted or worked for the Yes side in the 1995 divorce referendum. FitzGerald does a little better among those who want Fine Gael to move in a more liberal direction than among those who want it to become more conservative; the only other Taoiseach to whom this applies is Bruton, but here the difference is smaller. Even so, while it would be tempting to speak of a more conservative "old guard" and a more liberal wing (a "FitzGerald generation") among the membership, this would be to exaggerate the magnitude of the differences that actually exist. We also found that there is no relationship between support for FitzGerald and support either for further European integration or for replacing the PR-STV electoral system, both causes with which he is associated.

We noted earlier that optimists rate the Fine Gael former Taoisigh more highly than pessimists do, and this is especially marked in the case of John Bruton. Those who expect Fine Gael to overtake Fianna Fáil at an election in the next twenty years give him an average score of 72, those who expect Fine Gael to remain the second largest party give him 63, and those who think Fine Gael will be overtaken by Labour give him only 52. The last group epitomise the "demoralised" members cited by Bruton's opponents in early 2001 as part of their justification for launching a challenge to Bruton's leadership – though of course they are small in number, amounting to only 7 per cent of the members (Table 8.7). In general Bruton scores lowest among those who are unhappy about something within the party: among those who feel that Fine Gael does not make best use of its members, those who do not agree that existing candidate selection methods are best, and those who feel that Fine Gael pays little attention to its members.[16]

Turning to the Fianna Fáil former Taoisigh, we have already noted the considerable variation in their scores. Here too there are common patterns, some of which are entirely predictable: for example, those who would like Fine Gael to coalesce or merge with Fianna Fáil, and those who see no policy differences between Fine Gael and Fianna Fáil, tend to evaluate the Fianna Fáil former Taoisigh more favourably than other members do. Strength of support for Fine Gael is negatively related to evaluation of de Valera and Reynolds, who are evidently seen by the members as partisan Fianna Fáil figures, but is not related to evaluation of Lemass and Lynch, who attract a degree of respect across the board. Nor is there any pronounced relationship with members' views on Northern Ireland; one might expect Fianna Fáil former Taoisigh to be scored most highly by those Fine Gael members who want Irish governments to have special regard for Northern Ireland nationalists, but only in the case of Reynolds is this true. Haughey is highly unpopular with virtually all Fine Gael members, whatever their background or their views on other issues, with little variation across sub-groups. A quarter of members give him a score of precisely zero, and two-thirds give him a score of 10 or less.

De Valera, Lynch and Reynolds all tend to be rated most highly by members who voted against divorce and who want church influence in the education system to be increased. De Valera scores highest among older members, perhaps surprisingly, but scores a little lower among members who come from a Fine Gael family background (his score here is 32) than among members without this background (37). Lemass, unlike the other Fianna Fáil former Taoisigh, is evaluated most favourably by those with most education and also by readers of the *Irish Times*, which was never his favourite paper.[17] Lemass, a Dubliner, is also most popular with members from Dublin (they give a score of 58, while other members rate him at 52), while Lynch, though not noticeably more popular among members from his home province of Munster, is rated most highly (at 62) by readers of the *Examiner*, which is based in his beloved city of Cork.

Current politicians

We also asked members how they rate a number of current political figures: the leaders of the main political parties north and south of the border (see Appendix D for biographical notes). As Table 8.11 (in which John Bruton's score, already shown in Figure 8.2, is repeated for convenience) shows, attitudes vary widely. John Hume is by some way the most popular figure, and the high regard in which he is held crosses virtually all boundaries within the party. Along with Garret FitzGerald, he is the most popular political figure among Fine Gael members. The only groups with rather less esteem for him are non-Catholics (who rate him at 65) and those who believe that the government's Northern Ireland policy should show special regard for unionists, as shown in the table – both of these, of course, are small groups. Indeed, attitudes to Northern Ireland policy were, as we would have expected, quite a strong determinant of evaluations of Northern Ireland politicians. Among those who want government policy to favour nationalists, Gerry Adams, the Sinn Féin leader, is more popular than all other leaders except Bruton and Hume. In contrast, among those who want unionists to receive special treatment, David Trimble, the leader of the Ulster

Unionist party, is second only to Bruton.

The support profile of Bertie Ahern, who was Fianna Fáil leader and Taoiseach at the time of our survey, closely resembles that of the former Fianna Fáil Taoisigh whom we discussed in the previous section; he is least popular among those Fine Gael members who are most active, most strongly supportive of Fine Gael and most interested in politics, while he is most popular among those who would welcome a merger or a coalition with Fianna Fáil. The Labour leader, Ruairí Quinn, like his party, fares best among the strongest supporters of Fine Gael and among those who are most interested in politics. He is only marginally more popular among members on the left than among those on the right or in the centre, but does fare better among those who believe Fine Gael should move to the left (who give him an average score of 54) than those who want the party to stay where it is (they give him 50) or those who want it to move to the right (here he scores 45). Mary Harney, the leader of the Progressive Democrats, in contrast, fares better among those who want Fine Gael to move to the right, who oppose government measures to redistribute wealth, or who want further European integration. In all these respects her scores reflect the policy stance of her and her party, but in other respects the relationships are not as expected: she is strongest among those who believe the church has too little influence in the education system, among those who go to church most often, and among those employed by the state. She is stronger among *Irish Times* readers than among readers of other papers, but is marginally weaker among women than among men despite being the first female leader of an Irish political party.

The variation among members when it comes to evaluating Gerry Adams is greater than for other leaders. His support varies inversely with strength of support for Fine Gael (the strongest supporters give him 33, the weakest sup-

Table 8.11: Fine Gael members' evaluations of current politicians, by views on preferred Northern Ireland policy

| | Government policy towards Northern Ireland should | | | |
	Have special regard for nationalists	Be even-handed	Have special regard for unionists	All members
John Hume (SDLP)	76	77	54	75
John Bruton (FG)	62	66	66	66
Ruairí Quinn (Labour)	47	51	43	50
Mary Harney (PDs)	45	47	43	46
David Trimble (UUP)	37	44	58	44
Bertie Ahern (FF)	41	39	29	39
Gerry Adams (SF)	49	34	33	36
Ian Paisley (DUP)	14	15	28	15

Source: Fine Gael members' questionnaire, questions 51, 104 to 110.
Note: Figures are average thermometer scores. The maximum score is 99, denoting a very positive feeling, and the minimum is 0, indicating a very negative feeling.

porters give him 50) and with activism. He is weakest among non-Catholics (they give him an average score of 24), among those who favour dropping Irish neutrality (33) and those who believe that Northern Ireland policy is the main difference between Fianna Fáil and Fine Gael (31). Comparing Table 8.11 with Table 8.1 shows that Adams is considerably more popular than his party. Neither David Trimble nor Ian Paisley (the leader of the Democratic Unionist party) is much stronger among one sub-group than other, apart from those who want Irish governments to have special regard for Northern Ireland unionists (Table 8.11). Trimble receives a slightly cooler than neutral rating right across the board (50 is the score denoting neutrality) while Paisley, like Charles Haughey, is unpopular with members of all backgrounds and opinions.

Taking all these scores together, deeper exploration of the data by such techniques as correlation analysis and factor analysis can reveal whether the attitudes of Fine Gael members are simply a series of ad hoc responses to individual politicians or whether some fundamental structure underpins them. As the above discussion has strongly suggested, such analysis fails to discover any such basic structure. Consistent with our findings in earlier chapters, it is true that there are differences of opinion on certain questions – some members are more liberal and others are more conservative, some are further to the right and others further to the left, some are more nationalist and others are less nationalist when it comes to Northern Ireland policy – but we do not detect the existence of distinct ideological groups or factions among the membership, because the lines of division produced by each issue cut across each other rather than reinforcing each other. Two members who agree with each other on one issue are quite likely to disagree on another one.

When we compare members' attitudes to some politicians with their attitudes to others, we don't find very much that we would not have expected. Correlating the scores awarded to the various politicians shows, predictably, that those giving higher scores to one former Fine Gael Taoiseach also give higher scores to another, and the same is true on the Fianna Fáil side; this is especially marked for Lemass and Lynch.[18] These findings are consistent with what we have seen throughout this study, namely that opinions among the membership are not highly structured.

THE FUNCTIONING OF THE IRISH POLITICAL SYSTEM

The Irish political system, as far as we can tell, has been positively regarded by most citizens over the years since independence. However, at the time of our survey, in autumn 1999, the image of the system had definitely lost some of its lustre. The newspapers featured a steady flow of stories about corruption – proved or alleged – and a number of tribunals were sitting in order to try to find out how much money had been given by business interests to politicians and what favours if any had been received in return.[19] The long-term downward trend in general election turnout, from 77 per cent in 1973 to 66 per cent in 1997, was causing concern and a general sense that perhaps the institutions of the conventional political system were becoming less relevant to many people.

In order to measure the views of Fine Gael members towards the status quo and political reform, we asked eight questions (Q54 to Q61 on the questionnaire). One was a general question, asking members whether they felt that the Irish political system was working well, and we asked about specific reforms that have been proposed to the system. First, given that Ireland is generally seen as a country where government is exceptionally strong and parliament is exceptionally weak, we asked whether members felt that the Dáil should be reformed to allow the opposition parties more power. Second, we asked whether Seanad Éireann, the virtually powerless upper house, should be abolished. Third, we enquired about members' attitudes to increasing the power of local government. In addition, we asked an open question (Q61) inviting members to give their own suggestions as to what, if any, changes should be made.

The remaining three questions all concerned the PR-STV electoral system. Over the last twenty years, a number of politicians from the major parties have suggested that this system should be replaced, the essence of the argument being that the internal battles between candidates of the same party competing against each other for first preference votes force TDs into a pattern of behaviour that emphasises constituency work and an undue focus on local matters rather than attention on parliamentary work and national political matters. In addition, it is suggested, individuals of high calibre, looking at the large volume of constituency work they will need to discharge in order to be able to survive electorally so as to make a contribution to national politics, are inclined to shun a political career. Among those who have argued along these lines have been several prominent Fine Gael figures, such as former Taoiseach Garret FitzGerald and former ministers John Boland and Gemma Hussey, as well as leading Fianna Fáil politicians such as Charles Haughey, Albert Reynolds, Noel Dempsey and Micheál Martin.[20] Changing the electoral system, then, is probably the most widely offered recipe for curing the ills of the Irish body politic. Consequently we asked members whether they felt that the electoral system produces good quality TDs; whether it forces TDs to spend too much time on constituency work; and whether it should be replaced by another system that does not entail any intra-party competition for votes.

On the general question of whether the Irish political system is working well, we found a high degree of satisfaction; so high, indeed, that some might characterise it as complacency (see Figure 8.3). Fewer than a third of members feel that the political system is not working well. In general, those who are happiest with other things are the most likely to be satisfied with the political system. Those who feel that Fine Gael's candidate selection methods result in the best possible calibre of candidates (Q71), who feel that Fine Gael members have enough say in determining party policy (Q66), who see no need for gender quotas (Q77), and who feel that the low number of women being selected as Fine Gael candidates reflects women's relative lack of ambition rather than unfair treatment of aspiring women candidates, are all more likely than other members to express

Figure 8.3: Satisfaction with the Irish political system

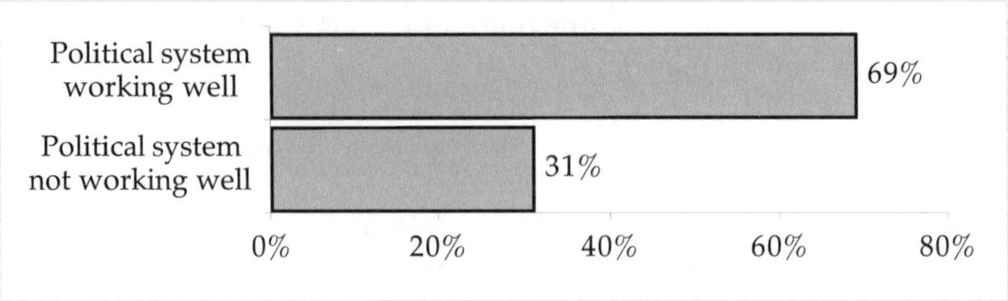

Source: Fine Gael members' questionnaire, question 60.

satisfaction with the operation of the political system. Those whose support for Fine Gael is strongest, or who hold party office, also have an above-average tendency to feel that the political system is working well. For example, among those who describe themselves as "very strong" supporters of Fine Gael, 72 per cent feel that the political system is working well; this figure drops to 68 per cent among "fairly strong" supporters, 59 per cent among "not very strong" supporters and a mere 41 per cent among those whose support is "not at all strong". Members who favour more European integration and the dropping of Irish neutrality are more likely than other members to agree that the system is working well, but with these exceptions evaluation of the system as a whole is not related to attitudes on other issues. Nor is satisfaction with the system related to class, age, education or region.

When it comes to specific reforms, those who are satisfied with the operation of the political system are, as we would expect, usually the least likely to see a need for change. Thus, those who feel that the existing system is working well are less likely than other members to want Dáil reform, abolition of the Seanad, or replacement of the electoral system; they are, though, more likely than other members to favour enhancing the power of local government. On this particular issue, as Table 8.12 shows, there is widespread agreement among the Fine Gael membership. Most of the other proposed changes divide the membership. There is widespread support for reforming the Dáil to give the opposition more power, a virtually even split on the question of abolishing the Seanad, and, on balance, opposition to the idea of dropping the PR–STV electoral system.

Three of these items (reforming the Dáil, abolishing the Seanad, and increasing the power of local government) can be seen as running together, since they each relate to the question of concentration of power (characteristic of what has been termed majoritarian democracy) versus diffusion of power (characteristic of consensus democracy).[21] Those who prefer majoritarian democracy and believe strongly in the idea that "governments must govern", preferably with as few obstructions as possible, would be likely to oppose Dáil reform and greater power for the opposition and to favour abolishing the Seanad. Those who favour consensus democracy, in contrast, can be expected to welcome the suggestion that the power of the government be checked by other actors such as the

Table 8.12: Attitudes towards reform of the Irish political system

	Balance in favour	Strongly agree	Agree	Neutral	Disagree	Strongly disagree	Total
Increase power of local government	+69	63	16	10	3	7	100
PR electoral system produces good quality TDs	+44	46	17	18	7	12	100
Reform Dáil to give opposition more power	+28	38	17	19	10	17	100
PR electoral system forces TDs to spend too much time on constituency work	+11	29	17	19	11	24	100
Abolish Seanad	+2	36	7	15	10	31	100
PR electoral system should be replaced	-12	26	10	16	11	38	100

Source: Fine Gael members' questionnaire, questions 54, 55, 56, 57, 58, 59.
Note: "Balance in favour" indicates the percentage agreeing or strongly agreeing, minus the percentage disagreeing or strongly disagreeing.

opposition in the Dáil, the Seanad, and an empowered local government system. However, the expectation that we will find support for these broad principles of governance underpinning members' responses to specific questions is not entirely fulfilled. It is true that those who favour reforming the Dáil are the most likely to favour strengthening local government, as we would expect. However, attitudes to the Seanad don't follow the same pattern. Being in favour of stronger local government is unrelated to whether or not a member wants the Seanad to be abolished, while those advocating Dáil reform to strengthen the position of the opposition are actually more likely than other members to favour abolition of the Seanad. This, though, is not to say that members' attitudes are inconsistent or internally contradictory; given the weakness of the Seanad, advocating its abolition could be defended on the ground that this would not in practice remove a check on the government of the day, and that if the position of the Dáil and local government were enhanced, there would be even less rationale for an upper chamber with few if any powers and little popular legitimacy.

In general, looking at attitudes to these three issues, we find a number of common patterns. Those who are most active within Fine Gael, most interested in national political issues, and strongest in their support for Fine Gael, are the most likely to agree with increasing the power of the Dáil, strengthening local government, and retaining the Seanad.[22] Some other variables are also related to attitudes on these issues, though not always in a predictable way. We would expect those who prioritise a national, Dáil-based role for TDs (in response to Q81) to be the most concerned about reforming the Dáil – but in fact it is the other way round, with those who prioritise a local activity role for TDs being most in favour of Dáil reform. Cynics might wonder whether the reason why so many Fine Gael members want the Dáil reformed so as to strengthen the role of the opposition is because they are pessimistic about their party's future and expect it to be in opposition for most of the time in the foreseeable future as it has been in the past. However, there is no sign of this: attitudes to Dáil reform are quite unrelated to expectations about the party's future prospects as measured by questions 82 and 83, which we discussed in the previous section. Rural members are more likely than urban ones to favour Dáil reform, but are neither more likely nor less likely to favour strengthening local government.

PR-STV electoral system

As we have explained, we asked three separate questions about the electoral system because of the extent to which PR-STV has come to be credited with great influence over the operation of the Irish political system. Its effect, either for good or for ill, may, of course, often be exaggerated – and most academic analyses suggest that this is indeed the case.[23] Nevertheless, it is a topic that engenders sporadic discussion among the political class, and it is very likely that the system would long since have been changed if this could be achieved by TDs alone without the need to secure the approval of the people in a referendum. Our questions were designed to measure attitudes to two of the most salient aspects of the debate. First, given the suggestions that potential able politicians are discouraged from even entering the fray by the patterns of behaviour engendered by the electoral system, does PR-STV produce good quality TDs or not?[24] Second, since so many of STV's critics allege that it takes TDs away from parliamentary work and forces them into an excessive concentration on local constituency work, we asked members whether they believed this was the case. Third, having asked about attitudes to these specific aspects of the debate, we asked whether Fine Gael members would favour replacing PR-STV by a new electoral system – one that would not have the key feature of competition for votes between candidates of the same party.

As Table 8.12 shows, on balance Fine Gael members evaluate the electoral system positively. They are inclined to agree that it produces good quality TDs, although they also agree, albeit by a much narrower margin, that it imposes a constituency-oriented pattern of behaviour upon TDs. On the substantive question of whether the system should be dropped, members are more likely to advocate retention than replacement, though not by a huge margin. Not surprisingly, attitudes to these three issues are inter-related. Those who believe that the electoral system produces good quality TDs are less likely to agree that it imposes an excessive burden of constituency work on TDs. As Table 8.13 shows, evaluations are clearly related to overall views on the retention or dropping of PR-STV. Those who feel that good quality TDs are produced by the electoral system are, not surprisingly, less likely to want PR-STV replaced by something different; those who believe that PR-STV causes too much emphasis on constituency work are the most likely to want it replaced.

At the same time, these factors evidently do not entirely determine Fine Gael members' views on the electoral system. Table 8.13 also shows that even among those who agree that the electoral system results in high quality TDs being elected, 31 per cent still want PR-STV replaced. Similarly, even among those who agree that PR-STV leads to excessive constituency demands on TDs, 37 per cent feel that it should be retained. For these members, other factors clearly outweigh the alleged advantages or disadvantages that our questions specifically highlighted.

Beliefs about the *impact* of PR-STV are related to a number of other variables, as we shall see, but these variables are not related to responses to the basic question of whether members want to *retain or replace* PR-STV. The factors that are usually related to members' attitudes simply do not show up significantly here; such variables as education level, age, level of activism, extent of support for Fine Gael, and opinion about whether TDs should prioritise their national or their local role have little or no bearing on whether a member wants to change the electoral system.

Attitudes to the *effects* of PR-STV, in contrast, do seem to be related to aspects of members' backgrounds and opinions. Those who are most likely to agree that the electoral system produces good quality TDs are, on the whole, those who are generally satisfied with the operation of the political system; they tend to be especially strong supporters of Fine Gael, they come from families with a long tradition of supporting Fine Gael, they have been members of the party for a long time, they are active members, they believe that the party makes the best use of its existing members, they are optimistic about Fine Gael's future, and they give a high score to the party's then leader, John Bruton. In addition, those members who have relatively little education, who attend church most fre-

Table 8.13: Attitudes to retention of PR-STV, by evaluation of effects of PR-STV

| | PR-STV should be replaced | | | |
	Agree	Neutral	Disagree	Total
PR-STV produces good quality TDs				
Agree	31	12	57	100
Neutral	38	30	32	100
Disagree	50	15	36	100
PR-STV compels TDs to spend too				
much time on constituency work				
Agree	47	16	37	100
Neutral	26	25	49	100
Disagree	26	10	63	100
All members	36	16	49	100

Source: Fine Gael members' questionnaire, questions 57, 58, 59.
Note: "Agree" and "Disagree" include those strongly agreeing / disagreeing.

quently, who live outside Dublin, or who read the *Irish Independent* are all the most likely to agree that PR-STV produces good quality TDs. In contrast, those members who believe that the most important role for a TD is playing a role in national politics and in the Dáil, as well as *Irish Times* readers, are the most likely to feel that PR-STV does not result in good quality TDs.

Responses to the question about whether PR-STV compels TDs to spend too much time on constituency work are related to some of the same factors. Thus urban members, members with most education, those who read the *Irish Times*, those who are most interested in national political issues, those who feel that the party's candidate selection methods need improvement, or those who do not feel that Fine Gael is making best use of its members are all more likely than other members to agree that PR-STV does indeed have this undesirable effect. In addition, those few Fine Gael members in our survey who are already councillors or TDs are especially likely to agree with the statement: 73 per cent of these members feel that the electoral system forces TDs to do too much constituency work, whereas only 45 per cent of other members feel this. Attitudes are quite strongly related to members' views about the priority for TDs. Among those members who believe that the national (Dáil) role is most important, 57 per cent agree with the statement that PR-STV makes TDs do too much constituency work and 25 per cent disagree; among members who believe that the TD's local and constituency role is most important, 36 per cent agree with the statement while 43 per cent disagree. It may be, then, that both groups of members agree that TDs do a lot of constituency work; they disagree over whether this is "too much". The first group feel that it is too much, while members in the second group believe that it is perfectly proper that TDs devote much of their time to this work.

Attitudes to the electoral system, then, to some extent follow the "fault line" in the party that we have identified in earlier chapters, especially in chapter 7. Not all of the factors that relate to one electoral system question necessarily relate to the others, but, generalising a little, we can sum up as follows. Those members who are long-serving and active, who are frequent church attenders, who are high in support for Fine Gael, who have relatively little education, who believe that a TD's most important role is looking after his or her constituents, or who come from a rural area, are likely to see merit in PR-STV. Those members who are Dublin-based, read the *Irish Times*, favour European integration and dropping neutrality, are liberal on church-related issues, have relatively high levels of education, or who believe that a TD's proper place is in the Dáil – in short, perhaps, those who are least likely to need the assistance of a TD in dealing with the state bureaucracy – are the most likely to feel that PR-STV has undesirable consequences. As we saw in table 8.13, these beliefs about the consequences of PR-STV do not necessarily determine a member's opinion about whether the electoral system should be changed. The overall picture is one of a fairly even split of opinion within the party, and if there were to be another referendum on changing the electoral system then, depending on exactly what alternative was being proposed and who was proposing it, we could expect the party organisation to show clear signs of division.

Members' prescriptions

We asked members for their views on a number of specific areas where the Irish political system could be reformed, and in addition we invited them to tell us in their own words what changes they would recommend. Around half of our respondents had a suggestion to make (or wrote that they had no suggestion), and we have categorised the ideas in the way shown in Table 8.14.

The change most widely hoped for, as the table shows, is one broadly involving more integrity – evidently a quality of great importance to Fine Gael members. This category, as we have defined it, embraces a desire for better, more honest and more plain-living politicians generally. Some members in this category had specific proposals in mind:

- Anyone involved in fraud, tax evasion, bribes etc should be disqualified from politics. Also tribunals should not give immunity to guilty sorts (beef tribunals)
- Attendance obligatory if elected to Dáil, too many TDs (jobs for the boys). Higher standards in public life, an effort is needed to get rid of corruption
- Parties should be centrally funded and prohibited from seeking funds privately
- Openness in candidates – tax clearance cert for all TDs and candidates
- Jail all corrupt politicians in every party – that's not a slogan, I mean jail them.

Others in effect simply hoped that a better state of affairs would come about or had rather vague suggestions as to how this could be achieved, such as checking that potential TDs are honest and honourable:

- Honesty, sincerity and good manners

Table 8.14: Members' recommendations as to what changes should be made to the Irish political system

	%
Greater honesty, integrity, transparency from politicians	27
Reduce number of TDs	18
Increase power and effectiveness of Dáil	9
More power for local government, separate national and local government more	9
Make politics less adversarial	4
Change electoral system	4
Other institutional or policy change	4
Other change	16
Don't know or none	9
Total	100

Source: Fine Gael members' questionnaire, question 61.
Note: Responses were received from 50 per cent of members (weighted). Since question 61 was completely open, the categories used are devised by the authors.

- Politicians when taking an oath should put honesty as a priority
- I would like to see honest men and women elected to the Dáil
- They should do more for the poor. Cut some of their expenses and live moderate like the rest of us.
- No it's not working well. The scandals are a disgrace and I hope Fine Gael will highlight this
- The system is okay but I think more openness and honesty is needed in our politicians
- Very difficult to say at the moment in view of all the scandals, misuse of money. It gets worse every day
- Honesty from parties in opposition about what they would do in government. It is easy to make promises in opposition and then break them when in government
- Elect more young people, and elected representatives that abuse their position should be removed from the party and receive no pension
- A system should be put in place so that no powerful institution should offer any monies to change laws to suit themselves, politicians should be watched very closely
- Break the connection between political parties and big business
- Potential TDs should be vetted to see if they are honest and honourable people
- Politicians should answer yes or no and not beat about the bush.

Rather surprisingly, the second most widely advocated step is to reduce the number of TDs which, at 166 for a population of about 3.8 million people, is by no means out of line with international norms.[25] Most respondents favoured this not simply for its own sake but because they believe that fewer would mean better, or they wanted the measure to be introduced in conjunction with other steps to improve the calibre of TDs or to enhance the role of a TD:

- Reduce number of TDs by half. Introduce "Professional Politician" as degree course
- Reduce number of TDs, increase allowances to attract quality candidates
- Reduce the number of TDs and give them more say through committees
- Reduce size of Dáil, abolish Senate, establish real local government
- Have fewer TDs and have them concentrate on national issues
- No Senate, less TDs, pay them a proper salary to induce better quality
- Reduction in number of TDs. Increase number of TDs attending debates in Dáil, compulsory for all parties
- Less TDs, possibly scrapping the Seanad, more powers to local authorities, weekend voting, less junkets, less cute hoorism
- Less and more educated TDs.

For a further 9 per cent, enhancing the power and role of the Dáil was the priority in itself. Some members aimed to achieve this by reforming the procedures and operation of the Dáil, while for others the best step would be to change the rules for election to ensure that only those of high calibre could be elected in the first place. In the first category, examples were:

- Opposition TDs to have more power to speak out against government on issues of concern

- Freer Dáil debates to replace the rigid question and answer format, elimination of the need for prior written questions to be submitted to ministers
- The holidays are too long. More legislation could be framed if there were more Dáil sittings
- All politicians to deliver a positioning (personal) statement at the start of each new Dáil, e.g. identify the issues they wish to influence, and then they can be reviewed for election
- More Dáil committees with real power. Less TDs and more focused working time in the Dáil
- Make more use of committee system – Public Accounts Committee an example.

Some of the recommendations in the second category could be seen as rather elitist – for example, demanding that election candidates have achieved a certain educational level or requiring them to pass some kind of test – while others were more concerned about getting younger people elected to the Dáil:

- Only people with qualifications should be allowed to stand for Dáil. When elected as TD all other jobs should be given up
- Every candidate standing for election should have passed his/her leaving cert
- Open competitive examination similar to Civil Service before nomination. Footballers do not make good Ministers of Finance
- Like any other employee each minister should have an appropriate college degree for the particular post they hold
- All councillors / TDs should hold weekly clinics. TDs should go on courses and attend all public information meetings
- Less formalities to raise Dáil issues. Endeavour to raise standards of candidates contesting local elections by making them prove that they understood the fundamentals of politics and national issues
- Older TDs to retire and make way for young blood
- Upper age limit for candidates
- TDs should retire after 2 terms
- No one over 60 should be allowed to run for any political party
- Should give TDs in the age group 25 to 45 more power and ask those over 50 to step down.

A further 9 per cent wanted more power for local government, often arguing for a greater separation of the duties of TDs and national government from those of councillors and local government, although some wanted TDs to be more in touch with local issues:

- More decisions should be allowed to be made at local government level
- Strengthen local government to allow TDs to devote more time to legislation
- TDs should not be members of local councils. Dáil full-time
- TDs should concentrate on legislation and should not be involved in local politics
- Spend less time in parish pump politics after being elected to the Dáil
- Remove the need for national politicians to get involved in day to day local matters
- Clear distinction between the role of local politicians and legislators and a list

system to promote quality candidates
- I am going against what I answered in Q58 now: I think when a person is elected TD he should not be a County Councillor
- More contact with the local voters and more emphasis on local issues
- Be more ready to entertain ideas from general public
- Public reps should visit branches more and get involved more at local level.

For some members, what was needed above all was not so much institutional reform as a new spirit of politics, one that would search for consensus and abandon what they see as the point-scoring adversarial format that has become established:

- The work of parties in opposition should not be opposing for the sake of opposing
- Encourage more cooperation between TDs of different parties representing their area
- Emulate the Belfast Agreement's system of power sharing, with monitoring committees
- Not just arguing a point for the sake of it, working together if necessary
- Too much disunion between parties
- Parliamentary procedure is divisive and argumentative, there should be more creative consensus
- Reduce the level of adversarial politics, all parties be required to state say 5 priorities, committees for consensus on these
- More public involvement, partnership, acknowledging people's involvement – partnership approach
- First, too much time goes into snapping and smarting at one another, and the poorer section have a terrible time and the government doesn't want to hear how they live
- Take more account of views of opposition
- There are times when the Tallaght Agreement should be used again.

Several members criticised the PR-STV electoral system; some of these would do away with PR altogether and move to a system based on single-member constituencies, while others would keep PR but move to a list system rather than continue with the single transferable vote:

- The present PR system results in too many hung parliaments giving rise to too many general elections
- Single seat constituencies, leadership quality test for candidates
- List system to be introduced to improve calibre of TDs
- Retain the PR system but reduce the number of Dáil deputies from 166 to 90–100, have some elected on the list system.

Some other institutional or policy changes were offered by a further 4 per cent:

- Ban opinion polls 14 days prior to election
- Fixed term government
- President should be abolished as it only adds extra cost to the country

- Consult women to ascertain what time of day, days of week etc, meetings should be held, as at the moment system caters for men.

Others had rather broader or more fundamental changes to offer which in some cases can hardly be termed "reforms":

- Coalition policy announced before election rather than after
- Restrict the right to vote to those who choose to inform themselves properly about our political system
- Ban Fianna Fáil from holding any power for at least 10 years
- It's too late now to be asking this, we have now sold out to Europe
- You would have to change the quality of the electorate
- It should be possible to get what is yours without having to get your local TD to intercede
- One should have a larger representation from the left and a lesser from the right
- Get rid of Bertie Ahern and put in Fine Gael that is decent
- Get on and govern, cut out all the nonsense
- Would prefer 2 parties, Democrat and Republican.

Finally, there were some respondents who either did not know how to put the system right or who did not think anything significant needed to be changed.

- Don't know enough about the strengths and weaknesses of other political systems to suggest improvements
- I don't know enough about the system but as farmers we are completely disillusioned with the powers that be
- If something is not done soon the youth won't vote, something very wrong
- At the end of the day, PR and multi-seat constituencies keep politicians in touch with the people unlike some European countries and UK, so none really
- It is hard to know, it seems to be working well at the moment
- Leave well enough alone.

Perhaps the clearest conclusion to come from this is that members' recommendations are very disparate and often concern the philosophy that underlies politicians' behaviour rather than the institutions within which these politicians operate. Many members, it is true, do favour changing the rules in one or more respects: banning private financial donations to political parties, introducing term limits for TDs, reducing the number of TDs, strengthening the Dáil, introducing formal education or other requirements for election candidates, giving more power to local government or changing the electoral system. But others want more than this: they want to see a new, constructive, altruistic and patriotic spirit in politics. They want more honesty, openness and sincerity in politics; they want politicians to approach politics in a non-party spirit. They want the government to listen more to the opposition and to the people, and they want the opposition not to oppose just for the sake of opposing. Tom Garvin's characterisation of the political culture of Fine Gael as "moralist", which we quoted earlier in this chapter, remains a good way to sum up the worldview of many members.

CONCLUSION

In this chapter we have examined Fine Gael members' perception of the political and party systems. We found that members have a view of the political world in which Labour is regarded sympathetically while other parties are viewed coolly, with the smaller parties being rated lowest of all. When it comes to government formation, the great majority of Fine Gael members do not wish to go into a coalition with anyone other than Labour, and they are especially hostile to the idea of a coalition with Fianna Fáil. Nevertheless, one in five would be prepared to contemplate a merger with Fianna Fáil at some stage in the future, and most would welcome a merger with the PDs. Fine Gael members seem fairly positive about the party's future, with widespread optimism that the long-awaited day when Fine Gael will overtake Fianna Fáil is less than twenty years away – though, perhaps worryingly, it is the oldest members who are most likely to believe this. Analysis of members' evaluations of current and former politicians largely reflects attitudes to these politicians' parties. There are some signs that liberal members have a different perspective from that of conservative members, and pro-European integration members from that of anti-integration members, but these differences are not so strong that we can talk realistically of distinct ideological groups within the party.

On the whole members are, or were when we conducted the survey, fairly satisfied with the performance of the political system. There is general support for certain suggested reforms, such as reducing the power of the government *vis-à-vis* the Dáil or enhancing the power of local government, but on balance there is opposition to changing the PR-STV electoral system. For the most part, members do not really feel there is a problem that needs to be solved here, and, in their view, while there may be minor adjustments or improvements to be made, the system generally does not need a fundamental overhaul. What many of them wish to see above all is a more honest, positive and constructive spirit in Irish politics.

9 Conclusion

What have we learned from surveying the membership of Fine Gael? In this final chapter we will review our main findings and consider what their implications are, for Fine Gael specifically and perhaps for political parties generally.

THE MAIN FINDINGS

Let us first summarise and reiterate some of the lessons to be drawn from earlier chapters. In chapter 3 we examined the role of membership in Fine Gael over the years and observed that the party was based largely on Cumann na nGaedheal, which was created in 1923 in a "top-down" way by members of parliament. There is an influential theory in political science that holds that members will always be more marginal in a party that came into existence this way than in one founded from the bottom up, and certainly in Cumann na nGaedheal the party organisation was unable to constrain ministers in any significant way. Some ministers, indeed, seemed to have a degree of disdain for their party and did not believe it had any valid role except to support uncritically whatever its leaders decided to do. In addition, and not necessarily in consequence, the pro-Treaty parties had difficulty from the start in attracting members and election candidates, and their organisation was always characterised as far less effective and dynamic than that of their rival, Fianna Fáil. Fine Gael was not, then, a party in which the members initially occupied centre stage and, with the possible exception of the first six or so years of Garret FitzGerald's leadership, there has been no golden age of internal party democracy or activity that can act as a yardstick or a beacon when the extent of membership involvement and activity today are discussed.

In chapter 4 we presented our findings about the backgrounds of Fine Gael members. Members are predominantly male and middle-aged; in urban areas they are mainly middle-class, but in rural areas there are more working-class members and, of course, many more farmers. Indeed, almost a third of Fine Gael members are farmers, and 29 per cent of members belong to a farmers' interest group, something that must inevitably have an impact on the kind of policies the party adopts towards the agricultural sector. Quite a high proportion of members joined the party for essentially non-political reasons, such as a desire to enhance their social life or as a result of the influence of family or friends. These members tend to be relatively uninterested in policy questions. The longevity of members is striking: about half have been members since before Garret FitzGerald became leader in 1977, and a quarter have been members since before Liam Cosgrave became leader in 1965. This indicates an impressive degree of loyalty, but it also points to the paucity of new, young members. Another striking aspect is that 63 per cent of members report that one or both of their parents were also party members, and 75 per cent come from families with a tradition of supporting the party that goes back to the treaty split eighty years ago. The party may be doing well in drawing on the loyalty of the pro-Treaty tradition, but it has evidently not been very successful in reaching out beyond that tradition.

In chapter 5 we attempted to assess just how active these members are. There seems to be more grassroots activity than some gloomy assessments, of Fine Gael and of political parties generally, might have led us to expect. Branches meet on average about three times a year, with an average of 11 members at each meeting, and over 80 per cent of members have been to at least one such meeting in the past year. Moreover, the organisation does not seem to be "inward-looking" or "talking to itself", conclusions reached by a commission that examined the party organisation in 1993 – in fact we find plenty of evidence of activity at and around elections, which after all involves communicating with the wider public. Nearly three-quarters of members had taken part in election campaigning in the previous four years, most had participated directly in candidate selection, and most fill a linkage role between citizens and the state by passing constituents' requests to a party TD. However, when we asked members whether they were becoming more active or less active over time, the results showed that on balance the membership is becoming less active. Not surprisingly, in the light of our findings in chapter 4, a major cause of this is old age or ill health, and given the low number of young members there is cause for concern for the party here. We explored the question of whether members were for the most part loyal to the party or loyal to an individual politician within the party. Nearly half of the members describe themselves as strong supporters of one local Fine Gael politician in particular, but we concluded that the party is able to harness these personal links rather than being weakened by them.

In chapter 6 we reported the views of members about how the party treats them. As in any large organisation, there are plenty of complaints: members want to be listened to more, to be told more about what's going on, and to be more involved. There are fewer complaints about candidate selection, which is significant as this is the area where party rules give members most input. Members are agreed that the party needs more members, especially more women and young members, but when they are asked how it should go about achieving this, very few accept that it is primarily the members' own responsibility to recruit. Instead, most have suggestions as to what someone else in the party, usually head office or public representatives, should do. Most members, too, are against introducing quotas for women among election candidates, though female members are (just) in favour. When we sought the views of branch secretaries specifically, we found that, notwithstanding the generally healthy picture we found when we asked about members' activity, a number report that their own branch is heading for extinction. Some secretaries go further and call into question the need for a branch structure in the twenty-first century. We also attempted to gauge the electoral impact of members, and reached the clear conclusion that members make a difference. Active members make most difference of all and, subject to the qualifications that must always be made about such an exercise, we estimate that each additional active member adds an extra 10 votes to the Fine Gael total, with an additional 100 active members adding around 5 per cent to Fine Gael's vote in a constituency.

In chapter 7 we discussed the political views of the members. Some of the findings were striking in themselves: the overwhelming preference for an even-handed approach towards the two communities in Northern Ireland, the vehement opposition to the idea of legalising marijuana, and the lack of enthusiasm for further European integration or for dropping Irish neutrality. There is scope for division within the party over the last two issues. When we compare the views of members with those of Fine Gael voters we find very little difference, contrary to the views of those researchers who have theorised that members are likely to be policy "extremists" compared with the more moderate voters. We asked Fine Gael members to place themselves on the left–right spectrum, and found that the great majority place themselves in the centre or on the right. However, members' self-placement on this scale seems to have little bearing on their attitudes to specific policy issues; there is no evidence here of an ideological underpinning for the opinions held, or of a structure in the attitudes that would enable us to speak of distinct groups, such as "liberals" and "conservatives", defined by different ideologies, among the Fine Gael members.

We also asked members to place the main Irish parties on the left–right spectrum, and this revealed that members collectively situate Fianna Fáil and Fine Gael in virtually identical positions. In chapter 8 we returned to the comparison between these two parties, and found that when Fine Gael members are asked directly to identify the main difference, the most common answer given is: integrity. Many Fine Gael members do not appear to believe that there are any great policy differences, but they do feel strongly that, as one member put it, "Fine Gael are honest, Fianna Fáil are completely dishonest". Yet, when we asked members about the prospect of a merger with Fianna Fáil, a remarkable 19 per cent said they would favour the idea – though, pending this unlikely event, feeling in the meantime is strongly against entering coalition with that party. Members generally seem quite optimistic about the party's future electoral prospects, though it is the older members who are most optimistic, and this optimism has to be set beside some of the pessimistic reports from branch secretaries that we encountered in chapter 6. We also examined members' evaluations of current and former politicians – John Hume and Garret FitzGerald were by some way the most popular – and of the main parties, which revealed that while Fine Gael is (of course) viewed positively and Labour neutrally, all other parties are seen in a negative light. We asked members to assess the functioning of the Irish political system, and found that on the whole they are satisfied with it – they are in favour of strengthening local government but against changing the electoral system.

DAYS OF BLUE LOYALTY OVER?

We pointed out in the preface that the title of this book came from a comment made by a party member in response to one of the questions in the survey. This member was pessimistic about the future of the organisation, and wrote "Days of blue loyalty over". Is this prediction in line with the evidence of this book, or is Fine Gael alive and well and set to prosper in the twenty-first century?

As we might expect, there are arguments to consider on both sides. On the negative side, some writers argue that the sun is setting on the world of political parties generally and that the political party as we know it today is a centralised, formally structured pyramidal body that evolved in and for the nineteenth century and the first half of the twentieth century and is now as redundant as steam trains, gas lamps and the electric telegraph.[1] If this line of thought is valid, Fine Gael is indeed on the way out, but so are Fianna Fáil and Labour; days of blue loyalty, green loyalty and red loyalty are all over. However, those who pronounce the imminent death of the political party don't offer any very plausible speculation as to what is likely to replace it, and we confidently expect political parties to continue to play a dominant role in structuring political life in Ireland and indeed in other European countries for the foreseeable future.

There are also more temperate argument on the pessimistic side that suggest that while parties as such will continue to thrive, these parties may not be quite the same as the parties of yesterday or even today. In particular, they may not have many members. There are two sides of this case: one stresses the *demand* side of the argument and says that parties have no real need for members any more, while the other stresses the *supply* side and says that even if parties do want members they will have great difficulty in finding and keeping them. We have already discussed many of these arguments, especially in chapters 1, 5 and 6, and here we will just review some of the main points briefly.

Taking the demand-related arguments first, the suggestion is that parties no longer need members in the same way or to the same extent as they used to. With the mass media as a campaigning vehicle and with public money provided by the state, the election work and the subscriptions formerly supplied by members are of diminishing value. Moreover, if members demand some policy "payment" for their services – in other words, if they use their power within the party to commit the party to a certain policy line or to select candidates of a certain policy outlook – then they could become a liability to the party leadership, as the danger is that the policy demands they make will render the party less electable. So writers such as Richard Katz and Peter Mair portray parties gradually withdrawing from civil society, fighting battles (often little more than mock or ritualistic ones) with each other in their own "party world" but no longer engaging with ordinary people.[2] Parties, in this view, are on the road to becoming "head without a body" organisations: they will have a strong well-funded head office and a powerful parliamentary group, but will neither have nor see the need for a vibrant grassroots membership.

Turning now to the supply-related arguments, it is often suggested that people are becoming ever less likely to join parties. Indeed, as we have pointed out, membership trends are downwards in virtually all European countries. Those who are thinking about joining a party for "solidary" reasons can nowadays find plenty of other and probably more appealing leisure and social opportunities; those who are motivated by policy should have little difficulty in finding a pressure group that is committed to the cause that concerns them. Moreover, if political parties generally are often regarded as going through a difficult time these days, then established, major parties seem to be in most trouble of all. With policy convergence between the main parties having taken place in many countries, none of these parties finds it easy to identify itself with a distinctive cause that will inspire and enthuse those outside its traditional recruitment pool. A citizen who feels strongly about a particular issue may not see much point in joining a large party on whose agenda this issue is just one of many issues and quite probably not the top priority. It might seem to make more sense to join a smaller party that gives central place to the subject the citizen is concerned about and in which one will not have to spend a lot of time fighting against general indifference to persuade the party to take the issue up. Or, perhaps, such a citizen may decide that the established political and institutional structures are not sufficiently flexible or responsive to their wishes and instead join a single-issue pressure group whose organisation is looser and less hierarchical than that of a party, or work at community level to try to change things on the ground.

Major political parties suffer a number of difficulties when trying to recruit new members and enthuse existing ones. Since they aim to be a dominant force in government, there are constraints on how they can behave; if they issue wild promises, or make spending commitments without soberly pointing out the revenue implications, they may be penalised by an electorate that demands a responsible government. Moreover, they are constrained by their past record; while of course some degree of policy evolution is inevitable, if they are to be taken seriously they cannot blithely advocate policies at one election that bear no relation to what they advocated previously.[3] However, while being consistent, level-headed, honest and responsible is all very well, it is not always easy to transform this into excitement. It becomes a little more easy if a party's main rival is none of these things. especially if that rival is in government. Then, ordinary virtues becomes appreciated as rare values that are under threat, and in such circumstances new members may flock to the party.[4] Fine Gael, as a party that has played the leading role in Irish governments on a number of occasions, clearly cannot adopt the garb of an outsider, a protest or anti-establishment party. On the other hand, many of its members evidently feel, as we saw in chapter 8, that the Fianna Fáil government with which they were confronted in 1999 did lack many of these ordinary virtues, and a desire to get and keep Fianna Fáil out of power is undoubtedly a galvanising factor for a significant number of members.

As those readers who have made their way this far through the book will know, we do not really subscribe to the pessimistic point of view that we have just outlined about the future of parties. Nonetheless, there is no doubt that the information on what is happening at the grass roots of Fine Gael is by no means all positive. As we saw in chapter 4, the membership is generally getting on in years, with only 13 per cent being aged less than 35. More members told us they are becoming less active than said they are becoming more active. In chapter 6, quite a number of branch secretaries made it clear that they saw little future for their particular branch, which had elderly memberships and had failed in all attempts to recruit fresh blood. (Moreover, some young members who had joined predominantly elderly branches reported feeling that they were not entirely welcome, especially when they tried to shake up the established way of doing things.) Some secretaries wanted amalgamation of small rural branches into larger units, while others suggested that the whole branch structure itself was no longer relevant. Branches, said some secretaries, belonged to a pre-telephone era when contact between members required regular face-to-face meetings, and to a time when people needed a local politically active person to act as a mediator in any dealings with authority – and those days are now gone.[5]

Why, then, do we feel that the days of blue loyalty are not over? Part of the reason has to do with our belief that parties themselves will survive, but there are more specific reasons. For one thing, parties in Ireland do seem to need members, and they know they need them; Fine Gael in particular has given serious consideration to how to attract them. The model according to which parties can exist solely as a clique in the nation's capital, communicating with the rest of the country only through the mass media, simply would not be sustainable in Ireland (or perhaps anywhere else). People expect parties to have a strong local presence at election times, and if parties have nothing on the ground between elections then there will be nothing to cajole into action when the election comes round. So the demand for members, and ideally for loyal members, is still there; Irish parties will continue to try to recruit members. And, for as long as internal conflict and competition exist within parties, individual politicians will have an incentive to recruit members to deploy in these internal battles – in Fine Gael's case, this applies most obviously over candidate selection. Moreover, as our survey has shown, there is no sign that members, in Fine Gael at least, are policy extremists who would tie the party to vote-losing policies. They are generally non-ideological and for the most part their views are firmly in line with those of party voters. If Fine Gael could attract thousands more members like those it has at the moment, the benefits would be great and the costs very minor indeed.

So the demand for members will remain in the future – but what about the supply? We have outlined the problems that Fine Gael (like most of the main Irish parties, and indeed parties elsewhere) faces in recruiting dynamic, vibrant young members who are willing to devote time and energy to the party, but let us finish on a positive note, one that we suspect would be valid for the other Irish parties as well. Many Fine Gael members may be elderly, but this is not entirely a bad thing. A party that has only young members is a party that clearly has difficulty in retaining the loyalty of its members once they enter middle age. What stands out about so many Fine Gael members is precisely their loyalty to the party through thick and thin. Some even speak of having been "born into" Fine Gael, and certainly most have inherited their allegiance from one or both of their parents. The pool from which members are drawn is in some ways disturbingly restricted, but at least within this pool loyalty levels are impressively strong. Members, it is true, have their complaints and have no difficulty in thinking of ways in which the party could treat them better, but for the most part they do not seem to be contemplating leaving.

Moreover, although we have outlined some of the disadvantages that large government-bent parties have when it comes to trying to convey a sense of excitement, large parties do have one huge advantage over small ones, namely that they have a realistic prospect of getting their hands on the levers of power. A member with a strong policy priority can have some hope that he or she might be able both to influence the policies and to advance the cause of the party, or of an individual politician within the party, and that the party, unlike a smaller one, will actually be able to get into government and implement some of its policies. Access to power is a vital attraction for a major party, so Fine Gael (and indeed Fianna Fáil) cannot afford to spend too much time in opposition; if that starts to look like its natural and inevitable position then its raison d'être will be increasingly called into question and the pessimistic arguments that we have outlined will hold increasing sway.

What of the future? Even with the most faithful of members, a party will die if it cannot recruit new blood. Here, clearly, there is no room for complacency, and concern has been expressed by many members in our survey that young people are not joining. It is little consolation that the other main parties might say much the same. However, the reservoir of pro-treaty loyalty from which so many current members have emerged continues to exist, and we can expect a good proportion of today's members to be followed into the party by their own children. Moreover, we suspect that the same concerns about the lack of young members would have been applicable at many points in time over the past seventy years. As we saw in chapter 4, membership over the years has not followed a linear trend. If there is any cyclical pattern, it is that it rises as a general election approaches and falls soon afterwards. Sometimes there does seem to be a long-term decline, and at such times there is no shortage of commentators to conclude that the party is nearing the end of its life. But then something happens: perhaps a new leader not only galvanises the faithful but also inspires the previously uncommitted to join, as in 1977, or the party gains a new lease of life simply by getting into government when a barren stretch in opposition seemed to loom, as in 1948.

Maybe, if absolutely nothing goes right for Fine Gael over the next ten to twenty years, the need for activists will be superseded by the need for obituarists. Developments in the Irish party system may work against Fine Gael no matter what the dedication of its members. It is much more probable, though, that the blue loyalty that has sustained the party for seventy years will remain a resource for it into the foreseeable future. And by supplying, indeed by constituting, this resource, the members of Fine Gael, like the members of all the other parties in the state, are making an important but often overlooked contribution to the Irish democratic system.

Appendix A: How the sample was constructed

This study uses the methodology of the large-scale sample survey. This has been employed to examine party members in many countries, most notably in Britain where surveys of the Labour and Conservative parties have served to undermine much of the conventional wisdom about each of them. The survey of Fine Gael members that we describe in this book was carried out at the end of 1999. Fine Gael is well set up for such a study because it maintains a national database of members that includes each member's name and address and the branch the member belongs to. This allows a national random sample to be selected with minimal difficulty. Here we explain the methodology and discuss some limitations of the data.

We first separated the 1,410 local branch secretaries from 18,542 other members so as to sample the two separately. This was done largely because we wanted to ask secretaries questions about their branch and for this exercise to be useful it required a much larger sample of secretaries than we would expect to obtain by chance. We also assumed that secretaries would be more likely to respond and wanted to ensure a reasonable sample size (this assumption was correct, though the difference in responses rates was minor, as Table A1 shows). We selected a simple random sample of 1,009 secretaries and 2,610 other members using the random sampling procedure in Data Desk 5.0. Leaving aside a small number of Dáil deputies selected in this way, we sent each individual a questionnaire (see Appendix B for this) along with a pre-paid envelope for returning it. We included an additional short questionnaire (also in Appendix B) in the mailing to secretaries. This was done at the start of October 1999. We followed this up with a postcard reminder a month later, and a further reminder and replacement questionnaire a month later again. Each mailing was spread out over several days for logistical reasons. Eventually, as Table A1 shows, 1,719 usable questionnaires were returned, 523 from those sampled as branch secretaries and 1,196 from other members. This is an overall response rate of over 47 per cent.

This was achieved largely before the end of 1999. In fact, 33 per cent of questionnaires came back in the first three weeks after posting, and 86 per cent were returned before the end of November with almost all remaining questionnaires returned beforeNew Year's day 2000 (week 12). The remaining 4 per cent dribbled in over the next several weeks. Both the first postcard, and to a lesser extent the second questionnaire, led to a spurt in responses following declining numbers. Figure A1 shows the proportion of responses, week by week from 11 October 1999 until the end of February 2000, after which only four

Table A1: Population and sample numbers and response rates

	Population	Target sample	Responses	Response rate (%)
Members	18,542	2,610	1,196	45.8
Branch secretaries	1,410	1,009	523	51.8
Total	19,952	3,619	1,719	47.5

more questionnaires were returned. The second and third spikes in the chart suggest the impact of the reminder postcard and then the second questionnaire.

The satisfactory response rate was due in no small part to support from Fine Gael. The party exhorted members through its newsletter, *Branch Lines*, to fill in their questionnaires, and we wrote to individual TDs informing them about the survey and asking them to do the same. We also explained to individual respondents that Fine Gael would be provided with our general conclusions, which may have had particular impact on those most committed to the party. However, we made it clear in a letter to each potential respondent that this was an independent and academic study which was not being carried out on behalf of the party, nor would any of the data collected on individuals be given to the party. We also suggested to each respondent that our study could make up for the fact that his or her voice was generally ignored in political debate. As an additional inducement, we promised a small donation (50p, i.e. 63 cents) to a charity for each completed questionnaire – potentially a sum of nearly IR£2,000 (2,540 euros). In this way we hoped to obtain responses from as many of the target sample as possible.

The population from which the sample of branch secretaries was taken was turned out to be an exaggerated one. The party's mailing list for secretaries errs on the side of inclusiveness to ensure that as many branches as possible get official communication. As well as current secretaries it probably contains some former secretaries as well as secretaries of some districts and Young Fine Gael branches. Official records for the time list only 992 branches, and thus where estimates are made from the secretaries' reports on branches we have aggregated up only to 992 branches and not 1,410.

In computing estimates of the views of members we have weighted the responses of

Figure A1: Week by week pattern of response

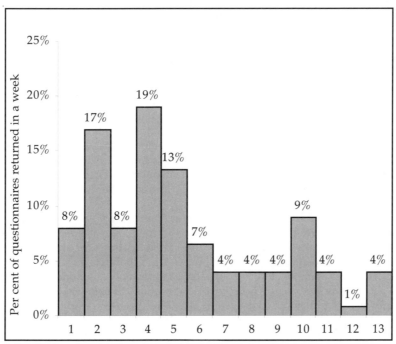

Number of weeks from initial posting when questionnaire returned

secretaries and other members according to their chances of being included in our sample so that our estimates take into account the fact we have a disproportionately large number of branch secretaries. The weighting factors are 0.92 for members and 0.08 for secretaries. For this reason we have not provided numbers of cases for the tables in the body of the book, since neither a weighted N nor an unweighted N gives the real picture. Calculations of statistical significance take into account the fact that estimates of secretaries' opinions come from around 500 cases, and those of other members from about 1,200 in most instances.

While we view this as a satisfactory and worthwhile sample, questions can be raised about the extent to which the sample is representative. This boils down to asking whether those who did not respond were in some way different from those who did. We see little reason to expect that this would be so in many respects. For instance, when it comes to views on political issues, or to social background, we do not see any good reason to expect significant distortion. There might be more reason to expect some link between whether or not a person responded and his or her commitment to, and extent of involvement in, the party – a factor that, of course, applies to virtually every survey. We have no way of assessing this directly. On the face of it, the fact that branch secretaries were more likely to respond than ordinary members suggests some link with activism. Even so, the difference is quite small, only 6 per cent. We are able to ascertain whether more active and involved members tended to answer more quickly. If so, it would strengthen the argument that less involved members may have delayed their response to a point where they then did not respond at all. Alternatively, if there is no link, if activism is not related to when the questionnaire was returned, then we can have greater confidence that we did not over-sample activists. In fact, there is only a very weak link, with a correlation of just -0.08 between activism and the date on which the questionnaire was returned. (The regression coefficient is 0.52. Since the range of the activism score is 15 points, this indicates that the least active member would, on average, take 7–8 days (15 times 0.52) longer than the most active member to respond.) Almost certainly there is some bias in the sample towards the more active and committed member but nonetheless we found a wide variety of degrees of interest in and commitment to Fine Gael in our responses. Many respondents were pretty inactive. Nor were they all strong supporters. Many said frankly that they were not.

We have little reason to question the sampling frame. A few people contacted us to explain why questionnaires were not returned. As might be expected in such a population, some members were deceased and others too ill to respond. More than twenty people complained they had not received the first questionnaire and were duly sent a second. One recipient informed us that he had not been a member for 10 years. There were less prosaic reasons for non-response, or delayed response. One respondent asked for another questionnaire after his dog had eaten the first one (after he had filled it in, moreover).

On some variables it is possible to compare the estimates from our sample with parameters in the target population. Where this is done, estimates are in all cases very close to known population figures. For instance, Table A2 shows the sample proportions of members by Euro-constituency and by gender. All differences are small. Those between estimated (sample) and real proportions of members by Euro-constituency are within plus/minus 2 per cent. Those for the proportions of men and women, amongst secretaries and other members, are even smaller. This gives us confidence in our figures for other characteristics. The secretaries' questionnaire asked branch secretaries to report on the number of members in their branch. If we total these estimates, and multiply the sum by 992/438 (438 secretaries answered this question) to make up for the fact that we

Table A2: Sample estimates and actual proportions – selected characteristics

	Sample %	Actual %	Difference %
All members by Euro constituency:			
Dublin	12.2	10.5	1.7
Leinster	22.8	22.3	0.4
Connacht–Ulster	25.5	27.1	-1.6
Munster	39.5	40.1	-0.6
Secretaries and other members, by gender:			
All members: %female	31.1	32.2	-1.0
Secretaries: %female	41.8	42.1	-0.3

Note: Actual membership figures by region are from official Fine Gael records, and gender breakdown for actual members and secretaries is calculated by the authors from the sampling frame.

have estimates from just under half the official number of branches (and not all secretaries answered this question), the estimated number of party members comes to just 20,533. This is a slight overestimate of the official figure of almost 19,232 for that time, but it is very close to the 19,952 names in our sampling frame. Secretaries almost certainly gave rounded figures rather than actual ones (there are spikes in the distribution of branch sizes at 15, 20, 25, 30, 40 and 50) that may inflate the figure marginally. Some might think it likely that secretaries from the larger, more successful branches would have been more likely to respond, but in that case we would have expected to overestimate the actual total number of members by a greater margin.

APPENDIX B: The questionnaires and the responses

This essentially reproduces both the member's and secretary's questionnaires, though the response boxes are excluded and it includes the weighted distribution of responses to each closed ended question.

NO SPECIAL KNOWLEDGE IS REQUIRED TO ANSWER THESE QUESTIONS ON WHICH WE ARE SURE THAT EVERYONE WILL HAVE AN OPINION

The questions inside cover a wide range of subjects. Most of them can be answered by placing an 'X' against the answer you would like to give. For example:
Were you a member of Fine Gael at the time of the last general election?

If you were a member at the time of the last election put a cross in the first row box as indicated. If not, put a cross in the second box.

1. Yes	X
2. No	

      In some cases we will ask you to indicate how strongly you feel about something by placing an 'X' in an appropriate column. For example, to answer the question "How important do you think it is for a TD to speak in Dáil debates?" you should put an 'X' in the appropriate column. The illustration below would show you thought it was very important.

	very important	quite important	not very important	not at all important
How important do you think it is for a TD to speak in Dail debates	X			

In a few cases you are asked to write numbers into boxes. For instance:

What year did you join Fine Gael *Write in*

1	9	6	8

Most of this questionnaire is designed to be machine readable, so whether you are asked to write an 'X' or a number in a box, please make sure that what you write fits INSIDE the box and does not overflow into any other box. Also, will you please use black or blue ink, or a heavy pencil

We want everyone to take part, not just those with strong views about a particular issue. The questionnaire should not take too long to complete and we think you will find it interesting and enjoyable. It should be completed only by the person to whom it was sent, so that responses will reflect all shades of opinion within the Fine Gael party.

When you have filled it in, please place it in the enclosed FREEPOST envelope and post it back as soon as you possibly can.

SECTION 1

1.   Would you call yourself a very strong supporter of Fine Gael, fairly strong, not very strong, or not at all strong?

1. Very strong	51
2. Fairly strong	38
3. Not very strong	9
4. Not at all strong	2

2.   Thinking back to the time you first joined Fine Gael, did you approach the party to apply for membership, or did Fine Gael approach you?

1. I approached the party	49
2. The party approached me	39
3. Don't remember	12

3.   In approximately which year did you join Fine Gael?

(Write in)   1976

4a.   Have you been a member continuously since that time?

1. Yes	93
2. No	7

4b. If you have NOT been a member continuously since you first joined, for about how many years have you been a member?

(Write in)   13 years

4c.   Are you, or have you ever been a member of Young Fine Gael?

1. Yes	12
2. No	88

5.   Before you joined the party, were either your father or mother a member of Fine Gael?

1. Father and mother were members	36
2. Father only was a member	22
3. Mother only was a member	5
4. Neither were members	38

6.   What was your most important reason for joining Fine Gael?
        Please put an X in ONE box only
Most important
1. To get Fine Gael into government, or keep it there   24
2. A belief in what Fine Gael stands for   43
3. A good way to meet interesting people and extend my social life 3
4. Opposition to Fianna Fail   9
5. As a first step in a political career   1
6. Influence of family and/or friends   18
7. Other (specify)   28

7.   Does your family have a tradition of supporting Fine Gael and Cumann na nGaedheal, going back to the civil war of 1922–23?

1. Yes   75
2. No   25

8.   Thinking back over the last twelve months, about how often, as far as you know, has your local branch met?

1. Not at all   3
2. Once or twice   33
3. 3-5 times   30
4. More than 5 times   24
5. Don't know   9

9.   And during the last twelve months, how often have you personally attended a local Fine Gael branch meeting?

1. Not at all   18
2. Once or twice   44
3. 3-5 times   25
4. More than 5 times   14

10.   Are you in frequent contact with a number of members of your branch through your work or social life?

1. Yes   74
2. No   26

11.   Do you live in the constituency where your branch is located?

1. Yes   93
2. No   7

12.   Thinking about the last local meeting you attended, how much time was spent on each of the following?

	No time	Some time	Most of the time	All of the time
1. Internal party organisation matters	12	69	16	3
2. Fund raising	9	70	9	2
3. Local political matters	3	46	45	5
4. National political matters	14	70	12	4

13.   How active do you consider yourself to be in Fine Gael, relative to the average member?

1. Very active	20
2. Fairly active	41
3. Not very active	29
4. Not at all active	10

14.   Are you more active or less active within the party than you were four years ago, (or when you joined if this was less than 4 years ago)?

1. More active	20
2. Less active	32
3. About the same	48

If you are now more active or less active:
15.   What is the most important reason why you are more active or less active than four years ago?
WRITE IN _____

16.   Approximately how much money do you give to Fine Gael every year, taking into account membership fees, Superdraw, and any other donations? [£1 = 1.27 euro]

1. Nothing	3
2. Less than £10	21
3. £10 to £50	49
4. £50 to £100	21
5 £100 or more	6

SECTION 2

17.   Over the last four years, have you found that you tend to get actively involved in the party only at election times?

1. Yes	57
2. No	43

18a.   Did you take an active part in any Fine Gael election campaigns during the last four years?

1. Yes 72
2. No   28

IF NO go on to question 20
IF YES

18b.   What form did your activity take? (Put an 'X 'against EACH activity you took part in)

1. Door to door canvassing   68
2. Mailing or distributing campaign literature   48
3. Other activities (specify below)   42
If Other: Please specify_____

19a.   If you worked in the last general election were you working primarily for the election of one particular candidate or equally for all the Fine Gael candidates?

1. One particular candidate   55
2. Equally for all candidates   45

If you were working for one particular candidate in the general election
19b.   Was that candidate known to you personally **before** the campaign?

1. Yes, known personally   91
2. No, not known personally   9

19c.   If you worked in the last local election were you working primarily for the election of one particular candidate or equally for all the Fine Gael candidates?

1. One particular candidate   55
2. Equally for all candidates   45

If you were working for one particular candidate in the local election
19d.   Was that candidate known to you personally?

1. Yes, known personally   92
2. No, not known personally   8

20.   Do you at present hold any branch or constituency organisation office(s) within Fine Gael (e.g. secretary, treasurer)?
1. Yes 56
2. No   44

IF YES, WRITE IN THE TITLE OF YOUR OFFICE _____
(If you hold more than one office, write in the name of the most important one)

If you do not hold any office at present:
20a.   In the last three years, have you held or stood for any branch or constituency office(s) within Fine Gael?

1. Yes	11
2. No	89

21.   How much time do you devote to party activities in the average month?

1. None	55
2. Up to 5 hours	37
3. More than 5 hours	9

23a.   Did you take part in a constituency convention to select Fine Gael candidates for the 1997 general election?

1. Yes	66
2. No	34

23aa.   Did you take part in a constituency convention to select Fine Gael candidates for the 1999 local elections?

1. Yes	72
2. No	28

23b.   Have you ever attended a European party conference and met members of Fine Gael's allied parties in the European Parliament?

1. Yes	18
2. No	82

24.   How interested would you say you are in national political issues?

1. Very interested	50
2. Quite interested	46
3. Not at all interested	5

25.   Have you ever stood for office on behalf of Fine Gael, in a local council election, or a Dáil election?

1. Yes	8
2. No	92

26.   Have you sought a party nomination to contest a local or general election?

1. Yes   9
2. No   91

27.   Are you, or do you hope some day to be, a TD or a local councillor, or aren't you interested in a political career?

1. Already a councillor or TD   2
2. Hope to be a public representative   10
3. Not interested in a political career   88

28.   At the divorce referendum in 1995, did you manage to vote, and if so did you vote Yes to permit divorce, or No to maintain the ban on divorce?

1. Did not vote   8
2. Voted Yes   59
3. Voted No   33

29.   Did you take an active part in campaigning during the referendum on divorce in 1995, and if so did you work for a Yes vote, to permit divorce, or did you work for a No vote, to maintain the ban on divorce?

1. Did not take an active part   75
2. Took an active part for a Yes vote   17
3. Took an active part for a No vote   8

SECTION 3

30.   Have you had any personal contact with any of the Fine Gael TDs for your constituency over the last 12 months?

1. Yes   75
2. No   25

31.   Have you had any personal contact with any of the Fine Gael councillors for your area over the last 12 months?

1. Yes   86
2. No   14

32.   Do you sometimes pass on requests for assistance from people in the constituency to any of the Fine Gael TDs for the constituency?

1. Yes   61
2. No   39

33.   Do you think of yourself as a strong supporter of one of the party's leading politicians in the constituency, or would you say you supported all of the party's politicians equally?

1. Strong supporter of one of the leading politicians	45
2. Support all the party's politicians equally	55

34.   Are you currently a member of any of the following groups or organisations?
Please indicate using an 'X' as many as apply:

34.1. Irish Farmers' Association or other farming association	29
34.2. A trade union (please specify)_____	15
34.3. Local residents' association	14
34.4. Local community association	19
34.5. Chamber of Commerce or Junior Chamber	3
34.6 The GAA	23
34.7.Irish Countrywomen's Association	5
34.8 Other (please write in)_____	11

We would now like you to give us some personal details.

35.   Are you male or female

1. Male	69
2. Female	31

36.   Which of these descriptions applies to what you were doing last week, that is, in the seven days ending last Sunday?
Please place an 'X' in ONE box only

1. In full-time paid work	42
2. In part-time paid work	8
3. Registered unemployed	2
4. Wholly retired from work	17
5. Looking after the home full-time	17
6. Other (please specify)_____	14

37.   Which type of organisation do you work for? (If you are not working now, please answer in terms of your LAST job): *Please place an 'X' in ONE box only*

1. Self-employed	43
2. A private company or firm	24
3. A semi-state company	7
4. The state *(including e.g. civil service, army, gardai)*	7
5. A local authority	3
6. A health board / hospital	5
7. Other *(please specify)*:_____	10

38.   What is the full title of your present job? (If you are not working now, please answer in terms of your LAST job)
Please write in _____

39.   If you are not the chief income earner in your household could you write in his or her occupation:
Please write in _____

40.   Do you ever think of yourself as belonging to any particular social class, and if so which one?

1. Upper class	1
2. Upper middle class	13
3. Middle class	56
4. Lower middle class	8
5. Working class	20
6. Other (please specify)_____	2

41.   Could you please indicate to which age group you belong?

1. Under 25	4
2. 25-34	10
3. 35-44	16
4. 45-54	25
5. 55-64	23
6. 65 or over	23

42.   Which of these types of educational institution did you LAST attend, FULL-time?

1. National school	26
2. Second level school	42
3. RTC or VEC	12
4. University	14
5. Other (please specify)_____	6

43.   Have you obtained any of the following qualifications?

1. Inter cert	45
2. Junior cert	11
3. Leaving cert	44
4. Technical qualification (e.g. Nursing diploma)	11
5. Teachers training qualification	4
6. University degree	12

44.　Think of the accommodation where you live now. Do you..?

1. Own it or are buying the property	83
2. Rent it from the local authority	2
3. Rent it from a private landlord	3
4. Live with family or friends	12
5. Other (please specify)_____	0

45.　Do you regard yourself as belonging to any particular religion, and if so which one?

1. Catholic	94
2. Church of Ireland	4
3. Presbyterian	1
4. No religion	1
5. Other (please specify) _____	1

46.　How often do you attend church?

1. Several times a week	13
2. Weekly	69
3. About once a month	6
4. A few times a year	8
5. Rarely or never	4

47.　Which daily newspaper do you read MOST?

1. Irish Independent	52
2. Irish Times	17
3. The Examiner	19
4. Evening Herald	2
5. I don't read a daily newspaper	7
6. Other daily newspaper (please specify) _____	5

SECTION 4

Now we would like to get your views on various issues.
First of all, to what extent do you agree or disagree with the following statements?
For each statement, please put an X in the appropriate column.

	Strongly agree 1	2	3	4	Strongly disagree 5
48.1 Government should intervene more decisively in the economy so as to transfer wealth and resources from the wealthy to the less well off	51	15	20	6	7
48.2 The use of marijuana should be legalised	7	3	9	6	74
48.3 There are too many immigrants being let into this country	29	8	28	13	23
48.4 The trade unions have too much power in this country	22	12	28	14	24
48.5 Job creation should be a top priority even when this means some damage to the environment	22	13	20	15	30
48.6 There should be tighter controls on farming practices so as to prevent harm to the environment	45	15	16	8	16

And now some other questions about various issues:

49.   Some say European Unification should be pushed further. Others say it has already gone too far. What is your opinion?

1. It should be pushed further	38
2. It has already gone too far	31
3. Don't know	31

50.   Should Ireland drop its neutrality, to take part in a common defence policy in the EU (European Union)?

1. Yes	40
2. No	44
3. Don't know	17

51.   With regard to Northern Ireland, should the Irish government of the day have special regard for the views and concerns of Northern nationalists, or for Northern unionists, or should it try to be even handed as between Northern nationalists and Northern unionists?

1. Special regard for the views and concerns of Northern nationalists	14
2. Special regard for the views and concerns of Northern unionists	3
3. Even handed as between Northern nationalists and Northern unionists	76
4. Don't know	7

52.   Do you feel that the Catholic Church has too much influence on the educational system in this country, about the right amount of influence, or too little influence?

1. Too much influence	34
2. Too little influence	8
3. About the right degree of influence	54
4. Don't know	4

53.   Which of the following phrases comes closest to your own opinion about abortion?

1. It should be allowed for any woman who wants it	14
2. It should be allowed in special circumstances	39
3. It should be allowed only where there is a threat to the mother's life	33
4. It should not be allowed in any circumstances	12
5. Don't know	3

Now we would like you to consider a number of questions about our political institutions.

Could you tell us, for each of the following, the extent to which you agree or disagree? *For each statement, please put an 'X' in the appropriate column.*

	Strongly agree				Strongly disagree
	1	2	3	4	5
54. The Dáil should be reformed so as to reduce the power of the government parties and allow the opposition to have greater input into decision-making	38	17	19	10	17
55. The Seanad should be abolished	36	7	15	10	31
56. Local government should have consid--erably more power than at present	63	16	10	3	7

	Strongly agree				Strongly disagree
	1	2	3	4	5
57. Our PR electoral system results in good quality candidates being elected to the Dáil	46	17	18	7	12
58. Our PR electoral system forces TDs to spend too much of their time on constituency work instead of national parliamentary work	29	17	19	11	24
59. Our PR electoral system should be replaced by a system that does not make candidates of the same party compete against each other for votes.	26	10	16	11	38

60.   In general, do you feel that the Irish political system is working well, or not?

1. Yes   69
2. No   31

61.   What changes, if any, would you recommend to improve the quality of the Irish political system? *Please write in*:_____

SECTION 5

People often talk about "the left" and "the right" in politics. In the scales below, the number '1' is used to denote left-wing and the number '10' to denote right-wing. Would you please indicate how you would place the following on such a scale by placing an 'X' in the appropriate column.

	Left-wing									Right-wing
	1	2	3	4	5	6	7	8	9	10
62. Your own views	3	1	4	11	25	14	14	12	3	12
63. The Fine Gael party	5	1	3	4	21	19	17	12	5	13
64. Fianna Fáil	6	2	4	8	16	16	14	15	8	12
641. Labour	16	13	22	22	13	5	3	2	1	3
65. The PDs	4	3	4	4	11	10	12	16	17	19

Now some questions on internal Fine Gael matters.

66.   Do ordinary members of the Fine Gael party have enough say in determining party policy?

1. Yes	25
2. No	75

IF NO to Q66 Which of the following would you suggest to improve matters:
Please indicate, by placing an 'X' in the appropriate square

67.1. Regular meetings with party TDs in the constituency to
ascertain the views of ordinary party members   66
67.2. Resolutions at Ard-Fheiseanna to be binding on the party's TDs   36
67.3. Regular regional conferences of party members to discuss party policy   54
67.4. Other (please write in)_____   9

68.   Do you think Fine Gael should move to the left in its economic policies, move to the right, or stay about where it is?

1. Move to the left	18
2. Move to the right	10
3. Stay where it is	72

69.   Should Fine Gael become more liberal on social issues, become less liberal, or stay about where it is?

1. Become more liberal	33
2. Become less liberal	9
3. Stay where it is	59

70.   If the next government had to be a coalition, one of these combinations below, which would be your first choice, and which your second, and which your third? *[cell entries show percentage ranked first]*

WRITE 1 BESIDE YOUR FIRST CHOICE, AND 2 BESIDE YOUR SECOND

1. Fine Gael and Fianna Fáil	7
2. Fine Gael, Labour and the PDs	24
3. Fine Gael and Labour	69

71.   Do you believe that Fine Gael's existing methods of selecting election candidates ensure that Dáil candidates are of as high a calibre as possible?

1. Yes	68
2. No	32

72.   What additional steps do you feel could be taken by the party that would help to attract better quality candidates to the party?
Write in: _____

Most election candidates of all parties, including Fine Gael, are men. Several reasons have been put forward to explain this. We would like to know your opinion of the following suggested reasons and ways of changing the balance:
For each statement, please put an X in the appropriate column.

	Strongly agree				Strongly disagree
	1	2	3	4	5
73. Women are not as politically ambitious as men are	19	17	16	13	36
74. Women candidates lose votes for the party and so are not chosen	6	5	9	16	64
75. Attitudes within the party mean that women don't get an equal opportunity	27	14	20	13	25
76. Most women have too many family commitments	33	20	19	11	19

77.   Should Fine Gael introduce 'quotas' so that at least a certain minimum percentage, say 33 per cent, of its election candidates are women?

1. Yes   41
2. No   59

78a.   Do you feel the Fine Gael organisation could take more steps to attract new members?

1. Yes   89
2. No   11

If YES to Q78a
78b.   What is the most important step it should take?
*Write in*_____

79a.   Do you believe the Fine Gael organisation makes the best use of the energy and commitment of its existing members?

1. Yes   48
2. No   52

IF NO to Q79a.
79b.   What is the most important way in which it could make better use of them?
*Write in*_____

SECTION 6

Next, here are some general statements about politics in Ireland
Could you tell us, for each of the following, the extent to which you agree or disagree?
For each statement, please put an 'X' in the appropriate column.

	Strongly agree				Strongly disagree
	1	2	3	4	5
80.1 The FG party leadership doesn't pay a lot of attention to the views of ordinary party members	36	19	23	12	11
80.2 Parties in general are only interested in people's votes, not in their opinions	44	23	17	8	9
80.3 The only way to be really educated about politics is to be a party activist	43	15	15	12	15
80.4 FG would be more successful if more people like me were elected to the Dail	21	9	23	13	35
80.5 Attending party meetings can be pretty tiring after a hard day's work	37	20	18	9	16

SECTION 7

81.   Thinking of the job of a TD, in your view, how important do you think the
following things are for a TD to be doing his or her job properly? **Please mark 1 beside
the one you think is most important and 2 besides the next most important.** *[cell entries
show percentage ranked first]*

81.1. Playing a role in national politics, by speaking in Dáil debates,
helping to make laws, or being active on Dáil committees   43
81.2. Playing a role locally, by keeping in touch with local party members,
holding regular constituency clinics, or helping constituents with
individual problems   49
81.3. Playing a role for the party, by defending party policy to the press,
radio and television, and voting with the party at all times in the Dáil   8

82.   Do you believe that Fine Gael will win more seats than Fianna Fáil at any general election in the next twenty years?

1. Yes   53
2. No   47

83.   Do you believe that the Labour Party will win more seats than Fine Gael at any general election in the next twenty years?

1. Yes   11
2. No   89

84.   If the Progressive Democrats wanted to merge with Fine Gael would you welcome this?

1. Yes   55
2. No   45

85.   If there were to be a merger between Fianna Fáil and Fine Gael in the next twenty years would you welcome this?

1. Yes   19
2. No   81

86.   In which of the following policy areas do you think Fine Gael and Fianna Fáil differ most from one another? *Please put an 'X' in only ONE box*

1. Northern Ireland   28
2. Taxation   19
3. Europe   5
4. Agriculture   11
5. No real policy differences   32
6. Other *(write in)*_____   5

87.   In your own words, what do you feel is the main difference between Fianna Fáil and Fine Gael today? Please write in._____

Here are some questions about politicians.
Please think of a thermometer scale that runs from zero to 99 degrees, where 50 is the neutral or middle point. This time, if your feelings are warm and sympathetic towards something or some-one, give them a score higher than 50; the warmer the feelings, the higher the score.
If your feelings are cold and unsympathetic, give them a score less than 50; the colder your feel-ings, the lower the score. A score of 50 means that your feelings are neither warm nor cold.

Write ratings of between 10 and 99 like this   50
Write ratings of under 10 like this   09

Please give a rating to each of the following former Taoisigh

88. William T. Cosgrave	67
89. Eamon de Valera	33
90. John A. Costello	59
91. Seán Lemass	53
92. Jack Lynch	59
93. Liam Cosgrave	66
94. Charles Haughey	15
95. Garret FitzGerald	75
96. Albert Reynolds	40
97. John Bruton	66

Now please give a rating on the same basis to each of the following political parties.

98. Fianna Fáil	34
99. Fine Gael	76
100. Labour Party	50
101. Progressive Democrats	40
102. Green Party	31
103. Sinn Féin	19

Finally, please give a rating to each of the following politicians.

104. Bertie Ahern	39
105. John Hume	75
106. Mary Harney	46
107. Gerry Adams	36
108. David Trimble	44
109. Ian Paisley	15
110. Ruairí Quinn	50

What types of activity at election times do you think are most effective in increasing the vote for a political party?
Please mark 1 beside the one you think is most important and 2 besides the next most important.
[cell entries show percentage ranked first]

111. Personal contact with voters, such as door-to-door canvassing, after-mass meetings, meeting voters at shopping centres etc.   79
112. Local activity such as putting up posters on lampposts, displaying posters in windows or cars, delivering leaflets through the letterbox, and party advertisements in the local press   2
113. National activity such as campaign speeches by party leaders, party political broadcasts on television, and party advertisements in the national press   19

114.   Finally, what in your opinion are the main issues, policy and/or organisational, that Fine Gael needs to face up to either at the present time or in the future?

_____

_____

_____

_____

_____

_____

This is the end of the questionnaire

Please check that you have answered all the questions

Thank you very much for your help

Dear secretary

According to the membership lists supplied to us by Fine Gael head office, you are the secretary of your branch. It would be very helpful to us if, after you've answered the main questionnaire, you could fill in the additional questions on this sheet. As we stress in our letter, all the responses to the questionnaire will remain confidential to us and will not be passed to party head office.

If there are any other aspects of the party's organisation that our questionnaire has not touched on, and that you feel are important, please feel free to write additional comments at the bottom of this sheet or on a separate sheet of paper.

Thank you
Michael Gallagher and Michael Marsh

Q1.For how many years have you been secretary of the branch?   7 years

Q2.How many members does your branch have?   21

Q3.On average, how many people attend a typical meeting of your branch?   11

Q4. Would you say that there is a "core group" in your branch that does most of the work between elections?

1. Yes	93
2. No	7

Q5. If Yes, how big is this core group – how many people does it consist of?   6

Q6. Could you rank the following (from 1-5) according to how important you think these are for your branch? *[cell entries denote ranked first]*

election campaigning and campaign planning	41
support work for the TD or Dáil candidate	26
recruiting new members	19
fund-raising for Fine Gael	5
discussing policy matters	9

Q7. Over time, has the role of the local branch in election campaigns changed?

become more important	29
become less important	49
has not changed	22

Q8. Of the members of your branch, how many would you say are

very active, coming to most branch meetings and taking part in election campaigns?	8 members
quite active, taking part occasionally in party activities?	7 members
completely or almost completely inactive?	7 members

Q9. At election campaigns, how important in your branch's area are people who are party supporters but not formally paid-up party members?

very important – supporters do most of the work	21
important – supporters do as much work as paid-up members	24
not very important – supporters do only a minor proportion of the work	23
unimportant – all the work is done by paid-up members	33

Q10. In non-election years, is there

a net flow of funds from your branch to party head office	37
a net flow of funds from party head office to your branch	2
no significant flow of funds	61

Q11. If there is a significant flow of funds, please indicate the approximate amount

(*average*) £93.00

Q12. Does your branch

freely share its branch mailing list with Fine Gael head office	88
keep certain information to itself, or delay in sending updated lists	12

Q13. Do local party members complain about the number of appeals for party funds that they now get?

Yes	45
No	55

Q14. Are there any additional comments that you would like to make?

_____

_____

_____

Appendix C: The activism scale

Operationalising activism among Fine Gael members

In chapter 5 we introduced an activism scale on which almost all of the Fine Gael members in our survey could be placed. We need to have a variable that measures activism so that we can, among other things, explore the determinants of activism. Constructing a scale can be done in a number of different ways, and we chose a method that is simple and straightforward.

Our survey included six different questions that measure aspects of activism:

Q9, which asks members how often they have attended branch meetings in the previous twelve months;

Q13, which asks members how active they consider themselves to be relative to the average member;

Q18a, which asks members whether they took an active part in any Fine Gael campaigns during the last four years;

Q21, which asks members how much time they devote to Fine Gael in the average month;

Q23a, which asks members whether they took part in selecting candidates for the 1997 general election;

Q23aa, which asks members whether they took part in selecting candidates for the 1999 local election.

A scale can be based on just one item, but its reliability is usually enhanced by basing it on a number of related items. For example, studies carried out on the main British parties used eight items in the case of Labour and nine items for the Conservatives.[1] In this case, the items listed above are indeed related. Not only do they look intuitively as if they are; reliability analysis shows that they are, with a Cronbach's alpha of .62, a reasonably satisfactory level.

After some exploration of the data we decided to base our scale on four of the six items listed above. The two that were excluded were Q9, relating to attendance at branch meetings (on the ground that this is partly determined by the frequency of branch meetings, something that varies considerably across the country, as we saw in chapter 5) and Q23a, relating to participation in candidate selection for the 1997 general election (on the ground that those joining since May 1997, and indeed earlier in those constituencies where candidates were selected well in advance of the election, had no opportunity to participate).

The four items employed, then, were whether members had been active in recent party campaigns, how much time they give to the party, whether they participated in candidate selection for the 1999 local elections just a few months before our survey, and how active they considered themselves to be. The rationale for including the last item was that some members might be active in ways not specifically covered in the questionnaire, but because it is a subjective measure it was given less weight than the other three items.

Respondents were given scores for each of the fully weighted items: a low score (1) for the minimum level of activism, a medium score (3) for medium levels of activism, and a high score (5) for high activism. In the case of the question asking respondents for their own assessment of their activity level, the half-weighting led to the awarding of scores of 1, 2 and 3 respectively for low (not very active or not at all active), medium (fairly active) and high (very active) levels of self-perceived activism. Thirty-three out of the 1,722 respondents did not answer two of more of the four questions, and these were excluded from the scale, being treated as missing cases. Sixty-four respondents answered three of the four questions; these were given a medium score for the item that they did not answer. The other 1,625 respondents answered all four questions.

As a result, each respondent, other than the thirty-three missing cases, achieved a score of anything from 4 to 18 across the four items. Based on their scores, the respondents were then divided into four groups of approximately equal size as follows:

Score	Category	Label	% in category prior to weighting of cases	% in category after weighting of cases
4–8	1	Not at all active	21.7	26.6
9–13	2	Not very active	31.6	34.0
14–15	3	Fairly active	25.0	22.1
16–18	4	Very active	21.7	17.2
		Total	100.0	100.0

As explained in Appendix A, cases were weighted according to whether or not they were a branch secretary, secretaries having been deliberately over-represented in our sample. Since secretaries tend to be more active than other members, the effect of weighting is to increase the proportion of cases in the least active group and reduce the proportion in the most active group.

The scale could, of course, have been constructed differently, but in the last analysis any alternative approach would have made little difference, given that all six activism-related variables are highly correlated with each other.

Note to Appendix C

1.   Seyd and Whiteley, *Labour's Grass Roots*, pp. 94–6; Whiteley et al, *True Blues*, pp. 102–5.

Appendix D: Historical data

Key events in the history of Fine Gael

1916–18	The Easter Rising and subsequent heightened nationalist feeling leave the Sinn Féin party as the dominant political force in nationalist Ireland
1919	On 21 January Sinn Féin sets up an Irish parliament (Dáil Éireann) and government
1921	On 6 December the Anglo–Irish Treaty is signed by representatives of the British and Irish governments; it provides for the establishment of a substantively independent Irish state, but this would be confined to twenty-six of the thirty-two counties of Ireland. Moreover, members of the Dáil will have to take an oath to the British monarch
1922	January. Sinn Féin splits over whether the Treaty is acceptable. A small majority of both ministers and members of parliament believe that it is (the pro-Treatyites); a large minority regard it as a betrayal of the full nationalist demand (the anti-Treatyites). An election in June is won by the pro-Treatyites, who form the government
1922–23	A civil war takes place between the pro-Treaty government forces and the anti-Treatyites; it is won by the government
1923	On 27 April the pro-Treatyites launch a new party, Cumann na nGaedheal ("League of Gaels"), under the leadership of William T. Cosgrave
1932	On 9 March, Cumann na nGaedheal loses office for the first time; it is defeated at an election by Fianna Fáil, the main representatives of the anti-Treaty tradition, led by Eamon de Valera
1933	On 8 September Cumann na nGaedheal merges with the smaller National Centre Party and with the extra-parliamentary National Guard (the Blueshirts) to form Fine Gael ("Tribe of Gaels"), led by Eoin O'Duffy, the National Guard leader
1934	O'Duffy is ousted as Fine Gael leader and replaced by the former Cumann na nGaedheal William T. Cosgrave
1948	After sixteen years of electoral decline in opposition, Fine Gael returns to government as part of a multi-party coalition that remains in office until 1951. A Fine Gael deputy, John A. Costello, becomes Taoiseach, and Fine Gael's electoral fortunes begin to revive
1957	Fine Gael loses office after leading a second multi-party coalition government (1954–57) and begins a second sixteen-year spell in opposition
1959	In October the dual leadership of Richard Mulcahy (leader of the extra-parliamentary party) and John A. Costello (leader of the parliamentary party) comes to an end; James Dillon becomes leader
1965	Fine Gael stands on its "Just Society" manifesto, which emphasises the need for social justice and is generally perceived as being well to the left of the party's traditional stance – though there are doubts as to whether the party leadership is genuinely committed to it
1965	On 21 April, following the election, Dillon resigns the leadership and is succeeded by Liam Cosgrave
1973	On 1 January Ireland joins the European Community and takes up 12 seats

	(later expanded to 15) in the European Parliament. The Fine Gael MEPs become part of the European People's Party (christian democratic) group
1973	On 14 March the National Coalition government takes over after 16 years of Fianna Fáil government; Liam Cosgrave becomes Taoiseach
1977	Election defeat brings to end the Fine Gael–Labour coalition government that has been in office since 1973. Fine Gael elects Garret FitzGerald as its new leader; FitzGerald is seen as liberal on church–state issues and as further to the left on socio-economic issues than previous party leaders. He initiates a vigorous organisational overhaul and recruitment drive
1987	FitzGerald's second government, a coalition with Labour that took office in 1982, ends when Labour withdraws in January. At the ensuing general election Fine Gael receives its lowest vote share since 1957, losing votes heavily to a new party, the Progressive Democrats (the PDs), who belong to Europe's liberal tradition. FitzGerald resigns as party leader
1990	On 13 November Alan Dukes, who succeeded FitzGerald as leader, is ousted following the presidential election, in which the Fine Gael candidate Austin Currie wins only 17 per cent of the votes. He is succeeded on 20 November by John Bruton
1994	On 15 December Fine Gael enters government after the Fianna Fáil–Labour coalition breaks up. Labour switches sides to take part in a new coalition with Fine Gael and Democratic Left (the "rainbow coalition") – the first time an Irish government has changed without a general election. John Bruton becomes Taoiseach
1996	On 30 November Fine Gael's Michael Lowry resigns as Minister for Transport, Energy and Communications following revelations about money he has secretly received from a leading businessman. His affairs come under increasing scrutiny, with discoveries about his involvement in the black economy and tax irregularities. In March 1997 he leaves Fine Gael; standing as an independent in the June 1997 election in his Tipperary constituency
1997	Following the election of 6 June, the rainbow coalition loses office, to a coalition of Fianna Fáil and the PDs
2001	On 31 January, after a run of unspectacular election results and poor opinion poll showings, John Bruton is ousted as party leader; he is succeeded on 9 February by Michael Noonan.

Key figures in Fine Gael's history

John Bruton (1947–). First elected to the Dáil in 1969 from Meath. Fine Gael leader 1990–2001, Taoiseach 1994–97. Inherited Fine Gael party when it was at a low ebb and despite best efforts left it in much the same state. Was seen as conservative on socio-economic issues while Minister for Finance in governments of the 1980s, but played successful consensus role as Taoiseach

Michael Collins (1890–1922). Leading figure in IRA (Irish Republican Army) and IRB (Irish Republican Brotherhood), and played a crucial role in the war of independence conducted against the British 1919–21. One of the signatories of the Treaty in 1921, though he realised that many IRA members would bitterly oppose it; his support was instrumental in securing significant support for the Treaty from the IRA. Described the Treaty pragmatically as not the embodiment of all nationalist aspirations but as "freedom to achieve freedom". Killed during an ambush at Béal na mBláth, Co Cork, in August 1922; one of the most revered figures within Fine Gael

Liam Cosgrave (1920–). Fine Gael leader 1965–77, Taoiseach 1973–77. Son of William T. Cosgrave. Regarded as pragmatic on socio-economic issues and as very clericalist on church–state issues; attached high priority to preserving the security and institutions of the state and to the need to be vigilant against paramilitary violence

William T. Cosgrave (1880–1965). Took part in 1916 rising, minister in Sinn Féin governments from 1919. After deaths of Collins and Griffith became leader of the pro-Treaty forces. Leader of Cumann na nGaedheal and Fine Gael (apart from a break from 1933–35) until his retirement in 1944, prime minister 1922–32. Seen as a conservative figure but played vital role in creating the institutions of government and establishing the new Irish state as a functioning liberal-democracy

Declan Costello (1926–). Son of John A. Costello, first elected to the Dáil in 1951. From the late 1950s he was the prime mover in what became known as the "Just Society" wing of the party, seeking to move Fine Gael well to the left of its previous conservative position. This had a certain impact during the 1960s, but it was only after Garret FitzGerald became leader in 1977, ironically just a few months after Costello had left politics to become a judge, that his views became mainstream party policy. He never held government office (though he was Attorney-General 1973–77) but was an influential and respected figure within Fine Gael

John A. Costello (1891–1976). Taoiseach (prime minister) in the two "Inter-Party" coalition governments of 1948–51 and 1954–57. Leading barrister first elected to Dáil in 1933, became Taoiseach in 1948 (even though he was not Fine Gael leader) at the request of the other parties in the coalition. As Taoiseach bore some responsibility for the misunderstandings and lack of communication within the government that brought about the "Mother and Child" affair, in which Minister for Health, Noel Browne, clashed with the Catholic bishops; Costello made clear his complete support for the church

James Dillon (1902–86). Son of John Dillon, the last leader of the Irish Parliamentary Party, whose MPs at Westminster pressed for Home Rule for Ireland until the party was swept away by Sinn Féin at the 1918 election. Dillon was elected as an independent TD in 1932, joined the National Centre Party when it was formed later that year, and became a Fine Gael TD and vice-president when that party was brought into existence in 1933. He left Fine Gael in 1942 because he favoured Ireland's participation in the second world war on the side of the allies, unlike the rest of the political establishment which preferred the policy of neutrality. As an independent, he was a minister in the first Inter-Party government of 1948–51, but he rejoined Fine Gael in 1952. He was elected party leader in 1959 and resigned following the 1965 election. He was an eloquent speaker and a dedicated parliamentarian, though unsuited to the television era, and his critics said that he would have been most at home in the House of Commons of the nineteenth century. Throughout his career he attracted special hostility and scorn from Fianna Fáil, which he fully reciprocated

Alan Dukes (1945–). First elected to the Dáil in 1981 from Kildare after working as an agricultural economist, and, unusually, was appointed a minister immediately on his election. A leading figure in Fine Gael for the next six years, serving as Minister for Finance from 1982 to 1986, he won the race to succeed Garret FitzGerald when the leadership became vacant in 1987. At that time he was seen as personifying the relatively social democratic wing of the party, following in FitzGerald's footsteps, whereas his main rival John Bruton was seen as standing for the more traditional large farmer element within the party. He committed Fine Gael to the "Tallaght

Strategy" under which Fine Gael, in opposition, would not bring down the minority Fianna Fáil government elected in 1987 provided that government adhered to prudent economic policies. However, his relations with party colleagues deteriorated, and following a disastrous presidential election campaign he resigned the leadership in November 1990 when on the verge of losing a motion of no confidence in his leadership

Garret FitzGerald (1926–). Trained as an economist, brought unprecedented levels of expertise to highest levels of Fine Gael when he became a TD in 1969. Minister for Foreign Affairs in 1973–77 government, succeeded Liam Cosgrave as Fine Gael leader in wake of heavy 1977 election defeat. Undertook active recruitment drive and overhaul of organisation, set up and encouraged Young Fine Gael. Led Fine Gael to unprecedented electoral heights in early 1980s. Taoiseach 1981–March 1982 and again from December 1982 to March 1987, but resigned leadership after Fine Gael's disastrous 1987 election result. Liberal on church–state issues, and his leadership was viewed with disfavour by a more conservative "old guard"

Arthur Griffith (1871–1922). Leader of Sinn Féin party from 1905 onwards; minister in Sinn Féin government 1919–22; not involved in violence; advocated the use of tariffs and protection by an independent Irish state to discourage imports and enable Irish industry to develop; seen (along with Collins) as one of the two leading figures on the pro-Treaty side an, as such, as a founding father of Fine Gael

Richard Mulcahy (1886–1971). A leading figure in the war of independence who took the pro-Treaty side when Sinn Féin split. A member of most Cumann na nGaedheal governments during the first decade of the state, though was compelled to resign in 1924 during the so-called "army mutiny", returning to government in 1927. Became leader (party president) of Fine Gael in 1944 following the resignation of William T. Cosgrave, and as such could have expected to become Taoiseach when Fine Gael entered government in 1948, but his civil war record made him unacceptable to some of the other parties in the government and Costello became Taoiseach instead, though it appears that Mulcahy played a major role in selecting the Fine Gael ministers. Resigned the leadership in 1959

Michael Noonan (1943–). First elected to the Dáil in 1981 from Limerick East, and became Minister for Justice in December 1982; senior figure in party ever since then. Took part in an unsuccessful "heave" against John Bruton's leadership in February 1994, but was nonetheless appointed to government when Fine Gael unexpectedly returned to office in December 1994. Launched another coup against the leader in January 2001, and this time Bruton was ousted; Noonan won the party leadership with 44 votes against 28 votes for his only rival, Enda Kenny

Eoin O'Duffy (1892–1944). Chief of police during the 1920s, he was sacked by the Fianna Fáil government in February 1933 and became leader of Ireland's quasi-fascist movement, known officially first as the Army Comrades' Association and then as the National Guard, and unofficially as the Blueshirts. Surprisingly, he was made leader of Fine Gael when that party was formed in September 1933 even though he was not even a member of parliament, but he was temperamentally unsuited to the role and was ousted the following year, after which he led a small band of supporters to fight on Franco's side in the Spanish civil war.

Other figures in Irish political life

Gerry Adams (1948–). Leader of Sinn Féin since 1983. Regarded with suspicion up to mid-1990s by many southern voters, especially Fine Gael supporters, given Sinn Féin connection with IRA, but played leading role in "peace process" in 1990s and often credited with attempting to lead republican movement away from violence and into conventional political activity

Bertie Ahern (1951–). Fianna Fáil leader from 1994, Taoiseach from 1997. Elected to Dáil in 1977 and worked his way steadily up party hierarchy. Personally popular, seen as seeker of consensus rather than confrontation, criticised by opponents for policy vagueness

Eamon de Valera (1882–1975). The dominant Irish nationalist figure of the twentieth century. Leader of the anti-Treatyites from 1923, founded Fianna Fáil 1926 and led the party until 1959. Taoiseach 1932–48, 1951–54, 1957–59; President 1959–73. Perceived by Fine Gael contemporaries as a very partisan figure, blamed by many of them for destructive role at time of Treaty negotiations and the subsequent split, seen as hypocritical. By the same token, a revered figure within Fianna Fáil, praised for his vision, judgement and patriotism, and for his successful execution of the policy of neutrality during the second world war

Mary Harney (1953–). Member of Fianna Fáil until 1985, then founding member of PDs; became party leader 1993, led party into government 1997 and became Tánaiste. Regarded as firmly within European liberal tradition, i.e. in favour of separation of church and state and of reduction in taxes and state spending

Charles Haughey (1925–). Fianna Fáil's most controversial leader (1979–92), Taoiseach 1979–81, 1982, 1987–92. Identified with the more nationalist wing of his party, dismissed from government by Lynch in 1970 on foot of allegations that he had connived at the importation of arms for use by the IRA in Northern Ireland (he was acquitted of all charges). Very divisive figure within own party and generally distrusted by supporters of other parties. Reputation fell following retirement as a result of revelations that he lived way beyond his means while a senior politician, being secretly bankrolled by business people and bank loans; tribunals of enquiry established to try to discover whether he granted political favours to those from whom he received money

John Hume (1937–). Leader of main Northern Ireland nationalist party, the SDLP, from 1979 to 2001. Good contacts with all southern parties and widely respected among southern voters. Was offered chance in 1997 to become President of Ireland as unopposed nominee of all main parties, but declined

Seán Lemass (1899–1971). Succeeded de Valera as Fianna Fáil leader in 1959, Taoiseach 1959–66. Was associated with the shift in Fianna Fáil, of which he was a founder member, from traditional nationalist policies to support for rapid economic development and with normalisation of relations with Britain and Northern Ireland. For this reason, regarded more favourably by non-members of Fianna Fáil than de Valera is

Jack Lynch (1917–1999). Succeeded Lemass as Fianna Fáil leader, Taoiseach 1966–73, 1977–79. Personally popular among voters across the political spectrum, resisted those within his own party who wanted a stronger nationalist line (including in some cases support for violence) when the Northern Ireland troubles re-emerged from 1969 onwards. For this reason and others, regarded warmly by many outside the ranks of Fianna Fáil supporters

Ian Paisley (1926–). Leader of Democratic Unionist Party, a long-standing critic of many aspects of southern state, uncompromising opponent of Good Friday Agreement and of Irish nationalism generally

Ruairí Quinn (1946–). Leader of Labour Party since 1997; Minister for Finance in rainbow

coalition 1994–97

Albert Reynolds (1932–). Fianna Fáil leader 1992–94, Taoiseach for same period. Played important role while Taoiseach in construction of Northern Ireland "peace process", but failure to handle coalition partners with sufficient sensitivity led to break-up of both coalition governments that he led

David Trimble (1944–). Leader of Ulster Unionist Party since September 1995. Led his party into support for 1998 Good Friday Agreement despite opposition from many unionists, including a substantial minority of own party.

Sources: Coakley and Gallagher, *Politics in the Republic of Ireland*, pp. 379–84; Boylan, *A Dictionary of Irish Biography*.

Table D1: First preference votes in Dáil elections by party, 1922–97, in per cent

Election	Fianna Fáil	Fine Gael	Labour Party	Others	Total
1922	21.7	38.5	21.3	18.4	100.0
1923	27.4	39.0	10.6	23.0	100.0
1927-1	26.1	27.5	12.6	33.9	100.0
1927-2	35.2	38.7	9.1	17.1	100.0
1932	44.5	35.3	7.7	12.5	100.0
1933	49.7	30.5	5.7	14.2	100.0
1937	45.2	34.8	10.3	9.7	100.0
1938	51.9	33.3	10.0	4.7	100.0
1943	41.9	23.1	15.7	19.3	100.0
1944	48.9	20.5	8.8	21.8	100.0
1948	41.9	19.8	8.7	29.6	100.0
1951	46.3	25.8	11.4	16.6	100.0
1954	43.4	32.0	12.1	12.6	100.0
1957	48.3	26.6	9.1	16.0	100.0
1961	43.8	32.0	11.6	12.5	100.0
1965	47.7	34.1	15.4	2.9	100.0
1969	45.7	34.1	17.0	3.2	100.0
1973	46.2	35.1	13.7	5.0	100.0
1977	50.6	30.5	11.6	7.3	100.0
1981	45.3	36.5	9.9	8.4	100.0
1982-1	47.3	37.3	9.1	6.3	100.0
1982-2	45.2	39.2	9.4	6.3	100.0
1987	44.1	27.1	6.4	22.4	100.0
1989	44.1	29.3	9.5	17.1	100.0
1992	39.1	24.5	19.3	17.2	100.0
1997	39.3	27.9	10.4	22.4	100.0
Average	42.7	31.3	11.4	14.6	100.0

Source: Coakley and Gallagher, *Politics in the Republic of Ireland*, p. 367.
Note: Fianna Fáil includes anti-Treaty Sinn Féin and Republicans (1922 and 1923), Fine Gael includes pro-Treaty Sinn Féin and Cumann na nGaedheal (1922–32).

Table D2: Seats won at Dáil elections by party, 1922–97

Election	Fianna Fáil	Fine Gael	Labour Party	Others	Total
1922	36	58	17	17	128
1923	44	63	14	32	153
1927-1	44	47	22	40	153
1927-2	57	62	13	21	153
1932	72	57	7	17	153
1933	77	48	8	20	153
1937	69	48	13	8	138
1938	77	45	9	7	138
1943	67	32	17	22	138
1944	76	30	8	24	138
1948	68	31	14	34	147
1951	69	40	16	22	147
1954	65	50	19	13	147
1957	78	40	12	17	147
1961	70	47	16	11	144
1965	72	47	22	3	144
1969	75	50	18	1	144
1973	69	54	19	2	144
1977	84	43	17	4	148
1981	78	65	15	8	166
1982-1	81	63	15	7	166
1982-2	75	70	16	5	166
1987	81	51	12	22	166
1989	77	55	15	19	166
1992	68	45	33	20	166
1997	77	54	17	18	166
Average	69	50	16	16	151

Source: Coakley and Gallagher, *Politics in the Republic of Ireland*, p. 368.
Note: Fianna Fáil includes anti-Treaty Sinn Féin and Republicans (1922 and 1923), Fine Gael includes pro-Treaty Sinn Féin and Cumann na nGaedheal (1922–32).

Table D3: Participation in government by Fine Gael and its predecessors, 1922–2001

Start date	Termination date	Composition of government	Taoiseach	Number of FG ministers	Total number of ministers
14.1.22	22.8.22	Pro-Treaty SF	Michael Collins	8	8
22.8.22	9.9.22	Pro-Treaty SF	William T. Cosgrave	9	9
9.9.22	6.12.22	Pro-Treaty SF	William T. Cosgrave	11	11
6.12.22	19.9.23	CG	William T. Cosgrave	10	10
19.9.23	23.6.27	CG	William T. Cosgrave	11	11
23.6.27	11.10.27	CG	William T. Cosgrave	10	10
11.10.27	2.4.30	CG	William T. Cosgrave	9	9
2.4.30	9.3.32	CG	William T. Cosgrave	9	9
18.2.48	13.6.51	FG, Lab, CnP, CnT, NLab, Ind	John A. Costello	6	13
2.6.54	20.3.57	FG, Lab, CnT	John A. Costello	8	13
14.3.73	5.7.77	FG, Lab	Liam Cosgrave	10	15
30.6.81	9.3.82	FG, Lab	Garret FitzGerald	11	15
14.12.82	10.3.87	FG, Lab	Garret FitzGerald	11	15
15.12.94	26.6.97	FG, Lab, DL	John Bruton	8	15

Source: Coakley and Gallagher, *Politics in the Republic of Ireland*, p. 376
Note: CG = Cumann na nGaedheal; CnP = Clann na Poblachta; CnT = Clann na Talmhan; DL = Democratic Left; FG = Fine Gael; Ind = independent; Lab = Labour; NLab = National Labour; SF = Sinn Féin. The term "Taoiseach" was introduced by the 1937 constitution; prior to that, the head of government was known as the President of the Executive Council.

Notes

Notes to Chapter 1

1. Sartori, *Parties and Party Systems*, pp. 3–13.
2. The fullest discussion of the names of the Irish parties can be found in Coakley, "The significance of names". Coakley observes (p. 181) that several Irish parties, including Fianna Fáil and Fine Gael, chose names that have connotations of community, a closely-knit collectively that can be regarded as a living organism, rather than names including a word such as "party", which implies a "more formal mechanical aggregate". "Fianna Fáil" is usually translated loosely as "Soldiers of Destiny", though "Soldiers of Ireland" would be equally valid. For the translation of "Fine Gael" see chapter 2, pp. 20–23.
3. Gallagher, Laver and Mair, *Representative Government in Modern Europe*, pp. 271–3.
4. Under the constitution, all members of the government must belong to either the Dáil or the Seanad; at most two may belong to the Seanad. In practice, virtually all ministers are TDs; only two Senators have been appointed to government since the constitution came into force in 1937.
5. Scarrow, *Parties and their Members*, p. 43.
6.. This is the argument of Katz and Mair, "Changing models of party organization".
7. See Seyd and Whiteley, *Labour's Grass Roots*, and Whiteley et al, *True Blues*.
8. These examples are from De Winter, "Belgium", p. 36; Koole and Leijenaar, "The Netherlands", p. 202.
9. Katz, "Party as linkage".
10. The benefits and costs of members are discussed in Scarrow, *Parties and their Members*, pp. 40–50.
11. Although for the most part we shall report our findings in the present tense, the fact that these findings date from late 1999 should constantly be borne in mind by the reader.
12. For a description of the contents of the archive see Helferty, "Irish political parties and research". Fianna Fáil's records have been systematically archived, and these archives are utilised by a number of the contributors to Hannon and Gallagher, *Taking the Long View*.
13. In *Changing Irish Party System*, chapter 3. We shall discuss Mair's conclusions about Fine Gael's organisation in chapter 3 of this book.
14. Garvin, "Local party activists"; Garvin, "Belief systems"; Mair, "Social factors"; Sacks, *The Donegal Mafia*; Bax, *Harpstrings and Confessions*.
15. Dunphy, "Group of individuals".
16. These studies are Seyd and Whiteley, *Labour's Grass Roots*; Whiteley et al, *True Blues*; Bennie et al, "Party members"; Rüdig et al, *Green Party Members*.
17. Most of these studies were conducted at around the same time as our own and publication of the findings is still forthcoming. There is some information available on the internet. A general description of these projects can be found at the web site of the Institute for the Study of Political Parties at the University of Sheffield; see www.shef.ac.uk/~pol/ispp. For Canada see www.mta.ca/faculty/socsci/polisci/scppm/index.html. For Norway see Heidar and Saglie, "A decline in party activity?".

18. To be precise, this was the final question on the additional one-page questionnaire sent to all branch secretaries.
19. Gallagher, "Parliament".
20. See Sinnott, "The electoral system" for a full description and assessment.
21. The historical record shows that most Fianna Fáil and Fine Gael TDs who seek re-election secure it, but among those who are defeated, almost half are ousted by a candidate of their own party. Gallagher, "Relatively victorious incumbent", p. 97.

Notes to Chapter 2

1. There are, after all, a number of substantial histories of Ireland during the last century, such as Lee, *Ireland 1912–1985* and Keogh, *Twentieth-Century Ireland*.
2. Lawrence, "Labour – the myths", p. 342. Italics in original.
3. Ibid, pp. 341–2.
4. Garvin, *Evolution of Irish Nationalist Politics*, p. 161.
5. Gallagher, "Pact election".
6. Garvin, *1922: the birth of Irish democracy*, p. 45.
7. For some discussion of whether class differences underpinned the split see Sinnott, *Irish Voters Decide*, pp. 127–31. The evidence suggests that in 1923 support for the pro-Treaty Cumann na nGaedheal was catch-all rather than class-based (ibid., p. 131).
8. Collins, *Cosgrave Legacy*, pp. 7–41.
9. Regan, *Irish Counter-Revolution*, p. 141.
10. Regan, *Irish Counter-Revolution*, p. 186; see generally ibid., pp. 163–97 and Lee, *Ireland 1912–1985*, pp. 96–105.
11. Lee, *Ireland 1912–1985*, p. 112.
12. Downs, *Economic Theory of Democracy*, chapter 8. On, say, the left–right dimension, the median voter is the one who has as many voters to his or her left as to his or her right.
13. Garvin, "Democratic politics", p. 362.
14. Gallagher, *Political Parties in the Republic of Ireland*, 45.
15. See Girvin, *Between Two Worlds* , for a discussion of the issues.
16. Regan, *Irish Counter-Revolution*, pp. 133, 313–14.
17. Sinnott, *Irish Voters Decide*, p. 133.
18. Gallagher, *Irish Elections 1922–44*, p. 157.
19. Regan, *Irish Counter-Revolution*, p. 339.
20. Regan, *Irish Counter-Revolution*, p. 332; Cronin, *Blueshirts*, p. 47.
21. Regan, *Irish Counter-Revolution*, pp. 291–5.
22. Gallagher, *Political Parties in the Republic of Ireland*, p. 46.
23. Manning, *James Dillon*, p. 79.
24. Coakley, "The significance of names", p. 174. "Fine Gael / United Ireland Party" is still employed in some parts of the country.
25. Ibid, p. 175.
26. Keogh, *Twentieth-Century Ireland*, p. 83.
27. For a full discussion of the issue see Bew, Hazelkorn and Patterson, *Dynamics of Irish Politics*, pp. 62–7; Cronin, *Blueshirts*, pp. 38–68; Manning, *Blueshirts*, pp. 211–44.
28. Manning, *Blueshirts*, p. 125.
29. Manning, *Blueshirts*, p. 102.
30. Manning, *James Dillon*, pp. 90–1.

31.   O'Higgins, *A Double Life*, p. 47.
32.   Cronin, *Blueshirts*, pp. 110, 128–9.
33.   Waters, *Jiving at the Crossroads*, p. 24.
34.   Manning, *Courage to Succeed*, p. 25.
35.   Joint meeting of parliamentary party and Standing Committee, 14 November 1945, UCD archives, P39/Min/2(225–9).
36.   UCD archives, P39/Min/4(206–8), 5 December 1945.
37   UCD archives, P39/Min/5, 5 May 1948.
38.   Manning, *James Dillon*, p. 294.
39.   Gallagher, *Irish Labour Party in Transition*, p. 57.
40.   UCD archive, P39/GE/125(11–12), 22 April 1965.
41.   Manning, *James Dillon*, p. 375; for a contrary view see FitzGerald, *All in a Life*, p. 70.
42   Gallagher, *Irish Labour Party in Transition*, p. 85.
43.   Lysaght, *Republic of Ireland*, p. 149.
44.   Collins, *Cosgrave Legacy*, pp. 148, 152.
45.   For FitzGerald's own account, see *All in a Life*, pp. 325–9; see also O'Byrnes, *Hiding behind a Face*, pp. 16–29.
46.   Brian Farrell, "The context of three elections", pp. 12–13.
47.   FitzGerald, *All in a Life*, pp. 424–5. For the misdemeanours see Joyce and Murtagh, *The Boss* and Collins, *Power Game*, especially pp. 119–225.
48.   Girvin, "The divorce referendum".
49.   See the accounts of those most closely involved: FitzGerald, *All in a Life*, pp. 621–5; Desmond, *Finally and in Conclusion*, pp. 313–20; Hussey, *At the Cutting Edge*, pp. 196–202.
50.   FitzGerald, *All in a Life*, p. 390.
51.   Brian Farrell, "The government", p. 187.
52.   Finlay, *Snakes and Ladders*, pp. 15–17.
53.   The previous TDs to have this distinction – Noel Browne, Kevin Boland and Martin O'Donoghue – all went on to leave or be expelled from their parties.
54.   Collins, *Power Game*, p. 170.
55.   Collins, *Power Game*, p. 176.
56.   On "Seven Ages", RTE television, 10 April 2000.
57.   The Tallaght strategy is discussed in Marsh and Mitchell, "Office, votes, and then policy", pp. 50–4.
58.   Desmond, *Finally and in Conclusion*, pp. 214, 320.
59   Mair, "The Irish party system into the 1990s", p. 219.
60.   For accounts of the events of these days see Collins, *Power Game*, pp. 263–86; Duignan, *One Spin on the Merry-Go-Round*, pp. 153–66; Garry, "The demise of the Fianna Fáil / Labour 'Partnership' government".
61.   See Girvin, "Political competition, 1992–1997", pp. 18–26.
62.   Collins and O'Shea, *Understanding Corruption in Irish Politics*, p. 26; Kerrigan and Brennan, *This Great Little Nation*, pp. 192–4.
63   Gallagher, "The results analysed", pp. 130–1.
64.   Marsh, "The making of the eighth president".
65.   MRBI poll 5444/01, 22–23 January 2001.
66.   *Irish Times* 30 January 2001.
67.   FitzGerald, *All in a Life*, p. 647.
68.   Coincidentally, two previous leaders had also been 57 when they became leader; comparing their ages at election to the leadership, Noonan was about eight months older than James Dillon and a few days older than Richard Mulcahy.

69. Foreword to Manning, *Courage to Succeed*, p. 3.
70. Manning, *Courage to Succeed*, p. 33.

Notes to Chapter 3

1. See Laver and Marsh, "Parties and voters", pp. 153–5 for a general discussion of Irish party organisation.
2. Details from Fine Gael, *Constitution and Rules*, p. 9. The party's *Branch Manual* has much useful information both on the rules and on what in practice branches are expected to do.
3. The reasons are too complicated to go into here; for some discussion see Gallagher, "Candidate selection in Ireland", pp. 492–5 and Katz, "But how many candidates should we have in Donegal?"
4. Galligan, "Candidate selection", p. 69.
5. Gallagher, "Ireland: the increasing role of the centre", p. 126.
6. "Some of them don't even know they *are* members" was one comment.
7. Fine Gael, *Constitution and Rules*, p. 34.
8. Waters, *Jiving at the Crossroads*, pp. 33–4.
9. FitzGerald, *All in a Life*, p. 74. Italics in original.
10. Manning, *James Dillon*, p. 339.
11. He was elected for the National Centre Party in 1933, and for Fine Gael in 1937, 1938, 1954 and 1957. In 1932, 1943, 1944, 1948 and 1951 he was returned as an independent; in 1932, when he stood in Donegal, he had the backing of the Ancient Order of Hibernians.
12. Gallagher, "Politics in Laois–Offaly", p. 660.
13. Scarrow, *Parties and their Members*, p. 186; see ibid., pp. 174–95 and Tanner, "Labour and its membership", especially pp. 252–9.
14. Duverger, *Political Parties*, p. xxxv.
15. Regan, *Irish Counter-Revolution*, pp. 131–2. Our account of the pro-Treatyites' organisations up to 1936 draws heavily on Regan's work.
16. Regan, *Irish Counter-Revolution*, pp. 143, 149.
17. Regan, *Irish Counter-Revolution*, pp. 154–60.
18. Regan, *Irish Counter-Revolution*, p. 160; Garvin, *Evolution of Irish Nationalist Politics*, p. 147.
19. Regan, *Irish Counter-Revolution*, pp. 203–4.
20. Regan, *Irish Counter-Revolution*, pp. 209–11.
21. Regan, *Irish Counter-Revolution*, pp. 213–14.
22. Regan, *Irish Counter-Revolution*, p. 238.
23. Regan, *Irish Counter-Revolution*, pp. 262, 306.
24. Fanning, *Independent Ireland*, p. 102.
25. Cumann na nGaedheal's approach to organisation is analysed by the first political scientist to study Irish politics, Moss, *Political Parties in the Irish Free State*, pp. 54–108.
26. Regan, *Irish Counter-Revolution*, p. 300.
27. Gallagher, "Politics in Laois–Offaly", pp. 667–8.
28. Mair, *Changing Irish Party System*, p. 121; see generally pp. 114–24.
29. Ibid, p. 119.
30. Ibid, pp. 123–4.
31. For just one example of many see Mulcahy's appeal to TDs to attend the Dáil more regularly and put down more questions, UCD archives P39/Min/4(215), 8 May

1946. At times Fianna Fáil too had difficulties in securing the attendance of its TDs, though, it seems, its difficulties were not on the same scale nor of the same persistence as those of Fine Gael. See Horgan, "Seán Lemass: a man in a hurry", p. 38.

32. Duverger, *Political Parties*, pp. 63–71.
33. See photograph section.
34. UCD archives, P39/Min/4(5), 31 January 1934.
35. UCD archives, P39/Min/4(30), 15 November 1934.
36. UCD archives, P39/Min/2(47), 5 July 1934 and P39/Min/2(91), 16 February 1935. Some at least of the organisers were back by December 1937.
37. UCD archives, P39/Min/4(46), 6 November 1935.
38. UCD archives, P39/Min/4(195), 18 July 1945.
39. UCD archives, P39/Min/5, 10 March 1949.
40. O'Higgins, *A Double Life*, pp. 156, 184.
41. Manning, *James Dillon*, p. 339.
42. Sacks, *Donegal Mafia*, pp. 180–95.
43. Chubb, *Government and Politics of Ireland*, pp. 89, 90.
44. UCD archives, P39/GE/119(94), 17 December 1963.
45. UCD archives, P39/GE/119(10), 20 March 1965.
46. After the death of the Clann na Talmhan TD Michael Donnellan in 1964, his son John stood and won as a Fine Gael candidate in the ensuing by-election and the entire Clann na Talmhan organisation in the constituency was integrated into Fine Gael.
47. Mair, *Changing Irish Party System*, pp. 119–20.
48. UCD archives, P39/GE/119(47), 19 March 1965.
49. UCD archives, P39/GE/125(11,12), undated.
50. FitzGerald, *All in a Life*, pp. 325–9; O'Byrnes, *Hiding behind a Face*, pp. 16–29.
51. For details, see Mair, *Changing Irish Party System*, p. 128; Gallagher, *Political Parties in the Republic of Ireland*, pp. 123-4.
52. See Table 4.1 in next chapter and Mair, *Changing Irish Party System*, p 104.
53. See Table 4.1 in next chapter
54. Mockler, "Organisational change in Fianna Fáil and Fine Gael", p. 170.
55. Fine Gael, *Report of the Commission*, p. 9.
56. Fine Gael, *Report of the Commission*, p. 9.
57. Fine Gael, *Report of the Commission*, p. 10.
58. Mockler, "Organisational change in Fianna Fáil and Fine Gael", p. 169.
59. Fine Gael, *Report of the Commission*, p. 39.
60. Fine Gael, *Report of the Commission*, p. 39.
61. Its discussion of the organisation can be found in Fine Gael, *Report of the Commission*, pp. 39–48.
62. Fine Gael, *Report of the Commission*, p. 42.
63. Fine Gael, *Report of the Commission*, p. 45.
64. Fine Gael, *Report of the Commission*, p. 46.

Notes to Chapter 4
1. Mair, *Changing Irish Party System*, pp. 102–6.
2. Chubb, *Government and Politics of Ireland*, p. 94.
3. Mair, *Changing Irish Party System*, pp. 102–6.
4. See Mair and van Biezen "Party membership"; Gallagher et al., *Representative Government in Modern Europe*, p. 275.

5. Analysis of the 1999 European Values survey supports this. Four per cent of those saying they would support Fine Gael in a general election also claimed to be party members. In 1991 the figure was 6.5 per cent. Differences between the two are not statistically significant.

6. Gallagher et al., *Representative Government in Modern Europe*, Table 10.1.

7. The average date when members say they joined is 1976. Recall of dates at such a distance is obviously a little unreliable. Our data shows members disproportionately claiming to have joined in end-of-decade dates such as 1960, 1970, 1980 and so on. Hence this table groups the time people claim to have joined around these dates.

8. Our information on age is recorded in ten-year bands, so estimates had to be made here by taking the mid-points of each age range.

9. Tom Garvin reported evidence from the late 1960 that indicated most members joined before they were 30, but this study covered only one constituency in Dublin (Dublin South-Central) and examined only activists: Garvin, "Local party activists", p. 377.

10. Numbers are too small to estimate usefully prior to 1956. In addition, it is likely that the older cohorts, who joined prior to 1955, may be confusing family support and activity with formal membership, if indeed formal membership mattered much in those days.

11. A simple simulation, in which it is assumed that all members leave the party at 70, provides some support for our argument. Taking a cohort's age at joining, increasing it by 10, 20 or 30 years as appropriate so as to correspond to the time of our sample, and dropping anyone passing the age of 70, produces a mean age which exceeds that for each cohort in our sample by only 1–2 years. This suggests that attrition could well account for most, if not all, of the apparent change over time.

12. Fianna Fáil, *Commission on the Aims and Structures of Fianna Fáil*.

13. Whiteley et al, *True Blues*, p. 42.

14. van Holsteyn et al., "Party membership in the Netherlands", Table 4.

15. Cross and Young, "The study of Canadian party members", http://www.mta.ca/faculty/socsci/polisci/scppm.

16. Galligan and Wilford, "Gender and party politics in the Republic of Ireland".

17. Urban areas are defined in this book as all the constituencies in greater Dublin, along with Cork North-Central, Cork South-Central, Kildare North and Limerick East.

18. Occupational groups are categorised here using the standard market research coding as follows: AB (upper middle class and middle class; professional, managers, employers with considerable seniority or authority over others), C1 (lower middle class; junior professionals, secretarial), C2 (skilled working class), D (other working class), E (those dependent on social security or state pensions), F (farmers, farm managers, farm workers).

19. This classification relies on the reported occupation of the head of household. In allocating members between the AB and C1 categories, we erred on the side of C1s when in doubt so the proportion of ABs here may be a slight underestimate. If insufficient information was given about the degree of responsibility of those such as teachers, or the size of companies for which people were "company directors", such people were classed as C1. Twelve per cent of members could not be classified at all and are excluded from these calculations.

20. For example; Manning, *Irish Political Parties*, chapter 2. Sacks, *Donegal Mafia*, p.

128 also found that a preponderance of Fine Gael members were of high social status.

21. "Others", where they specified their job, were fairly evenly divided between public and private sector, plus some who simply said "housewife".

22. These are sets of state examinations and certificates are given for fulfilling minimum requirements. Junior, later called intermediate certificate, exams are taken at around age 15 and leaving certificate at 17–18.

23. Lansdowne JNRR Readership Survey 1999–2000.

24. Sacks, *Donegal Mafia*, p. 132.

25. For example Meals on Wheels, juvenile badminton supervisor; craftworks association, have worked on schools committee; church choir; drama group; Muintir na Tíre; Nautical institute; town traders association; Opus Dei; Organic Farming Association; Organisation of National Ex-Servicemen and Women; Square One theatre group; Senior Citizens, Mental Health Support group; Parent on school board of management; Parish Committee; Womens' group; Bridge club; Golf club; International Police Association.

26. In addition to the 522 secretaries who returned questionnaires, a further 38 "ordinary" members also turned out to be branch secretaries and are included as such in Table 4.7.

27. This is not true of incumbents of offices in general, who look much more like the general membership.

28. Garvin, "Local party activists", pp. 376–7, who also cites Bax, *Harpstrings and Confessions*, p. 228.

29. Sinnott, *Irish Voters Decide*, pp. 131–7.

30. We used the Lansdowne/RTE exit poll from the 1997 general election for gender, class and age. This was a particular large survey and so provides data on over 700 Fine Gael voters. However, this survey is very limited in the range of variables included. Other comparisons had to made with smaller 1999 European Values Survey, though it contained only 171 Fine Gael voters.

31. Widfeldt, "Party membership and party representativeness", pp. 146–60.

32. Seyd and Whiteley, *Labour's Grass Roots*, p. 39.

33. Whiteley et al, *True Blues*, p. 50.

34. Authors' own analysis of data from the European Values Study 1999.

35. Brady et al, "Beyond SES – a resource model of political participation".

36. Wilson, "Volunteering"; Verba et al, *Voice and Equality*, chapter 13.

37. Clark and Wilson, "Incentive systems"; Seyd and Whiteley, *Labour's Grass Roots*, pp. 56–68.

38. Conservative figure from Whiteley et al, *True Blues*, p. 78; Labour figure from Seyd and Whiteley, *Labour's Grass Roots*, p. 84 (those who don't remember are apparently excluded from the calculation).

39. Brady et al, "Prospecting for participants".

40. Whiteley et al., *True Blues*, Table 4.6; Seyd and Whiteley, *Labour's Grass Roots*, Table 4.5.

41. Heidar and Saglie, "A decline of party activity?" pp. 22–3; van Holsteyn et al., "Party membership in the Netherlands", Question 10a.

42. Cross and Young, "The study of Canadian party members", http://www.mta.ca/faculty/socsci/polisci/scppm.

43. Interestingly, only 4 per cent report that only their mother was a member, compared with 22 per cent who report only their father as a member and 37 percent who say both parents belonged to the party. This suggests that, at least in the past,

few married women belonged to Fine Gael unless their husband also belonged.

44. Yet these people, and those whose families have a record of long support for Fine Gael, are no more likely than other members to report that the party approached them to become a member.

45. Gallagher et al., *Representative Government in Modern Europe*, p. 279.

46. Though only a small minority of such people mention a career motive for joining.

Notes to Chapter 5

1. Michels, *Political Parties*, p. 370.

2. Ware, "Activist–leader relations", p. 79.

3. Wolinetz, "Reconstructing Dutch social democracy", pp. 106–7.

4. Fine Gael, *Report of the Commission*, p. 39.

5. Svåsand et al, "Change and adaptation", pp. 109–10.

6. A caveat that we should enter at this point is that by definition these figures relate only to our respondents, and it is possible that inactive members, who may be less interested in politics or elderly and in poor health, were simply less inclined to return the questionnaire, in which case our data understate the proportion of inactive members in the party. Of course, the same applies to the surveys of members in other countries with which we are comparing our own data. See Appendix A for details of the sampling and for further discussion of this point.

7. It was clear from the responses that, despite the wording of Q9, some respondents had counted meetings not only of their local branch but also of other bodies such as a constituency or district organisation.

8. Seyd and Whiteley, *Labour's Grass Roots*, p. 89; Whiteley et al, *True Blues*, p. 68.

9. Information from the Canadian party member survey web site at www.mta.ca/faculty/socsci/polisci/scppm/index.html, Q12a.

10. Whiteley et al, *True Blues*, p. 248.

11. Rüdig et al, *Green Party Members*, p. 41.

12. Lawson, "Political parties and linkage", p. 3.

13. Katz, "Party as linkage", p. 143.

14. Katz and Mair, "Changing models of party organization", p. 16.

15. For an overview see Gallagher and Komito, "Constituency role of TDs".

16. Desmond, *Finally and In Conclusion*, p. 45.

17. Scarrow, *Parties and their Members*, pp. 115, 146.

18. Crewe and King, *SDP*, p. 273. For a general discussion of groups that seek members who will pay fees without donating any time see Jordan and Maloney, "Manipulating membership".

19. Whiteley et al, *True Blues*, p. 258.

20. These figures represent 10.20 euros and 3.80 euros respectively.

21. In 1965 a candidate selected at a Fine Gael convention withdrew his name, saying that "this was a rich man's party and he had not the money necessary to be a candidate". Other parties, he said, supplied the deposit and expenses to their candidates. UCD Fine Gael archives P39/GE/119(65), 18 March 1965. In 1987 the Dublin South-West Fine Gael organisation was said to be insisting that candidates contribute £3,000 towards the cost of the election campaign and one candidate withdrew for this reason (*Irish Times* and *Irish Press* 19 January 1987).

22. Laver and Marsh, "Parties and voters", p. 157.

23. Under the OMOV system all members may take part, but only if they turn up at the convention – there is no provision for postal voting. In a geographically large

constituency this makes the selection of a venue an important decision, since aspirants whose main base is a long way from the venue will feel themselves to be at a disadvantage.

24. Scarrow, *Parties and their Members*, p. 181; Scarrow, "Parties without members?", p. 94.
25. Maor, *Political Parties*, p. 115.
26. Gallagher, Laver and Mair, *Representative Government in Modern Europe*, pp. 275–6.
27. Whiteley et al, *True Blues*, p. 249.
28. Seyd and Whiteley, *Labour's Grass Roots*, p. 228; Bennie et al, "Party members", p. 139; Whiteley et al, *True Blues*, p. 249.
29. Laver and Marsh, "Parties and voters", pp. 170–1; generally, see Sinnott, *Irish Voters Decide*.
30. Seyd and Whiteley, *Labour's Grass Roots*, pp. 97–9; Whiteley et al, *True Blues*, pp. 105–7; van Holsteyn et al, *Party Membership in the Netherlands*, p. 5.
31. Komito, "Brokerage or friendship?".
32. Fine Gael, *Report of the Commission*, pp. 67, 43, 40.
33. Whiteley et al, *True Blues*, p. 247.
34. Fine Gael, *Branch Manual*, p. 23.
35. Of course, members' experiences may not be as overwhelmingly unfavourable as this suggests, given that those who are dissatisfied with some state of affairs are always more likely to voice complaint than those who are satisfied are to express their contentment.
36. Sacks, *Donegal Mafia*, p. 117.
37. Coakley, "Society and political culture", p. 53.
38. Sacks, *Donegal Mafia*, p. 19; Chubb, *Government and Politics of Ireland*, p. 52.
39. Decalo, *Coups and Army Rule*, p. 6.
40. Carty, *Party and Parish Pump*, pp. 141, 130, 138.
41. Schlesinger, "Political party organization", p. 781.
42. Carty, *Party and Parish Pump*, pp. 134–8.

Notes to Chapter 6

1. A comprehensive review is Gallagher et al., *Representative Government in Modern Europe*, chapter 10.
2. Katz, "Party as linkage".
3. Mair and van Biezen, "Party membership in twenty European democracies".
4. This was attempted by party head office in the mid-1990s. Members were circulated and asked what they could contribute, but the response rate was extremely low (less than five per cent).
5. Brendan Grace is a well known Irish entertainer, whose appeal, it would be fair to say, is primarily to the middle-aged and to pensioners.
6. Note the contrast with the member quoted on p. 92 above who felt that it is in the first instance up to those at the bottom to get things right.
7. "The Branch should not wait for New Members to come to them. It is the responsibility of every member of the Party to seek New Members". Fine Gael, *Branch Manual*, p. 23.
8. Although the question asked, which was "what should the Fine Gael organisation do?", may have encouraged members to focus on what others could do.
9. See Q6 of secretaries' questionnaire in Appendix B.
10. On Britain, see Scarrow, *Parties and their Members*; on Norway see Heidar and

Saglie, "Predestined parties?", passim.

11. Fine Gael, *Renewing the Party*. This was the report of an implementation committee appointed by the leader, John Bruton and chaired by Frances Fitzgerald TD
and which comprised Michael Lowry TD (chairman of the parliamentary party),
Senator Maurice Manning (Leader in the Senate), Councillor Mary French
(Secretary of the Council of Local Representatives), Gina Menzies (national executive), Séan Murray (a trustee), Michael O'Reilly (from the Joyce Commission)
and Ivan Doherty (general secretary of the party).

12. Although at present Senators, who are indirectly elected (mainly by county councillors), are among those electing the leader and their claim to a democratic mandate is certainly arguable.

13. The policy committee was duly established, and its role is described in Fine Gael,
Constitution and Rules, p. 23.

14. Many who had answered that the system was fine went on to explain how it
could be improved. These people were much more likely to point to the lack of
certain types of candidate than those who were dissatisfied (41 per cent as against
25 per cent), and less likely to suggest changes in the procedures (25 per cent as
against 43 per cent).

15 Galligan, "Candidate selection", p. 67.

16. Chubb, "Going about persecuting civil servants".

17. Phillips, *The Politics of Presence*.

18. Galligan, "Candidate selection", p. 77.

19. See Galligan and Wilford, "Gender and party politics".

20. Academic evidence on this is mixed. Galligan, Laver and Carney in "The effects
of candidate gender" argue that women candidates are as successful as men. A
contrary conclusion is arrived at by Gallagher, "The results analysed" p. 123 and
Marsh, "Electoral evaluations of candidates ", p. 70.

21. Galligan and Wilford, "Gender and party politics", p. 153.

22. Galligan and Wilford, "Gender and party politics", pp. 158–9.

23. Mair, *Changing Irish Party System*, p. 137.

24 Fine Gael, *Branch Manual*, pp. 35–43.

25. We have used the percentage of the electorate rather than percentage of the valid
vote in Figure 6.2 since we think it is the absolute rather than the relative level of
support that should respond to member activities. If we use raw vote numbers
we run the risk of obscuring the real relationship behind the obvious fact that,
other things being equal, bigger constituencies are likely to have more Fine Gael
voters and more Fine Gael members simply because they contain more people.
However, taking an overall turnout rate of 65 per cent, 1.5 per cent of the electorate works out also at 2.3 per cent of the valid vote, or 1003 votes in an average
constituency.

26. See Sinnott, *Irish Voters Decide*, pp. 137–8.

27. The R^2 for 1992 was 0.58. This statistic indicates on a scale from 0 to 1 how closely
two things are related in terms of how far one value (Fine Gael support) can be
predicted from another (percentage of farmers). It is 0.37 for 1997, using 1992
class data again.

28. The multiple regression equation here is: Fine Gael vote as a percentage of the
electorate = 5.0+1.3 (Members in hundreds) + 0.11 (%Farmers) + 0.37
(%Professional). R^2 (adjusted) = 0.57.

29. The correlation is 0.75 as opposed to 0.61.

30. Seyd and Whiteley, *Labour's Grass Roots*, pp. 181–200.

Notes to Chapter 7

1.   For example, Duverger, *Political Parties*, pp. 182–202.
2.   Katz and Mair, "Changing models of party organization".
3.   May, "Opinion structure of political parties".
4.   Seyd and Whiteley, *Labour's Grass Roots*, pp. 52–5.
5.   Whiteley et al, *True Blues*, p. 64.
6   Norris, "May's Law"; Holmberg, "Dynamic opinion representation"; Narud and Skare, "Are party activists the extremists?".
7.   Strøm, "A behavioral theory"; Ware, "Activist–leader relations".
8.   Scarrow, *Parties and their Members*, pp. 44–5.
9   Mair, "Party competition and the changing party system".
10.   Sinnott, *Irish Voters Decide*, pp. 160–4.
11.   Sinnott, *Irish Voters Decide*, p. 161.
12.   Of course, in all these surveys respondents were given no direction from the researchers as to how to interpret the terms "left" and "right".
13.   This is Pearson's correlation coefficient; a value of 1 would indicate a perfect relationship, while a value of 0 would indicate no relationship at all.
14.   Knutsen, "Value orientations", pp. 72–3.
15.   Coakley, "Society and political culture", pp. 41–4, 61–3; Hug, *Politics of Sexual Morality*.
16.   Of course, given turnover among members, the 1995 and 1999 memberships are not identical. But as we explained in chapter 4 we estimate that turnover is low given the overall stability in membership figures and the long tenure of existing members.
17.   This factor explains 42 per cent of the variance. The loadings are not especially strong, ranging from .33 up to .52.
18.   Donoghue and Devine, "Is there a gender gap?", pp. 250–60.
19.   Gallagher, "Ireland: the referendum as a conservative device?", p. 96.
20.   Kennelly and Ward, "The abortion referendums", pp. 129–30.
21   Garvin, "Belief systems", p. 45. Garvin concludes that "in Ireland ... the political shorthand terms 'left' and 'right', in so far as they mean anything, tend to be attached to Church–State issues rather than to issues of welfare or wealth redistribution".
22.   Those on the left are those who, in answer to Q62, placed themselves at points 1–4 inclusive on the 10-point scale; those on the right are those who indicated positions 7–10 inclusive.
23.   Of course, our survey can only show how this issue is viewed by the left and right within Fine Gael; it does not establish that the issue may not divide national political opinion along left-right lines.
24.   For example Laver, "Are Irish parties peculiar?", pp. 365–9.
25.   Keatinge and Laffan, "Ireland: a small open polity".
26.   *Irish Times*, 2 February 2001.
27.   Mudde, "Defining the extreme right party family".
28   For example Inglehart, *Silent Revolution*.
29.   When politicians were surveyed on this issue in 1995–96 as part of the European Representation Study, attitudes among Fine Gael TDs and MEPs were very similar to those of members in 1999.
30.   The 1997 Lansdowne / RTE exit poll produced very similar figures. It drew responses from 782 Fine Gael voters, of whom 11 per cent placed themselves on the left, 54 per cent in the centre and 35 per cent on the right.

31.   For details, see MRBI polls of 6 May 1992, 8 June 1992 and 9 November 1992.

32.   Crewe and King, *SDP*, p. 278.

Notes to Chapter 8

1.   Whiteley et al, *True Blues*, pp. 178–9.

2.   To express this another way, the correlation between evaluation of Labour and self-placement on the left–right spectrum is -0.10. The meaning is the same: there is a slight tendency for members on the left to rate Labour more highly than do members who place themselves on the right.

3.   Desmond, *Finally and in Conclusion*, p. 81.

4.   Duignan, *One Spin on the Merry-Go-Round*, p. 49.

5.   Garvin, "Belief systems", pp. 52–3.

6.   Manning, *James Dillon*, p. 341.

7.   Mair, "Party competition and the changing party system".

8.   Nor, in order to keep the list manageable, did we include any option including the Greens – who, as the thermometer scores showed, are not at all popular with Fine Gael members.

9.   There is no significant relationship between optimism / pessimism and whether a member has had contact with a TD in the last twelve months.

10.   It should be noted that the wording of the two question was slightly different. Regarding the PDs, members were asked, in effect, how Fine Gael should respond if the PDs indicated a desire to merge with Fine Gael. In the case of Fianna Fáil, where the prospect of a merger was not on anyone's agenda in 1999, the question asked whether members would welcome a merger if this were to take place in the next twenty years.

11.   Garry and Mansergh, "Party manifestos", pp. 91–2.

12.   We do not show the breakdown among those who gave other responses since, as we saw in Table 8.5, the numbers in these other categories are small.

13.   This familiar broad-brush generalisation is subjected to scrutiny, but by no means dismissed, in Horgan, *Seán Lemass*, chapters 6–11.

14.   Coakley, "Appendices", p. 382. Lynch died on 20 October 1999, just a few weeks after our questionnaire was mailed to members. At this stage only about a quarter of our eventual respondents had sent back their questionnaires. Lynch's death and the extensive obituaries that he received undoubtedly boosted the regard in which he was held; his average score of 54 before his death rose to 62 among those questionnaires completed after his death. Even before this, though, his popularity was clearly markedly higher than that of other Fianna Fáil Taoisigh apart from Lemass.

15.   Collins, *Power Game*, chapter 11.

16.   Q80.1. Among those strongly agreeing with the last of these statements, Bruton's average score was 63; among those strongly disagreeing with it, it was 74. We discussed responses to Q80.1 and related questions in chapter 6.

17.   For example, see Horgan, *Seán Lemass*, p. 207.

18.   It is clear, indeed, that to some extent members who gave higher scores to one person tended to give higher scores to another person; some members simply gave higher "marks" than others, even though all were given the same guidance about the scale and were told, for example, that 50 was the score denoting a feeling of neutrality.

19.   Murphy, "A culture of sleaze"; O'Halpin, " 'Ah, they've given us a good bit of stuff'".

20. Sinnott, "The electoral system", p. 118.
21. See Lijphart, *Patterns of Democracy*, for a general examination of these two models of democratic regime.
22. Age and education are related to attitudes to reform, though in a slightly unexpected manner. We found that younger and newer members are simply less likely to have an opinion on these questions, and more likely to place themselves at the neutral position 3 on the 5-point scale. Similarly, when it comes to education, the main impact is that those with the least education are the most likely to express strong opinions, one way or the other, while those with most education tend to give one of the less forceful responses. For example, on the question of whether the Dáil should be reformed, 74 per cent of those with national school education either strongly agree or strongly disagree and 26 per cent give one of the middle three responses, whereas among those with university education only 38 per cent express strong agreement or strong disagreement and 62 per cent place themselves in the centre of the scale or adjacent to it on the 5-point scale.
23. See, for example, Sinnott, "The electoral system"; Gallagher, "Electoral systems".
24. Although the electoral system is proportional representation by means of the single transferable vote (PR-STV for short), we did not use this phrase in our questions, since the system is widely known in Ireland simply as "PR", as if there were no other kinds of PR electoral system. Instead, the questions refer to "Our PR electoral system".
25. Advocates of this measure tend to compare the ratio of population to MPs in Ireland with that of larger countries, especially the United Kingdom, but for a whole host of practical reasons this ratio is higher in smaller countries (applying the United Kingdom ratio Ireland would have a parliament of 42 members and Luxembourg one of just 5). A study covering twenty-one stable, developed democracies found that the size of parliament is closely related to the cube root of the population (Taagepera and Shugart, *Seats and Votes*, pp. 174–5). On this basis we could expect the Dáil to have about 156 TDs (the cube root of 3.8 million, which is the population of the Republic of Ireland), only ten fewer than the actual number.

Notes to Chapter 9

1. For the argument that pyramidal organisations such as traditional political parties are having to give way to loosely structured groups such as women's and environmental networks, see Mulgan, *Politics in an Antipolitical Age*, pp. 124–5. See also the discussion in Webb, "Are British political parties in decline?"
2. Katz, "Party as linkage"; Katz and Mair, "Changing models of party organization".
3. Anthony Downs in *An Economic Theory of Democracy*, pp. 103–7, terms this "responsibility".
4. Thus the British Labour party, confronted by a Conservative government whose behaviour offended large swathes of British society, recorded a large increase in membership from 1991 to 1997. See Seyd and Whiteley, "Towards a more responsible two-party system", p. 5.
5. Interestingly, none of our respondents suggested adopting the model of organisation preferred by the Joyce Commission, which we discussed in chapter 3.

References

Books and articles

Bax, Mart, *Harpstrings and Confessions: machine-style politics in the Irish Republic*. Assen: Van Gorcum, 1976.

Bennie, Lynn, John Curtice and Wolfgang Rüdig, "Party members", pp. 135–53 in Don MacIver (ed.), *The Liberal Democrats*. Hemel Hempstead: Prentice Hall, 1996.

Bew, Paul, Ellen Hazelkorn and Henry Patterson, *The Dynamics of Irish Politics*. London: Lawrence and Wishart, 1989.

Boylan, Henry, *A Dictionary of Irish Biography*, 3rd ed. Dublin: Gill and Macmillan, 1998.

Brady, Henry E., Sidney Verba and Kay L. Schlozman, 'Beyond SES – a resource model of political participation", *American Political Science Review* 89:2 (1995), pp. 271–94.

Brady, Henry E., Kay L. Schlozman and Sidney. Verba, "Prospecting for participants: rational expectations and the recuitment of political activists", *American Political Science Review* 93: 1 (1999), pp. 153–68.

Carty, R. K., *Party and Parish Pump: electoral politics in Ireland*. Waterloo, Ontario: Wilfrid Laurier University Press, 1981.

Chubb, Basil, "Going about persecuting civil servants: the role of the Irish parliamentarian", *Political Studies* 11:3 (1963), pp. 272–86.

Chubb, Basil, *The Government and Politics of Ireland*. London: Oxford University Press, 1974.

Clark, Peter B. and James Q. Wilson, "Incentive systems: a theory of organization", *Administrative Science Quarterly* 6 (1961), pp. 129–66.

Coakley, John, "The significance of names: the evolution of Irish party labels", *Études Irlandaises* 5 (1980), pp. 171–81.

Coakley, John, "The foundations of statehood", pp. 1–31 in John Coakley and Michael Gallagher (eds), *Politics in the Republic of Ireland*, 3rd ed. London: Routledge and PSAI Press, 1999.

Coakley, John, "Society and political culture", pp. 32–70 in John Coakley and Michael Gallagher (eds), *Politics in the Republic of Ireland*, 3rd ed. London: Routledge, 1999.

Coakley, John, "Appendices", pp. 364–87 in John Coakley and Michael Gallagher (eds), *Politics in the Republic of Ireland*, 3rd ed. London: Routledge and PSAI Press, 1999.

Collins, Neil and Mary O'Shea, *Understanding Corruption in Irish Politics*. Cork: Cork University Press, 2000.

Collins, Stephen, *The Cosgrave Legacy*. Dublin: Blackwater Press, 1996.

Collins, Stephen, *The Power Game: Fianna Fáil since Lemass*. Dublin: O'Brien Press, 2000.

Crewe, Ivor and Anthony King, *SDP: the birth, life and death of the Social Democratic Party*. Oxford: Oxford University Press, 1995.

Cronin, Mike, *The Blueshirts and Irish Politics*. Dublin: Four Courts Press, 1997.

Decalo, Samuel, *Coups and Army Rule in Africa: motivations and constraints*, 2nd ed. New Haven and London: Yale University Press, 1990.

Desmond, Barry, *Finally and In Conclusion: a political memoir*. Dublin: New Island, 2000.

De Winter, Lieven, "Belgium: democracy or oligarchy", pp. 20–46 in Michael Gallagher and Michael Marsh (eds), *Candidate Selection in Comparative Perspective: the secret garden of politics*. London: Sage, 1988.

Donoghue, Freda and Paula Devine, "Is there a gender gap in political attitudes in Ireland?", pp. 240–68 in Yvonne Galligan, Eilís Ward and Rick Wilford (eds), *Contesting Politics: women in Ireland, north and south*. Boulder, CO: Westview and PSAI Press, 1999.

Downs, Anthony, *An Economic Theory of Democracy*. New York: Harper and Row, 1957.

Duignan, Seán, *One Spin on the Merry-Go-Round*. Dublin: Blackwater, 1995.

Dunphy, Richard, " 'A group of individuals trying to do their best': the dilemmas of Democratic Left", *Irish Political Studies* 13 (1998), pp. 50–75.

Duverger, Maurice, *Political Parties*, 3rd ed. London: Methuen, 1964.

Fanning, Ronan, *Independent Ireland*. Dublin: Helicon, 1983.

Farrell, Brian, "The context of three elections", pp. 1–30 in Howard Penniman and Brian Farrell (eds), *Ireland at the Polls 1981, 1982, and 1987*. Durham NC: Duke University Press, 1987.

Farrell, Brian, "The government", pp. 167–89 in John Coakley and Michael Gallagher (eds), *Politics in the Republic of Ireland*, 2nd ed. Dublin: Folens and PSAI Press, 1993.

Farrell, David M., "Ireland", pp. 389–457 in Richard S. Katz and Peter Mair (eds), *Party Organizations: a data handbook*. London: Sage, 1992.

Fianna Fáil, *Commission on the Aims and Structures of Fianna Fáil: final report*. Dublin: Fianna Fáil, 1993

Fine Gael, *Report of the Commission on Renewal of Fine Gael [the Joyce Commission]*. Dublin: Fine Gael, 1993.

Fine Gael, *Renewing the Party: the next decade*. Dublin: Fine Gael, 1994.

Fine Gael, *Constitution and Rules*. Dublin: Fine Gael, 1999.

Fine Gael, *Branch Manual*. Dublin: Fine Gael, 2001.

Finlay, Fergus, *Snakes and Ladders*. Dublin: New Island, 1998.

FitzGerald, Garret, *All in a Life: an autobiography*. Dublin: Gill and Macmillan, 1991.

Gallagher, Michael. "The pact general election of 1922", *Irish Historical Studies* 21:84 (1979), pp. 404–21.

Gallagher, Michael, "Candidate selection in Ireland: the impact of localism and the electoral system", *British Journal of Political Science* 10:4 (1980), pp. 489–503.

Gallagher, Michael, *The Irish Labour Party in Transition 1957–82*. Manchester: Manchester University Press, 1982.

Gallagher, Michael, *Political Parties in the Republic of Ireland*. Manchester: Manchester University Press, 1985.

Gallagher, Michael, "Ireland: the increasing role of the centre", pp. 119–44 in Michael Gallagher and Michael Marsh (eds), *Candidate Selection in Comparative Perspective: the secret garden of politics*. London: Sage, 1988.

Gallagher, Michael, *Irish Elections 1922–44: results and analysis*. Limerick: PSAI Press, 1993.

Gallagher, Michael, "Electoral systems", pp. 499–520 in Constitution Review Group, *Report of the Constitution Review Group*. Dublin: Stationery Office, 1996.

Gallagher, Michael, "Ireland: the referendum as a conservative device?", pp. 86–105 in Michael Gallagher and Pier Vincenzo Uleri (eds), *The Referendum Experience in Europe*. Basingstoke: Macmillan, 1996.

Gallagher, Michael, "Parliament", pp. 177–205 in John Coakley and Michael Gallagher (eds), *Politics in the Republic of Ireland*, 3rd ed. London: Routledge and PSAI Press, 1999.

Gallagher, Michael, "Politics in Laois–Offaly 1922–92", pp. 657–87 in Pádraig G. Lane and William Nolan (eds), *Laois: history and society*. Dublin: Geography Publications, 1999.

Gallagher, Michael, "The results analysed", pp. 121–50 in Michael Marsh and Paul Mitchell (eds), *How Ireland Voted 1997*. Boulder CO: Westview Press and PSAI Press, 1999.

Gallagher, Michael, "The (relatively) victorious incumbent under PR-STV: legislative turnover in Ireland and Malta", pp. 81–113 in Shaun Bowler and Bernard Grofman (eds), *Elections in Australia, Ireland, and Malta under the Single Transferable Vote: reflections on an embedded institution*. Ann Arbor: University of Michigan Press, 2000.

Gallagher, Michael and Lee Komito, "The constituency role of TDs", pp. 206–31 in John Coakley and Michael Gallagher (eds), *Politics in the Republic of Ireland*, 3rd ed. London: Routledge and PSAI Press, 1999.

Gallagher, Michael, Michael Laver and Peter Mair, *Representative Government in Modern Europe: institutions, parties and governments*, 3rd ed. New York: McGraw-Hill, 2001.

Gallagher, Michael and Michael Marsh (eds), *Candidate Selection in Comparative Perspective: the secret garden of politics*. London: Sage, 1988.

Galligan, Yvonne, "Candidate selection", pp. 57–81 in John Coakley and Michael Gallagher (eds), *Politics in the Republic of Ireland*, 3rd ed. London: Routledge and PSAI Press, 1999.

Galligan, Yvonne, Michael Laver and Gemma Carney, "The effect of candidate gender on voting in Ireland, 1997", *Irish Political Studies* 14 (1999), pp. 118–22.

Galligan, Yvonne and Rick Wilford, "Gender and party politics in the Republic of Ireland", pp. 149–68 in Yvonne Galligan, Eilís Ward and Rick Wilford (eds), *Contesting Politics: women in Ireland, north and south*. Boulder CO: Westview Press and PSAI Press, 1999.

Garry, John, "The demise of the Fianna Fáil / Labour 'Partnership' government and the rise of the 'Rainbow' coalition", *Irish Political Studies* 10, pp. 192–99, 1995.

Garry, John and Lucy Mansergh, "Party manifestos", pp. 82–106 in Michael Marsh and Paul Mitchell (eds), *How Ireland Voted 1997*. Boulder CO: Westview Press and PSAI Press, 1999.

Garvin, Tom, "Local party activists in Dublin: socialisation, recruitment and incentives", *British Journal of Political Science* 6:3 (1976), pp. 369–80.

Garvin, Tom, "Belief systems, ideological perspectives and political activism: some Dublin evidence", *Social Studies* 6:1 (1977), pp. 39–56.

Garvin, Tom, *The Evolution of Irish Nationalist Politics*. Dublin: Gill and Macmillan, 1981.

Garvin, Tom, *1922: the birth of Irish democracy*. Dublin: Gill and Macmillan, 1996.

Garvin, Tom, "Democratic politics in independent Ireland", pp. 350–63 in John Coakley and Michael Gallagher (eds), *Politics in the Republic of Ireland*, 3rd ed. London: Routledge and PSAI Press, 1999.

Girvin, Brian, "The divorce referendum in the Republic, June 1986", *Irish Political Studies* 2 (1987), pp. 93–9.

Girvin, Brian, *Between Two Worlds: politics and economy in independent Ireland*. Dublin: Gill and Macmillan, 1989.

Girvin, Brian, "Political competition, 1992–1997", pp. 3–28 in Michael Marsh and Paul Mitchell (eds), *How Ireland Voted 1997*. Boulder CO: Westview Press and PSAI Press, 1999.

Hannon, Philip and Jackie Gallagher (eds), *Taking the Long View: 70 years of Fianna Fáil*. Dublin: Blackwater Press, 1996.

Heidar, Knut and Jo Saglie, "Predestined parties? Organizational change in Norwegian political parties", paper presented at the ECPR Joint Sessions, Grenoble, 6–11 April 2001.

Heidar, Knut and Jo Saglie, "A decline of party activity? Intra-party participation in Norway 1991–2000", paper presented at the 1st ECPR general conference, Canterbury, 6–10 September 2001.

Helferty, Séamus, "Irish political parties and research: the records of the Fine Gael party", *Irish Archives Bulletin – Journal of the Irish Society for Archives* 9–10 (1980), pp. 24–31.

Holmberg, Sören, "Dynamic opinion representation", *Scandinavian Political Studies* 20:3 (1997), pp. 265–83.

Horgan, John, "Seán Lemass: a man in a hurry", pp. 36–44 in Philip Hannon and Jackie Gallagher (eds), *Taking the Long View: 70 years of Fianna Fáil*. Dublin: Blackwater Press, 1996.

Horgan, John, *Seán Lemass: the enigmatic patriot*. Dublin: Gill and Macmillan, 1997.

Hug, Chrystel, *The Politics of Sexual Morality in Ireland*. Basingstoke: Macmillan, 1999.

Hussey, Gemma, *At the Cutting Edge: cabinet diaries 1982–87*. Dublin: Gill and Macmillan, 1990.

Inglehart, Ronald, *The Silent Revolution: changing values and political styles among Western publics*. Princeton: Princeton University Press, 1977.

Jordan, Grant and William A. Maloney, "Manipulating membership: supply-side influences on group size", *British Journal of Political Science* 28:2 (1998), pp. 389–409.

Joyce, Joe and Peter Murtagh, *The Boss*, 2nd ed. Dublin: Poolbeg, 1997.

Katz, Richard S., "But how many candidates should we have in Donegal? Numbers of nominees and efficiency in Ireland", *British Journal of Political Science* 11:1 (1981), pp. 117–23.

Katz, Richard S., "Party as linkage: a vestigial function?", *European Journal of Political Research* 18:1 (1990), pp. 143–61.

Katz, Richard S. and Peter Mair, "Changing models of party organization and party democracy: the emergence of the cartel party", *Party Politics* 1:1 (1995), pp. 5–28.

Katz, Richard S. and Bernhard Wessels (eds), *The European Parliament, National Parliaments, and European Integration*. Oxford: Oxford University Press, 1999.

Keatinge, Patrick and Brigid Laffan, "Ireland: a small open polity", pp. 320–49 in John Coakley and Michael Gallagher, *Politics in the Republic of Ireland*, 3rd ed. London: Routledge and PSAI Press, 1999.

Kennelly, Brendan and Eilís Ward, "The abortion referendums", pp. 115–34 in Michael Gallagher and Michael Laver (eds), *How Ireland Voted 1992*. Dublin: Folens and Limerick: PSAI Press, 1993.

Keogh, Dermot. *Twentieth-Century Ireland: nation and state*. Dublin: Gill and Macmillan, 1994.

Kerrigan, Gene and Pat Brennan, *This Great Little Nation: the A–Z of Irish scandals and controversies*. Dublin: Gill and Macmillan, 1999.

Knutsen, Oddbjørn, "Value orientations, political conflicts and left–right identification: a comparative study", *European Journal of Political Research* 28:1 (1995), pp. 63–93.

Komito, Lee, "Brokerage or friendship? Politics and networks in Ireland", *Economic and Social Review* 23:2 (1992), pp. 129–45.

Koole, Ruud and Monique Leijenaar, "The Netherlands: the predominance of regionalism", pp. 190–209 in Michael Gallagher and Michael Marsh (eds), *Candidate Selection in Comparative Perspective: the secret garden of politics*. London: Sage, 1988.

Laver, Michael, "Are Irish parties peculiar?", pp. 359–81 in J. H. Goldthorpe and C. T. Whelan (eds), *The Development of Industrial Society in Ireland*. Oxford: Oxford University Press, 1992.

Laver, Michael, "Party policy in Ireland 1997: results from an expert survey", *Irish Political Studies* 13 (1998), pp. 159–71.

Laver, Michael and Michael Marsh, "Parties and voters", pp. 152–76 in John Coakley and Michael Gallagher (eds), *Politics in the Republic of Ireland*, 3rd ed. London: Routledge and PSAI Press, 1999.

Lawrence, Jon, "Labour – the myths it has lived by", pp. 341–366 in Duncan Tanner, Pat Thane and Nick Tiratsoo (eds), *Labour's First Century*. Cambridge: Cambridge University Press, 2000.

Lawson, Kay, "Political parties and linkage", pp. 3–24 in Kay Lawson (ed.), *Political Parties and Linkage: a comparative perspective*. New Haven and London: Yale University Press, 1980.

Lee, J. J., *Ireland 1912–1985: politics and society*. Cambridge: Cambridge University Press, 1989.

Lijphart, Arend, *Patterns of Democracy: government forms and performance in thirty-six countries*. New Haven and London: Yale University Press, 1999.

Lysaght, D. R. O'Connor, *The Republic of Ireland*. Cork: Mercier Press, 1970.

Mair, Peter, "Social factors in the maintenance of party loyalty", *Social Studies* 4:2 (1975), pp. 152–61.

Mair, Peter, *The Changing Irish Party System: organisation, ideology and electoral competition*. London: Frances Pinter, 1987.

Mair, Peter, "The Irish party system into the 1990s", pp. 208–20 in Michael Gallagher and Richard Sinnott (eds), *How Ireland Voted 1989*. Galway: PSAI Press and Centre for the Study of Irish Elections, 1990.

Mair, Peter, "Party competition and the changing party system", pp. 127–51 in John Coakley and Michael Gallagher (eds), *Politics in the Republic of Ireland*, 3rd ed. London: Routledge and PSAI Press, 1999.

Mair, Peter and Ingrid van Biezen, "Party membership in twenty European democracies, 1980-2000", *Party Politics* 7:1 (2001), pp. 5-21.

Manning, Maurice, *Irish Political Parties: an introduction*. Dublin: Gill and Macmillan, 1972.

Manning, Maurice, *The Courage to Succeed*. Dublin: Fine Gael, 1983.

Manning, Maurice, *The Blueshirts*. Dublin: Gill and Macmillan, 1987.

Manning, Maurice, *James Dillon: a biography*. Dublin: Wolfhound Press, 1999.

Maor, Moshe, *Political Parties and Party Systems: comparative approaches and the British experience*. London: Routledge, 1997.

Marsh, Michael, "Electoral evaluations of candidates in Irish elections, 1948–82", *Irish Political Studies* 2 (1987), pp. 65–76.

Marsh, Michael, "The making of the eighth president", pp. 215–42 in Michael Marsh and Paul Mitchell (eds), *How Ireland Voted 1997*. Boulder CO: Westview Press and PSAI Press, 1999.

Marsh, Michael and Paul Mitchell (eds), *How Ireland Voted 1997*. Boulder CO: Westview Press and PSAI Press, 1999.

Marsh, Michael and Paul Mitchell, "Office, votes, and then policy: hard choices for political parties in the Republic of Ireland, 1981–1992", pp. 36–62 in Wolfgang C. Müller and Kaare Strøm (eds), *Policy, Office or Votes: how political parties in western Europe make hard decisions*. Cambridge: Cambridge University Press, 2000.

May, John D., "Opinion structure of political parties: the special law of curvilinear disparity", *Political Studies* 21:2 (1973), pp. 135–51.

McGarry, Fearghal, *Irish Politics and the Spanish Civil War*. Cork: Cork University Press, 1999.

Michels, Robert, *Political Parties: a sociological study of the oligarchical tendencies of modern democracy*. New York: Dover, 1959 [originally published 1912].

Mockler, Frank, "Organisational change in Fianna Fáil and Fine Gael", *Irish Political Studies* 9 (1994), pp. 165–71.

Moss, Warner, *Political Parties in the Irish Free State*. New York: Columbia University Press, 1933.

Mudde, Cas, "Defining the extreme right party family", *West European Politics* 19:2 (1996), pp. 225–48.

Mulgan, Geoff, *Politics in an Antipolitical Age*. Cambridge: Polity, 1994.

Murphy, Gary, "A culture of sleaze: political corruption and the Irish body politic 1997–2000", *Irish Political Studies* 15 (2000), pp. 193–200.

Narud, Hanne Marthe and Audun Skare, "Are party activists the extremists? The structure of opinion in political parties", *Scandinavian Political Studies* 22:1 (1999), pp. 45–65.

Norris, Pippa, "May's Law of Curvilinear Disparity revisited: officers, members and voters in British political parties", *Party Politics* 1:1 (1995), pp. 29–48.

O'Byrnes, Stephen, *Hiding behind a Face: Fine Gael under FitzGerald*. Dublin: Gill and Macmillan, 1986.

O'Halpin, Eunan, " 'Ah, they've given us a good bit of stuff ...': tribunals and Irish political life at the turn of the century", *Irish Political Studies* 15 (2000), pp. 183–92.

O'Higgins, T. F., *A Double Life*. Dublin: Town House and Country House, 1996.

Phillips, Anne, *The Politics of Presence*. Oxford: Clarendon Press, 1995.

Regan, John M., *The Irish Counter-Revolution 1921–1936: Treatyite politics and settlement in independent Ireland*. Dublin: Gill and Macmillan, 1999.

Rüdig, Wolfgang, Lynn G. Bennie and Mark N. Franklin, *Green Party Members: a profile*. Glasgow: Delta, 1991.

Sacks, Paul M., *The Donegal Mafia: an Irish political machine*. New Haven and London: Yale University Press, 1976.

Sartori, Giovanni, *Parties and Party Systems: a framework for analysis, Vol 1*. Cambridge: Cambridge University Press, 1976.

Scarrow, Susan E., *Parties and their Members: organising for victory in Britain and Germany*. Oxford: Oxford University Press, 1996.

Scarrow, Susan E., "Parties without members? Party organization in a changing environment", pp. 79–101 in Russell J. Dalton and Martin P. Wattenberg (eds), *Parties without Partisans: political change in advanced industrial democracies*. Oxford: Oxford University Press, 2000.

Schlesinger, Joseph A., "Political party organization", pp. 764–801 in James G. March (ed.), *Handbook of Organizations*. Chicago: Rand McNally, 1965.

Seyd, Patrick and Paul Whiteley, *Labour's Grass Roots: the politics of party membership*. Oxford: Clarendon, 1992.

Seyd, Patrick and Paul Whiteley, "Towards a more responsible two-party system", paper presented at the Annual Conference of the American Political Science Association, Washington, 31 August–3 September 2000.

Sinnott, Richard, *Irish Voters Decide: voting behaviour in elections and referendums since 1918*. Manchester: Manchester University Press, 1995.

Sinnott, Richard, "The electoral system", pp. 99–126 in John Coakley and Michael Gallagher (eds), *Politics in the Republic of Ireland*, 3rd ed. London: Routledge and PSAI Press, 1999.

Strøm, Kaare, "A behavioral theory of competitive political parties", *American Political Science Review* 34:2 (1990), pp. 565–98.

Svåsand, Lars, Kaare Strøm and Bjørn Erik Rasch, "Change and adaptation in party organization", pp. 91–123 in Kaare Strøm and Lars Svåsand (eds), *Challenges to Political Parties: the case of Norway*. Ann Arbor: University of Michigan Press, 1997.

Taagepera, Rein and Matthew Soberg Shugart, *Seats and Votes: the effects and determinants of electoral systems*. New Haven and London: Yale University Press, 1989.

Tanner, Duncan, "Labour and its membership", pp. 248–80 in Duncan Tanner, Pat Thane and Nick Tiratsoo (eds), *Labour's First Century*. Cambridge: Cambridge University Press, 2000.

van Holsteyn, Joop, Ruud Koole and Joe Elkink, "Party membership in the Netherlands:

the Dutch survey and some tentative results". Paper presented at Party Membership conference, Sheffield, 26–27 May 2000.

Verba, Sidney, Kay Lehman Schlozman and Henry E. Brady, *Voice and Equality: civic voluntarism and American politics*. Cambridge: Harvard University Press, 1995.

Ware, Alan, "Activist–leader relations and the structure of political parties: 'exchange models' and vote-seeking behaviour in parties", *British Journal of Political Science* 22:1 (1992), pp. 71–92.

Waters, John, *Jiving at the Crossroads*. Belfast: Blackstaff Press, 1991.

Webb, Paul D., "Are British political parties in decline?", *Party Politics* 1:3 (1995), pp. 299–322.

Whiteley, Paul, Patrick Seyd and Jeremy Richardson, *True Blues: the politics of conservative party membership*. Oxford: Oxford University Press, 1994.

Widfeldt, Anders, "Party membership and party representativeness" pp. 134–82 in Hans-Dieter Klingemann and Dieter Fuchs, *Citizens and the State*. Oxford: Oxford University Press, 1995.

Wilson, J, "Volunteering", *Annual Review Of Sociology* 26 (2000), pp. 215–40.

Wolinetz, Steven B., "Reconstructing Dutch social democracy", *West European Politics* 16:1 (1993), pp. 97–111.

Archives

Fine Gael archives, University College Dublin.

Internet

www.finegael.com. Site of the Fine Gael party

www.mta.ca/faculty/socsci/polisci/scppm/index.html. Site of the Canadian Political Party Members study, conducted by Bill Cross and Lisa Young.

www.shef.ac.uk/~pol/ispp.. Site of the Institute for the Study of Political Parties at the University of Sheffield, England, maintained by Patrick Seyd.

www.tcd.ie/Political_Science/cgi. Site of the Irish opinion poll archive, maintained by Michael Marsh.

Index